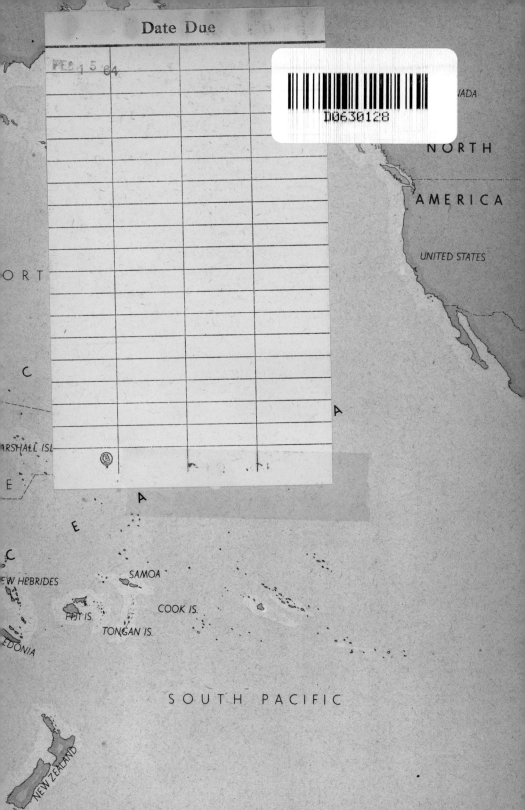

D0630128

NORTH

AMERICA

UNITED STATES

ORT

C

A

MARSHALL ISL

E

A

E

C

NEW HEBRIDES

SAMOA

FIJI IS.

COOK IS.

TONGAN IS.

EDONIA

SOUTH PACIFIC

NEW ZEALAND

POPULATION AND PEACE
IN THE PACIFIC

BY WARREN S. THOMPSON

SCRIPPS FOUNDATION · MIAMI UNIVERSITY

POPULATION AND PEACE IN THE PACIFIC

UNIVERSITY OF CHICAGO PRESS · CHICAGO

University of Chicago Press · Chicago 37

Agent: Cambridge University Press · London

Copyright 1946 by The University of Chicago. All rights
reserved. Published 1946. Composed and printed by the
University of Chicago Press, Chicago, Illinois, U.S.A.

PREFACE

THIS book was originally intended to be a revision of the author's *Danger Spots in World Population*, published in 1929, as the latter had been out of print since about 1934. The work of revision had not progressed far, however, before it became clear that revision was not practicable. The fundamentals of the problem discussed had not changed, but the materials relating to the population and economy of the Pacific Region had so expanded in the meantime that it seemed best to concentrate on the problems of the Pacific, although it was recognized that they were not separate from world problems—indeed, were simply one aspect of them.

In final form, then, this book is closely related to its predecessor in being an exposition of the view that the changes in population growth and in social (economic) organization taking place in the world should be taken account of in developing a political organization which will encourage peace rather than war. The trends in growth discernible at that time only to those especially interested in them are now much better known and have begun to attract considerable attention on the part of the informed public.

Regarding the general purpose of this book I cannot do better than quote a few passages from this earlier work, which centered discussion on two types of changes: "changes in the organization of a people which bring about new needs; and changes in size which bring about increased needs. . . . . In the world of today far more than in past ages these two types of changes . . . . are going on simultaneously and are far more rapid" (p. 5).

"Today, however, some of those peoples who until recently were living quite outside the influences leading to increase in both wants and numbers are beginning to feel impulses altogether new to them. They are developing industries modeled after those of the West, and they are also undergoing the growth of population which comes when a certain measure of modern sanitary practice is first introduced among backward peoples. . . . . They are conscious of growing human power, and many of them are becoming painfully aware that they have not the resources to make this power effective and respected in a world where force is dominant. . . . . We have the spectacle of nations holding on to vast economic resources (lands) after there ceases to be any reasonable hope of their being able to hold them through actual settlement on the land. . . . . That some such attempts [to dislodge the possessors of lands which they cannot settle] will be made within the next few decades seems certain. . . . . But it should be noted here that the acquisition of new lands today, if effected by force, will involve far more serious conflict than in times past. Indeed, there is good reason to think that world wars will result from the attempted seizure of new lands by the expanding powers. It is for this reason that the most serious consideration should be given to some plan for the redistribution of resources which will avoid war" (pp. 6–13).

This situation still exists. Much water has flowed under the bridge in the last sixteen years, and in this book an attempt is made to give an up-to-date version of the need for a better and a more just distribution of the world's resources in the Pacific Region if we are seriously determined to maintain the peace. A conscientious effort has been made not to overemphasize the role of the differential population growth of nations and differentials in resources in promoting conflict between them. The reader will have to be the judge of whether, in his anxiety to gain consideration for population growth as a fundamental factor in determining international relations, the author has overshot the mark. There is certainly no intention to minimize the development of industry as an important element in the situation, but a long and careful consideration of probable development in this field has led the writer to be less optimistic about what it may do to relieve differential population pressures than many men are.

It will no doubt appear to many readers that there are serious gaps in the discussion. A detailed statement of a scheme for the handling of the present colonies in the postwar world if the colonial system is abolished will be desired by some; a more adequate discussion of the race problems which will arise if large migration into the present colonial areas from the crowded countries of Asia is allowed will be desired by others; fuller treatment of the role of industrial development in caring for population increase and of the chances for the spread of birth control in "backward" areas will be wanted by still others. It is not because these additions are not needed that they are omitted. The excuse the writer offers is, first, space and, second, his own judgment that it is more important at this stage of the discussion to gain consideration for the changing population pressures arising in the world than to attempt a statement of solutions which we know beforehand will have to be subject to continuous adjustment in the light of economic and social changes which cannot be foreseen. Naturally, there will be wide differences of opinion on this point.

The wealth of material now available has made it necessary for the author to rely on assistants for the gathering of many of the data used. He is indebted to the Rockefeller Foundation for aid in employing these assistants and wishes to express his great appreciation for it. He also wishes to express his great indebtedness to the assistants—to Doris Vance Shaffer, Jane Frederiksen, Isabelle Brittain, Ruth W. Smith, and, above all, to Evangelyn Dine Minnis—for the unflagging interest they have taken in the work and the painstaking efforts they have put forth to assemble the relevant facts. To Mrs. Minnis has also fallen the burden of seeing the book through the press and of preparing the Index.

Since the above portion of the Preface was written, the atomic bomb has been used. It is not possible at this time to assess fully the significance of this event. Much foolishness has been talked about the new sources of power it makes available to mankind; in particular, the assumption is frequently made that this power will be available soon for everyday use. The statements I have seen by responsible scientists talk in terms of decades rather than in terms of years. But there can be little doubt that the atomic bomb is a weapon which is likely to make future wars as terrible as H. G. Wells imagined. Moreover, to judge from the spread and use of scientific discoveries in the past, it seems highly probable that the use of atomic energy in war will become the common property of all peoples by the time of the next war, if it comes.

This makes it all the more incumbent on us to develop some form of world organization capable of dealing with the problems discussed in this book. Injustice and discrimination in the allotment of resources and in the treatment of other peoples must be corrected voluntarily in accordance with laws freely accepted by all peoples, or we must expect force to be used by the underdogs to remove their handicaps. With the atomic bomb available to all moderately industrialized peoples within a comparatively short time, we do not have long to mend the errors of our ways. Even a relatively weak power, as weakness is measured today, may destroy a great power by surprise. Either we must remove the causes which make people willing to resort to war to settle differences by some kind of world organization controlling the use of the world's resources or we may expect future Pearl Harbors which will destroy a great nation and a whole continent in a few moments.

As I see it, then, the atomic bomb does not eliminate the problems of differential population pressures and unequal resources dealt with here; rather it increases the urgency of dealing with them wisely and quickly.

It may be said that this view ignores the possibility that the incredible cheapness of atomic energy will make man's present economic problems of no moment in the future, that to talk of coal and iron and copper, etc., is out of date. This may be so several decades hence; but, until those who know best are in position to assure us that we can use these new sources of energy at a cost far below that of our present sources of energy and that we can convert abundant and at present almost useless minerals into useful goods by the use of this energy, we must assume that men will go on demanding coal and iron and oil and wheat and cotton and meat and the myriad other products we are now using and that they will fight for them when they want them badly and see no other way to get them. Until the use of atomic power removes all scarcities and points the way to abundance everywhere, man will scramble for what he needs, and this will lead to war—to more awful wars than we have dreamed of in the past.

This probability only makes more immediate the necessity of removing the causes of war as far as we can now see them and of being as bold in devising new social and political controls as our scientists have been in tapping new sources of energy.

WARREN S. THOMPSON

OXFORD, OHIO
October 15, 1945

TABLE OF CONTENTS

I. The Danger in the Pacific 11

II. The Differential Growth of Peoples 22

III. Tropical Oceania 36

IV. Australia and New Zealand 52

V. Manchoukuo 78

VI. Japan: The Population of the Empire 93

VII. Japan: The Food Supply of the Empire 109

VIII. Japan: The Mineral Resources of the Empire 122

IX. Japan: Modern Industrial Development 134

X. Japan: Foreign Trade 148

XI. Japan: Economic Future 165

XII. China: Population and Agriculture 176

XIII. China: Mineral Resources and Industry 192

XIV. China: Economic Future 207

XV. India: Population and Agriculture 218

XVI. India: Mineral Resources, Industry, and Economic Outlook . 236

XVII. The Colonies of Southeast Asia. I 251

XVIII. The Colonies of Southeast Asia. II 274

XIX. The Colonial System in South and East Asia 297

XX. Migration and Population Pressure in South and East Asia . . 319

XXI. Peace and Population Growth in the Pacific 329

XXII. The Stake of the United States in the Pacific 344

Selected Bibliography 362

Index 385

Chapter I

THE DANGER IN THE PACIFIC

IN THESE days of world-wide and almost instantaneous communication and of air transport girdling the globe in a few days, the problems of peace are no longer local or even regional. Conditions likely to disturb peace between two or more great powers or even between lesser powers anywhere are now a world danger. For this reason all danger spots in the world today assume a vastly greater importance than ever before. If in this book attention is devoted to a particular region, it is not because it is the only danger spot but because space and time and a special interest make this necessary; besides, a fuller analysis of the factors affecting war and peace in one region will enable us to understand better the *oneness* of the world peace problem.

Perhaps the most dangerous of all these danger spots is the Pacific Region—not only because the problems it represents are of such tremendous magnitude but because if we do not deal with them now, it will forever be too late. By the "Pacific Region," I mean the area extending from Hawaii on the east to India on the west, but not including the Soviet Far East. In this great expanse, to which we in the West have turned our eyes so recently and so late, the major problems are not merely military but concern a gigantic population increase now taking place and likely to continue for the next few decades and the probable social and economic development of the peoples living there. (India added 50 million to her numbers between 1931 and 1941.)

The development of these peoples in the next few decades may very well determine whether there will be a third world war, and yet we pass it by with a brief glance while we concentrate attention on Europe and her problems. Since such a statement naturally demands justification, our main task here is to investigate the evidence for believing that the germs of another world war are inherent in the future development of the Pacific Region, *if this development is along the lines that have been followed in the past.*

It is my hope to offer convincing proof that toward the peoples of the Pacific Region a course of action quite different from that of the past is essential if we are to avoid frictions that will lead to war. Of course, even if we adopt new methods of dealing with the economic, political, and social problems of the peoples of this region, there can be no complete assurance that we can avoid war—but we must at least try to find better ways of handling these problems. It is my contention that we can make little headway in forestalling war in the western Pacific unless we take into account the probable population growth of this region and devise means, if possible, both for controlling this growth and for raising the region's production to provide a decent living for all its people.

POPULATION GROWTH IN THE PACIFIC REGION

The facts of actual population growth in the Pacific Region are incontestable for most of the countries and areas and are of vital interest, since they make clear what is happening. For judging population growth in China and Inner Asia, where facts are few and uncertain, we can draw upon the recent experience of other Asiatic countries where the facts are established, and thus obtain some basis for conclusions as to what has probably happened there during the last half-century. As to future growth of population in the Pacific Region, the experience of the Western world since 1800 shows the trends in population growth which can be expected here during the next few decades.

My conclusion from the study of these facts is that most of the countries of South and East Asia have already entered upon a period of population expansion quite similar to that which took place in the Western world after 1800 and that a similar growth in those lands for which data are unsatisfactory only awaits the establishment of internal peace, the development of a moderately effective health service, the improvement of transportation, and the expansion of agriculture through irrigation and better farm practice, all of which these lands hope for in the near future. This growth of population in South and East Asia, which contain all but a small part of the population of the Pacific Region, coupled with the fact that in much of the West the birth rate is no longer high enough to maintain present numbers (to say nothing of providing colonists for tropical areas), means that a large part of the population growth of the world during the next few decades will almost certainly take place in this region.

The whole argument centers so largely around the social and economic effects of this population growth on the establishment and maintenance of peace that it calls for a word on the contrast between the conditions encountered by the expanding Europeans of 1800 and those being encountered today by the peoples of South and East Asia. When population began its rapid growth in the West—about 1800—there were probably somewhat fewer than 200 million Europeans in Europe and in the areas then being settled by them. With minor exceptions there were only small native populations in the Americas, Australia, New Zealand, and South Africa, which were the chief areas open to European settlement at that time. At present there are between 1,000 and 1,100 million people in South and East Asia, and there are no more Americas to be settled. Even the unsettled, or thinly settled, tropical areas of South and East Asia (Borneo, New Guinea, Sumatra, Celebes, and parts of the Philippines and the Indo-Chinese peninsula, and, I think, tropical Africa should be included) are largely colonial areas not open to free settlement and exploitation by these Asiatics.

Today there is no emigration outlet for these peoples which can for a moment be compared with that available to Europeans in 1800. This is a fact no one can dispute. But I hasten to add that in my opinion even if these colonial areas were opened to Asiatic migration, they would do little to relieve the actual pressure of population in the more crowded Asiatic countries—for the population needing outlets is five to six times as great as that of Europe in 1800, and the lands available are relatively small and not so richly endowed as the Americas.

Furthermore, Western experience with emigration is to the effect that, when populations are large and while birth rates and death rates remain high, even the emigration of considerable numbers does not do a great deal to relieve population pressure, unless at the same time industry is developing fast enough to absorb the major portion of the natural increase. What happens in a *poverty-stricken* population like that of the western Pacific, where new industry is developing slowly, is that, while the birth rate is little changed by emigration, any temporary relief of pressure on subsistence reduces the death rate so that more of the children born survive, and the gaps caused by emigrants are quickly filled by those children saved from an early death.

In a population as great as that in South and East Asia there is, then, little chance of relief through emigration, except in certain relatively small areas. In great countries like India and China, emigration will produce no significant effect. However, increasing the freedom of these peoples to settle in unused areas in this region and to exploit their resources might very well have a beneficial psychological effect in helping to remove the feeling of discrimination, of being treated as inferiors. The good-will thus gained would be out of all proportion to the economic effects of emigration, whereas the feeling of bitterness now permeating all the relations of East and West will almost certainly grow more intense in the future if the West insists on retaining its present controls over South and East Asia.

THE MEANS OF SUPPORT

Obviously in a region where from 75 to 85 per cent of the people are agriculturalists, where the population is already dense, and where the level of living is very low, any large and rapid increase of population at once raises the question of how these additional millions are going to be fed, clothed, and sheltered. In general, the situation is this: while several political units, notably the Netherlands East Indies and the Philippines, appear to have an abundance of land for some time to come, China, India, and Japan are already badly crowded, and the outlook for increasing their food and clothing much faster than their population grows is far from encouraging. Apparently there will not be much easing of pressure among the agricultural populations of these countries, or of certain other areas like the rice deltas of the Indo-Chinese peninsula, within the next few decades—under the present system of outside control in the colonial areas, at least, or in China without an agricultural revolution.

But, of course, agriculture is not the only source of the goods man needs for a better living. What are the possibilities of more efficient industrial production? The evidence of actual development of modern technologies, and of machine industry, in each of the countries in question shows that modern industry is spreading in this region, although the spread has been slow. Only Japan can be said as yet to possess a sufficient amount of modern industry to have any significant effect upon the level of living of the majority of the people. Furthermore, improved technologies have as yet had little influence on agriculture anywhere, except in certain types of plantation production. In spite of this industrial backwardness, the knowledge and use of modern technologies is making some headway, and during the years immediately ahead their use will undoubtedly continue to spread in most of this region at a considerably accelerated pace.

But it should be noted that the influence of modern technology is not confined to actual production. Up to the present it can be plausibly argued that modern communication and transportation, although only slightly developed, are exercising more influence on the mental lives of these peoples than actual machine production. Their attitudes toward their own problems, toward their colonial masters, and toward other Western controls are changing faster than might be assumed from their backwardness in adopting more efficient productive processes.

In addition, if modern machine industry is to ameliorate the living conditions of these peoples, they must have the raw materials with which to work. Do the peoples of South and East Asia possess the minerals which are essential to a modern industrial system? The conclusions that we arrive at are not so definite as could be desired; but, even so, I believe we are justified in saying that, while South and East Asia do not possess the "vast" or "unlimited" mineral resources so often attributed to them and while no country seems to be well endowed with all the major minerals, there are sufficient quantities of most of them to support a steady but slow growth of machine industry in the more important countries. For the next few decades the growth of machine industry in South and East Asia is probably more dependent on overcoming social obstacles and man-made economic difficulties than on the lack of natural resources, although China's lack of good iron ore and India's lack of copper and probably of good coking coal cannot be overlooked.

China and India likewise offer conspicuous examples of social and economic difficulties. The organization of Chinese society around the family and the values attached to belonging to a class which does not have to work with its hands are very great obstacles to the development of machine industry. The family ideal makes corporate organization unbelievably difficult, since members of the family to the nth cousin must be provided with good jobs regardless of training and ability. The loss of status by one who soils his hands also makes the growth of a class of competent technicians and managers very slow. In India the caste system, of course, places great impediments in the way of organizing effective industrial production. I am not saying that these obstacles cannot be battered down—let us not forget what Japan has accomplished in this respect in the last fifty years—but I am saying that these and many other aspects of life in these countries do retard, and will for some time yet continue to retard, industrial development.

On the more purely economic side one must ask: Where is the capital to come from which is needed to build railways, highways, steamships, communication facilities, steel mills, cotton mills, and a hundred other types of factories, to open mines and build smelters, and to establish credit facilities for agriculture as well as industry? Do we have it? Does Europe have it? If it is available, under what conditions will it be loaned and to whom? Will we loan to the governments of these countries or to private interests, and will you and I loan our savings directly or will we want them guaranteed by our own government? Do we want foreign loans to be used to secure "spheres of influence" as in the past? What about trade between these countries and the rest of the world? Are they going to erect tariff barriers to protect "infant industry" which will make foreign trade practically impossible, and are we going to shut out all their products which in any way compete with our own?

When these matters are considered, I do not see how we can possibly conclude otherwise than that the development of modern machine industry will be rather slow in the countries of the Pacific Region. This is a very important matter, because the speed with which industrial expansion takes place will probably determine the speed of improvement in the level of living, which in turn is closely related to the development of effective control of population growth.

These conclusions, which follow inevitably from the facts, are probably of less interest from the human standpoint than the secondary conclusions which in turn follow from them.

THE RELATION OF EAST TO WEST

The absolute economic needs of the peoples in South and East Asia are increasing rapidly and will increase even more rapidly in the foreseeable future. As population grows, the demand for the mere necessities of life, since these peoples now live on a near-subsistence basis, will grow in like measure. But perhaps even more important will be the relative increase in the need for capital and for minerals and for industrial crops, which are essential to modern industry. Moreover, any significant industrial development will lead most of these countries to assess carefully and for the first time the sufficiency of their natural resources to provide for their future industrial expansion. In doing this, a considerable body of people in most of these countries will be made aware of the lack of certain important minerals and the rather scanty supply of others. They will at the same time become keenly aware of the lack of land for the expansion of agriculture as a national, rather than as a merely local, problem. This will be particularly true in India and China (Japan has already gone through this stage of development), where population is quite dense and new areas open to settlement are relatively small and for the most part of inferior quality.

We can predict with a high degree of certainty that the need for more land and mineral resources will shortly, perhaps in two or three decades, be felt by a larger and larger proportion of the people. It will no longer be confined to a small educated ruling class, for it is a simple fact that the need of these larger resources is never widely felt until they come into wide use, and this only comes about as modern machine industry develops and more and more people become dependent on nonagricultural work for their living.

A similar conclusion of great significance is that, even though the development of industry will be slow and even though in most of these countries it may be limited in certain directions by the lack of basic resources, most of the countries of South and East Asia, particularly India and China, will become relatively much stronger industrially and economically, and therefore militarily, within the next three or four decades. It is also certain that, as economic strength grows, national unity will become greater, that the people will come to feel that they belong to China or India or Burma and not merely to their own family and village. In the future we shall have to reckon with these peoples as growing nations. All modern cultural and economic development is moving in this direction, and there is abundant evidence that this nationalistic development will make rapid progress as communication and transportation improve, as education spreads to the masses, and as the dependence on factory industry increases.

Still another point of vital importance is that the growth of population and industrial strength in South and East Asia and a relatively stationary population in much of the West will result in a shift in the balance of power toward the East. Just how rapidly this will take place and how far it can go no one can tell, but that it will take place seems inevitable. Can anyone doubt that if the West does not undertake to make voluntarily the adjustments this shift in power renders necessary, they will be made by force as soon as the Asiatic peoples feel strong enough to undertake them? Japan has shown clearly her attitude in this matter. Why should we suppose that China and India will feel differently when the time comes that they have the power, or believe they have the power, to force a favorable decision for themselves if the Western powers have not rendered them elementary justice?

In the light of all these considerations it seems only simple common sense to conclude that now is the time to plan for a new order in South and East Asia. The Western powers are still strong enough to enforce such conditions as they deem fit. They should use this power to inaugurate a new period of co-operative democratic development in this part of the world—a development which in the course of a few decades will render the present system of force unnecessary. If this is not done, we can only expect that force will be used to change the status quo whenever and wherever any people grows powerful enough to believe it can correct what it regards as injustice, or where ambitious leaders can convince their people that they deserve to rule over a wider area and over peoples less powerful than themselves. Only essential justice and a thorough training of the masses of people in the processes of deciding their own destiny can prevent the organization of nations by a ruling class to enforce their demands on weaker peoples.

Since the entire colonial system denies the right of the subject people to decide their own destiny, it has no place in a democratic future. As long as it exists, it will remain a constant aggravation to the colonial peoples and a constant temptation to any growing power to take colonies from a weaker power for its own exploitation. Moreover, the colonial system can offer no solution for the population pressure it has done so much to encourage in the East. The necessities of successful colonial exploitation have released to some extent the customary positive checks to population growth in much of the East but have done nothing to develop a sense of responsibility among these peoples for the overpopulation which has been developing and which is steadily becoming more acute.

POPULATION PRESSURE AS A CAUSE OF WAR

It is often denied that population pressure, no matter how acute it may become, is a cause of war, or even a contributory cause. It is said that if population pressure led to war, China and India rather than Japan should have been the most aggressive peoples in recent decades, because every informed person knows that population pressure is much greater in these lands than in Japan.

This argument fails to recognize the true nature of population pressure. It is not an absolute quantity which can be measured by persons per square mile of arable land, or by per capita consumption of rice, or by some other objective standard of consumption; it is as much, if not more, a psychological factor, a feeling which cannot be measured accurately by any known economic standard.

For myself, I would admit at once that the most poverty-stricken peoples are not likely to be aggressive disturbers of world peace, both because they do not have the means to undertake the conquest of lands held by more opulent peoples with better weapons and a more effective political organization and because the mass of the people in these poor countries are not generally aware of the existence elsewhere of resources (land and minerals) which might relieve their poverty even if brought under their national control. The Chinese peasant does not read, does not listen to the radio, does not know anything at all about the world beyond the limits of his neighborhood, and, therefore, cannot be aroused to aggressive action against a neighboring country even assuming that the government had the means to support him as a soldier. But since the government does not have the economic means to put much of an army in the field even for home defense, as we have seen, and does not have the political control to direct the gathering and training of a national army to attack a neighbor, this problem scarcely arises. A country in the position of China in the past century has not constituted any serious threat to world peace, except as her very weakness invited interference by stronger outside powers and a scramble for spheres of influence under the political system that has prevailed. This has been even more true of colonial areas.

It is not, therefore, absolute poverty which measures the degree of population pressure as a danger to peace but the *felt* lacks, the *felt* pressure on resources, the *felt* discriminations in the access to the resources of the world. Perhaps it will help us to understand the role of *felt* population pressure as a cause of war if we draw an analogy between the struggle for a better distribution of national income in our own country and the struggle between nations for a larger share of the world's resources.

Who are the people most aggressive in demanding a larger share of our national income? They are not the poorest and most poverty-stricken of our people. Those who are loudest in their demands and who are in position to force and do force consideration of their claim for better living are the strong labor unions and the well-organized farm groups made up of the more prosperous workers and farmers. Share-croppers, casual laborers, unorganized clerical workers, and others who really have much inferior living conditions not only do not get much consideration but do not even make much trouble. The people who make demands for better living conditions and who fight for them effectively are the people who have already attained a substantial share of the good things of life, who are convinced that they and their fellows are entitled to a still larger share, and who are able to organize to press their demands against the intrenched interests which oppose a "new deal."

The situation is much the same between nations. It is those nations which have already made considerable progress in developing effective economic organization, whose workers have emerged from the dire proverty of mere subsistence and know something about the improvements in living they might gain if the resources of the world were more fairly divided, that are likely to take aggressive action to secure a larger share of these resources. Only as the people of a nation become aware of their relative inferiority in resources and in national power can they be effectively aroused to support aggressive action against strong outside powers. People who have tasted some of the sweets of a more productive economy can be told with some show of reason that if they had larger resources, more coal, more oil, more copper, more aluminum, etc., they could live better. They can also be told and apparently convinced that in the world as it has been organized there is only one way to get these larger resources and that is to take them by force from other people now controlling them.

This is what happened in Japan. Her people have come to *feel* the pressure of population on resources far more keenly than those of China and India, not because they are poorer, but because they have come to know more about world conditions and their relative poverty in resources, because they have been eating better and more certainly and wish to eat still better and be even more secure in their food supply, because they have begun to use electricity and automobiles, to wear better clothes, and to enjoy certain small luxuries and want more of them just as all the rest of us do. Thus the Japanese have come to *feel* the lack of the resources from which they can make more goods far more keenly than the Chinese, who do not even know that most of these new goods exist, or that they might have a public health service, or that the chance to emigrate might improve their lot. It will certainly be some time before the Chinese will come to feel that aggressive military action might be to their advantage, but it would be extremely unwise to assume that they will not come to feel this way a few decades hence if they are kept from sharing justly in the exploitation of the world's resources.

Finally, I believe we must recognize that fundamental changes in the manner of life of the peoples in South and East Asia cannot be stopped. In the course of a few decades these peoples will, like the

Japanese, become aware that the Netherlands East Indies have oil and tin and coal and iron which they cannot exploit under the present colonial system, will cast covetous eyes upon the large unsettled areas in Borneo and New Guinea and elsewhere, which are forbidden them as long as Europeans maintain their control, and will resent the fact that their trade is interfered with at the pleasure of Western nations whenever it becomes truly competitive. As they come to know more about these conditions, they will also come to feel that the existing distribution of basic resources among nations is unjust and that, if the European possessors are not willing to remedy this injustice voluntarily, recourse to force will be necessary.

The only way to plan for peace in the Pacific Region is to begin now to plan for a more equitable distribution of the resources of this region. How can we expect any help from these peoples in maintaining peace unless we show a willingness to share the good things of the world with them? How can we expect any honest and effective effort on their part to control their population growth unless we convince them by our fairness, while we are yet strong, that they do not need large battalions to gain a fair share of the good things of this world?

I cannot see how we can honestly hope to avoid future wars and at the same time doom these Asiatic peoples to a poverty-stricken existence while we exploit the resources of this region which they need so badly to enable them to rise a little above the subsistence level.

Chapter II

THE DIFFERENTIAL GROWTH OF PEOPLES

IN THE preceding chapter I have stated certain conclusions regarding population growth in the Pacific Region and in the world—conclusions on which the argument of this book rests. Here I will describe, albeit briefly, the population growth of the world in the last century in order to show the position of the Pacific lands in a world setting. The population growth of particular lands and countries and the factors affecting it will be set forth in the chapters relating to these countries.

THE MODERN POPULATION GROWTH CYCLE

Before the development of the more efficient methods of machine production in Western countries and before the accompanying agricultural revolution got under way, steady and rapid population growth was the exception rather than the rule. There was a severe struggle for mere subsistence. When for some reason conditions were favorable, when there was a series of good crop years, when favorable "runs" of fish appeared, or when disease was less prevalent than usual, there was an increase in population, its rate depending on how favorable these conditions were at that time. But, when dearth and disease came, the death rate rose and population did not grow or even declined.

The data for Finland, which are generally considered quite reliable, illustrate the nature and magnitude of these fluctuations even in a well-governed country as late as the second half of the nineteenth century. In the decade 1856–65, Finland's population grew from 1,689,000 to 1,843,000, or by 154,000 (145, I, 14).[1] In the three and one-half years from 1866 to the middle of 1869 it declined by 109,000, although there was little emigration. Thus, instead of an average annual increase of more than 15,000, there was an average annual decrease of about 30,000 in these three and one-half years of famine and disease. This loss was made up in the ensuing four "favorable" years, because the famine had taken off many of the weak and sickly and the death rate temporarily dropped to a new low, while the birth rate

[1] Except in a few instances, references to sources are by number as they appear in the Bibliography.

soon regained the level of pre-famine years. Exactly the same pattern of growth as the result of famine and war is found in Sweden in 1771–77 and 1807–14.

But in these highly organized and well-advanced countries the death rates were already well below those of most of the world. The rate of recovery from famine, war, and pestilence was generally much slower in less developed areas and might not take place for many decades or even centuries. Europe is not supposed to have again attained the population it had just before the Black Death (1347–50) until about 1700. These facts, coupled with the observation of population growth

TABLE 1*

POPULATION OF THE WORLD BY CONTINENTS, 1800–1939
(In Millions)

Continent	1939	1900	1850	1800
World.....................	2,080	1,527	1,091	919
Asia......................	1,097	839	664	600
Europe...................	542	390	266	188
Africa....................	157	141	100	100
North and Central America...	184	110	39	15
South America.............	89	41	20	14
Oceania..................	11	6	2	2

* Data for 1800 and 1850 are from Walter F. Willcox, *Studies in American Demography* (Ithaca, N.Y.: Cornell University Press, 1940), pp. 30 and 45; those for later years are from a number of official yearbooks and the *Aperçu de la démographie des divers pays du monde, 1929–1936* (La Haye: Office Permanent de l'Institut International de Statistique, 1939).

in the nonindustrialized nations of today, lead us to believe that in pre–Industrial Revolution days all death rates were high and averaged very little lower than the birth rates; otherwise there would certainly have been far more than 900–920 million people on the earth in 1800. They also lead us to conclude that never before 1800, or a little earlier, had any people enjoyed a relatively long and continuous period of steady death rates, to say nothing of a long decline in death rates leading to a fairly long and steady growth in numbers. A violently fluctuating death rate with a very slow increase of population over long periods probably characterized most peoples before the advent of the Industrial Revolution. There must also have been many places and times when population did not grow at all and even when it declined largely.

The modern cycle of population growth can be said to have begun when man's labor became more productive both in agriculture and in

MAP I

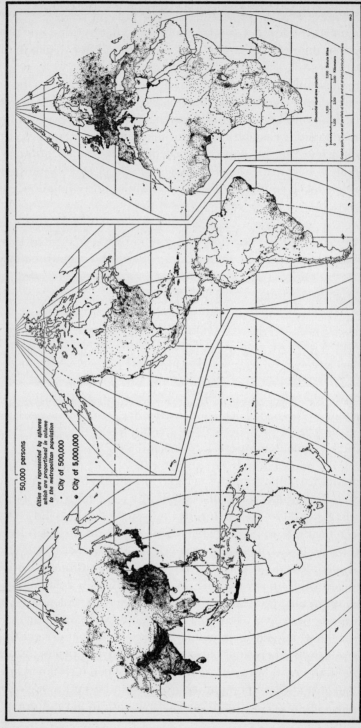

50,000 persons

Cities are represented by spheres which are proportional in volume to the metropolitan population

● City of 500,000

● City of 5,000,000

Sinusoidal equal-area projection

Statute Miles
1,000   2,000   3,000

Kilometers
1,000   2,000   3,000

Graphic scale, true on all parallels of latitude, and on straight (vertical) meridians

Compiled and drawn in the Department of State, Division of Geography and Cartography, by Mr. Clarence B. Odell

DISTRIBUTION OF WORLD POPULATION

industry following the industrial and agricultural revolutions. Because of this greater productivity, man was able to save a small surplus against bad years and to support a government strong enough to move local crop surpluses to areas of deficit, and thus he began to live a little better and a little more securely. He also had the means to introduce a small measure of sanitation. These improvements began in the early days of the Industrial Revolution and paid almost immediate dividends in lower death rates.

There were, of course, occasional setbacks in times of famine and war which also brought on disease, as in Finland and Sweden, but, on the whole, there was a fairly steady, if slow, decline in the death rate as soon as man's economic conditions began to improve. On the other hand, for some decades after the decline in the death rate began there was little decline in the birth rate; and, when it did set in simultaneously, as in Finland, it was generally as slow as, or even slower than, that in the death rate for several decades.

The data for Sweden show the pattern of a growing natural increase for several decades after the birth rate began to decline (Fig. 1). Here the natural increase—birth rate minus death rate—was greater every decade from 1851 to 1911 than in the corresponding decade a century earlier, although there can be no doubt that Sweden's birth rate had begun to decline as early as 1830. In Finland, on the other hand, where the decline in the birth rate, as well as in the death rate, seems to have been present from 1750 onward and where these declines were about equal, there was comparatively little change in the rate of natural increase for a hundred and sixty years (1750–1910), except for years of famine and war.

This period of an increasing margin between birth rate and death rate, or of a rather large but steady margin, as in Finland, is in time succeeded by a period generally shorter but varying considerably in length from country to country, in which the rate of natural increase begins to decline because the birth rate is falling faster than the death rate but during which natural increase still remains quite high.

After 1910 and the disturbances occasioned by World War I, the birth rate in most Western lands continued to decline about as it had been declining; but, since the death rate could no longer be reduced at its former pace in most of them, a period of rapidly declining growth set in. The birth rate in most of the more industrialized countries has now declined to the level at which they have very little or no natural increase.

Thus the modern cycle of population growth in industrialized lands is completed and the population again approaches the stationary or has too few births to maintain itself, as it was in pre-industrial days— although it no longer fluctuates largely between excess and deficit as in earlier days. The failure of population to grow today is not because of the high and fluctuating death rate, as was usually the case in the past,

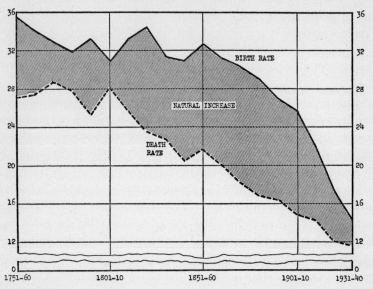

Fig. 1.—Crude birth and death rates and natural increase of Sweden, 1751–1940 (ten-year averages).

but because of the low birth rate. This is the general picture of population growth in the Western world during the last hundred to a hundred and fifty years.

CLASSIFICATION OF NATIONS IN THE CYCLE OF GROWTH

Because the industrial and commercial development of all peoples has not proceeded uniformly since pre-industrial days, different peoples have been and now are at different stages in the cycle of population growth just described. This has resulted in a differential growth of peoples and of regions which seems likely to continue for a considerable time in the future, since the factors which produced it are still at work. In the hundred to the hundred and fifty years before World War I, they operated to enhance the growth of Europeans more than that of the other peoples of the earth, because of the earlier improvement in Europe's level of living. At present, with the more and more secure control of the birth rate in the West, the differential growth of peoples is changing, and it is in this change in population growth as it affects the Pacific peoples that we are interested here.

Since we cannot consider the population prospect in all countries here, but since we do need to see population growth in the Pacific Region in relation to world population growth, let us see where the chief countries of the world would fit into the cycle of population growth described above.

It will be sufficient to distinguish three broad classes of countries based on the character of their present demographic processes (1935–39). The first group consists of those which have about completed the cycle and now have a natural decrease, a low rate of increase, or a birth rate now declining so fast that their natural increase seems certain to disappear shortly. These may be called "stationary" countries.

The second class consists of those in which the death rate has already fallen significantly and is well below the birth rate. In them the death rate is still declining more rapidly than, or as rapidly as, the birth rate, although there may be clear evidence that the birth rate has also begun to decline. As a consequence these countries have a relatively large natural increase, and in many of them it is growing larger. These are the "expanding" countries.

The third group will then include all other countries, both those which are definitely in the pre-industrial era and those which have so recently entered upon a period of higher productivity that their control of death rates is not yet securely established (see Map II). They are characterized by high birth rates and high death rates, and their rate of increase is so dependent on the accidents of a precariously controlled death rate that it is highly unpredictable and may vary greatly from year to year. These countries presumably have ahead of them nearly all of that period of large and steady growth which has characterized so much of the West since about 1800. For the sake of brevity we will call these "pre-industrial" countries, although some of them have already developed some modern industry.

It should be said here that the lines of demarcation between these classes are not clear and well defined. Actually many peoples are on the margin of each class, and it is to a considerable extent a matter of opinion whether they should be called "stationary" or "expanding" or "pre-industrial." Any difference of opinion would rest primarily on a

MAP II

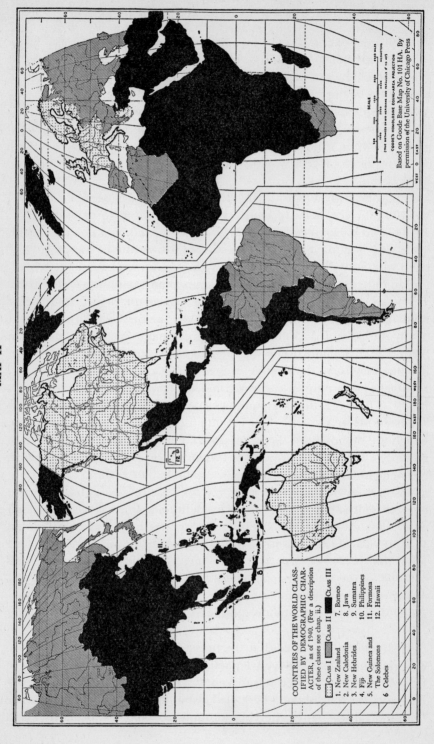

COUNTRIES OF THE WORLD CLASS-
IFIED BY DEMOGRAPHIC CHAR-
ACTER, as of 1940. (For a description
of these classes see chap. ii.)

CLASS I   CLASS II   CLASS III

1. New Zealand   7. Borneo
2. New Caledonia   8. Java
3. New Hebrides   9. Sumatra
4. Fiji   10. Philippines
5. New Guinea and   11. Formosa
   The Solomons   12. Hawaii
6. Celebes

SCALE

Based on Goode Base Map No. 101 HA. By
permission of the University of Chicago Press

different evaluation of the extent to which the death rate and the birth rate of a given people have come under assured voluntary control.

In the following discussion of the probable growth of the peoples in these three classes the basic assumption is that the general pattern of population growth as described above will be repeated wherever industrial and social development somewhat similar to that of the West takes place. It will not be assumed, however, that the length of time needed to complete the cycle will be the same everywhere.

THE "STATIONARY" PEOPLES

In this class we find the United States, the United Kingdom, France, Scandinavia, Holland, Germany, Austria, Czechoslovakia, Hungary, the Baltic countries, Belgium, Finland, Switzerland, Italy, Canada, Australia, and New Zealand.

These countries are, in general, characterized by low death rates and low birth rates which are declining faster than their death rates, so that as a class they have little real increase. In most of them the present excess of births over deaths is due to the relatively large number of young persons (under middle age) in their populations as a consequence of a fairly rapid growth up until about 1910–20.

In view of the steady and long-continued decline of birth rates in the countries in this group which still have enough births to maintain numbers—for example, Italy and Holland—and in view of the increasing difficulty they will all have in further lowering their death rates, it seems reasonable to assume that this group as a whole will soon reach the stage where it will no longer have any real growth.

Only a definite increase in the average number of children born per woman can prevent this group from becoming stationary in a few years; after this they will begin to decline. With the *possible* exception of Germany, there is no evidence that the average number of children born per woman has ceased to decline in any of them. In the case of Germany there is some slight indication of an increase in third- and higher-order births. But this evidence is not conclusive and even if a true increase has been achieved, by 1939 it was sufficient only to maintain a stationary population and not to support a growing one.

There is nothing inevitable, or outside man's control, in this probable decline of the "stationary" peoples. Man can change this pattern of growth if he really wants to do so, but, until there is evidence that he really does want to change it and has started to do so by having larger families, the logical assumption is that the decline in the birth rate will continue in those more industrialized lands and that all other lands as they pass through the social and economic development characteristic of the West will also pass through this growth cycle.

In 1940 the estimated population of the "stationary" countries was about 430 million. In 1913 it was about 356 million. Thus the gain amounted to 74 million, or 20.8 per cent, in twenty-seven years and may be compared with a gain of almost 47 million, or 15.1 per cent, in the preceding thirteen years—a period only half as long. In 1940 these countries contained a little over one-fifth of the world's population, assuming the world's population was 2.1 billion. This is the same proportion as in 1913. From now on it is almost certain that they will become a smaller and smaller proportion of the world's total.

So far as I can ascertain, these low rates of population growth and decline in numbers *due to low birth rates* are unprecedented in human history, except for small groups or classes. It will be of some interest, therefore, to inquire briefly into the causes of this change. The reduction in the birth rate did not manifest itself in most Western countries for several decades after industrialization began. In England and Wales there is no clear evidence of a decline before about 1878, and in Germany it was not evident before 1900. In the United States and France it appears to have been present throughout the nineteenth century, although in the United States the birth rate remained high, according to present standards, until 1900.

Gradually, as more and more people came to live in cities and to work at nonagricultural jobs, the birth rate began to decline everywhere. There is evidence in the number of children 0–4 per 1,000 women 16–44 in the early censuses of the United States that there was a significant difference in the birth rates of rural and urban women as early as 1800. Thus the decline of the birth rate appeared first in cities and was, and is, greater in cities than in rural areas. This is true of all countries in which industry has made much headway. Thus we can conclude that industrialization, with its accompanying urbanization, furnished relatively new and powerful motives for the control of births and that these new conditions of living also fostered the development of means by which this control could be accomplished.

Within the city the decline in the birth rate came first among the classes in which the improvement in living conditions was greatest— among the comfortable and the well to do—and there is still a significant difference in the size of families of the well to do and the better educated, on the one hand, and those less comfortable and with less schooling, on the other. This difference is now diminishing, however.

Because the decline in the birth rate has been so closely associated with industrialization in the West, it is more than likely that the development of similar social and economic conditions in other lands will also be effective in reducing their birth rates. This is an important point, for, to be concrete, it appears probable that as the Soviet Union, or the peoples in the Balkans, or the Chinese, or any other group, become industrialized and as their people come to live more and more in cities, their birth rates will decline until they become quite similar to those of the West. There is no good reason to suppose that the same motives which have led us to control births will not come into operation in these other lands. This does not mean, of course, that the birth rates and death rates will be identical, but rather that they will be of much the same general magnitude and that they will be held at a low level for much the same reasons.

THE "EXPANDING" PEOPLES

The countries that fall in this class are Spain, Portugal, Greece, Yugoslavia, Bulgaria, Rumania, Poland, South Africa (white), Japan, the Soviet Union, and *possibly* also French North Africa (Algeria, Tunis, and Morocco), Brazil, Argentina, and Uruguay. The term "possibly" is used in regard to these latter countries because there is some doubt as to just what is happening to their birth and death rates. But what evidence there is indicates that their death rates have begun to come under control; therefore, they belong in the group of countries with populations likely to grow rather steadily and rapidly during the next several decades.

The "expanding" peoples, in general, are characterized by fairly high but declining death rates and by high and fairly steady birth rates, although in most of them the birth rate also has begun to decline in certain segments of the population. As a group they represent the earlier stages of population growth in countries now being industrialized. Some of them are considerably farther along in the cycle of growth than others, but they share the common characteristic of having a sufficiently firm control over their death rates so that, except for unforeseen catastrophes, they should be able to keep them well below what they have been in the past. It is reasonably certain, therefore, that they will continue to grow rapidly for several decades after the "stationary" countries have begun to decline.

The population data for most "expanding" countries are not of much value before 1900, and even at that time estimates have to be used in several cases. But if we assume that all the countries enumerated above belong in this class, their population in 1900–1901 in territory approximately as it was in 1939 was about 269 million and constituted 17.6 per cent of that of the world. They grew rapidly up to World War I, and in 1913 they numbered about 345 million—about one-fifth of that of the world. By 1940 their population was approximately 438 million, or slightly more than one-fifth (21.1 per cent) of the world's. They then contained a somewhat larger number than the "stationary" countries. Whereas the latter grew only 15.1 per cent between 1900 and 1913, the former grew 28.2 per cent. The rates of growth for 1913–39 were 20.8 and 27.0 per cent, respectively, in spite of an extraordinary loss of life of 20 million or more by war, famine, and disease in Russia alone, and almost equal losses, proportionally, in the Balkans.

The probable future rates of growth in "stationary" and "expanding" countries are illustrated by some calculations recently made by the Office of Population Research (346). The group of countries which it called Northwestern and Central Europe are all in our "stationary" group and had a population of 234 million in 1940. They can be expected to increase to about 237 million in 1950 and then to decline to 225 million in 1970, assuming the continuation of inter-war trends. In general, this region includes the lower-birth-rate countries of our "stationary" group, which as a unit will probably increase by not more than 10–15 per cent by 1970.

On the other hand, the Soviet Union, which has a somewhat higher rate of growth than the remainder of our "expanding" group, but which constituted about 40 per cent of it in 1940, can, according to these calculations, be expected to increase from 174 million (346, p. 312) in 1940 to 251 million in 1970—an increase of 77 million, or more than 44 per cent in thirty years. Making no allowance for the effects of the war, this seems a reasonable calculation. If the whole "expanding" group were to grow at this rate, it would amount to about 630 million in 1970 compared with 474 million in the "stationary" group, allowing for a 10 per cent increase in the latter. This is not merely an exercise in arithmetic; it is a highly probable development. The figures, of course, are not exact, but there is little doubt among population students that the differential will be of about this magnitude.

In these calculations no account has been taken of the effects of the present war on population growth. Such effects are highly problematical, but, as regards relative increase, I know of no good reason to assume that the war will do more to slow up the rate of growth in "expanding" countries than in "stationary" countries during the next thirty years, hence the ratio of the two classes to each other should develop about as indicated although the totals may be somewhat smaller.

THE "PRE-INDUSTRIAL" PEOPLES

If the population of the world amounted to about 2.1 billion in 1940, then the peoples in the two preceding classes comprised about 42 per cent of the total. The remainder, or 58 per cent, would belong in the third class. From a demographic standpoint this group is characterized by high and largely uncontrolled birth rates and death rates, although neither of these is ever wholly uncontrolled. In this group birth rates of 40–50 are the rule rather than the exception, and death rates are generally very high, although they are quite variable from year to year.[2]

Since control over the death rate in these countries is very insecure, it frequently fluctuates violently from year to year and even from region to region within a country in the same year. There may be famine and severe epidemics in parts of China today, and the death rate may be as high as 50 or more per 1,000. In the same area next year there may be good crops and relatively little disease, and the death rate may fall to 30 or below, while in the country as a whole there may be little difference in death rates in these two years.

In consequence of the almost negligible, or highly uncertain, control over the death rates in this class, it is impossible to feel sure of any prediction of population growth in them. However, one can say under what conditions their populations are almost certain to grow if one assumes, as seems altogether reasonable, that the conditions prevailing in these countries today are closely similar to those which prevailed throughout most of the world before about 1800, and if one further assumes that in due time they, too, will industrialize, as has happened in the West. This assumption seems quite justified in view of the facts adduced in following chapters.

There may have been some reason three or four decades ago to doubt whether the course of population growth in these "pre-industrial" lands and particularly in the East would follow a similar pattern

[2] For a more specific account of the population growth in some of the larger "pre-industrial" lands see population sections in the chapters that follow.

to that which had been developing in the West, but this is not true to-day. Japan, the first country in the East to industrialize to any signifi-cant degree, has already proceeded a long way from this status and has now reached the phase of the cycle characteristic of an "expanding" people (see chap. vi).

The expansion of population in these "pre-industrial" countries will depend largely on the speed with which they can industrialize, can improve and extend their agriculture, and on the success they attain in the control of disease. Although highly efficient industrial techniques are available which would make very rapid industrialization possible in these countries, it is not at all certain that the basic resources needed by such a vast population can be found. This "pre-industrial" group is already five to six times as large as was the European population of 1800. Furthermore, the experience of Japan and the Soviet Union clearly proves that, although industrialization can proceed at a faster pace today than it could a century and a half ago, the control of dis-ease can also be greatly accelerated.

The *possibility* of quickly reducing the death rate in these countries is, therefore, greater than ever before in man's history; but the *prob-ability* would seem to be less than in the Europe of 1800 because of the very magnitude of the population we have to commence with—1.2 billion—and of the more limited supplies of new land and resources available for their settlement. There are no more North and South Americas to be settled, and the islands of the Pacific Ocean, great as they are, together with the thinly settled but tillable areas of Africa, cannot furnish the relief to the present populations of these "back-ward" lands that the Americas and Australasia did to Europe through-out the nineteenth century and that many parts of South America still furnish.

PROSPECTIVE GROWTH OF DIFFERENT PEOPLES

Judging from the time it took Western lands to develop effective birth control, it may be a century or more before the populations in most "pre-industrial" lands cease to expand about as rapidly as their increasing productivity decreases their death rate. During this time there will be, as we have said, large differentials in the rates of growth of different nations and regions. The "stationary" countries will grow but little in the near future unless they admit large numbers of immi-grants of lower levels of living from the "expanding" or "pre-indus-trial" countries. The "expanding" countries will continue to grow at a fairly rapid rate for several decades, since it is not humanly possible to spread the effective practice of birth control among such masses of people in a few years. "Pre-industrial" countries must remain something of an enigma, but it is quite certain that it will require several decades longer for them to develop any effective control of their population growth than will be needed by the "expanding" countries.

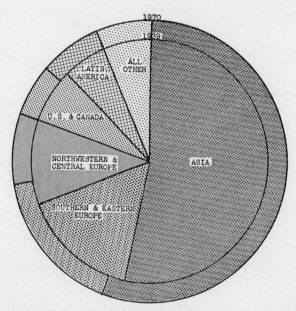

Fig. 2.—Distribution of the world's population by selected areas in 1939 and estimated distribution in 1970. Data for Europe in 1970 based on estimates of future population taken from Frank W. Notestein *et al.*, *The Future Population of Europe and the Soviet Union* (Geneva: League of Nations, 1944). Other estimates by the Scripps Foundation for Research in Population Problems.

Figure 2 gives us a good idea of the probable future growth of the regions of the earth during the next thirty years. If population growth goes forward in this way, as now seems probable, the "stationary" peoples who expanded so rapidly in the century preceding World War I will grow but little, the "expanding" peoples will grow for two or three decades about as during the past two or three and then begin to pass into the "stationary" group, while the "pre-industrial" peoples will begin to move into the "expanding" group. This will result in a significantly different ratio between these groups *even in a quarter of a century*, and after that for several decades it will become steadily greater in favor of the "pre-industrial" peoples.

Chapter III

TROPICAL OCEANIA

THE islands included under this title are those lying between the west coast of the Americas on the east and the Celebes, the Philippines, and Japan on the west, but not including New Zealand and Australia. Oceania thus defined is almost entirely tropical. Furthermore, with the exception of New Guinea, these islands are all relatively small, the largest being New Britain with about 13,000 square miles. Their total area, including New Guinea, is about 400,000 square miles, New Guinea alone constituting about four-fifths of the whole. The other islands or groups of islands of sufficient size to be of more than strategic interest, or of interest solely because of specific resources, are: Solomons (14,500), New Ireland (3,000), Hawaii (6,454), Fiji (7,083), New Hebrides (5,700), New Caledonia (9,475), French Establishments (1,520), Samoa (1,193—American and Western), and Japanese mandates (830).

Most of the islands large enough to support a population of more than a few hundreds are mountainous and have relatively large areas of unusable land. The valleys and more level lands are, however, generally very fertile and, when properly cultivated, will raise large crops of nearly all tropical products.

THE POPULATION OF OCEANIA

The present population of Oceania is about 2.7 million, although it must be recognized that no real count of heads has ever been made in many of the larger islands or in most of the smaller ones. About 2,086,-000 of the inhabitants are natives, and about 230,000 are Japanese, of whom almost 70 per cent are in Hawaii and most of the remainder in the Japanese mandate. The whites number about 142,000, of whom about 73 per cent are in Hawaii and about 12 per cent in New Caledonia, leaving only about 15 per cent in the remaining islands. There are also about 98,000 Indians who settled in Fiji after their period of indenture on the sugar plantations had expired, about 52,000 Filipinos in Hawaii, and about 40,000 Chinese, of whom about 72 per cent are in Hawaii. The small number unaccounted for are largely of mixed blood, with a few Malays from the Netherlands East Indies and a few Tonkinese from Indo-China.

It will be noted that, although all these islands have long been under the control of the white man, except the small Japanese mandate, whites constitute less than 6 per cent of the total population and, outside of Hawaii (25 per cent white) and New Caledonia (31 per cent white), are only about 1 per cent of the total.

Rather than go into the history of population trends in these islands since the white man came, we will simply note that those who have studied the matter quite generally believe that the coming of the white man and his efforts to exploit the natives was a major population catastrophe to most of these peoples (383). In addition to the direct attempt to use the natives for plantation work (probably a minor factor), the white man brought whiskey, tuberculosis, syphilis, and clothes, all of which were deadly to people not accustomed to them. But, above all, he broke up the traditional modes of tribal life and thus robbed the natives of their most precious social heritage. The result was a large and rapid decline in population in many of these islands, which has now been arrested in most of them but which went so far as to lead to practical extinction in some of them.

There were probably 3.5 million people (251, p. 43) in these islands when the white man came, about a million more than the total population today, and about 1.4 million more than the present-day natives. This large and rapid decline in natives was one of the first effects of their contact with the whites.

In Polynesia a native population estimated at 1.1 million when the whites came dropped to about 180,000 by 1890 and then began to increase slowly, rising to about 330,000 by 1938—perhaps *one-third* of what they were early in the nineteenth century. In Micronesia—the Carolines, Marshalls, and Marianas—the fluctuation in population was not so violent, probably because contact with the white man was never very close. Here a native population estimated at 200,000 at the end of the eighteenth century declined to about 80,000 by the end of the nineteenth century and is now presumed to be a little over 100,000. In Melanesia—New Guinea and the larger islands near it reaching east to Fiji—the population declined from about 2.2 million to perhaps 1.2–1.3 million and is now growing again, being estimated at about 1.4 million in 1939. On a number of these islands, however, particularly in Polynesia, the population is believed to be still declining.

The policies of the whites toward the natives have improved over the years, but clearly the latter have no reason to feel grateful for the treatment they have received. From the very beginning the white man has acted on the assumption that he had a God-given right to exploit these peoples and their land for his own profit. It is not surprising that as a consequence he is neither trusted nor respected by the more influential natives, although he may be feared. Moreover, where the white man went ahead vigorously with his exploitation, Hawaii and Fiji being the best examples, he introduced other alien (Asiatic) peoples and thus complicated both the economic and the population problems of the area.

THE POPULATION OF HAWAII UNDER WHITE CONTROL

What the white man has done to the population of Hawaii in his eagerness to exploit its agricultural riches is well worth examining, since it would probably furnish the pattern for any rapid development in other areas.

It is generally thought that in 1850 there were about 70,000 native Hawaiians in the islands (203, p. 17). This is supposed to be not more than one-third of the pre-white Hawaiian population (251, p. 49) and about half of that in 1800. In 1850 there were only about 2,000 foreigners in the islands, of whom about 1,200 were whites.

Here, as elsewhere, the natives were very reluctant to work on the plantations which some of the whites were beginning to establish, so a few Chinese were brought in as early as 1852. It was not until after the reciprocity treaty of Hawaii with the United States in 1875, however, that a rapid plantation development took place, the number of Chinese growing from 6,045 in 1878 to 18,254 in 1884.

It soon became clear to the white owners that the Chinese would not long remain docile plantation laborers. If given opportunity, they left the plantations and penetrated quickly into many phases of the economic life of the islands. This brought them into more or less direct competition with the whites. In small business, in particular, they were very successful because they had a lower level of living and were more industrious than the whites. As soon as the plantation owners saw this, they began to look for another labor supply. The exclusion of the Chinese from Hawaii in 1887 and 1888 (by passport requirements) was no doubt hastened somewhat by the troubles between whites and Chinese in the United States, but the underlying reason for their exclusion from Hawaii was the belief that the position of the landowners would be made more secure if no more Chinese were brought in. Since 1887 the growth of the Chinese in Hawaii has been considerably less than their natural increase because of the return to China of many of those who had come earlier.

The next group brought in for work in the fields were the Portuguese. They numbered only 424 in 1872, but by 1930 they had increased to over 27,000, and the number of Caucasian-Hawaiians, of whom a large part are Portuguese crosses, had increased to over 15,000. The census for 1940 does not separate the Portuguese from other Caucasians, but there is little doubt that they have continued to increase.

However, the number of Portuguese entering Hawaii was never adequate to meet the increasing demands for field labor after the exclusion of the Chinese, and about that time the plantation owners also began to bring in Japanese laborers—over 3,000 a year between 1885 and 1894. Their number increased very rapidly until 1906, after which time they were excluded for much the same reasons that earlier led to the exclusion of the Chinese. By 1910, however, there were over 79,000 in the islands, and, since "picture brides" continued to enter in considerable numbers until 1924 (over 14,000 between 1909 and 1924), natural increase alone rapidly expanded the Japanese population. By 1940 the number had increased to 158,000, or well over one-third of the total population, including the military establishment.

With the stopping of Japanese immigration after 1906 it was necessary to find a new source of field labor, and this time the planters turned to the Philippines. The Filipinos were already American citizens (with certain limitations), and it was again hoped that a sufficiently abundant and docile labor supply had been tapped. (The plantation owners seemed to have learned little or nothing from their previous experience.) The Filipinos, who formed only about 10 per cent of the plantation labor in 1910, had become 70 per cent by 1930, declining to about 60 per cent of the farm laborers in 1940 (294, p. 325).

But the Filipino plantation laborer, like the Chinese, Portuguese, and Japanese before him, did not long remain a peon if he had a chance at some other work. He might have been a little slower to get into other kinds of work, but, in spite of the fact that he had more severe competition in making the transition than the Chinese and Japanese had encountered earlier, by 1940 almost one-third had left farm work. The total number of Filipinos declined by almost 17 per cent between 1930 and 1940, and there has been much agitation in recent years to find still another source of cheap and docile labor. The latest group of field workers has come from Puerto Rico, but the number has been small and is by no means sufficient to take the place of the departing Filipinos.

The racial results of the efforts to maintain the plantation system by bringing in cheap labor from wherever it could be had are apparent in the data in Table 2 and call for little explanation. The Hawaiians,

TABLE 2

DISTRIBUTION OF HAWAIIAN POPULATION BY SEX AND RACE, 1890–1940

Race	Total	Male	Female	Total	Male	Female
	1940			1930		
Hawaiian..........	14,375	7,413	6,962	22,636	11,311	11,325
Part-Hawaiian......	49,935	24,650	25,285	28,224	14,042	14,182
Caucasian..........	103,791	64,473	39,318	80,373	48,706	31,667
Chinese............	28,774	16,131	12,643	27,179	16,561	10,618
Filipino............	52,569	40,791	11,778	63,052	52,566	10,486
Japanese...........	157,905	82,820	75,085	139,631	75,008	64,623
Other races........	15,981	8,857	7,124	7,241	4,446	2,795
Total...........	423,330	245,135	178,195	368,336	222,640	145,696
	1910			1890		
Hawaiian..........	26,041	13,439	12,602	34,436	18,364	16,072
Part-Hawaiian......	12,506	6,250	6,256	6,186	3,085	3,101
Caucasian..........	44,048	24,782	19,266	18,939*	10,897*	8,042*
Chinese............	21,674	17,148	4,526	16,752*	15,343*	1,409*
Filipino............	2,361	2,160	201	....	....	....
Japanese...........	79,675	54,784	24,891	12,610*	10,219*	2,391*
Other races........	5,604	4,536	1,068	1,067*	806*	261*
Total...........	191,909	123,099	68,810	89,990	58,714	31,276

* Hawaiian-born children of foreigners distributed racially by estimate and included with parents, 7,495 in 1890.

who had been declining in numbers rather rapidly for a long while before 1890, continued to decline up to 1940. However, the rate of decline, which had been diminishing prior to 1930, rose precipitately between 1930 and 1940, and Hawaiians now number only a little over 14,000 and constitute only 3.4 per cent of the total population. On the other hand, the part-Hawaiians increased about 75 per cent during the last ten years, which suggests the probability that a considerable number of persons who had been reporting themselves as Hawaiians before 1940 reported themselves as part-Hawaiians at that time. In any event, there can be no doubt about the steady and rapid increase of part-Hawaiians during the last thirty to forty years.

There is no way of telling exactly where the large increase in Caucasian stock in recent years has come from, but it seems reasonably certain, because of the high and increasing proportion of males, that the increase in "Caucasians," from 54,742 in 1920 to 80,373 in 1930 and to 103,791 in 1940, was due chiefly to the strengthening of the military forces in the islands and, to a minor extent, to bona fide migration from the mainland.

The more important changes in the ratios of children to women in the different racial groups in Hawaii between 1930 and 1940 are those taking place in the Chinese and Japanese populations. In both groups the ratios were less than half as high in 1940 as they were in 1930 (Chinese 982 in 1930 and 421 in 1940; Japanese 1,112 and 550 in the same years). Since it took about 440 children 0–4 to 1,000 women 20–44 to maintain the white population of the United States in 1930 and about 430 in 1940, it can be seen that the Caucasians, with a ratio of 362 in 1940, are dying out, that the Chinese are scarcely maintaining themselves, and that the Japanese are still increasing quite rapidly (although at a very modest rate as compared with their rate in 1930). The Filipinos (with 1,429 and 1,411) and the part-Hawaiians (with 1,661 and 1,231), on the other hand, showed a large increase at both times.

The figures on the Chinese, Japanese, and Filipinos in the islands speak for themselves. The Chinese have never increased very rapidly, in the past, chiefly because of the small number of women in the group and of the return of older Chinese to their homes. In 1940 there were still 128 males to each 100 females.

As a result of these differential rates of growth, assuming no immigration into Hawaii in the future, the "Caucasians" would become a rapidly diminishing part of the population, the Chinese would about hold their own, the Japanese would increase slowly, while the Filipinos and Hawaiians (including part-Hawaiians) would grow rather rapidly. Thus under a political system in which all native adults are citizens, the control of the islands would certainly pass out of the hands of the "Caucasians," largely Anglo-Saxons, who have exercised it hitherto, and into the hands of the Asiatic groups which they have brought in to work the plantations. If this political shift were to take place, it would be a matter of only a few decades at most until the "Caucasian" group would also lose its economic dominance.

The strategic importance of Hawaii to the United States will undoubtedly determine its political status for some time to come, but the economic dominance of the white population can be maintained only by denying the fundamental rights of democracy to the descendants of the peoples who made the rapid economic development of the islands possible. The inevitable processes of population growth in Hawaii are bringing about a change in the numerical relation of whites and Asiatics which must be faced.

This rather long description of the growth of Hawaii's population and the indication of its future trend is important because it illustrates what happens when whites come into contact with Asiatics. It is happening in Fiji and in the French Establishments and will happen wherever the Asiatics are used to develop the plantation system or to exploit the mineral resources, if they are allowed to bring women with them and to remain when their indenture contracts expire.

Nowhere in this whole region has the white man actually taken hold of the job of development himself, unless it is among the descendants of the convicts in New Caledonia. He does not actually "possess" the land, raise crops, and dig minerals, as he does in Australia, New Zealand, the United States, and other temperate latitudes, and, above all, he does not reproduce. The small Australian sugar industry, highly subsidized, and the permanent residence of the few dominant families of Hawaii do not constitute true exceptions. The dilemma of this "colonial" system will not be fully apparent, however, until we have examined the economic life of the region.

AGRICULTURE IN OCEANIA

The crops actually being grown in Oceania can be divided into two classes: those being grown on a commercial scale for world trade and those being grown for local consumption and with which we need not much concern ourselves. The former consist chiefly of coconuts (shipped mostly in the form of copra—dried coconut meat), sugar cane (shipped as raw sugar), and pineapples (chiefly canned). There are also a number of other commercial crops such as rubber, vanilla, cotton, coffee, and certain spices and fruits (bananas); but, as yet, they are of comparatively little importance.

For the most part the commercial crops are grown on large plantations by hired labor or, as in Fiji, by farmers (Indians) on contract and under the direction of a large corporation. The crops are generally concentrated for shipment on the plantation or at some convenient point near by. However, there are very considerable differences between the different islands in the organization of their agriculture; for example, on a number of them a large part of the coconut production is in the hands of native growers, but the processing and sale is likely to be in the hands of Europeans. This is essential to insure uniform quality in the product.

In general, it may be said that the greater the need for uniform quality in commercial crops and the greater the difficulty of achieving it, the more these crops are grown on plantations owned and managed by Europeans. The fact that the native peoples of this region do not take kindly to steady work on the plantation has greatly retarded its agricultural development. Then, too, the dying-off of the native populations in many of the islands would have resulted in a shortage of labor even though they had been willing to work. The result of these conditions, as we shall see, is that commercial agriculture has never made much headway except when laborers were imported from Asia in rather large numbers.

At the present time Oceania contributes significant amounts of only three crops to the commercial agricultural production of the world: about 12–13 per cent of the copra (251, p. 322), about 6.5 per cent of the sugar (251, p. 324), and perhaps half or more of the pineapples. There is not the least doubt, however, that production of these items as well as of many other tropical crops can be increased many fold.

Even the most highly developed islands in Oceania are far from being completely used. In 1939 Hawaii, which is far ahead of any of the others in agricultural production, had only 184,600 acres harvested, 123,000 for future harvest (cane and pineapples), and 104,000 of fallow or plowable pasture (185, p. 18). The total land available for crops is given as a little over 413,000 acres, which is about one-tenth of the total area and about one-sixth of the total land in farms (2,486,-000 acres). Since the islands are quite mountainous, a large porportion of the land can never be tilled, but there are many people who believe that the present tilled area could be doubled without much difficulty (although not under the present system of large plantations).

In 1940 there were 114 farms of over 1,000 acres—a total acreage of 2,384,000, or about 95 per cent of all the land in farms. The value of these large farms, including their buildings, was $99,000,000, while the value of all farms in the islands was only $113,000,000. Clearly, only land which can be used for commercial crops in large-scale farming will be tilled as long as the ownership of usable land is thus concentrated. There cannot be the least doubt that a more diversified farming, in which the farmer produces for his own needs as well as something for sale, would make it possible to extend the tilled area and to support a much larger agricultural population at as good or better levels of living than at present (185, p. 25).

The other island group (aside from the Japanese mandate) which has developed a considerable amount of commercial agriculture is the Fiji Islands. Here the development is far behind Hawaii, but sugar, copra, bananas, and a number of other crops are grown largely by Indians who were brought in originally on indenture to the sugar companies. After their indenture expired, many of them stayed; now they are almost equal to the natives in number and are growing much faster, so that numerically they will soon be the dominant group in the islands. Most of the work on the plantations is done by Indians either as hired hands or as lessees of land from the sugar company. Many of the Indians now own small plots of land and grow their own food while giving some space to commercial crops. Ownership of land in Fiji is not nearly so concentrated as in Hawaii.

In all the rest of this vast region it can be truly said that there is only the merest beginning of commercial (plantation) agriculture and that the area under crops for native use, although small, accounts for most of the tilled area. It is doubtful if the entire tilled area exceeds 2,000–3,000 square miles, and it certainly cannot exceed 5,000, while the total area is about 400,000 square miles. If at present 4,000 square miles are tilled (1 per cent) and if 20 per cent can be tilled, we can see that the possibilities of expansion are enormous. Twenty per cent as an estimate of tillable land is guesswork, of course, since most of this land is on New Guinea, and no comprehensive survey of that island has ever been made. But, as one reads descriptions of it, one gets the general impression that perhaps one-fourth or more of it can be tilled. Naturally, one wonders why so little of the land in Oceania is now tilled or ever has been tilled.

The answer seems to be that the natives were always relatively few, and they had become accustomed to a modest self-sufficing tribal life which required but little steady agricultural work. Consequently, they used only the land necessary to meet their simple needs. Indeed, in some parts of Oceania most of the agricultural products needed required no cultivation: sago palm, coconuts, breadfruit, and even taro. In other parts fish and pork were important articles of diet, but even they were not "raised"; they just "growed." It is not surprising, therefore, that native agriculture never has occupied, and does not now occupy, any significant proportion of the tillable land of Oceania and that there are no dense native agricultural populations in this whole region.

EXPLOITERS AND/OR SETTLERS

The situation in the mandate (Australia) of New Guinea shows what is happening and is likely to happen in the exploitation of this region under the colonial system without the importation of Asiatic labor on any significant scale such as has taken place in Hawaii and Fiji. This mandate, including the islands of New Britain, New Ireland, and some of the northern Solomons, contains about 91,000 square miles. It came under the control of Australia shortly after the outbreak of World War I, having been a German colony previously.

In 1941 the European population numbered a little over 4,000, of whom about three-fourths were British, chiefly Australians, many of whom had come to the new gold fields during the later 1920's and early 1930's. The number of Chinese was about half that of the Europeans. The natives are supposed to number between 850,000 and 950,-000, made up of about 670,000 (including 39,000 indentured laborers) who presumably have been counted and an estimated 200,000–250,-000 not counted. The natives live in tribal groups and produce only for their own needs. The plantation agriculture in this mandate is almost entirely in the hands of the Europeans (354, 1942, p. 267).

In 1940 there were about 272,000 acres of cultivated land in plantations, or less than 0.5 per cent of the area of the mandate. The labor on these plantations is given as 339 whites, 99 Asiatics, 21 half-castes, and 20,477 indentured persons (natives). This represents the total accomplishment during almost sixty years of colonial effort, about thirty years of German possession, during which most of the plantation development took place, and an almost equal length of Australian control. There has been only a very slow advance in plantation agriculture since World War I.

The development of plantation agriculture depends on getting enough labor to bring land under cultivation and to care for the crops. The common complaint here, as everywhere in Oceania, is that the natives do not want steady work. It now seems obvious that the supply of native labor is going to increase very slowly unless far greater pressure is put upon them to enter into indenture contracts than has been done since New Guinea has come under Australian control. It is true that the wages offered—about $2.00 (10 shillings) per month with "found"—are pitiably small according to European standards, but they undoubtedly enable the native worker to live somewhat better from our point of view than he does in the tribe. The point here is not the low wages, however—they are probably as high as can be paid if plantation agriculture is to be profitable—it is rather that, regardless of wages, very few natives are willing to contract for the two or three years for which anyone starting a plantation feels he must be assured of his labor supply before it is worth while to undertake this task. There seems to be little prospect, therefore, of any rapid development of plantation agriculture in this colony by native labor as long as the present humane policy is followed.

An interesting contrast to this stagnation is offered by the Japanese mandate. This mandate consists of many small islands the total area of which is only about 830 square miles, less than 1 per cent of the size of the mandate of Australia in New Guinea. Almost 70,000 Japanese had settled there by 1939—almost twice the number of whites in the whole of Oceania outside Hawaii. Furthermore, most of these Japanese are real farmers, not mere exploiters of labor; nor are they soldiers in disguise. They have gone into the production of sugar cane and coconuts, and they produce much of their own food in spite of the fact that these islands are mountainous and have much waste land. About 10 per cent of their total area is now under cultivation.

In 1937 the total production of sugar cane amounted to over 200,000 tons (240, 1940, p. 566) and that of copra to over 14,000 tons. Phosphates are also being mined, the production amounting to more than 140,000 tons annually. Thus the Japanese development of their Oceanic mandate stands out against the development of any of the areas under white control, except Hawaii and Fiji, and it differs from these in that the governing group is of the same race as the people who actually do the work of development.

The slow development of New Guinea and the rapid development of the Japanese mandate illustrate the difference between control of an area by a people who will exploit it only as a colony and control by a people who will actually settle it and work the land with their own hands because they need it. We in the United States, Canada, Australia, and New Zealand should have no trouble in recognizing the fundamental differences between the actual settlement of a country by people who work the land, open the mines, build the railways, and operate the factories and the exploitation of colonies by a small master-class using cheap native or imported labor; but we seem to have forgotten it rather quickly. On the other hand, we now claim that natives' rights must be respected as against the Asiatics—*who*, as this book will show, *can use these lands and will almost certainly feel the need for them badly in the not distant future.*

We might expect more consideration for this view if its actual operation did not so obviously contribute to the enrichment of the white masters. We should not forget that never in our own expansion has the possession of the land by a few people using it meagerly been considered an adequate reason for allowing them to retain it when a more numerous people with a higher level of technology, and therefore with greater military power, wanted to occupy it either for settlement or for the mere economic advantage of a small class. Can the white man, having taken what he wanted of Oceania in the past and now having attained a position of pre-eminence in this region, *freeze* his position and prevent other peoples from emulating his past conduct?

MINERAL RESOURCES

The proved mineral resources of tropical Oceania are not large. The phosphates on some of the Society Islands, on Nauru and Ocean islands, and in the Japanese mandate are of importance, but mining them supports only a small population. Thus Nauru, which supplies almost half the total shipments of phosphate of the entire region, had a population of only 3,500 in 1939. Of these, about half were natives, about 43 per cent Chinese, and about 6 per cent Europeans.

Gold is the most widely mined mineral in Oceania. It is found in the Fiji Islands, New Guinea, New Caledonia, Guadalcanal, and some of the other islands. In 1938 production amounted to about 12 million dollars (251, p. 25).

New Caledonia appears to have the greatest variety and amounts of proved mineral resources. It has nickel, chrome, cobalt, iron, manganese, copper, mercury, and coal. Its nickel and chrome are of special importance; its production of the former is second largest in the world (12 per cent), although a long way behind Canada. Reliable estimates of the reserves of these minerals are lacking, however, so we do not know whether they are great enough to support any considerable industrial development.

New Guinea is also supposed to be rich in minerals, but only gold and copper are mined in significant amounts. At present all that can be said is that New Guinea is quite commonly thought to be worth thorough prospecting. A considerable amount of money has already been spent in searching for oil, but the results have been disappointing.

Altogether it would seem not unlikely that the mineral resources of southwestern Oceania are considerable and at some time in the future may prove of much value. But, at present, one must assume that agriculture will remain the chief support of population in these islands and that their development, in the future in which we are interested, will depend primarily on the agricultural policies pursued, provided they remain European colonies.

TRADE

A brief examination of the trade of some of the more developed parts of Oceania will also help us to understand the economic development of the region and particularly to appreciate the nature of the colonial plantation system.

It has already been noted that the chief agricultural products of the region are sugar, pineapples, and copra; consequently, they are also the chief exports. Following them are the gold of Fiji and New Guinea, the phosphates of some of the smaller islands, and the nickel and chrome of New Caledonia.

The imports, of course, are of far greater variety. If sugar cane is to be made into raw sugar, there must be machinery to do the work; if coconuts are to be dried, there must be driers; if minerals are to be mined, there must be mining equipment; and, if pineapples are to be canned, there must be cans and canneries. The people who manage this work will want a variety of goods which cannot be produced in these nonindustrialized lands, and as much of them as their means will allow. Finally, there must be reasonably good transportation if any trade at all is to be carried on, and the equipment for this must all be imported.

Hawaii, as the most developed of these islands agriculturally and as the largest processor of agricultural products, may be looked upon as the pattern the rest would follow under the present colonial system if conditions were favorable. The exports of Hawaii consist chiefly of raw sugar and pineapple products. Of total exports of Hawaiian products to the United States in 1939, over 106 million dollars out of 109 million dollars consisted of these products; coffee, canned fish, molasses, and fiber board account for most of the remainder, but their total value was only about 2.1 million dollars (453, p. 674). Nearly all of Hawaii's export trade is with the United States, as might be expected, since it is within our customs boundaries.

The imports of Hawaii show what a plantation area needs. The clothing, the machinery, the vehicles, the gasoline and oil, and the many luxuries of modern life are about what would be expected. The one exception, and a surprising one to many, is the great import of agricultural products. Of total goods imported from the United States in 1939, about one-fourth consisted of foods, feeds, and beverages. If tobacco is added, the proportion becomes about 27 per cent.

Clearly the plantation agriculture of Hawaii is a highly specialized agriculture which makes no provision for food crops. Although more than half the population consists of rice-eating people from Asia, almost no rice is grown; and although nine-tenths of the area is untilled, only a few beef cattle are raised, and the dairy cattle have to be fed imported grain. Even the native crops of coconuts and taro (a tuber from which porridge is made) are no longer grown in any significant quantity. This situation is not peculiar to Hawaii, although, having more commercial agriculture, it has a somewhat higher degree of dependence on outside food than most of the other islands.

In Fiji, where the Europeans constitute only about 2 per cent of the population, the situation is not very much different. The Indians do the plantation work, and many of them also have small plots of their own on which they can raise their food; but apparently they are far from being self-sufficing in food and feed. Its advantage over Hawaii lies in having a large number of small farms worked by Indians who have settled there after having worked out their labor contracts.

In 1937, before the export of gold became of much importance, about 89 per cent of the exports of Fiji consisted of sugar, copra, and bananas. There were also small amounts of other tropical crops but not enough of any one to be of much significance. Fiji's total exports in 1939, aside from gold, amounted to about 7 per cent of those of Hawaii, although its total area is somewhat greater, and it apparently has a somewhat larger proportion of tillable land. If Fiji had a large protected market for commercial agricultural products like Hawaii, it would probably be about as dependent on outside food as the latter.

In the mandated (Australia) territory of New Guinea it is the same story. The plantations produce commercial crops only (copra), while the natives, when living undisturbed in their tribal organization, produce only for their own use. Thus the plantation workers as well as the whites have to be fed largely on imports from outside. In this territory in 1937 about one-third of all the imports consisted of food, drink, and tobacco (about $400 per head of the European population of some 4,000, or a little over $37 per head for all indentured laborers, Chinese and Europeans). The agricultural exports consisted largely of copra. The largest export, however, was gold.

Even in the Japanese mandate about one-fifth of the imports are food, drink, and tobacco, with rice far in the lead.

At present and for some decades to come it appears that the amount of trade in Oceania is likely to depend on the extent to which the area is developed along lines followed by Hawaii if the present colonial system continues to operate. The more intensive the plantation development, the greater the volume of trade. But it must be remembered that the large per capita trade of Hawaii—$530 per capita for exports and imports combined—was possible because of two conditions, only one of which could be duplicated by any of the colonies even if it chose to do so. These conditions were the willingness to disregard completely the social and political problems raised by using Asiatic laborers to develop plantations and the existence of a great market for tropical products in which the territory had a preferred position. Any colonial power in this region could probably secure the Asiatic labor needed for rapid plantation development, but none of them can assure planters in Fiji or New Britain or New Guinea a market big enough to absorb their product or prices high enough to insure a profit.

THE FUTURE OF OCEANIA

The development of the economy of Oceania is so closely tied up with what is to be done about the labor supply and with whether the world will move toward freer trade or toward greater autarchy and with decisions still being made about its political future, and thus with the future of the whole colonial system, that little can now be said about what may happen. But it does seem clear that the whole colonial system as exemplified in the development of this area has reached a dead end. Apparently the white man can never be more than a bird of passage in this region—in which case the system he has established to exploit lands he cannot settle is bound to be almost equally transient unless he is able to establish a pattern of society which looks upon the bird of passage as necessary to the welfare of the mass of the people and can convince this mass that he should be paid at high European standards for his work. It is not sufficient for the European to be convinced of his own indispensability. The people themselves must believe that the system which gives him power and, not infrequently, wealth is desirable and is to their advantage. Otherwise only by the exercise of force and by establishing a fixed caste system can he remain white and maintain power; and then only if he will also reproduce.

In this book our interest in tropical Oceania centers in whether it may be so used as to enhance the hope of a more durable peace than followed World War I. As already shown, the cultivated area in Oceania can be greatly extended. To say that it can support ten times its present population in far greater comfort and health than any people in this region, or in Asia, now enjoys is undoubtedly a large understatement. Will it be so used? The answer to this question will be attempted after we have examined the conditions in the colonies and the countries of the western Pacific (chap. xx).

Chapter IV

AUSTRALIA AND NEW ZEALAND

AUSTRALIA is almost as large as the continental United States, but in 1940 it had a population of only seven million, practically all white. It might appear to many Americans at first thought that Australia is only now at the stage of settlement reached by the United States about 1810, when our population was a little over seven million and when our period of white settlement had been going on for only a little longer than Australia's has at present. There are many reasons, however, why such a comparison is misleading.

The first and most striking difference between Australia and the United States is that of climate. Only a small part of Australia has a rainfall of over 30 inches, and a considerable part of this lies within the tropics in a region of seasonal rainfall and drought, where it is of little value for crop production. The tillable area consists of a narrow coastal belt along the eastern, southeastern, and southwestern shores (Map III). Once the mountains are passed, the Australian pioneer, unlike his prototype in the United States, finds himself entering an arid region which becomes almost useless for agriculture before he has proceeded many scores of miles. The ultramontane area, of 20–30-inch rainfall, is very small when compared with that of the United States lying between the Appalachians and central Kansas and Nebraska. When the American pioneer had passed the Appalachians in his westward trek, he entered the largest domain of fertile tillable land in the temperate zone, if not in the entire world. He had no need to think of drought as a constantly threatening factor until he passed west of the hundredth meridian in central Kansas, where the rainfall fell below 20 inches per year. About 30 per cent of Australia has a rainfall of 10–20 inches (434, p. 54) and may be likened in this respect to our "dust bowl," our western wheat lands, and our grazing lands east of the Rockies, while another 36 per cent of Australia has a rainfall of less than 10 inches. Moreover, since a large proportion of the 10–20-inch rainfall area in Australia lies in the tropical and subtropical belt, only a very small part of it can be classed as agricultural or even as reasonably good grazing land.

MAP III

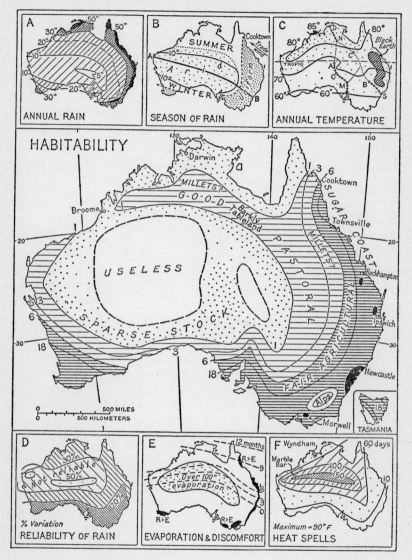

FUTURE SETTLEMENT OF AUSTRALIA, SHOWING APPROXIMATE LINES OF
EQUAL POPULATION (TO THE SQUARE MILE)

Small maps: A, annual rainfall; B, seasonal rains (the line *AB* separates summer from
winter rains); C, temperature (the suggested railway routes are indicated from Alice
Springs, *A*, or Bourke, *B*, to Newcastle Waters, *N*, Marree, *M*); D, rain reliability; E,
evaporation and discomfort; F, regions experiencing long periods of heat (days over 90° F.).
(Reproduced from Isaiah Bowman, *Limits of Land Settlement* [New York: Council on Foreign
Relations, 1937], Fig. 5, p. 209. Used by permission of the Council on Foreign Relations.)

Australia's population was estimated at a little over 7,000,000 on December 31, 1940, about 400,000 less than that of New York City at the 1940 census and a little more than that of the state of Ohio. At the time of the last census (1933) it was 6,600,000. Of this, over 99 per cent were full-blood Europeans and the rest were non-Europeans and half-castes. In addition, there were also (in 1933) about 60,000 full-blood aboriginals who are not listed with the census population. In 1940 this group was estimated at about 48,000, a decline of some 12,000 in seven years (17, 1941, pp. 280 and 285).

TABLE 3*

POPULATION AND INCREASE AND PROPORTION OF INCREASE DUE TO
NATURAL INCREASE AND IMMIGRATION, AUSTRALIA, 1860–1940

| YEAR | POPULATION | POPULATION INCREASE | | | | RATIO NATURAL INCREASE TO NET IMMIGRATION |
		No.	Per Cent	Natural Increase	Net Immigration	
1940	7,068,689	567,938	8.7	535,696	32,242	16.6
1930	6,500,751	1,089,454	20.1	776,481	312,973	2.5
1920	5,411,297	986,214	22.3	778,643	207,571	3.7
1910	4,425,083	659,744	17.5	619,259	40,485	15.3
1900	3,765,339	613,984	19.5	589,105	24,879	23.7
1890	3,151,355	919,824	41.2	537,083	382,741	1.4
1880	2,231,531	583,775	35.4	391,971	191,804	2.0
1870	1,647,756	502,171	43.8	335,606	166,565	2.0
1860	1,145,585	....	...	......	......	......

* Source: 17, 1901–20, pp. 1140–42, and 1941, p. 297.

In the early years of settlement Australia's population grew very rapidly, and as late as 1880–90 it increased by over 41 per cent in a decade. Since that time the rate of increase has generally been less than 20 per cent, and in the last decade it fell to a little over 8 per cent (Table 3). Like the United States, Australia has had until recently a relatively high ratio of net immigration to natural increase, so that a very considerable part of her population growth from decade to decade has been due to immigration. Since 1890, however, immigration has played a smaller part in the increase of population than in earlier years. This accounts in some measure for the much lower rate of increase since that time, but the greater part of the decline is due to the falling birth rate, for Australia, like most of Europe, now has a birth rate declining much faster than her death rate, and this decline has already reached the point where there is no true natural increase.

The fairly large excess of births over deaths which now exists and which will continue for several years even with present low birth rates is due to the favorable age composition of the population. Mainly because of the higher birth rates of the past, the proportion of young adults is considerably larger now than it will be in 1960–65; thus births are more numerous than they will be in twenty years unless there is an increase in the average number of children born to each woman. Deaths are also fewer now than they will be then.

The general effect of these changes in age composition will be to lower the rate of population growth rather slowly during the decade 1940–50 and then more rapidly so that there will be comparatively little growth after 1960. In brief, Australia now belongs to that group of European peoples which were placed in the "stationary" category. Her total population cannot reasonably be expected to increase much beyond eight million by the end of the present century unless there is a much larger net immigration in the future than there has been in the recent past or unless the birth rate increases.

What immigration might mean to Australia in absolute population growth over a period of years can be seen by applying to her immigrants, 1921–30, some calculations made by the Scripps Foundation for the United States. When it was assumed that there would be a net immigration of 500,000 into the United States in each five-year period from 1945 to 2000 and that these immigrants would have the same age and sex composition as our actual immigrants during 1925–29 with the estimated death rates and birth rates of the native population, it was found that such an immigration would increase the population of the United States by about 7.2 million by the end of the century. Since our birth rates and death rates are not greatly different from those of Australia, an annual immigration of 31,000, such as occurred between 1921 and 1930, would result in a total addition by the year 2000 of about 2,400,000, or about 30 per cent, to the population otherwise to be expected—a very significant increase. An immigration of 50,000 a year would add over 3.5 million by the year A.D. 2000.

For a relatively young country Australia's population tends to concentrate very heavily in urban districts. Almost half (47 per cent) of the total population lived in the six metropolitan areas in 1933. (A metropolitan area in each state includes the capital city and the adjoining urban municipal areas.) In addition, a little over 18 per cent lived in urban places of 2,000 or more outside metropolitan areas. Thus it would appear that almost two-thirds of Australia's population could be called urban in 1933. Our United States census classifies as "urban" people living in places of 2,500 or more, and in 1940 our urban population amounted to only 56 per cent. Even using the same standard, Australia's urban population may very well have exceeded 60 per cent of the total by 1940. And this in spite of the fact that Australia has little industry as compared with the United States, her chief industries having to do with the processing of her agricultural products.

From a demographic standpoint this high proportion of urban population is important because among Europeans everywhere the birth rate is lower among urban people than among rural. This is undoubtedly one of the most significant factors in the very rapid decline in Australia's birth rate during the last fifteen or twenty years and needs to be emphasized because it unquestionably will have a very direct bearing upon the probable growth of Australia's population in the future.

AGRICULTURE IN TEMPERATE AUSTRALIA

To understand her agricultural possibilities, we must look further into the climate and rainfall of Australia. From the standpoint of temperature and rainfall, the total area in Australia suitable for wheat is estimated at only 500,000 square miles (434, p. 162 n.). However, much of this is not suitable for cultivation from the standpoint of soil and topography, and another estimate (485, p. 333) would reduce this area by far more than one-half, putting the total area suitable for agriculture at only a little over 220,000 square miles. This is slightly over 7 per cent of the entire area (Table 4).

Since many Australians would hold even this estimate too high and since the argument here is strengthened by an underestimate rather than an overestimate of the agricultural area, I will assume that Australia has only 100 million acres of tillable land, or about 5 per cent of the total area. This may be compared with an actual crop area of about 22.2 million acres in 1939–40 and an average of about 21.7 million acres in 1935–40.

What are the more important agricultural products of this temperate area? In 1939–40 there were only about 13.3 million acres of wheat grown, and the wheat acreage has only occasionally surpassed 14 million, although it rose to about 18 million acres in 1930–31 (17, 1941, pp. 477 and 487; 267). I have been unable to find any very satisfactory estimate of the probable wheat area taking account of topographic and soil conditions as well as temperature and rainfall, but it would not seem unreasonable to assume that Australia could produce three or four times the amount it now does. Since the 1931–40 average was 177,758,000 bushels, it would appear that Australia might well produce somewhere between 500 and 700 million bushels. This amount would be sufficient to supply the needs of a population ten to fifteen times as great as the present population of Australia. As a matter of fact, in 1938–39 Australia exported close to two-thirds of the total

TABLE 4*

AREA, LAND ALIENATED, TILLABLE LAND, AND LAND IN CROPS, BY STATES
AUSTRALIA, 1939–40

STATE OR TERRITORY	TOTAL AREA ACRES (Millions)	PER CENT OF AREA ALIENATED AND BEING ALIENATED	PROBABLE AREA CULTIVABLE †		CULTIVABLE AREA UNDER CROPS	
			Acres (Millions)	Per Cent of Total Area	Acres (Millions)	Per Cent Probable Area
New South Wales....	198.0	34.5	40.0	20.2	6.4	16.0
Victoria............	56.2	58.9	25.0	44.4	5.0	20.0
Queensland.........	429.1	6.5	23.0	5.4	1.7	7.5
South Australia......	243.2	6.1	15.0	6.2	4.5	30.3
West Australia.......	624.6	5.2	35.0	5.6	4.3	12.4
Tasmania...........	16.8	37.7	2.0	11.9	0.3	12.9
Northern Territory...	335.1	0.1	2.0	0.6	....	....
Federal Capital......	0.6	17.7	0.1	16.7	....	8.1
Total..........	1,903.7	9.6	142.1	7.5	22.2	15.7

* Source: 17, 1941, pp. 79 and 473.
† Source: 485, p. 333.

wheat crop, or enough, since the seed is already provided for, to supply bread to a population nearly four times as great as it now has.

In most other lines of agriculture the possibilities of expanded production are probably much less than in the case of wheat, and for that matter there is little doubt that even an expansion in wheat acreage to 50 million would make inroads on some of the better pasture land in the Commonwealth. However, this might be compensated for by the more extensive use of the grain sorghums and cultivated grasses for fodder crops, as we do on our semiarid lands in the West. If this were done, the numbers of cattle and sheep in temperate Australia might not be much diminished by the extension of the tilled area. Indeed, they might be considerably increased in some of the tropical and semitropical parts of northern Australia, because the Australians (if they can really work in this climate as they claim they can) could produce much larger feed crops.

In the production of sheep Australia is far ahead of any other country in the world, with over 119 million head in 1939, more than twice as many as in the United States. The slaughter of sheep and lambs runs to 18–20 million annually, and 25–30 per cent of the meat is exported, while about three-fourths of the wool production of the country—averaging about a billion pounds annually—is exported. In addition, 13–14 million sheep hides are exported each year, of which about 12 per cent are with wool. Thus it can be said that Australia produces enough wool for a population about four times as great as her own and enough mutton for a population about one-third greater at the present very high standards of Australian consumption (17, 1941). A very large proportion of these sheep are raised in temperate Australia.

Australia also has 9.5–10.0 million beef cattle and annually slaughters 3.0–3.5 million, or almost one-half head per person (20, p. 52). The Australians consume about three-fourths of their beef and veal and, next to the New Zealanders, are the greatest beef-eaters in the world, using more than twice as much per capita as we do in the United States. At present most Australian cattle are range cattle, comparatively few being farm fed. The possibility of an increase in beef cattle, as in dairying, would seem to lie in cultivating a larger proportion of the feed crops and relying less on natural pasturage. It should not be difficult to add somewhere from 50 to 100 per cent to present beef production—in other words, to supply from two to three times the present population with a very abundant beef supply. However, a considerable proportion of Australian cattle are raised in the tropics, perhaps 40 per cent, so that a large increase in cattle-raising would depend in considerable measure on the willingness and the ability of the Australians to live and work in the tropics.

Butter and cheese production in Australia is likewise greatly in excess of home needs. About half the butter produced is exported and considerably more than half the cheese. Since her per capita consumption of butter is about twice that of the United States, it would require but little increase in dairying to furnish adequate supplies of dairy products to a population at least three times as great as Australia now has.

Australia also exports considerable quantities of many other agricultural products—pork products, poultry and eggs, sugar, barley, wine, many kinds of fruits, a wide variety of canned goods, etc. There can be little question that increases of most of these products amounting to several fold can be attained without greatly raising their unit cost.

This very cursory examination of Australia's agricultural possibilities has dealt largely with the temperate zone, but it should not be closed without saying a word about tropical Australia and its use. Of a total area of about 407,000 square miles in Australia having a rainfall of 30 inches or more, over 80 per cent lies in the tropics. Unfortunately nearly one-third of this is of almost no value agriculturally (see Map III) because all the rainfall comes in the summer, with the result that there is a long, hot, dry winter during which everything burns up. Queensland, however, has large areas suitable for intensive tropical agriculture as well as for rather extensive cattle-raising. If out of Queensland's 153,000 square miles with a rainfall of over 30 inches, only one-tenth is suited to tillage, this would still amount to more than 9,000,000 acres, or over five times its present crop area.

In all Australia only about 360,000 acres are now in sugar cane and 23,000 acres in bananas; these are the only tropical crops of any importance, and a considerable part of them is not raised within the tropics but in the subtropical coastal area lying south of the tropic of Capricorn. In fact, almost nine-tenths of the population of Queensland lives between Rockhampton (near the Tropic of Capricorn) and the northern border of New South Wales, which is about the latitude of Tampa, Florida, and Corpus Christi, Texas. Most of the remainder lives on the coast, where the heat is much tempered by the trade winds.

In view of these facts it is by no means clear that the white Australian can develop his tropical areas in spite of his vigorous claims to this effect. The tropical character of much of the area suitable to more intensive agriculture can be put down as one of the important obstacles to the more rapid settlement of the country under prevailing immigration policies. Although as a rule the northern European in the tropics does not want to work with his hands, it may not be physically impossible for him to do so, as certainly some Australians do. At the present time, however, the production of sugar, the chief tropical crop, has to be heavily subsidized in order to hold even the small labor force it now employs.

But there is no doubt whatever, and this is the important point here, that only a very small part of the land of tropical Australia suited to intensive culture is now being used. Tropical production could be increased many times if this land were tilled in family-sized farms for general agriculture, such adaptations being made as would be needed in the tropics. It should be emphasized again in this connection that the Australians are very certain that they can work in the tropics and do their own development in this region. The fact is, however, that they are doing very little to exploit the agricultural resources of this area, and it seems highly improbable in the light of their probable future population growth that they will do much in the next several decades.

When one tries to weigh these many and varied possibilities of Australian agriculture in terms of its ability to support people, no definitive figure emerges. Taylor (432, p. 441) has estimated Australia's population-carrying capacity at European standards at over 60 million, and no one is more familiar with the climatic handicaps than he. Although there are estimates as low as 13 million (8, November, 1931, p. 9), they undoubtedly assume a somewhat higher standard of living than that prevailing in Australia today. It does not seem far-fetched to assume that, so far as agricultural products are concerned, Australia can support three to four times her present population—that is, somewhere between 22 and 30 million—at a very good standard of living. Even now it would appear that Australia's agricultural produce feeds and clothes two or more times the present population.

If Australia has such agricultural possibilities, why is it that her agricultural development has almost stopped in recent years and that there are only about 253,000 agricultural landholdings (17, 1941, p. 532), with about 550,000 persons occupied in agriculture (17, 1939, p. 388)? Several factors merit some consideration at this point.

AUSTRALIA'S EARLY AGRICULTURAL SETTLEMENT

In the first place, Australia's land policy from the very beginning encouraged large holdings with extensive types of farming, largely sheep- and cattle-raising and wheat-growing, rather than the family-sized farm given over to more general farming and primarily concerned with family subsistence during the period of pioneering. Thus a large part of the land suitable for general farming early fell into the hands of a few people and was used for large-scale farming. Much of it is still so used.

The latest data on size of holdings where the land has been alienated

or is in process of alienation show that 67.0 per cent of the holdings are
under 500 acres but that they contain only 12.3 per cent (Table 5) of
the alienated land.[1] Since the large alienated holdings quite early included most of the better agricultural land, there was never the same
chance for the immigrant or even for the children of Australian farmers to "move west" and to take up new land as there was in the United
States or Canada. Australia in its "closer settlement" schemes has had
to buy back the land from the large landholders or to open up new
and less fertile land not well suited to the establishment of self-sufficient
family farms.

TABLE 5*

ALIENATED HOLDINGS BY SIZE, AUSTRALIA, ABOUT 1937

Size of Holdings (Acres)	No.	Per Cent	Size in Acres (in Thousands)	Per Cent
1–49	51,450	22.1	982.6	0.5
50–99	23,479	10.1	1,712.1	0.9
100–499	81,105	34.8	19,766.7	10.9
500–999	33,613	14.4	24,059.0	13.3
1,000–4,999	38,970	16.7	75,047.9	41.6
5,000–9,999	2,943	1.2	19,664.7	10.9
10,000–19,999	988	0.4	13,302.2	7.4
20,000–49,999	440	0.2	12,932.6	7.2
50,000 and over	137	0.1	13,101.2	7.3
Total	233,125	100.0	180,569.0	100.0

* Source: 17, 1939, p. 98.

As a result, Australia's land policy has created a small but powerful
group of holders of large tracts who have always been opposed to close
settlement because it would adversely affect their commercial farming.
In the United States, on the other hand, the small farmer, who if he did
not want free or cheap land for himself wanted it for his children, and
even the large landholder, who was a speculator and not a farmer,
had an interest in getting the land into the hands of settlers who
would actually improve the family-sized farm and thus raise land values in the community.

I would not give the impression, however, that the method of alienation of the public lands was the only reason why closer settlement in

[1] Much the larger part of the land in agricultural holdings in Australia is under lease.
Whereas there are 920 million acres in rural holdings, there are only about 180 million
acres of alienated land in such holdings. There can be little doubt, however, that nearly
all the 100 million acres estimated above as suitable for agriculture are included in the 180
million acres in alienated holdings (17, 1939, p. 98).

Australia did not follow much the same pattern as in the United States and Canada. A second factor, perhaps of as great importance, was the stage of economic development prevailing in that part of Europe from which Australia drew its settlers. From the very first Australia depended almost entirely upon Great Britain, and particularly England, for its settlers, but the Great Britain from which Australia was ready to draw large numbers of settlers after about 1860 and particularly after 1880 was a vastly different Great Britain from that from which the United States had been drawing settlers for more than two centuries.

Great Britain was steadily becoming more industrialized and less agricultural. She no longer had a large agricultural population fitted to pioneer in undeveloped lands. As her agriculture had become more and more commercialized with the growth of her cities, the farmer became less and less ready to go out to new land with only the prospect of subsistence for himself and family, particularly when the chance to get free land was almost nil. The English farmers' standards of living were no longer subsistence or near-subsistence standards as they had been earlier. Besides, the United States and Canada were still offering free land. The habits of life that made the British farmer of the eighteenth century and the early half or more of the nineteenth able and willing to pioneer in a new land had undergone a change, and he no longer made a good pioneer.

In the United States this change in the attitude of British farmers and the inadequacy of the number of emigrants Britain could send out was clearly recognized in fact, if not deliberately. We not only accepted but encouraged immigrants from Germany, Scandinavia, and other Central and Western European countries and gave them the same opportunity to acquire land as the native. Whether consciously or not, we recognized that the peasants from a number of these Continental countries were fully able to meet the requirements of pioneer living for some decades after the British farmers ceased to be interested in such opportunities. Australia never tapped these sources of peasant pioneers on the Continent to any appreciable extent, and it is one of the important reasons why closer settlement made such slow progress there.

The great Australian gold rush of the 1850's also had an adverse effect on the island's agricultural development. In the very nature of the case these gold-seekers were not of the temperament to make good farmers. They were not interested in making a meager living by steady hard work; they were looking for a bonanza. Besides, many of them did not bring their families with them. They were a vigorous and energetic group, but they were not selected with the idea of developing the farm lands of the colony. The preponderant urban development of Australia can very likely be attributed in significant measure to the gold-seekers, as may also a certain amount of the large-scale cattle- and sheep-raising and wheat-farming, which are so characteristic of the country. Moreover, in Australia, as in our own West, the interests of the cattle and sheep men were jeopardized by the encroachments of general farming; but, unlike our cattle and sheep men, the Australian ranchers have had great political power and have held back the tide of settlement far more effectively.

These are perhaps the chief factors which have retarded the more effective use of Australia's land suitable for close settlement, although there are other "historical accidents" which have also contributed to this result.

But even if it is possible for Australia by closer land settlement to supply the food and fibers needed by a population of 25–30 million, it by no means follows that it can support such an increased number at the level of living now prevailing in the country. In the modern world we want much besides food. We think of a good standard of living as involving the use of a great variety of goods which come from the factory as well as from the farm. Let us then inquire into Australia's mineral resources, particularly as to whether she has the iron, the coal, the copper, the oil, etc., which will enable her to produce a large part of the industrial goods that this larger population would need to maintain a high level of living.

AUSTRALIA'S MINERAL RESOURCES[2]

Australia is known to have rather large deposits of both black and brown (lignite) coal. The reserves of the former are estimated at 16.5 billion tons and of the latter at over 40 billion (20, p. 59). This is not a large amount as compared with that of the United States or Canada, but the black coal alone would last for about twelve hundred years at the present rate of mining. Moreover, much of this black coal is suitable for metallurgical purposes. The greater part of it is located in the area near Sydney in southeastern Australia, in the vicinity of one of the better farming regions. The bulk of the lignite is found in Victoria, also near one of the better farming regions. Other large deposits of black

[2] In most cases the weights and measures of different countries have been converted into those in common use in the United States. This has not been done in a few cases in which the comparison of interest is a percentage increase or decrease and the absolute size of the quantity is of little significance.

coal are found in Queensland (the chief tropical state), with smaller deposits in Tasmania and Victoria. Large lignite deposits are also found in northwestern Australia. It can safely be said, therefore, that Australia's industrial development will not be hampered for a long time to come by a shortage of fuel even if there should be a large increase in population and if industrial development should proceed at a much accelerated rate.

As far as is known at present, however, Australia has no petroleum deposits of any importance. There are considerable beds of oil-bearing shale, but even if these should prove to be large, the extraction of the oil from shale is a relatively expensive process and the oil thus obtained cannot compete in price with imported oil at present. The liquefaction of coal would seem to offer the best opportunity for Australia to become independent of outside sources of petroleum. The use of fuels made from agricultural products might change the situation somewhat, but Australia, like the United States, is a relatively high-cost producer of crops and could only produce fuel alcohol at a price far above that of imported oil. The more intensive development of sugar in tropical Australia might result in cheaper supplies of molasses for the manufacture of alcohol, but, as will be shown later, such a development will probably await a decisive change in Australia's population policy.

Much less is known about the iron deposits of Australia than about its coal and oil. A recent survey indicates that Australia may have as much as a billion tons of ore, but only two fairly large deposits are now considered workable (20, p. 60). They are located on or near the coast in South and West Australia. The one in South Australia is believed to contain about 150 million tons and that in West Australia about 100 million tons (17, 1941, p. 420). But on the basis of present knowledge it must be said that the long-term development of heavy industry in Australia will be definitely handicapped by the rather meager known supplies of good iron. If the iron deposits of New Caledonia and New Guinea should prove to be large and readily accessible by water, heavy industry in Australia might attain large proportions. Nevertheless, this lack of iron must be taken into account in considering Australia's industrial development.

As far as other minerals are concerned, Australia has long been one of the world's important producers of gold, silver, zinc, and lead; she also produces significant quantities of tin, copper, and tungsten ore. There does not seem to be any bauxite. The reserves of these different minerals are not definitely known, but Australia would seem to have rather large quantities of the first four. Besides, with her favorable position as regards coal, she appears to be in position to make economical use of the minerals found in New Caledonia and New Guinea.

On the whole, it would seem that Australia's mineral resources are somewhat less adequate than her agricultural resources. However, with an abundance of coal and with valuable mineral resources in New Caledonia and New Guinea which can be drawn upon, it is not unreasonable to believe that Australia can care for the mineral needs of a much larger population at relatively high standards. She would not have to export a great deal of wool, or meat, or manufactured goods to secure the iron and bauxite and other minerals she might need from abroad. Her coal, much of it near tidewater, should also provide cheap power for the production of magnesium from sea water as is now being done in this country. Apparently she will have to rely largely on coal for home-produced power of all kinds.

AUSTRALIAN INDUSTRY

As would be expected, Australian industrial development was rather slow from the beginning of white settlement up to World War I. Until that time the mining and refining of gold and silver and of the minerals found with them had occupied much of the enterprise and capital which might otherwise have gone into industrial development, while agriculture of the bonanza type still attracted much capital. Furthermore, the dominant economic interests in Great Britain were anxious to keep Australia as a source of cheap foods and raw materials and as a market for their manufactures. Thus the usual obstacles placed in the way of industrial development in colonies were operative in Australia. Capital was not made easily available for industry, and the protection of "infant industry" was opposed not only by the British manufacturers and traders but by the great landholders, who depended so largely on British markets. As was inevitable, however, the measures employed to retard industrial growth became increasingly irksome and gradually had to be relaxed or abandoned. The very great dependence of Australian agriculture (sheep, cattle, and wheat) on the British market and the concentration of commercial agriculture in comparatively few but powerful hands made Australia willing to play ball with the British industrialists longer than would have been the case if agricultural production had been less commercialized.

World War I gave great impetus to the development of Australian industry. When goods could no longer be imported from Great Britain, their manufacture at home became necessary. The growth in employees engaged in manufacturing from 320,000 in 1911–12 to 428,000 in 1924–25 and to 650,000 in 1940–41 shows this relatively rapid industrial development, as does also the increase in number of factories (17, 1941). The change in the character of the imports and exports, particularly the former, also shows the increasing extent to which Australian industry was coming to supply its own market for manufactures, even beginning to put out feelers for export markets.

The forces retarding industrial development in Australia were so powerful, however, that, in spite of the fillip industry got during World War I, there seems to have been little expansion between 1923–24 and the onset of the depression of the 1930's. The number employed in factories reached a high point (452,184) in 1926–27 and then declined until 1931–32 and did not pass the 1926–27 level until 1935–36, after which it grew rapidly to 650,073 in 1940–41. In recent years war industries have boomed in Australia as elsewhere. The iron and steel industry has grown with great rapidity, as have all industries producing munitions and ships. The industrial development of the country is being encouraged in every way possible, and, although there will no doubt be a considerable slackening of the war rate of development, it seems likely that a considerable part of the gain achieved will persist in postwar years as after World War I. But Australia cannot expect to keep increasing her tariffs against foreign goods, to impose import quotas, to require balancing agreements, and to impose other restrictions on imports and yet sell a large part of her agricultural produce abroad.

Furthermore, in producing for a home market of only seven million people, many of Australia's industries will inevitably be high-cost industries; hence it will be difficult for Australian manufactured goods to compete in world markets unless these industries are heavily subsidized.

The economic impasse in Australia implied in this analysis brings us inevitably to a consideration of Australia's population policy and its relation to the economic development of the country.

AUSTRALIA'S CLOSER SETTLEMENT POLICY OF RECENT YEARS

When the people of Australia became really concerned about "closer settlement" (1880–90), it was found that most of the land suitable for such settlement was already in private hands. It was necessary to purchase it from large holders at relatively high prices. This necessity would have made closer agricultural settlement a very expensive and difficult matter in any event, but the fact that Australian agriculture had already become highly commercialized, depending heavily on the export of wool, wheat, hides, and meat, made it seem natural to establish most new farmers on commercial farms similar to those already in operation. The original cost of such farms is extremely high, quite apart from the cost of the land, and the chances of failure (financially) are very great both because such farms require quite different training and management from that most immigrant settlers could be expected to have and because the wide fluctuations of agricultural prices in world markets render such farmers peculiarly liable to failure when they have heavy interest charges to meet, as most such new settlers did.

In the last forty to fifty years Australia has tried to build up a class of new farmers under closer settlement quite different in economic status from the pioneers who settled the United States, Canada, and most other regions where Europeans have sought land for homes. She has tried to turn settlers immediately into commercial farmers with a heavy money investment. She has, therefore, shown little interest in the land-hungry peasants of Europe (non-British) who would settle on land given them with the primary purpose of making a home for themselves, as in the United States.

It is not surprising under these circumstances that there does not seem to have been any rapid increase in recent years in the number of agricultural holdings or in the crop area, although not more than one-fourth and perhaps much less of the tillable area is now under crops. The number of holdings in the five states for which data are available (New South Wales, Victoria, South Australia, West Australia, and Tasmania) near 1910 was about 202,000. This number seems to have included about 19,000 small holdings (18, 1927–28, p. 682) in New South Wales which were not agricultural and were later omitted from returns; but, if we subtract these, we still have 183,000. In 1940 the total number of agricultural holdings reported is 253,000, but this includes 42,000 in Queensland, which is the sixth state and is not included in the 1910 report (17, 1941, p. 532). In the five states, therefore, the increase could not have been more than 28,000–29,000—from 183,000 to about 211,000. Supposing that a half of the holdings in Queensland were taken up between 1910 and 1940, the total increase could scarcely have exceeded 50,000—from about 205,000 to 253,000.

The increase in the area in crops has, apparently, been greater than that in holdings—from 11.9 million acres in 1910–11 to 22.2 million in 1939–40. This is a perfectly normal development in view of the rapid improvement in the machinery used in commercial agriculture. The area in wheat alone, which grew from 7.4 million acres in 1910–11 to 13.3 million in 1939–40, and that in oats accounts for almost a fourth of the remaining gain.

These facts seem to indicate that the settlement policies of Australia can scarcely be considered a success during the last thirty years if the increase of the agricultural population was its chief purpose.

The fact is that no country has ever been really settled by commercial farmers. Elsewhere—in the United States, Canada, and South Africa, where European settlement has succeeded—pioneer farmers have been *subsistence* or *near-subsistence* farmers who first lived off the land and only gradually came to participate in the flow of agricultural produce into commercial channels. We must conclude, I think, that Australia's settlement policies in recent years have not been calculated to build a large and a strong agricultural population but only a small class of commercial farmers. Since the area suitable for crops appears to be four to six times as large as the present crop area, possibly even more, it is easy to see that Australia's settlement policies would have to be radically altered in order to secure fairly full use of her tillable land in the foreseeable future.

THE MEANING OF "WHITE AUSTRALIA"

It is clear from this discussion of Australia's "closer settlement" policies that their success is closely bound up with that aspect of population policy which determines the kind of settlers wanted. Australia's population policy as regards kind of settlers wanted is commonly called the "White Australia" policy.

This policy received its name when it was decided not to admit any more Chinese, Japanese, or other colored peoples from Asia and thus keep Australia a white man's land. It still retains this name, although it is not a very accurate description of the immigration policy actually in operation. The actual policy pursued during the last two or three decades would be better described as a "non-British-exclusion policy."

In 1911 there were only about 74,000 "other" Europeans in Australia (other than British origin), or less than 1.7 per cent. This fell to 71,000, or 1.3 per cent, in 1921 but rose to 95,000, or 1.4 per cent, in 1933 (17, 1910–20, p. 1139; 17, 1941, p. 278). During 1936–40 there was a net gain of 27,000 "other" Europeans through migration. This may have brought the total "other" European population to 110,000–115,000 in 1940, or about 1.6 per cent. Moreover, a considerable proportion of this group was of northwestern European origin. But because this slight increase in this non-British group included a few thousands of Italians (12,000), there was a great outcry against their admission, and only to a lesser extent against the Yugoslavs, Greeks, and Poles, of whom even fewer entered. The "White Australia" policy had become in effect a "British Australia" policy.

Inevitably such a policy limited the group from which "settlers" could be drawn and almost as inevitably doomed any rural settlement policy to failure. Pioneers must be drawn from wherever they can be found and the British, the Americans, and even the children of Australian farmers are no longer good pioneers. They are not willing to become *subsistence* farmers as their grandparents and earlier ancestors were. Only people who are now subsistence or near-subsistence farmers, but who believe that they, or, if not they themselves, their children, may improve their lot a little by going elsewhere to settle on new land, are suited to pioneering. It has been such people who have done all Europe's true agricultural pioneering.

As for the demographic effects of a "White Australia," the facts show very clearly that Australia can expect to grow but little in the next several decades by natural increase of her present population unless there is a definite reversal of present birth-rate trends. Such a reversal is possible, but the evidence available at present regarding the ability of modern states with high levels of living to increase their birth rates indicates that it is not very probable.

Besides, the British immigrants, who are few in number to begin with, are not farm people and have a birth rate as low as or lower than that of the Australians. They cannot be expected to add much to the natural increase of Australia's population in the future. An almost purely British Australia will certainly be a small Australia, probably little more than eight million by the end of the century and almost certainly less than ten million. Australia's industry cannot be expected to absorb any considerable increase in numbers unless there is a much larger home market for its products, and this in turn is in large measure dependent on a substantial increase in the population, particularly on the land.

It is highly probable, therefore, unless Australia is willing to admit fairly large numbers of the southern and eastern European peasants who have low levels of living, who are accustomed to subsistence agriculture, and who still have fairly high birth rates, that she stands little chance to achieve "closer" settlement.

The consequences of the "White Australia" policy on settlement are especially marked in the tropical parts of the country. Queensland, which contains most of the land on which tropical or subtropical agriculture is possible, is still largely a grazing country, having almost half of the 13 million cattle in Australia in 1939 and nearly one-fifth of her 119 million sheep, although the majority of these are not actually within the tropics.

The area in distinctly tropical crops is still very small (17, 1941, pp. 506–8)—less than 600 square miles in 1940, of which about 95 per cent was in sugar cane and most of the remainder in bananas and pineapples. In 1933 (last census) there were only 5,600 (male) sugar-planters in tropical Australia and only 2,500 cane-cutters. The total number of males in Queensland engaged in agricultural pursuits, not including those in pastoral pursuits, was only 24,700.

Quite obviously the Australians are settling on and cultivating the land in tropical and subtropical Australia even more slowly than in the remainder of the continent. Here, even more than elsewhere, the farmer is a commercial farmer. There seems to be almost no settling on the land with the idea of making a home.

Thus if Australia wants to remain white and still develop her tropical areas, she will have to look for Europeans who seem more likely to carry on tropical and subtropical agriculture for the sake of direct family support than are the British or the Australians. The most likely sources of such immigrants are Portugal, Spain, and Italy—and, the arguments of the Australians to the contrary notwithstanding, the balance of the evidence is against the belief that northern Europeans can make an all-round success of living in the tropics.

As noted above, there was a great outcry in Australia when a few thousand Italians migrated thither during the 1920's and 1930's. Measures were taken to stop such an influx of "foreigners" (non-British peoples). It was maintained by many Australians that the admission of "foreigners" even in such small numbers would destroy the distinctive cultural features of Australian life as well as lower the level of living of the masses of the people.

To the outsider trying to look at the future of Australia in the light of larger world trends, it appears that Australia's choice is not whether she will remain essentially as she is, racially, socially, and economically, or allow a relatively large amount of non-British immigration, but whether she would prefer the changes in her manner of life produced by a rather large non-British immigration of southern and eastern Europeans selected and controlled by herself, or *those introduced by an Asiatic conqueror*. Australia must either increase her population to the point where she can make reasonably full use of her resources and thus develop the power to protect herself from outside attacks, or she will be conquered and settled by some of the Asiatic peoples. More of this later.

NEW ZEALAND

The Dominion of New Zealand lies wholly in the temperate zone some 1,200 miles east of Australia. It consists of two large and several smaller islands with a total area of 103,935 square miles. It contains a little over twice the area of New York State.

In the North Island, high mountains occupy approximately one-tenth of the surface. In the South Island, mountains occupy a large proportion of the area, and because they run almost its entire length, exert a marked influence on its climate and rainfall. For many years the mountains also constituted a formidable barrier between the east and west coasts.

New Zealand has a cool, temperate, moist climate without marked seasonal variations in temperature or precipitation. The rainfall varies from 28 inches in the east to over 100 inches on parts of the west coast, but, even where the rainfall is very heavy, intervals between rains are generally frequent and prolonged enough to insure adequate drainage and in some areas even to interfere with the growth of crops. On the whole, climate, soil, and rainfall are all suitable for fairly intensive agriculture.

New Zealand's population, like that of Australia, grew very rapidly in the early days of white settlement. It continued to grow rapidly until after 1921, never falling below an average of 2 per cent per annum until the decade 1921–31. The lower rate for this decade is due to the decline both in the birth rate and in immigration after 1926 (Table 6). Since that time New Zealand's population, in common with most other northwestern European populations, has had a much lower increase.

New Zealand's birth rate has long been declining and was only 18.36 per 1,000 in 1936–40. This is the lowest rate for any five-year period in the dominion's history except at the depth of the recent depression (16.98). Since New Zealand has an extremely low death rate (9.20 in 1936–40), the excess of births was still over 9 per 1,000; but, as in the case of Australia, this figure is deceptive because of an age composition highly favorable to few deaths and many births. When corrections are made for these conditions, New Zealand had only 95 per cent enough births in 1935–36 to maintain its numbers.

Although this rose to about 107 per cent in 1939 and still higher in 1941 (127), it can be said with considerable assurance that New Zea-

TABLE 6*

POPULATION AND INCREASE AND PROPORTION OF INCREASE DUE TO NATURAL
INCREASE AND IMMIGRATION, NEW ZEALAND, 1861–1941

YEAR	POPULATION	POPULATION INCREASE		PER CENT OF INCREASE DUE TO—	
		Number	Per Cent	Natural Increase	Net Immigration
1941......	1,543,982	101,432	7.0	98.2	1.8
1931......	1,442,550	227,873	18.8	68.7	31.3
1921......	1,214,677	209,092	20.8	76.7	23.3
1911......	1,005,585	235,281	30.5	63.5	36.5
1901......	770,304	145,849	23.4	81.9	18.1
1891......	624,455	136,566	28.0	86.7	13.3
1881......	487,889	232,961	91.4	43.1	56.9
1871......	254,928	157,024	160.3	30.6	69.4
1861......	97,904	71,197	266.6	....	....

* Source: 341, 1943.

land will soon have little or no excess of births over deaths. Therefore, unless there is a very considerable immigration into New Zealand within the next few years, it is almost certain that its population will not much exceed two million by 1975 or 1980 and after that it will probably begin to decline.

NEW ZEALAND'S AGRICULTURE

New Zealand, even more than Australia, is a pastoral and agricultural country, but in proportion to its area it is much more closely settled. It has only a little over one-thirtieth of the area of Australia but has over one-third as many landholdings of one acre or more. From the standpoint of agriculture the chief difference between New Zealand and Australia is that the former has only a small area in which the climate and rainfall, or lack of water for irrigation,[3] render the land unsuitable for a fairly intensive agriculture, although large areas, because of their mountainous character, cannot be cultivated.

Up to the present, sheep- and cattle-raising and dairying are the principal types of farming. In 1941–42, of nearly 20 million acres of "cultivated" land, over 17 million were in sowed pasture and only about 2 million were used for crops. In addition to the 20 million acres "cultivated," there were 23.2 million acres of unimproved land in the "occupied" classification. ("Occupied" land in New Zealand seems to be much the same classification as "land in farms" in the United States.)

New Zealand agriculture naturally has many close resemblances to that of Australia, but it should be noted that New Zealand has very little dry barren land and no tropical land. A much larger proportion of New Zealand than of Australia is, therefore, suitable for fairly intensive general farming by Europeans. The land policy of New Zealand, like that of Australia, has, however, encouraged large pastoral holdings—although not so large as in Australia—which, together with the highly commercialized character of the farming, has led to extensive rather than intensive use of the land, to its use for pasture rather than for cultivated crops.

In 1941 there were only 86,000 agricultural holdings in New Zealand, and over 11,000 of these contained less than 10 acres each. Most of these may be regarded as homesites rather than farms. The holdings of 10–999 acres numbered about 68,000 and contained over 14 million acres, or about 33 per cent of all the land in holdings of over 10 acres. These are the farms on which a fairly intensive general agriculture is likely to be practiced. The remaining holdings (6,911) each had 1,000 acres or more, for a total of almost 29 million acres, and contained 67 per cent of all occupied land.

Since New Zealand early alienated a large part of its better lands, it, too, has had to buy back what is needed for "closer" settlement. Thus it faces many of the same financial difficulties as Australia in settling more people on land suitable for general farming. Moreover, New Zealand's agriculture, even more than that of Australia, is dependent on foreign markets for the disposal of its products. Since about 1933 almost 70 per cent of the gross farm income of New Zealand has come

[3] Areas now irrigated and those surveyed as suitable for irrigation and for which water can be obtained comprise 700,000–1,000,000 acres, i.e., from one-third to one-half of the present crop area.

from exports and only 30 per cent from domestic sales (341, 1943, p. 258).

This would seem to indicate that New Zealand could supply an abundance of agricultural produce to at least three times its present population with almost no extension of the tilled area. If the tilled area can also be increased several fold, and this admits of little doubt, it is highly probable that New Zealand could readily supply a population four or five times its present size, or from six to eight million persons, with an abundance of food.

The chief difficulties in the way of such a development are the same as those encountered in Australia. The settling of the country with full-fledged commercial farmers from Great Britain is an impossible task, but the New Zealanders, like the Australians, refuse to face the facts and continue to spend great amounts of money on elaborate settlement schemes and on subsidizing commercial farmers whose attitude toward their land is that of exploiters rather than that of home-builders.

MINERALS AND INDUSTRY IN NEW ZEALAND

Although there are rather large possibilities for agricultural expansion in New Zealand—possibilities which might well permit it to support several times its present population—it is not so certain its mineral resources will enable it to support as large a population as its agriculture could provide for at the high level of living now current.

Its coal supply is ample for a long time to come, except for metallurgical purposes, particularly in view of the fact that the climate is mild and there is a large amount of water power available. Its iron deposits, however, are in the form of iron sand, and as yet no means have been found to use these economically. This lack of a good grade of iron ore coupled with the lack of coking coal make it appear unlikely that New Zealand can develop any heavy industry in the near future except behind a high tariff barrier and/or with the aid of large subsidies to offset the added costs of the transportation of raw materials and the high costs involved in producing for a small home market.

The islands also lack copper, manganese, and most other important industrial minerals. The only mineral of which they appear to have a considerable amount is gold.

But in determining New Zealand's industrial future, fully as important as its comparative poverty in minerals is its small home market. Even with a population of six to eight million—four to five times its present numbers—it would still have too small a home market to enable it to attain a volume of production in the heavier industries sufficient to insure low costs. In many lines of production where volume of output largely determines unit cost, New Zealand is almost certain to remain at a disadvantage.

In addition to these difficulties, New Zealand is still in the position where it must sell a large part of its agricultural produce abroad— about 70 per cent in value, as noted above. Any effort to become even self-sufficient in manufactures will be met, as it has been in the past, by the threat from Great Britain of buying agricultural products elsewhere. This would be a most serious blow to New Zealand's whole economy and, if carried out, would certainly result in a greatly lowered level of living.

The only way New Zealand can avoid this in the long run is to increase its population to the point where it will use a considerably larger proportion of its agricultural produce and thus become less dependent on foreign markets. The increasing subsidization of industry is no solution of this problem, although there seems to be a strong belief in both Australia and New Zealand that it is. A subsidy to industry or agriculture may be justified at times as a means of bringing about a change in the distribution of the national income, that is, as a social reform, or as assistance to an "infant" industry during its period of weakness, but as a permanent policy widely applied as seems to be happening in New Zealand and Australia it is another case of trying to lift one's self by one's bootstraps. It cannot succeed in maintaining enduring prosperity where fundamentals are unsound.

In the case of New Zealand, perhaps even more than in that of Australia, an effort is being made to retain a commercial system—agriculture largely dependent on export—and at the same time to develop industry not only adequate to supply the home market but large enough to export a substantial quantity of manufactured products. These aims are mutually antagonistic. Both could not be achieved even if New Zealand had adequate mineral resources. Only when the population of New Zealand becomes large enough to use its land fairly fully and to consume most of its own agricultural products can it hope to develop a sound industrial structure leading to as large a measure of economic self-sufficiency as may be possible for any country with New Zealand's rather meager mineral resources.

This should not be interpreted to mean that New Zealand cannot develop more nonagricultural industry than now exists. The development which has been going on will, no doubt, continue, and war developments will hasten New Zealand's industrial growth in certain respects; but we must not forget that, year in and year out, no country can sell much more than it is willing to buy. It is not reasonable to suppose that Great Britain will continue to buy New Zealand's agricultural produce as in the past if New Zealand does not continue to buy British manufactures much as she has. New Zealand's industrial development will be relatively slow as long as she depends so largely on export markets for the disposal of her agricultural produce. The obstructions being placed in the way of her industrial development by British manufacturers are far less fundamental than those arising from the slow growth of population for which the New Zealanders themselves are entirely responsible. The New Zealanders do not seem to realize this, and, until they do, they will continue to blame the British manufacturers for obstructing the industrial development of their country and will not come to grips with the more basic problem of population.

NEW ZEALAND'S SETTLEMENT AND POPULATION POLICIES

Nearly all that was said about the settlement policies of Australia applies to New Zealand. Climatic conditions in New Zealand would, however, make it possible for northwestern Europeans to settle anywhere in the country. But it should be remembered that any settlement in rural New Zealand calculated to change the present predominance of pastoral agriculture into a predominance of general agriculture based on increased tillage of the land would involve pioneering conditions for these settlers for some years. I seriously doubt that any appreciable number of northwestern European farmers are able, or are willing, to settle in New Zealand under these conditions.

New Zealand, like Australia, must seek immigrants who are now living much as pioneers must live if she is to settle her lands more closely and increase the crop area to any great extent. This means bringing in peoples who speak other languages, who have other habits of life and conduct, who will remain clannish for some time, who will compete with the natives in certain "unfair" ways, and who will have larger families and will thus adulterate the Englishness of the population— now more than 90 per cent British (341, 1939, p. 944). Judging from our experience in the United States with immigrants and their children, there is nothing to be frightened at in contemplating these changes, particularly if definite plans for their settlement and assimilation are made in advance.

Certainly most people would agree that the alternative of having to face the rapidly growing Asiatic peoples needing land is much more to be feared. Can there be any reasonable doubt that Australia and New Zealand with thirty to forty million people living at high standards, with a highly productive agricultural and industrial system, would be in far better shape to maintain their position in the Pacific against Asiatic pressure than they would be with ten million? In a world which is rapidly filling up, a thinly settled, underdeveloped land is a constant temptation to more densely settled peoples who believe they could use these undeveloped resources to good advantage. This is especially true when the undeveloped land is clearly a rich land and when its people are living at a relatively high level, as is the case in both Australia and New Zealand.

There is no need to enlarge upon this point in connection with the situation in New Zealand. All that has been said about the need for immigration into Australia and the sources from which it might be derived applies equally to New Zealand.

Chapter V

MANCHOUKUO

SINCE Manchoukuo was a part of China before 1931 and since we fully expect that it will again become part of China, it might seem that a survey of her people and economy should be included in that portion of our discussion relating to China. However, in 1931 Manchoukuo came under complete Japanese control and since then has been treated as an integral part of the Japanese Empire. It is essential, therefore, to the understanding of Japan's recent development that we know what has been happening in Manchoukuo since that time. Hence it has seemed best to make a survey of Manchoukuo before undertaking to discuss the population and the economy of Japan in relation to the problems of peace in the Pacific Region.

Manchoukuo, as defined by Japan, contains about 550,000 square miles (240, 1934, p. 571). It lies between latitudes 38° 43′ and 53° 30′ north; in North America it would reach from a little south of Kansas City to about 250 miles north of Winnipeg. It has short hot summers and long cold winters, except for the small Kwantung peninsula, whose climate is somewhat modified by the surrounding waters. Its rainfall comes with the ocean winds in summer like that of all of East Asia. In winter, cold dry winds from the interior of Asia dominate its climate. Its chief mountains are in the northwest and southeast, although there are several secondary ranges in the east and northeast. Between these mountains lie vast plains which are in many respects like those of Nebraska, the Dakotas, and the prairie provinces of Canada.

POPULATION

There are no reliable data on the growth of Manchoukuo's population during the last forty years. One estimate for 1905 is 21 million (224, 1929, p. 410), while the Ministry of the Interior at Peking estimated only 15 million five years later (1910). The Maritime Customs guessed the population at 19 million in 1912, and the South Manchuria Railway estimated it at over 25 million in 1924. By the end of 1932 the *Japan-Manchoukuo Yearbook* (240, 1934, pp. 804–5) was giving the population as 31 million, and the 1940 edition places it at 37 million at the end of 1937, while the 1941 edition gives a population of almost 39.5 million at the end of 1939. A so-called "second census" on October 1, 1940, gives a population of 43.2 million (369, July, 1942, p. 189). It is my own belief that these wide variations merely reflect the actual uncertainties, and I am therefore not disposed to use any definite figure but rather to speak of the population of Manchoukuo as falling somewhere within rather wide limits, let us say, 35–40 million in 1940. The reasons for this opinion are these:

If we start with a population of 31 million at the end of 1932 and accept the figure of 43.2 million in October, 1940, this increase would have to be accounted for about as follows: Chinese immigration into Manchoukuo for the years 1933–39 amounted to a net of 1,283,000 (134, Part I, p. 26). If we assume that immigration in 1940 was a little higher than in 1939 (595,000), let us say 617,000 to round off the total figure, then the gain by immigration in the eight years 1933–40 amounted to 1.9 million. This leaves a gain of 10.3 million (12.2 million minus 1.9 million), of which possibly 300,000–400,000 came from Japan and an equal number from Korea. Therefore, about 9.5 million persons must have been added to Manchoukuo's population during these eight years by an excess of births over deaths. This means that the rate of natural increase was about 34 per 1,000 per year. Perhaps such a rate is not impossible, but certainly it has never been known before in any large population. It may have existed in relatively small populations where the age groups were very favorable to a high birth rate and where economic and social conditions were highly conducive to very low death rates, as was the case for some decades in the early days of settlement in the United States; but no one who has visited Manchoukuo will believe that the conditions there are conducive to a death rate of 15–17 per 1,000, although he will have little difficulty in believing that the birth rate is very high, possibly between 45 and 50 per 1,000. In order to maintain a natural increase of 34 with a birth rate of 50, the death rate would have to remain at 16. As I say, this is not impossible, but no one familiar with what the maintenance of such a death rate involves in the way of sanitation and medical care in a population with a birth rate of 50, and who has also seen the way the Chinese live in Manchoukuo, can believe that such a rate of increase prevails.

In my judgment a rate of half that size (17) would be an extremely high rate for Manchoukuo during this period, while it would stretch my credulity to accept a rate of 12–15 per 1,000 per year over a period of eight years immediately following a military conquest of the country. After Japanese control had become well established, after the economic life of the country had been more efficiently organized, and after the government had had time to get a fairly good health service in operation, it is not impossible that the rate of natural increase might rise to equal the highest recorded in Formosa—28 per 1,000—but that it has already risen to anywhere near this level surpasses belief.

If this position is correct and if the Japanese "census" in Manchoukuo in 1940 is the best estimate of Manchoukuo's population we possess, we are forced to conclude that most previous estimates must have been far too low. The recorded immigration into Manchoukuo in 1933–39, together with an estimated immigration of 617,000 in 1940 and a rate of natural increase of 15 per 1,000, would only have raised a population of 31 million at the end of 1932 to about 37 million at the end of 1940, or over 6 million fewer than the "census." There is no need to pursue this point further.

In regard to the growth of Manchoukuo's population during the *next* few decades it may be said that it will depend chiefly on the amount of immigration allowed and the degree of control over the death rate that can be established, since there is no reason to believe that the birth rate will change significantly. It is assumed, of course, that Japanese control will end with the close of the war, so only the probable growth of Manchoukuo as a part of China need be considered here.

China has a relatively dense population living in great poverty. The Chinese from two of the large northern provinces, Hopei and Shantung (estimated population 60–70 million), have long been accustomed to move back and forth between their homes and Manchoukuo in considerable numbers, a certain proportion remaining there permanently. There is no reason to suppose that this movement will not be resumed, or continued, after the war. The means of travel both by road and by railway have been greatly improved since 1931 and the opportunities for settlement and for industrial work have also been much increased.

The dislodging of the Japanese has apparently resulted in less destruction of industrial equipment than was to be expected, hence the opportunities for immigrants in industry will probably be somewhat greater than before 1931. Agricultural opportunities will also be enlarged because of improved transportation if banditry can be kept down. In addition it seems reasonable to assume that some of such gains as may have been made in public health will be retained. Therefore, since there is no reason to anticipate any significant decline in the birth rate for several decades, it would appear that the population of Manchoukuo will increase fairly rapidly for most of the remainder of this century. The 35–40 million of today might very easily become 70–80 million by the year A.D. 2000 with a considerably smaller net immigration than has been taking place during the last forty years.

THE LAND AND AGRICULTURE

The total area of cultivated land in Manchoukuo is estimated at about 41.5 million acres (240, 1940, p. 710) and the total tillable area at about 101.7 million, or about 30 per cent of the total area. In other words, only about two-fifths of the tillable area is under cultivation. The forest area is estimated at a little less than one-fourth of the total and the unclassified area at about 44 per cent. Even though these estimates may be considerably in error, there can be little doubt that Manchoukuo still contains much land suitable for settlement and that its forest resources are large as compared with most of the remainder of China. It seems reasonable, therefore, to assume that Manchoukuo can supply adequate food for a considerably larger population than it now has at existing levels of living.

Unlike most of East Asia, but like parts of northern China, Manchoukuo has large areas favorable to extensive mechanized farming, and its chief crops—soybeans, millet, kaoliang, wheat, and corn— lend themselves well to such farming. An American farmer from North Dakota or the prairie provinces of Canada, set down in Manchoukuo, would know what to plant and how to go about using this land, although he would do his farming in quite a different manner from the Chinese farmer, who is accustomed to only a small amount of animal power and has never used modern machinery of any kind.

The chief point to notice here is that Manchoukuo does not belong to the rice region of East Asia. But since it has been settled by northern Chinese, its agricultural economy has been transplanted from North China. It will be very difficult to introduce more extensive agriculture in the areas still to be settled, although they may be suited to an American type of cultivation. However, we should not overlook the possibility that Manchoukuo might become the granary of a highly industrialized nation, an area comparable to the Middle West in the United

States with a relatively small (25–35 per cent) agricultural population supplying the food and raw materials for a large nonagricultural population. On the other hand, it may become just another North China with a dense poverty-stricken agricultural population such as is now developing.

At present about 85 per cent of the population of Manchoukuo is agricultural, and this proportion is not likely to decline greatly unless there is a definite effort on the part of the government to organize Manchuokuoan agriculture for the use of modern techniques and to see that the industrial development proceeds rapidly enough to absorb most of the natural increase as well as a large part of the immigrants from China. If Chinese immigrants are allowed to enter as freely as in the past and if new land is opened to them as fast as needed, even on the same onerous terms as in the past, the tillable portions of Manchoukuo will within two or three decades be about as densely settled as northern China with a people living at only a slightly higher level.

From the standpoint of agricultural production alone, Manchoukuo can probably support a population of 100 million or more at current levels of living. For the time being, therefore, the food supply is not a strongly limiting factor in population growth here as it is in China. Thus it was not unreasonable for the Japanese to expect to import large and increasing amounts of food from Manchoukuo once they had secured complete control. Even if Manchoukuo's population were to increase rapidly, the Japanese were safe in counting on large imports of soybeans, bean oil, millet, corn, and wheat for two or three decades. But if immigration could have been checked and if farming could have been partially mechanized, using cheap Chinese labor under Japanese direction, they might reasonably have expected large imports of food for two or three decades longer. Furthermore, under these conditions it was not overoptimistic for them to expect to settle some millions of Japanese immigrants on new lands which could be opened up and to use some additional millions in Manchoukuoan industries.

However, without some check on Chinese immigration and without agricultural subsidies, there is little chance that the Japanese can settle Manchoukuo either as agriculturists or industrial workers in competition with the Chinese. Migration in the mass always flows from areas of high pressure and low levels of living to areas of larger opportunity and higher levels of living. One can say with a high degree of assurance, therefore, that Japanese farmers and industrial workers would not migrate to Manchoukuo in any considerable numbers if they were forced to compete with the Chinese for land or jobs on equal terms.

But, of course, the advantage to Japan of holding Manchoukuo, even apart from strategic considerations, was by no means confined to the food she might have expected to get from such a colony or the migrants she might have sent to it. It will be well, therefore, to postpone consideration of the importance of Manchoukuo in the economy of the Japanese Empire until after we have examined Manchoukuo's other resources.

MINERAL RESOURCES

Before the Japanese seizure of Manchoukuo (1931) the country was known to contain considerable quantities of coal, iron, and gold and

TABLE 7

MINERAL RESOURCES, MANCHOUKUO, 1938 AND 1930

(Millions of Tons)

Mineral	1938*	1930[†]
Coal.....................	20,000[‡]	4,800[‡]
Iron ore..................	1,669 (2,500)[§]	1,000
Oil shale.................	8,408	5,300
Magnesite................	5,512	....
Fire clay.................	110	....
Aluminum shale...........	2,756	....
Gold ore (troy ounces).......	193	129[‖]
Manganese................	10[¶]	....

    * Source: 240, 1940, p. 751

    † Or nearest to 1930 possible. Source: 8, November, 1930, pp. 300 and 332.

    ‡ Source: 130, 1942, p. 185

    § Source: 403, p. 404.

    ‖ Source: 240, 1934, p. 643.

    ¶ 461, 1940, p. 583 (1940 estimate).

was believed to be rich in other useful minerals, but its resources had never been carefully explored. The Japanese have done a great deal of exploratory work since 1931, and the reports indicate that they have been highly successful in their search for new and better mineral resources.

We need not go into detail regarding the finds of new resources in Manchoukuo since Japanese occupation, but it will be of interest to compare the estimates of certain important minerals in Manchoukuo in 1938 with pre-1931 estimates.

The new minerals (those not known to exist in commercial quantities before 1931) of greatest importance are magnesite, manganese, and aluminum shale. But more important from the standpoint of the immediate future of industry in the Japanese Empire were the additional reserves of coal and iron which were discovered. Some of these are not only fairly large in amount but are also said to be of better quality than those already in use. The proximity of the best of these new reserves to great water-power developments on the Yalu River, which forms the boundary between Korea and Manchoukuo, promises well for low-cost production. Since the iron and coal reserves in this Tungpientao region have not yet been thoroughly surveyed, the aforementioned estimates may be materially changed in the near future, but there seems little doubt that the coal and iron reserves recently found are large and that a considerable proportion of them is of better quality than those known hitherto.

As a result of finding large mineral resources in Manchoukuo, the Japanese government of the region had planned their development on a large scale. Much of the construction needed to carry out these plans was nearing completion or was under way at last reports, which are generally for a date not later than 1940. As a part of the Japanese Empire, Manchoukuo's resources would have contributed much to an extensive industrial development; how the Japanese were using and were planning to use these minerals will form the subject of the following section.

THE DEVELOPMENT OF TRANSPORTATION

Except for the railways and some river traffic, transportation was in a primitive condition in Manchoukuo prior to 1931. It was practically impossible to get outside even the larger cities more than a few miles by automobile. The wheelbarrow and the cart were the chief means of local transport, and roads as we know them were nonexistent. The two chief railways were those built by Russia before the Russo-Japanese War (1904–5). One provided a short cut from the Trans-Siberian near the northwestern Russia-Manchoukuo border across northern Manchoukuo to Vladivostok (Chinese Eastern). Its direction was east-southeast. The second ran south from Harbin, located near the middle of the first line, to Dairen and Port Arthur in the Gulf of Pechili. There was a third line, built by the Japanese at the time of the Russo-Japanese War, running from Mukden southeast to the Korean border (South Manchuria).

The secondary rail lines consisted largely, although not entirely, of lines built by the Chinese, running north and south—mostly west of and parallel to the South Manchuria Railway. From the standpoint of the economic development of Manchoukuo all these railways were of great importance, first, in making possible a rapid settlement of the country and, second, in providing reasonably good and cheap transportation for its chief export crops.

Even before the seizure of Manchoukuo, the South Manchuria Railway was a large and powerful organization. In March, 1931, it had investments of over 742 million yen, almost half of the total Japanese investment in the country. Since it had a hand in many enterprises—iron and steel, coal, oil mills, flour mills, hotels, etc.—not directly connected with transportation, it was quite natural for it to take a most active part in the development of Manchoukuo once the country came under Japanese control.

Almost immediately after the military occupation of Manchoukuo had been completed (March, 1933), all its railways were placed under the control of the South Manchuria Railway. The total mileage of railways at that time, including the Chinese Eastern, in which the Soviet Union still had an interest, but which it sold to the Manchoukuoan government in 1935, was about 3,500 miles. A vigorous program of consolidation, reorganization, and extension was at once begun, and by the end of 1939 a well-unified system of over 6,200 miles had been developed, and about 870 million yen had been expended in the process (130, 1942, p. 182). The new lines added during this period were chiefly of strategic importance, being built to strengthen Japan's position against the Soviet Union in the north and west and to give more ready access to northern Manchoukuo through northern Korean ports. However, a considerable number of connecting lines, chiefly of economic importance, were also built. The job of providing Manchoukuo with reasonably good rail transportation seems to have been done quickly and well.

At the same time that the rail system of the country was being reorganized an extensive program of road-building was undertaken, and it, too, seems to have been carried through with vigor. This can be seen from the fact that, whereas there were practically no roads usable the year round by automobiles in 1931, there were about 6,000 miles of roads over which bus lines were operated by the end of 1937 (240, 1940, pp. 685–88) and a considerably longer mileage of highways had been somewhat improved.

This development of highways had two purposes: In the first place, banditry had been very widespread in Manchoukuo for many years, and there was little chance of suppressing it until troops could be moved quickly into the areas where forays were being made. No doubt opposition to Japanese occupation increased banditry in 1931 and 1932 and made local transportation even more essential. In the second place, the exploitation of the agricultural and forestry resources, as well as of the mineral resources, required far better transport than existed in many localities where it was not feasible to build railways. The building of highways could be pushed rapidly because an abundance of cheap coolie labor was available. Very little other expense was involved in making roads, whereas the laying of rails and the supply of equipment for a railway required a heavy capital outlay.

THE DEVELOPMENT OF INDUSTRY

Little need be said of the industrial development of Manchoukuo prior to 1931. Until that time Manchoukuoan industry was in the same rather primitive state as most of northern China outside the treaty ports. The chief development of modern industry was to be found in the territory leased to Japan known as the Kwantung Leased Territory, a peninsula of 1,200–1,300 square miles extending south into the Gulf of Pechili, with Dairen and Port Arthur at the southern tip, as well as in the South Manchuria Railway Zone, a zone lying along the railway and containing 100–150 square miles. In this Japanese-controlled area the South Manchuria Railway was the dominant economic power. In addition to its actual railway properties, it had the ports under its control. It had also made a beginning in iron and steel manufacture, was producing several million tons of coal annually, and was distilling oil from the shale which overlay this coal. Within this sphere of Japanese influence were to be found the few modern private factories of Manchoukuo—some cotton mills, some improved plants for processing soybeans, some modern flour mills, and most of the other power-operated factories. Aside from these developments in the Japanese-controlled area, Manchoukuoan industry was largely limited to the simple types of hand industry essential to the mere existence of a poverty-stricken oriental people.

Under the loose and arbitrary control of the war lord Chang Tso-lin there was little incentive to establish industry or even to explore the country for exploitable mineral deposits. The restrictions under which Japanese and other foreigners were allowed to prospect for minerals and to exploit them were so burdensome and property was so insecure that any active efforts for the industrial development of the area by foreign capital were practically precluded. Since Chinese development was unlikely because of lack of capital, management, skilled labor, and, above all, the general insecurity of life and property which prevailed over much of Manchoukuo, industrial development had been and was likely to be very slow.

This virtual exclusion from the unused resources of Manchoukuo by the Chinese authorities was one of the important causes of Japanese irritation with China. If this irritation at the tactics of Chang Tso-lin was the chief reason for his "accidental" death in 1928, the Japanese must have been much disappointed in his successor, for the accession to power of his son, Chang Hsueh-liang, rendered the general situation as regards the exploitation of Manchoukuo by the Japanese even less favorable. The "young marshal" was much affected by the growing force of Chinese nationalism and was determined that Japan should not gain further hold upon the resources and industry of Manchoukuo, but he seems to have lacked the vigor of his father, so that life and property outside the Japanese zones were even less secure than in his father's day.

The industrial development of Manchoukuo since 1931 need not be detailed. For the first few years, until about the end of 1937, it appears that the chief achievements were in transportation, although some progress was made in ironmaking and coal-mining, in which the South Manchuria Railway had already been engaged for some years. The military authority, the Kwantung Army, appears to have been determined to build a totalitarian state in which all economic power as well as all political power was to remain in its own hands. Quite naturally the economic oligarchy of Japan did not take kindly to such a scheme and were reluctant to invest heavily in enterprises over which they would have little control.

"Conditions began to improve in the second half of 1936," says Schumpeter, "although the real reversal of policy came more than a year later under the stimulus of a wartime economy. . . . . The final phase in the transition from a system of rigid state control, anti-capitalist in its outlook, to one which welcomed private capital and gave it unusual opportunities for profit was the formation of the Manchuria Industrial Development Company in December, 1937" (403, p. 394).

Because of the reluctance of the great Japanese capitalists to invest heavily in Manchoukuo before 1938, almost three-fifths of the new capital invested there through 1937 came from or through the South Manchuria Railway (Table 8), the total investment from this source amounting to about 850 million yen (403, p. 848). There can be no doubt that the relaxation of the rigid military control over economic enterprise which took place in 1936–37 was intended to conciliate the

TABLE 8*

JAPANESE INVESTMENTS IN MANCHOUKUO, 1932–39

Year	Total Japanese Investments (Millions of Yen)	Per Cent S.M.R. Investments Are of Total Japanese Investments
1932–39............	3,053.2	40.0
1939..............	1,103.7	26.3
1938..............	439.5	17.6
1937..............	348.3	46.2
1936..............	263.0	44.1
1935..............	378.6	65.0
1934..............	271.7	61.1
1933..............	151.2	53.7
1932..............	97.2	66.9
Prior to 1932........	1,617.0	48.0

* Source: Elizabeth B. Schumpeter (ed.), *The Industrialization of Japan and Manchoukuo, 1930–1940* (New York: Macmillan Co., 1940), pp. 398 and 848.

capitalist groups which had been holding more or less aloof up to that time; in this it appears to have been fairly successful. The Japanese investment in Manchoukuo in the two years 1938 and 1939 was larger (1.6 billion yen) than in the six preceding years (1.46 billion yen), and a little less than one-fourth came through the South Manchuria Railway. Over 1.2 billion yen came from other sources, chiefly through the Manchuria Industrial Development Company and the Manchoukuo government (403, p. 846).

The large and increasing share of the M.I.D.C. in the industrial development of Manchoukuo after 1937 measures the extent of the concessions of the Manchoukuoan government to the financial oligarchy of Japan. But even the rather abrupt "about face" in the economic policy of the Manchoukuoan (army) government could hardly have been expected to lead to the desired volume of new investment after the attack on China in 1937, since this war necessitated a very large additional investment in industry at home and also opened up a large and promising field of investment in North China, where army control was less rigorous than it had been in Manchoukuo before 1937. Nevertheless, the Chinese war did stimulate the industrial development of Manchoukuo up to a certain point because of the greatly increased need for the products of her heavy industries and mines.

INDUSTRIAL PRODUCTION IN RECENT YEARS

In terms of goods the actual achievements of the large investments in Manchoukuo during the period 1931–39 have not been reported in detail since 1936 or 1937. That they have been disappointing in absolute amount goes almost without saying. Investments in transportation must precede by several years the increase in goods to be hauled, and investments in mines and steel mills, in aluminum factories and shale-oil distillation, etc., do not yield returns until sometime after they are made, even where it is merely a matter of expanding going businesses. Where the investments are in new mines and new mills often using new and untried processes, it may well be several years before there is any large increase in production. This is clearly recognized in the following quotation from a Japanese source:

"The aggregate results of this heavy spending [3 billion yen] are still largely unapparent, however, in that most of the vast construction projects have not arrived at the point of completion. The full effect of the present schemes will come, therefore, at an increasingly rapid rate in the next few years. By the end of 1941 it is estimated in this regard that the economic bloc of Manchoukuo and Japan will be fully self-sufficing in iron and coal, while several other indispensable industrial products will follow in rapid succession" (240, 1940, p. 850).

The last sentence of this quotation was probably overoptimistic, as the following survey will show, but, even so, there is little doubt that the production of heavy basic goods in Manchoukuo was increasing quite rapidly and that it was large enough to be of substantial aid to Japan in her war effort.

In 1930–31 Manchoukuo produced an average of about 10 million tons of coal. By 1938 it appears to have increased to about 16 million tons and in 1941 to 22 million tons (130, 1942, pp. 184–85). But in spite of such increases it was falling considerably behind schedule. The original five-year plan called for about 19 million tons in 1938, and 28 million tons in 1941. The revised plans both called for 42 million tons in that latter year. This deficiency in production came from the inability to secure qualified labor, the shortage of transportation, and the lack of mining equipment. It appears that there has recently been some shortage of good coking coal and that Manchoukuo is now looking to North China for a part of its needs for such fuel.

Even before 1931 the South Manchuria Railway was producing oil from the shale overlaying the coal deposits at Fushun, but the amount was relatively small. Since 1935 the distilling capacity has been much increased, and production in 1940 was believed to have reached 470,-000 tons (148, p. 77). Almost certainly the original five-year-plan goal of 880,000 tons was not attained. Coal liquefaction had scarcely begun at last reports (130, 1942, p. 185), although the construction of four plants was going forward, and two were believed to be in production on a small scale in 1941. Before the disruption of Japanese shipping service by our armed forces it was far cheaper to ship oil from Borneo and Sumatra than to produce it either from shale or from coal in Manchoukuo; it scarcely seems likely that much effort has been expended on coal liquefaction or shale distillation since 1941.

The production of pig iron in Manchoukuo in 1930–31 averaged about 380,000 tons (240, 1940, p. 756). This rose to about 700,000 tons in 1936 (403, p. 388) and to 837,000 tons in 1939 (130, 1942, pp. 184–85). Since 1939, several new blast furnaces have been completed and additional equipment has been installed for concentrating low-grade ores. It is not possible to say with any assurance what the production of pig iron in Manchoukuo was at the end of 1941, but it may have been as much as 2 million tons (130, 1942, p. 184). It is quite commonly believed that the opening of new iron and coal fields in Tungpientao on the Manchoukuo-Korean border may have increased the output of pig iron some since 1941. The revised five-year plan called for an annual production of 5.5 million tons in 1941.

Steel ingots are not listed as being in production in Manchoukuo before 1935. In 1937 production amounted to 470,000 tons and in 1939 to 639,000 (130, 1942, pp. 84–85). In 1941 it is believed to have been about 1,000,000 tons. If these figures are anywhere nearly correct, iron and steel production in 1941 was far behind the original goal set for that year (steel 2.5 million tons), to say nothing of the second revised goal of 6.1 million tons (240, 1940, p. 855). But this failure to achieve the plan should not blind us to the fact that iron and steel production in Manchoukuo was progressing rapidly through 1941 in spite of the war with China and has probably continued to expand since that time.

Magnesium and aluminum were produced only in small quantities as late as 1939, but several new plants had been completed, and the prospects for future development were good. Both the quantity and the quality of Japanese airplanes would lead one to believe that at the close of the war Japan was producing considerable quantities of these metals, and it seems probable that the early stages of their production took place chiefly in Manchoukuo.

The generation of electric power had been stepped up quite rapidly, but, as far as is known, the increase has been less than half that scheduled through 1939 (403, p. 415). The original plan called for a tripling of 1937 generating capacity between 1937 and 1941, while the last revision of the plan called for about six times the 1937 capacity.

MANCHOUKUO'S PLACE IN THE JAPANESE ECONOMY

It is apparent from the preceding survey, brief as it is, that the industrial development of Manchoukuo was going forward quite rapidly in the years immediately preceding Pearl Harbor, but it is also apparent that Manchoukuo was not yet actually contributing very substantially to Japan's industrial strength. Indeed, it would appear that as late as 1940 or 1941 Manchoukuo was drawing more from Japan in the form of capital goods (equipment) than she was contributing to Japan through increased exports of foods, raw materials, and semifinished goods. What has happened since 1941 is not clear, but at last reports it appeared that Manchoukuo would be compelled to forego much further increase in mining and plant expansion and perhaps to leave unfinished many of the plants begun before Pearl Harbor, devoting her chief efforts to the more efficient use of the existing plants with a view to providing more coal, iron, oil, aluminum, etc., to the industries of Japan and more agricultural products for food and for industrial uses.

This exploitation of Manchoukuo as a colony in the orthodox manner ill suited the Kwantung Army authorities, who had every intention of making Manchoukuo largely independent of Japan Proper economically, although it would, of course, remain an integral part of the Empire. Quite obviously the military clique in control would have far more power if Manchoukuo were to become economically strong and nearly self-sufficing under its tutelage than it could hope for if Manchoukuo were to become merely another colony serving as a supplier of food, raw materials, and semimanufactured goods, on the one hand, and as a market for Japan's manufactures, on the other.

But we are not primarily interested here in the tussle between the army and the capitalists for the economic control of Manchoukuo. We are more interested in the fact that, up to the end of the war, *the economy of Manchoukuo had not been so fully integrated with the life of Japan that its loss as a colony will work any great hardship on her economy as a whole*, provided the way is left open for a fair amount of trade between them in the future. Manchoukuo had not yet become as vital a part of Japanese economy as had Formosa and Korea.

Chapter VI

JAPAN: THE POPULATION OF THE EMPIRE

THERE is no need now to dwell at any length on the location and climate of Japan, since we have learned much about the physical characteristics of the country during the last two years. It will suffice to say that Japan is largely mild-temperate to subtropical in climate and belongs in the rice area of monsoon Asia.

The population of Japan is not known with certainty before 1920, at which time the first actual count was made. The census of October 1, 1920 (242, 1927, p. 44), showed a population approximately two million smaller (55,963,000) than the "legal "population which had been estimated from the local population registers for the end of that year (57,919,000). In view of the fact that this difference was no larger, the series of population estimates for the years since 1872 (Table 9) may be considered indicative of the general trend of growth during the preceding half-century.[1]

JAPAN PROPER—GROWTH IN THE PAST

In the quarter-century prior to 1872 it appears probable that there was an increase of about 5 million, from about 27 million (407, p. 296) to about 32 million, or a gain of 18–19 per cent in twenty-six years. This would yield an annual rate of growth of about 0.7 per cent. For the century and a quarter preceding 1846 the general belief among Japanese scholars is that there had been little change in numbers, the population varying only from about 25 to 27 million; but the progress was by no means continuous. The variations from year to year depended upon whether the harvest had been good or bad, whether such diseases as cholera, dysentery, typhoid fever, and smallpox took more or less than their customary toll, and whether there had been any severe plagues (bubonic plague, pneumonic plague, Asiatic cholera, etc.) of more than local extent.

From about 1872 or a little later the rate of growth of population in Japan mounted steadily and averaged over 1.1 per cent a year between 1872 and 1900 and 1.2 per cent between 1900 and 1920. From 1920 to

---

[1] Reductions in the estimates usually given for 1872–1910 were made in order to arrive at the census population for 1920 while preserving the trend shown by the earlier estimates. Otherwise the decade 1910–20 would have shown a decided drop in rate of growth, whereas our knowledge of the factors at work would lead to the belief that there was no such decline but rather an increase.

1935 the annual rate of increase was a little over 1.4 per cent, but after 1935 the rate fell and for 1935–40 amounted to only 1.1 per cent annually.

It is often assumed that such a rate of population growth as that just noted is unusual. As a matter of fact, Japan's population growth even in recent years has never equaled that of several European countries at the time of their industrial expansion and their establishment of health work and has never remotely approached that of the United States before the Civil War. From 1872 to 1920 Japan's rate of growth was less rapid than that attained by England and Wales from 1801 to

TABLE 9*

Population of Japan, 1721–1940

(In Thousands)

Year	Number	Year	Number
1940.........	73,100	1890.........	39,700
1935.........	69,254	1880.........	34,955
1930.........	64,450	1872.........	32,000
1925.........	59,736	1846.........	26,908
1920.........	55,963	1798.........	25,471
1910.........	50,743	1750.........	25,918
1900.........	44,285	1721.........	26,065

* Sources: 286, 1940–41; 234, 1939, p. 4; 234, 1925; 407, pp. 300–301. Adjustments have been made for years 1872–1910. See note on p. 93.

1841, but it was rising steadily and by 1920–35 had attained approximate equality with that of England and Wales at this earlier period.

In Japan, as elsewhere, the modern *vital* revolution manifested itself in a rather sudden and rapid population growth brought about by a reduction of the death rate due primarily to the improvement of economic and sanitary conditions. The reduction in the death rate was small at first, but, as economic conditions improved and experience in public health work accumulated, the reduction was accelerated until the death rate fell as much as 12–16 per 1,000 below the birth rate and remained at this level for some years. In Japan, just as in a number of European countries, the recorded birth rate increased at the same time, thus making it appear on the surface that an increase in the birth rate was also a consequence of the changing economic and sanitary conditions and was in part responsible for the increasing rate of population growth. There is, however, good reason to think that most of this recorded increase in the birth rate, if not all, was due to the registration of an increasing proportion of the births rather than to an actual increase in the rate. Moreover, for some time after the birth rate did begin to decline, the death rate continued its downward course just as rapidly so that the rate of natural increase (birth rate minus death rate) remained at about the same level, again following the pattern of the West. Although Japan's attack on China (1937) resulted in a rather abrupt decline in the birth rate, the student of population could already recognize the signs of an approaching decline in the rate of population growth.

The evidence indicates that Japan's birth rate began to decline during the 1920's, almost fifty years after that of England and Wales and perhaps twenty to twenty-five years after that of Germany. In view of the fact that Japan had passed through that part of the modern cycle of population growth preceding a decline of the birth rate in a shorter time than most Western nations, it seems reasonable to believe that she will also complete the remainder of the cycle in a shorter time if her industrial and commercial development is not too much interfered with by the war.

RURAL AND URBAN DIFFERENTIALS IN BIRTH RATES

The chief reasons for expecting a continuation of the decline in Japan's birth rate are found in the social and economic development on which the country is embarked. Japan is becoming an industrial country much more rapidly than is generally realized, and its urban population is expanding at an even faster rate than our own of twenty to thirty years ago. Whereas 19.9 per cent of the Japanese people lived in communities of 30,000 or more in 1920, 28.5 per cent lived in such communities in 1930 and 38.4 in 1940 (242, 1937, p. 50).

The same trend is shown by the declining proportion of the occupied population engaged in agriculture. This group declined from 52.4 per cent in 1920 to 43.7 per cent in 1936, and its decline has apparently been accelerated since 1936 by reason of the rapid expansion of war industry. Probably not over 40 per cent of the occupied population of Japan is now engaged in agriculture. In the United States we reached this stage of agricultural employment at some point between 1890 and 1900.

From the standpoint of Japan's future population growth the main importance of this industrial-urban development lies in the rapidly declining birth rate in the urban population.

Unfortunately, it is not possible to get as clear cut a picture of urban and rural birth rates in Japan as in the United States, but the following facts show that much the same large differentials exist in Japan as in the Western world. In 1921 (235, 1921, pp. 4–5) the reported birth rate for Japan as a whole was 35.05 but about 28.5 for all cities. In 1936 the birth rate for Japan had fallen to 29.9, while that for all cities was 25.1 (235, 1938). Since all communities of over 30,000, which are almost but not quite identical with all "cities," contained only 19.9 per cent of the total population at the end of 1920, the noncity population would have needed a birth rate of about 37 to yield a rate of 35.05 for the total population. Thus it appears that even as early as 1920 the birth rate of the noncity population was over one-fourth greater than that of the city population. The census of 1935 showed that about one-third of the population was in communities of over 30,000 (33.8 per cent) and that this proportion was increasing at the rate of about 1 per cent a year. "Cities" had a slightly larger proportion. If it is assumed that the proportion in "cities" was 35 per cent in 1936, the noncity birth rate must have been 32.5, or almost 30 per cent above the "city" rate (about 25.07), to yield a rate of 29.9 for the total population.

These figures leave no doubt about the existence of a large rural-urban differential in the birth rates of Japan, but they also show that the noncity birth rate is declining in much the same manner as the city birth rate. In the more rural prefectures, however, the birth rate is still quite high. In 1933 the five northern prefectures on the main island had an average birth rate of 39.7 per 1,000 and an average death rate of 19.6, leaving a natural increase of 20.1, which is far above that for Japan as a whole. Furthermore, in Japan as in Western countries, the urban population has a much higher percentage of young adults than the rural population so that the differences in birth rates noted above by no means tell the whole story. A birth rate adjusted to take account of these age differences would show an even larger difference between rural and urban communities.

It is rather important to bear in mind the "naturalness" of these urban-rural differentials in the birth rate, for many people seem to think that the Japanese do not respond as we do to the urban-industrial influences which have led to the control of the birth rate in the West. Actually the Japanese are responding to urban life, to the individual wage system, to the desire to attain a better level of living, to the opportunity to move from class to class (economically and occupationally), to the broadening of interests outside the home, and to the growing independence of women, just as we do. Furthermore, the impact of modern city living is beginning to break up the Japanese family in much the same way it did the European family, and the payment of individual wages for a given amount of work is creating in Japan, as elsewhere, a situation in which children are a handicap to economic and social advancement. The effects of all these changes on the birth rate are already unmistakable.[2]

THE SPREAD OF CONTRACEPTION

Another factor to be taken account of in forming an opinion of the probable trend of the birth rate in Japan during the next few decades is whether contraception is likely to spread as rapidly there as it did in the West after about 1880. Any statement of what *will* happen in this respect must necessarily be only an opinion, but why should we seriously doubt that the decline in the birth rate of Japan just noted is due in large measure to voluntary control? The earlier decline in the West certainly arose chiefly from such control. But it is unrealistic to expect Japan to have achieved in four or five decades a control over birth rates and death rates as effective as the Western industrialized countries have achieved in twice that period. Japan was several decades behind most Western lands in the development of her industry and in the growth of her cities, and the decline in her birth rates and death rates could reasonably be expected to lag in about the same measure. Birth control apparently did not make much headway in England and Wales for about a century after British industry began its growth and the cityward movement was well advanced. The lag in Germany was not as long because her urbanization and industrialization was more rapid; also the means of contraception were better developed and the communication of such knowledge from person to person was far easier. For the same reasons the spread of contraception appears to be even more rapid in Japan than in Germany. But, even so, its general adoption in Japan will take some years, at least two or three decades.

THE TREND IN THE DEATH RATE

There is still opportunity for considerable decline in Japan's death rate; consequently, the rate of natural increase will probably not decline as fast as the birth rate falls. As we have seen, Japan's death rate began to decline as soon as she began to improve her productive capac-

[2] Since the above was written, an article, "The Dynamics of Population in Japan," by Drs. Irene B. Taeuber and Edwin G. Beal, *Milbank Memorial Fund Quarterly*, July, 1944, pp. 222–55, gives some reproduction rates for Japan which indicate a somewhat larger rural-urban differential than that suggested here but which do not change the picture in essentials.

ity and introduced some measure of modern sanitation. It continued to decline as sanitation improved, as better medical care was provided, and as productivity increased. (The Japanese data show an increase in the average death rate for the years 1914–23 over preceding years, but this does not seem to invalidate the general statement just made because this rise is probably due to the increasing completeness of death registration rather than to an actual increase in the death rate.) By 1924–28 the death rate had fallen to 20.1; in the five years 1929–33 the average was 18.5, and in the period 1934–38 it was 17.4.

It appears, then, that in the period just prior to Japan's heavy involvement in the war her death rate (17.4) had fallen to about the level reached in the United States and England and Wales in 1900. Since then we have gained still further control over our death rate, and while it may be that the low death rates attained in the more advanced countries of the temperate climates cannot be attained in subtropical areas such as the southern part of Japan, there is no good reason to believe that her latest pre-war death rates cannot be considerably reduced. Indeed, for several years they might well be reduced as fast as the birth rate declines so that there would be no significant decline in the rate of natural increase.

JAPAN PROPER—GROWTH IN THE FUTURE

Following the attack on China in 1937 the Japanese birth rate declined rapidly, but it recovered in 1940 and 1941 until it was about as high as in 1934–36. The death rate, according to official figures, kept on declining and was 15.4 in 1941. This death rate applies only to the civilian population and probably does not allow for the decline in population due to soldiers being sent abroad, so it is of little value. Since 1941, if Japan follows the usual pattern in a country long at war, we would expect the birth rate to decline and the death rate to rise so that the rate of natural increase would have been considerably reduced. When allowance is also made for military losses, it seems probable that there has been a much smaller increase in numbers than for some years past.

Following the war the pattern to be expected would be about as follows: for perhaps the second and third years after demobilization the birth rate will rise rapidly, possibly even exceeding that in the more normal years before 1937. This might occur in 1947 and 1948. After this we would expect a rather rapid decline in the birth rate so that within two or three years it would be about what one studying trends in 1936 would have predicted for 1949 and 1950. The death rate would be expected to resume its decline almost at once after the war unless, of course, Japan's economy is so badly disrupted that unusual hardship persists for some years. In this case the death rate might even rise.

When these different factors are taken into account, it seems quite likely that Japan's population will keep on growing for several decades but at a decreasing rate and that it probably will reach a total of between 85 and 95 million sometime between 1975 and 1985. Dr. Uyeda has estimated that it will number about 88 million in 1970, and the Population Institute of Japan has estimated it at about 105 million in the same year (215, p. 12). In virtually adopting Dr. Uyeda's estimate, I indicate my expectation of a rapid decline in the birth rate in the future and of a lack of official interference with the "natural" course of growth as determined by the operation of the social and economic factors mentioned above.

There is always the possibility, however, that a certain amount of control over population growth may be exercised by governmental agencies, e.g., that the birth rate might be lowered more rapidly by making contraceptive devices cheap and easy to procure and by the establishment of birth-control clinics to instruct the public in their use. On the other hand, it might be raised by economic and social inducements for large families and by penalties for failure to marry and rear children, as in Germany, and possibly by an urgent appeal to patriotism if they suffer a "hard" peace. But we must recognize that there are limits within which these deliberate efforts at control can be made effective at any given time (Fig. 3).

In order to understand more adequately what such a growth of population as that just indicated will mean for Japan in the future, it will be necessary to examine briefly the economic means by which Japan has supported her people and raised their level of living well above that of other Asiatic peoples during the last five or six decades and to try to evaluate the prospect of a continuance of this process. Before we do this, it will be well to look into the population growth of Japan's colonies (Korea and Formosa) and to take account of the emigration of Japanese during the past few decades.

THE POPULATION OF KOREA

Using the most commonly accepted figures, Korea's population was 13.3 million in 1910 (242, 1937, p. 977), 17.3 million in 1920, 21 mil-

lion in 1930 (240, 1940, p. 48), and 24.3 million in 1940. Since the
1910 and 1920 figures are estimates, no real census having been taken
until 1925 (19.5 million), and since the rates of increase—30 per cent
between 1910 and 1920 and 21.3 per cent between 1920 and 1930—

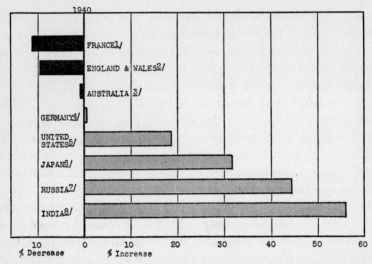

Fig. 3.—Estimated population increase or decrease in selected countries, 1940–70.
(1) Fertility and mortality rates remain same as in 1935; no immigration (Alfred Sauvy,
"Perspectives statistiques sur la population, l'enseignement et la chomage," *Journal de la
societe de statistique de Paris*, No. 6, June 1937, pp. 16–17). (2) Estimates assume fertility
and mortality rates same as in 1933; no immigration (Enid Charles, *The Effect of Present
Trends in Fertility and Mortality upon the Future Population of England and Wales and upon Its
Age Composition* [London: Executive Committee of London and Cambridge, Economic
Service, August, 1935]). (3) From 1938 to 1963 fertility rates decline at a rate equal to
one-half of the decline experienced during 1925 to 1930, then stabilize; same mortality
rates as 1932–34; no immigration (S. H. Wolstenholme, "The Future of Australian Population," *Economic Record*, XII, No. 23 [December, 1936]), p. 205. (4) Same number of
births (1,162,000) as in 1927; same mortality rates as 1924–26; no immigration (Friedrich
Burgdörfer, *Volk ohne Yugend* [Berlin: Vowinckel, 1935], p. 135). (5) Medium birth rates
and medium death rates; no immigration (National Resources Planning Board, *Estimates
of Future Population of the United States, 1940–2000* [Washington: Government Printing Office,
1943]). (6) Average of the 1970 estimates of the Institute for the Research of Population
Problems in Japan and of Dr. Teijiro Uyeda (Masaji Inouye, *Population of Japan* [Tokyo:
Bureau of Social Affairs (Kojimachi-Ku), 1937]). (7) Frank W. Notestein, "Some Implications of Population Change for Post-war Europe," *Proceedings of the American Philosophical
Society*, Vol. LXXXVII, No. 2 (1943). (8) It is assumed that India will continue to grow
at the rate of 15 per cent per decade as between 1931 and 1941 (Burma is not included.)

are higher than seems reasonable in the light of the economic and
health conditions prevailing in Korea and of the sketchy information
available on birth rates and death rates, we are justified in assuming
that these early estimates are considerably too low (242, 1921–22, p.

573; 234, 1933, p. 15). Furthermore, it is known that there has been a rather large emigration from Korea to Japan, to Manchoukuo, and even to the Soviet Far East, most of which has taken place since 1910. The total number of Koreans living abroad in 1940 was probably somewhat more than 2 million.[3]

Thus even if it is assumed that the population of Korea in 1910 was a million or even a million and one-half larger than the estimate usually given (13.3 million) and was a half-million to one million larger in 1920, there can be no doubt that there has been a very rapid increase in Korea's population since 1910. It may not have doubled, as it appears to have done when official figures plus emigrants are considered, but it very probably did increase by 80–90 per cent during these three decades.

The reasons for this rapid increase of population in Korea are fundamentally the same as those accounting for Japan's own increase, although the ingredients are not mixed in the same proportions. Since Japanese occupation (1910) the sanitary conditions of Korea have been much improved, especially in the larger cities. The efficiency of her agriculture has been increased and the area extended, thus at least temporarily raising the standard of living of part of the population. In addition, a reasonably good transportation system has been built and a small amount of modern industry was established even before 1937. These improvements reduced death rates below their customary level, while birth rates remained about as they were. As a consequence the rate of natural increase expanded at an unprecedented pace and has remained high up to the present time. The prospect is that Korea's death rate will continue to decline, although the decline may well be slower in the next two or three decades than in the last two or three.

Since Korea has been and still is largely an agricultural country, there is less reason to expect a rapid decline in the birth rate than in Japan in spite of official data (234, 1940, pp. 10–11) which indicate a most remarkable decline from about 38.0 for the years 1929 and 1930 to about 28.7 for the years 1936 and 1937. Although there is probably some mistake here, the census counts in 1930, 1935, and 1940 indicate that there must have been either a rather substantial decline in the birth rate in the last half of the 1930's or a much larger emigration

[3] There were 419,000 Koreans living in Japan in 1930 (240, 1940, p. 50) and 800,000 in 1939 (134, Part I). In addition, there were 931,000 (240, 1940, p. 604) in Manchoukuo and a considerable number in the Soviet Far East. Gradjanzev (167, p. 58) estimates a total of about 2,300,000 Koreans living abroad in 1939.

than usual. Whereas there was an increase of 1,840,000, or 8.7 per cent, between 1930 and 1935, there was an increase of only 1,430,000, or 6.2 per cent, between 1935 and 1940. There is no way to tell whether emigration or decline in the birth rate is the more important factor.

Hence, though it appears not improbable that Korea's birth rate is declining in spite of the fact that it is still largely an agricultural country,[4] it would perhaps be wise to remain skeptical of the large decline shown by the official data until more evidence becomes available.

In spite of the uncertainties of the data, the demographer would expect that Korea would continue to grow in numbers fairly rapidly for several decades yet, unless she encounters some great catastrophe. Korea's population may very well increase by one-third or more by 1970—from a little over 24 million in 1940 to 32–36 million by 1970. Even this would be a significantly slower rate than that which prevailed in the past. This belief in the probability of a lower rate of growth in the future seems justified by the fact that Korea is becoming modernized and is beginning to industrialize. Her cities are growing rapidly in spite of the manifest intention of the Japanese to keep her in a colonial status as a producer of cheap food and raw materials and as a consumer of Japanese manufactures.

It is true that the rapid industrialization of Korea might lead to a more rapid reduction in the birth rate than now seems probable and would also enhance the ability of the country to support this increase in population for some years at an improving standard; but whether it can be achieved fast enough to prevent an increased death rate in the not distant future seems rather doubtful at the present time, although we assume that Korea will become independent in the near future and thus will become free to develop her industry without hindrance by a colonial master.

THE POPULATION OF FORMOSA

The population of Formosa, like that of Korea, has been growing rapidly during the last three or four decades from an estimated 3,040,-000 in 1905 (240, 1940, p. 527) to 3,993,000 in 1925 and to 5,872,000 in 1940 (369, VII [1941], 318). Thus it has almost doubled in thirty-five years, with about two-thirds of the increase taking place in the last fifteen years since the data have become fairly reliable. Here again

[4] Approximately three-fourths (79.5) of the Koreans depend upon agriculture for their living (242, 1937, p. 977).

we see the familiar pattern of a relatively slow increase for some years after a "backward" area is brought within the sphere of influence of a more industrialized "mother"-country and following this a much more rapid growth as sanitary measures essential to the economic exploitation of the area are introduced and the security of life and income becomes greater. A brief review of Formosa's vital statistics will throw light on the processes of population growth in such an area.

Formosa's population is largely Chinese (about 94 per cent) so that anything said about its population as a whole or about its native population really applies largely to a Chinese population. These Chinese came from the central part of the eastern coast of China, chiefly from Fukien province; Foochow is only about a hundred miles distant. This is a point of some importance because the vital statistics of Formosa, deficient though they may be, not only show the trend of birth rates and death rates in this island but also indicate something about those of a Chinese population—the only Chinese population of more than a few thousands for which even moderately reliable data are available.

The earliest year for which birth rates and death rates for Formosa are given is 1915, and it can be taken for granted that these rates are highly deficient. For the years 1915–19 the average birth rate is given as 40 per 1,000 and the death rate as 30 (242, 1921–22, p. 593). In the next five years the recorded rates are 41.4 and 25.7, respectively (242, 1927, p. 641). For the last five years for which the writer can find data —1933–37 (163)—the birth rate for the natives is 45.6 and the death rate 20.6. The census confirms these high rates of natural increase in recent years, since the population increased by about 28 per cent between 1930 and 1940, a rate of approximately 2.5 per cent per year. This is an extremely high rate and would lead to a doubling of the population in about twenty-nine years. It may be somewhat too high, although there is generally greater deficiency in registering births than deaths.

Unless something happens to raise the death rate, Formosa's population will probably continue to grow at a very rapid rate for the next few decades. The war and the disruption of the administration which will follow upon Japan's defeat may so disturb the sanitary control and the steady development of agriculture which has been attained under Japanese direction that there will be little or no growth in the immediate postwar period. But we can be fairly sure that any decline in Formosa's population growth in the near future will be due to an increase in the death rate arising from the breakdown of governmental controls rather than to any decline in the birth rate. There is as yet no evidence whatever of such decline in Formosa.

The course of population growth in Korea and Formosa since Japanese occupation is of significance not only because of the increase in numbers but also because they are good examples of the way population is likely to grow in almost any simple agricultural community when a small measure of sanitation is introduced, when agriculture is improved, when the tilled area is extended, and when security of life and property is established.

THE JAPANESE AS COLONISTS

The Japanese have exercised a large measure of control over Korea since the close of the Sino-Japanese War in 1894–95, although it was not formally made a part of the Empire until 1910. The movement of Japanese into Korea prior to the Russo-Japanese War was quite small, but the number of Japanese increased to 172,000 by 1910 (242, 1937, p. 977) and then about doubled in the next ten years, reaching 348,000 in 1920. Since then the number has grown more slowly and was estimated at 630,000 in 1937 (240, 1940, p. 505).

This slower growth of the Japanese in Korea in recent years is considered by many people as proof (a) that there was no great population pressure in Japan and (b) that the Japanese do not make good colonists. In my opinion these are erroneous interpretations of the facts; but, before discussing these general aspects of the contact of the Japanese with their colonial subjects, it will be well to describe briefly the contacts which do actually exist.

In 1938 the 630,000–640,000 Japanese in Korea gained their livelihood from the major types of work shown in Table 10. Since many of those occupied in agriculture were managing estates and irrigation projects and were engaged in forestry rather than in farming (167, pp. 56–57), there were perhaps not over four thousand farm families among the Japanese in Korea in 1938. Most of the remainder were engaged in what might be termed "sheltered" occupations—occupations where they did not actually come into competition with the Koreans. The Japanese have made very little headway in settling on the land in almost forty years of control of the country; they have remained in these "sheltered" jobs and for the most part live in the larger cities.

The reason for this situation is quite understandable and is illustrative of the generally valid principle that, when peoples having different levels of living come into actual competition, those with the higher level are always driven out in the course of time by those having the lower level. In agriculture the Japanese peasant would come into real competition with the Korean peasant, and he is not yet so hard put to it at home that he is ready to accept Korean standards. In the non-agricultural occupations, on the other hand, the Japanese do not, as yet, have to compete with the Koreans. Their jobs are reserved for

TABLE 10*

OCCUPATIONAL DISTRIBUTION OF JAPANESE
IN KOREA, 1938

Occupation	Per Cent
Agriculture	5.3
Fishing	1.5
Mining	2.3
Industry	16.6
Commerce	23.4
Communications	5.9
Public and professional services	38.1
Other occupations	2.9
No occupation	4.0
Total	100.0

* Source: 167, p. 56.

them, and they are paid at a rate to enable them to maintain and even to improve upon the level of living they could reasonably hope for in Japan.

In Formosa the situation is almost identical. In 1905 there were about 60,000 Japanese (240, 1934, p. 508) living there. This number increased rather rapidly during the next fifteen years, and in 1920 there were 167,000 (234, 1925, p. 148). By 1930 the number had only risen to 232,000, and at the end of 1938 it was estimated at 309,000 (163, p. 25). The occupational distribution of the Japanese in Formosa is very much like that in Korea: they are almost entirely in "sheltered" occupations where they do not come into competition with the Chinese.

The same story with slight variations is repeated in Manchoukuo. Different bureaus of the Japanese government give different figures for the number of Japanese settled in Manchoukuo, but the following account is believed to be substantially correct. In 1904, before the Russo-Japanese War, there were only a few hundred Japanese in

Manchoukuo. Ten years later, in 1914, there were over 100,000, and by 1931, but before the occupation of Manchoukuo by Japan, the number had increased to 233,000 (240, 1934, pp. 73–74), not including the army. At the end of 1937 the number was estimated at 593,000 (240, 1940, p. 604). Thus the number of Japanese in Manchoukuo had considerably more than doubled in the first seven years of occupation. Here, as in Korea and Formosa, very few Japanese were engaged in agriculture—only 2.4 per cent of the total Japanese population. The latest available data (240, 1941, p. 413) show that there were about 24,000 agricultural settlers from Japan in Manchoukuo at the end of 1939. In addition, there were about 29,000 Youth Volunteers on the land: boys sixteen to eighteen years of age who were being trained in Manchoukuoan agriculture at the same time that they were being used as guards by the police authorities.

Clearly, up to 1940 the Japanese were almost as chary of going into agriculture in Manchoukuo as in Korea and Formosa, although here there could be no question whatever of land being available. This slow movement into agriculture is all the more significant because very grandiose schemes for the settlement of Japanese in Manchoukuo were laid out not long after the Japanese occupation of the country, and in 1935 a twenty-year plan involving the settlement of one million Japanese families (five million persons) was adopted. The figures on agricultural settlers given above come from Japanese sources and certainly do not indicate any large success in Japanese agricultural settlement in Manchoukuo up to 1940.

The war with China and later with the United Nations no doubt completely upset previous immigration plans for Manchoukuo, but the Japanese have shown definitely that they cannot compete with the Koreans and Formosans in growing crops quite similar to those of Japan, so there seems very little likelihood that Japanese farmers can compete with the Chinese farmers in Manchoukuo, where the climate and the crops are quite different from those to which they are accustomed.

WHY THE SMALL MOVEMENT OF JAPANESE TO THEIR COLONIES

The situation of the Japanese vis-à-vis the Chinese in Manchoukuo is much like that of the Germans and the Poles in western Poland while this region was still a part of Prussia. The Germans found that they could not compete with the Poles even after being settled by the government of Prussia under conditions which amounted to being subsidized. The Poles steadily pushed them back by buying their land at fabulous prices and by raising larger families. Bismarck frequently complained that the Poles so outbred the Germans that the latter had no chance to hold this area against them.

The Japanese encountered exactly the same situation when they came into actual competition with Chinese or Korean farmers in their colonies. If it is urged that this belief is not supported by the experience of the Japanese in the Philippines (Davao), in their mandated islands, in parts of South America (notably in Brazil), and in Hawaii and the United States, the answer is that only in the Philippines did they settle among a people with as low a level of living. Even here they managed to maintain such a separate economy that they did not actually come into competition with the natives. Besides, the Moros are not an agricultural people to the same degree as most other Filipinos. In South America the Japanese are generally believed to be undermining the standards of the natives, if one may judge by the opposition in these countries to further Japanese immigration. As regards the Japanese in the United States there has never been any question in the minds of most people in this country that the lower level of living among the Japanese made it impossible for American farmers with higher standards to compete with them.

Where peoples having different levels of living, based on somewhat similar processes of making a living (technologies), come into competition on the land, it always seems to work out that those willing to work the hardest, live on the least, and raise the largest families, supplant those whose level of living demands more leisure, more consumption goods, and smaller families. This is the basis for the belief that the Japanese could make little headway as agriculturists in Manchoukuo, Korea, or Formosa.

It is true that the Japanese do go to their colonies in much greater numbers than Europeans go to their colonies in the Pacific Region and that they take less desirable jobs than Europeans would consider; but, even so, the total number emigrating is small, as we have seen, probably not exceeding 1.3 million or a little over a single year's increase of the period 1931–35. Besides, we must not forget that the Japanese migration to Korea is more than matched by Korean migration to Japan.

It should be made clear, however, that the failure of the Japanese to migrate in large numbers to their colonies and Manchoukuo does not mean that they cannot become successful colonists. It is only an illustration of a very general principle of migration: that only a small exploitative migration flows from areas with a higher level of living to areas with a lower level unless the area of destination is a relatively un-inhabited area like the United States and thus offers large opportunity for the migrants to determine their own level. The movement of a few thousands or even of a few hundreds of thousands of British, Dutch, and Japanese officials, technicians, and managers into colonial areas does not raise problems of economic competition with the natives; at least, it does not raise them for some decades. This is a fact which must be borne in mind when trying to estimate the value of any area for pur-poses of mass migration from the homeland.

In view of these general conditions governing the success of mass mi-gration, I do not see how we can fail to conclude that the Japanese col-onies, and even Manchoukuo, never have offered any substantial op-portunity for Japanese migration, however valuable they might be in other respects. The same line of reasoning would lead us to conclude that no really large Japanese migration was to be expected into any of the fairly densely settled areas of the Orient—China, Formosa, Indo-China, Siam, Burma, Java, the Malay Peninsula, or most of the Philippines. In these areas the Japanese would have to compete with natives having as low a level, if not a lower level, of living.

But if there was little likelihood that the Japanese could migrate to the settled lands of southern and eastern Asia in any considerable num-bers, there is no good reason to doubt that they could settle in relative-ly large numbers in such sparsely inhabited areas as Borneo, Celebes, and New Guinea and succeed in agriculture, mining, and industry. Here they would not encounter any serious competition from the na-tives, and they have proved by their actual settlements in the tropics that they can live and work in such regions, that they can "possess" such lands just as our ancestors "possessed" the United States. The Netherlands East Indies alone contain about 735,000 square miles (286, 1940–41, p. 16), of which only about 50,000–60,000 (Java, Madura, and some of the smaller islands) are really densely settled. The British island possessions in the Pacific Region (not including Australia and New Zealand) amount to almost 300,000 square miles, of which only a few thousands have any population worth mentioning.

Attention is called to these facts at this point because they need to be considered when discussing the growth of population in Japan. Mere mention will suffice for the present, since more attention must be given to the possibilities of settlement when we come to consider the larger problem of peace in the Pacific (see chap. xxi).

Chapter VII

JAPAN: THE FOOD SUPPLY OF THE EMPIRE

U NTIL about 1880 Japan was almost wholly an agricultural country with perhaps 75 per cent or more (78.9 per cent in 1872 according to Nasu [335, p. 7]) of her people dependent directly on agriculture. As late as 1904 almost two-thirds of the families were classified as farming families, although a considerable number of them also had subsidiary occupations. The first real census, in 1920, listed 52.4 per cent of the occupied persons as in agriculture. This had fallen to 47.7 per cent in 1930, and estimates for 1936 indicate (403, p. 76) that it had declined to 43.7 per cent by that time. It has probably declined significantly since 1936, because the industrialization of Japan had been greatly accelerated by the war and the army had taken a large part of the rural youth.

THE CHARACTER OF JAPANESE AGRICULTURE

Before the modern era the agricultural practices of Japan had become firmly stabilized to supply the traditional needs of a population growing slowly or not at all and considerably less than one-half as large as at present (see chap. vi). She had then a relatively static agricultural civilization with the low level of living characterizing all oriental peoples at that time. Much the greater part of the agricultural work was performed by hand in the traditional ways which had prevailed for centuries.

The greater part of the work on Japanese farms is still done by hand, with the hoe and the spade and the sickle. The number of cattle has increased from about a million in 1903 to 1.97 million in 1939 (169), and the number of horses has increased from 1.1 million to 1.4 million. But even if the cattle were used for draft purposes alone, there would still be only a little over one-half as many possible draft animals as farms. Furthermore, the latest Japanese yearbooks and treatises on her agriculture make no mention of tractors or modern tillage machinery, so these must at least be a negligible factor in production. It could not well be otherwise, for we find that the increase in the average size of farm was only about .27 of an acre between 1903 and 1937, rising from

2.40 acres to 2.67 acres (240, 1940, p. 286). The fact that Japanese agriculture is still an intensive hand agriculture is undoubtedly one of the chief reasons why there had been no significant change in the absolute size of the agricultural population since 1920, unless since 1937.

At this point it will be well to explain that throughout the Orient where the climate is mild enough and the rainfall is high, or irrigation can be practiced, a significant part of the land produces two crops a year. North of the frost line and where the rainfall is sufficient, which includes all but the southern part of Japan, the summer crop is generally rice and the winter crop wheat or barley. South of the frost line the winter crop also may be rice, though this is not common. Over a goodly part of Japan and much of central China and Korea the rice is planted a plant at a time by hand—much as we plant tomatoes, cabbage, and other garden plants—in fields (paddies) which are flooded with water and are kept flooded, if possible, until almost harvest time. Obviously, such a system of cropping makes a large amount of hand labor necessary, and the fields which must be level for flooding are quite certain to remain too small to make much use of modern machinery as long as there is a dense rural population and the naturally level areas are small.

This two-crop system (especially where both crops are rice) rather than high yields per acre makes possible a very dense population in many parts of the Orient, since everywhere practically all the grain raised is used for human food. The draft animals live on such forage as they can find on the fields, the dikes surrounding them, and along the roads and paths, while the hogs and chickens live almost entirely as scavengers.

TILLABLE LAND

But the fact that Japanese agriculture has made little progress in the use of machinery and animal power to increase the productivity of human labor does not mean that it has remained static in other respects. The most obvious change in Japanese agriculture since about 1875 has been in the extension of the tilled area from about 10.5 million acres in 1877 to 14.9 million in 1939; but there has also been about the same proportional growth (42 per cent) in irrigated land.[1]

[1] There is much confusion in the Japanese figures on the area of tilled and irrigated land, so that the figures given here must be considered only approximate. Thus the figure for tilled land in 1877 is sometimes given as 10.1 million acres (335, p. 68) and at other times by the same generally reliable author as 11.0 million acres. In the above calculation I have used an average of these two figures. There is the same difficulty with regard to irrigated land; in view of all the uncertainties I am disposed to think it very doubtful that

The proportion of irrigated land which produced two crops a year was given as 37 per cent in 1903 (242, 1907, p. 324) and by a different authority as 43 per cent in 1939 (335, p. 94). This would indicate a substantial growth in such practice, and the large amount of attention given to the improvement of irrigation works makes such an increase in double-cropping appear reasonable. There cannot be any reasonable doubt that the total area available for intensive cultivation has increased by as much as 40 per cent in the last sixty years and may have increased by considerably more; the increase in nonirrigated land would vary between one-fourth and almost two-fifths. But this makes little difference, since in Japan such land can never support a very dense population. The addition of 1.5–2.0 million acres of nonirrigated crops would scarcely supply food to a two years' increase of Japan's population at the 1930–40 rate of growth even at the level of consumption prevailing.

It is of importance for our purposes, however, to note that most of this increase in the crop area of Japan took place before 1920. Indeed, on the basis of the figures given in Japanese official publications (240, 1940, p. 286) there appears to have been a slight decline in tilled area since 1920, probably apparent rather than real.

The failure to make any substantial gain in tilled land since 1920 is not due to lack of effort. Much money and labor have been spent on reclaiming and irrigating new land—but the demand for level land for the extension of cities, for new roads, railroads, canals, airfields, etc., and the destruction of crop land by earthquakes and floods has been so great in recent years that the net addition to agricultural lands is negligible. The withdrawals from cultivation just about equal the additions.

In addition, comparatively little increase in tilled land is to be expected in the future unless the people undertaking the exploitation of new lands are prepared to accept a distinctly lower level of living than that now prevailing among Japanese farmers, or unless the government is prepared to pay heavy subsidies to those undertaking this exploitation. The reasonably good land in Japan is already under tillage.

By way of calling attention to the significance of even a 50 per cent

there has been any proportional increase in irrigated land. This view seems to be confirmed by the figures used by Schumpeter (403, p. 119) for 1935, 53.1 per cent; by Pelzer (134, Part I, p. 114) for 1937, 52.8 per cent; and by Grajdanzev for paddy fields in 1939, 52.9 per cent (169, p. 17).

increase (using the most favorable figures) in tilled land between 1880 and 1920, it may be noted that Japan's population grew from about 35 million to 56 million during this same period—an increase of 60 per cent. Since 1920 the population has grown from 56 million to 73 million in 1940, or 30 per cent, while there has been no significant increase in tilled land.

Fortunately for Japan the efforts to improve the yields of the staple crops have been more successful than those to extend the tilled area. The rice yield rose by about 65 per cent from 1878–82 to 1934–38 (335, p. 108, and 240, 1940, pp. 286–87). During the same period wheat and barley yields have more than doubled, and certain other crops, notably potatoes (sweet and Irish), show substantial gains. On the other hand, millet and beans show little increase in yields.

But a large part of this increase in yields, like the increase in tilled area, took place before 1920. It was attained in Japan, just as elsewhere, by more intensive use of fertilizers, by the development of better varieties of seed, by improved farm practices, and by providing for a more certain water supply. Up to a certain point these improved practices add to yields more than in proportion to cost (increasing returns), but after the first large increments additional gains are less and may soon cost more than they are worth (diminishing returns). The yields of many Japanese crops are not by any means the highest known, but those of rice and wheat are considerably in excess of those in most other countries where these are major crops.

Because the increases in yields could not be maintained after 1920, Japan has been compelled to turn more and more to outside sources of supply for some of her staple foods, particularly rice. That these foods have come increasingly from Korea and Formosa (within the Empire) rather than from foreign sources does not alter the fact that Japan Proper seems to have approached the practicable limits of food production. To secure rice, sugar, and bananas from colonies within the Empire did, of course, simplify the problems of trade and exchange in the pre-war period, but it may render the food situation of Japan highly precarious in the postwar world when Formosa and Korea are no longer colonies.

In contrast with an almost stationary cereal crop in Japan Proper in recent years there has been a rather large percentage increase in meat and dairy products. This is often pointed to as indicating that

Japanese agriculture is not nearing its limits of expansion. The error here is that a large proportional increase is assumed to be the same as a large absolute increase. The fact is that the total production of these foods in Japan is so small as to be of almost negligible significance in the diet of the people. Thus meat (beef and pork) consumption in Japan is about 4 pounds per capita per year (240, 1940, p. 295) and the yearly milk consumption is less than one gallon per capita. These are negligible amounts and would have to increase many hundred fold before attaining a position of any significance in the Japanese food supply. At present no one expects that home-produced meat, milk, cheese, and butter will increase fast enough to have any noticeable effect on the ability of Japan Proper to supply herself with food.

There can be no reasonable doubt that there has been an improvement in the general level of living in Japan in recent decades, and it probably continued up to about the time of the attack on China (1937)—but this improvement arose chiefly from the expansion of Japan's industry, the growth of her fisheries, and the exploitation of her colonies (Korea and Formosa), and only to a minor extent from the expansion of agricultural production at home, since her population increased faster than home production. If for any reason Japan Proper had to rely entirely on her own agriculture and her local fisheries for her food, there would be a marked falling-off in the adequacy of the Japanese diet. We will deal with this point again after a look at the agricultural development of Korea and Formosa and after the industrial expansion of Japan has been discussed.

THE AGRICULTURE OF KOREA

Korean agriculture is much like that of Japan in that it is largely dependent on hand labor and in that the chief crop is rice grown on irrigated land. Other cereals, however, are relatively more important in Korea than in Japan, as are also sweet and Irish potatoes. There are about the same number of cattle (1,700,000) in Korea as in Japan but only about 3 per cent (50,000) as many horses. Since the tilled area is about 70 per cent of that of Japan, it would appear that the Koreans do an even larger part of their farm work by hand.

Korean agriculture, like Japanese, is relatively intense—about one-third, or a little less, of the irrigated land (229, p. 111; 167, p. 74), yielding two crops a year. Being colder and having a lighter rainfall in most sections than Japan, the second crop is generally a winter cereal (wheat, barley, rye) with rice as the dominant summer crop.

Crop yields are usually only one-half to one-third those of Japan (167, p. 7), probably because less fertilizer is used and farm practices are poorer, although the smaller proportion of tilled land that is irrigated may account for a part of the difference in yields, particularly for crops other than rice.

In general, it may be said that the development of Korean agriculture since 1910, and especially since 1920, has been directed by the colonial government with a view to making it supplement that of Japan rather than serve the best interests of the Koreans. Rice and cotton have been much encouraged because they were needed by Japan, and thus commercial farming has made much greater headway than might be expected in a population which is still about three-fourths agricultural (167, p. 55).

Korea is mountainous like Japan but has a larger proportion of tillable land, somewhat over 20 per cent (167, p. 13) as compared with a little over 15 per cent. The possibilities of future additions to tilled area are also greater in Korea than in Japan: probably 2.5–3.0 million acres remain to be brought into cultivation. The actual increase since 1920 has amounted to only about 500,000 acres, raising the total tilled area to 11,064,000 acres in 1938 (167, p. 12)—an increase of only about 4.4 per cent in eighteen years during a period in which the population has increased by about 40 per cent.

What proportion of this possible increase is irrigable is not known, but, in the light of the slow increase of irrigated land since 1919, it would appear doubtful that any large proportion of any future increase in tilled land can be irrigated. But since the increase in irrigated land that has taken place was all in two-crop land, a total of about a million acres or a little more has been added to the irrigated crop area since 1920. This is an increase of about 23 per cent in the irrigated crop area (167, p. 14) and is a more rapid increase than has taken place in Japan during the same period, but even this has not kept pace with the growth in Korea's population.

In addition to the increase in tilled land in Korea, there has also been a substantial increase in the yields of her staple crops, although far less than in Japan. The increase in rice yields is almost one-fourth since 1919, but that of the other cereals, chiefly wheat and barley, amounts to only 5 or 6 per cent in the same period. The total increase in rice production during the period 1916–20 to 1936–38 was only about 32 per cent, and in wheat, barley, and other cereals it was only about 34 per cent.

In Korea, as in Japan, there has also been a considerable increase in cattle, swine, and poultry in recent years, but their total production is still so small that they must be considered an almost negligible factor in the Korean diet. Nor are the imports of any of the chief items of diet, except millet, large enough to be of significance.

The other chief food crops on which data can be obtained, potatoes and sweet potatoes, have been increasing rapidly in recent years: 59 per cent and 127 per cent, respectively, between 1926–30 and 1936–37 (234, 1940, p. 19). But in the last two years for which data are available, 1936–37, the per capita production was a little less than 0.4 bushel of sweet potatoes and about 1.2 bushels of Irish potatoes. Since a considerable but unknown amount of the potatoes is used for the making of alcohol and starch and since potatoes grown for home consumption are less likely to be reported than the staple crops, it is impossible to say how far they may be replacing rice and other cereals in the Korean diet.

FOOD AND POPULATION GROWTH IN KOREA

Between 1920 and 1940 the population of Korea increased 35–40 per cent (this range being used because of some uncertainty in the figures before 1925), while the increase in the production of all cereals was only 32–34 per cent. Thus even if the entire cereal crop of Korea had been consumed at home, the per capita consumption would have declined slightly (no allowance being made for changes in imports). But, as a matter of fact, the export of rice from Korea to Japan grew rapidly during this time: in 1919–21 about 20 per cent of Korea's rice was sent to Japan, and by 1936–37 this percentage had risen to about 46 per cent. The net result for Korea was that, while she had an average of over 59 million bushels of rice left in the country after export in the years 1919–21, she had an average of only 51 million in the years 1936–38, although the population grew by approximately 7 million in the interval. It is clear that Korea's rice ration per capita must have declined greatly—from about 3.4 bushels in the former years to about 2.1 bushels in 1936–38. Nor has this decline in rice been compensated for by the increase in other cereals, for, as noted above, their production has increased only one-third, while population has grown over one-third. Besides, they have constituted a minor part of the Korean diet at all times (167, p. 37).

The general picture of agricultural Korea which emerges is that of a country being exploited as a colony to provide food and raw materials to the governing power with only such concern for the welfare of the natives as is dictated by the needs of this exploitation. Such increase in consumption of agricultural products as there is must be in vegetables and root crops, for which there are no data.

But, in spite of this deterioration in the Korean diet, one must not forget that the death rate has been reduced by the efforts of a well-organized government, through the introduction of a few elementary sanitary measures, through the extension of irrigation, through providing better transportation, and through encouraging a more efficient agriculture. These are facts beyond dispute, and I have found that even ardent Korean patriots who are very bitter against Japan recognize their truth. They also recognize that, even though the economic situation of Koreans may have been deteriorating recently, they are still living better than the Chinese in North China and Manchoukuo.

On the other hand, it did not look as though the continuance of Korea's present colonial status had anything to offer in the way of better living for the mass of Koreans. But we must not forget that, however much Korea has been held back by Japanese exploitation, her level of living is also being held down by the rapid increase of her population. Even with an all-Korean government having no interest but in the welfare of the masses, Korea will have a difficult time expanding her agriculture and her industry to maintain her present standards, to say nothing of improving them, if her population keeps on growing as during the last thirty years. If she ceases to send rice and cotton to Japan, she will have more for home use, but she will thereby lose the manufactured imports which she is now receiving in exchange for these goods.

It is possible, although by no means certain, that the sale of her present exports on a free world market would bring her more goods than she got as an integrated part of the Japanese Empire. But if she sells them at all, she will have no more to live on than now, and it is altogether possible—and, in this writer's opinion, rather probable—that the severance of her close economic relations with Japan will result in a definite deterioration of her general economic situation for some years. This is presented not as an argument against Korean independence but merely as a consideration to be taken into account now, when the postwar relations of Japan and Korea are up for determination. We must not forget that Korea's poverty is not due solely, or directly, to Japanese exploitation but rather indirectly to the rapid growth of population arising out of the developments essential to successful exploitation.

THE AGRICULTURE OF FORMOSA

Formosa is a mountainous island containing about 13,000 square miles—a little larger than Massachusetts and Connecticut combined—lying about a hundred miles off the coast of China between 21° and 26° north latitude.

The general agricultural situation in Formosa is quite similar to that in Korea in that it has been exploited as an agricultural dependency of Japan. Since Formosa is tropical, however, there is a significant difference in crops and in methods of exploitation, although rice is the chief crop in both.

Because of its mountainous character, it is officially estimated (163, p. 43) that not much over one-fourth of Formosa can be tilled, and, since about 24 per cent is already under cultivation, there is little room for further expansion. Estimates of land that remains to be brought into cultivation vary from about 100,000 acres (163, p. 44) to about 250,000 acres (335). In any event, the amount is small for a population of almost six million which is growing rapidly.

As was the case in Korea, the expansion of the cultivated area was quite rapid in the early years of Japanese occupation if official reports are accepted. It now seems probable, however, that much of this early expansion must be credited to more adequate administration of the land tax and to more complete surveys rather than to actual extension of the tilled area. If 1904 is taken as the starting-point for comparisons rather than some earlier year, the total increase of tilled land up to 1938 was from 1,545,000 (163, p. 42) acres to 2,120,000, or 37 per cent. During the same period the population increased 85–90 per cent. But since almost the whole increase in tilled land was in irrigated land, and since a considerable part of this increase was in two-crop fields, the total area available for intensive rice cultivation about doubled during this period and thus kept pace with population growth. This is an important fact because "irrigation almost doubles the crop [rice] while irrigation and double cropping combined increase the annual yield about three and one-half times" (163, p. 45).

Because of the increase in the irrigated area and the use of more effective methods of irrigation, because of better varieties of rice, more intensive fertilization, and other improved farm practices, the yield of rice per acre has increased by 50 per cent or a little more since 1905, and the total rice crop has more than doubled during this time. However, the exports to Japan have grown rapidly from about 3,200,000 bushels in 1905 to an average of almost 24 million in 1936–39. They now account for from 45 to 50 per cent of the entire crop (163, p. 55). As a result, the amount of rice available for consumption in Formosa has fallen in recent years from about 6.4 bushels per capita in 1905 to about 4.3 bushels in 1936–39.

The second crop in importance in Formosa, from the standpoint of its colonial function in the Japanese Empire, is sugar. This has increased greatly in the last thirty-five years. The total yield in sugar increased from an average of 192,350 tons in 1909–14 (286, 1928, p. 70) to an average of about 1.0–1.1 million tons in 1937–38. But again the sugar available for consumption in Formosa did not increase by this amount, since a large part of it was and is exported, chiefly to Japan. The average exports for 1909 and 1913 were 173,000 tons, and for 1937 and 1938 they were about 988,000 tons, or about nine-tenths of the total sugar production (286, 1928 and 1940–41).

Other crops important from the standpoint of Formosa's food supply are sweet potatoes, bananas, and pineapples. Large proportions of both bananas and pineapples are exported (two-thirds to three-fourths), and a considerable percentage of the sweet potatoes is used for industrial purposes (starch and alcohol) (240, 1940, p. 536).

Animal products from the farm are a much more important element in the diet of Formosans than in that of the Japanese or Koreans. The number of pigs, hens, geese, and ducks has been increasing rapidly and is large enough to add significantly to the food supply. In 1936 there was one pig to five Japanese farm families, one to two Korean farm families, but four to each Formosan farm family. While the poultry ratios were not so heavily favorable to Formosa, there were two or three times as many chickens, geese, and ducks combined per farm family as in Japan. The catch of fish has also been increasing rather rapidly in Formosa in recent years.

FOOD AND POPULATION GROWTH IN FORMOSA

When the food situation in Formosa is regarded as a whole, it appears probable that the people there have been enjoying a slow but steady improvement in diet although using less rice than formerly.

The diet is probably more varied, and, even if it includes more sweet potatoes, it also includes more meat, poultry, fruit, and probably more vegetables. But with a population increasing 28 per cent between 1930 and 1940 and 25 per cent between 1920 and 1930 and little new land to be tilled, it seems rather unlikely that the food supply of the island can long continue to improve unless there is a slowing-up of population growth.

Here, as in Korea, attention must be called to the fact that merely stopping exports of food from Formosa to Japan may not improve the general economy of the colony as much as is commonly assumed. It is true that if Formosa had 24 million bushels more of rice and 900,000–1,000,000 more tons of sugar, her people could have more to eat, but not this much more because some of this food is traded for fertilizers and for machinery for plantations and for experimental work in developing better crops and better farming. Besides, the improvement in health conditions shown in the falling death rate can be maintained only by taking a certain amount of the produce of the land for the support of this service.

In other words, no matter how bad the exploitation of Formosa by Japan may be, it has been accompanied by certain improvements in living which are generally approved and which can be paid for only out of the increased productivity made possible by the conditions the Japanese have heretofore supplied. The Formosans should not expect to gain any large and immediate economic advantage by being detached from Japan and made a part of China. Indeed, it is likely that they will be worse off for a time. The greater political freedom may well be worth the temporary deterioration of economic conditions, but it should be emphasized that a small island like Formosa without any considerable unused agricultural resources cannot long provide for a population increasing at 25–28 per cent each decade. Within a decade or two the Formosans must either reduce their birth rate or must expect a return of a death rate about equal to their high birth rate.

JAPANESE AND KOREAN FISHERIES

Before passing to the consideration of the future food supply of Japan Proper, a word should be said about the expansion of Japanese and Korean fisheries in recent years (58). Fish constitute the second most important item in the Japanese diet (286, 1939–40, pp. 78–79). The catch of Japan Proper amounted to about 25–27 per cent of the total world catch in 1935, while that for the Japanese Empire amounted to about 40 per cent of the total. The increase in the catch of the Empire has been rapid in recent years, but it is not clear just how much of this increase has gone to improve the diet of the people and how much has gone into cans for export and into fertilizer. In 1939 the total value of fish and of the manufactures of fishery products in Japan Proper was given as about 778 million yen and the value of exports was 175 million (130, 1943, p. 99), or almost one-fourth as great. This does not mean that one-fourth of the catch was exported, but rather that the value of the exports has been increasing rapidly and that they absorbed a significant proportion of the total increase, although, no doubt, considerably less than one-fourth of the total. The fact that nearly a million and a half people are employed in the fishing industry, about one-fourth as many as in agriculture, also indicates its very great importance for Japan (240, 1940, p. 312).

On the other hand, Dr. Herre (130, 1943, p. 100) believes that the point of diminishing returns has already been reached in fishing in Japanese waters. The use of larger boats and floating canneries has made it possible for Japan to extend her fishing operations far from home and thus to increase the catch of deep-sea fish, but there is considerable doubt as to whether the increased catch of recent years can be maintained and, hence, whether further improvement in the Japanese diet from this source can be expected. The 100 per cent increase in catch between 1920 and 1936 (403, p. 183) certainly is not likely to be duplicated in the next fifteen years.

Fish also constitute an important item in the Korean diet, and the Korean catch, like that of Japan, has increased rapidly in recent years. It is not possible to say to what extent the enlarged catch, from an average of 715,000 tons in 1925–29 (286, 1932–33, p. 57) to 1,860,000 tons in 1934–38 (167, p. 46), has improved the Korean diet, but it seems likely that the consumption of fish per capita has increased appreciably in recent years in spite of the increased use of fish for other purposes and in spite of much of the catch in Korean waters going to Japan.

Fish are much less important in the diet of the Formosans than in that of the Japanese and Koreans.

THE FUTURE FOOD SUPPLY OF JAPAN

Considering the food supply of the Japanese Empire as a whole, it would appear that only a fairly intensive exploitation of the colonies

(Korea and Formosa) by Japan Proper enabled the Empire to remain relatively self-sufficing in food up to World War II. It would also appear that the possibilities of further agricultural development either at home or in the colonies are small compared with what has been accomplished in the last thirty to forty years. Japan has already enjoyed the first and cheapest fruits of the modern agricultural improvements available to an intensive hand agriculture and has now reached the point where, if her population at home and in the colonies continues to grow at the rate that now seems probable, she is going to have to depend more and more on outside sources of supply—that is, outside the pre-1931 Empire.

The continued and more intensive exploitation of Manchoukuo as a part of her Empire might have postponed this dependence for a time, but if, to accomplish this exploitation of Manchoukuo, it became necessary to establish conditions which would reduce the death rate there to the level of that in Korea and Formosa, the natural growth of population in Manchoukuo would rise far above what it has been in the past, and the total increase would probably be greater than in the past even if immigration were forbidden. A population of 40–43.2 million at the end of 1940 (Manchoukuo) having a natural increase of about 25–28 per 1,000 per year, as in Formosa, 1920–40, would grow to 80 million or more by 1970.

This would mean that in Manchoukuo, as in Korea and Formosa, the limit of exports of food would be reached in a comparatively short time and Japan would have to count on increasing imports from outside her enlarged empire. Thus she would need still more colonies or would have to trade more and more of her manufactured goods for food—and if Japan Proper had to buy food outside the Empire the terms of trade would almost certainly be somewhat less favorable than those she obtained within the Empire, in which she could completely control the conditions of exploitation.

In order to trade outside the Empire for the food she would need, Japan would have to be assured of larger and larger foreign markets for her manufactures; and, before we can form any useful judgment as to whether Japan Proper could cover her future food needs in this way, it will be necessary to make an appraisal of her natural resources other than agricultural, her industrial development, the outlook for trade, and the probable terms of the peace. Final appraisal of Japan's food outlook must be postponed until we have surveyed these other aspects of her economy.

Chapter VIII

JAPAN: THE MINERAL RESOURCES
OF THE EMPIRE

JAPAN PROPER is one of the poor countries of the world as regards her mineral resources. This is shown clearly in Figure 4, which gives the proportions of the leading minerals produced at home, in the colonies, in Manchoukuo, and imported from abroad in 1936. Coal, copper, and sulphur are the only three minerals of which large amounts are used in industry and of which Japan produced most of her requirements. But in order to appreciate fully the problems she faced in developing her industry, let us examine Japan's position with regard to each of the more important minerals individually.

FUEL AND POWER

Even before the recent development of heavy industry Japan Proper found it necessary to import considerable amounts of coal for metallurgical purposes. Any significant increase in the iron and steel industry, or in the metal industries as a whole, would necessarily require greater imports. The most optimistic figure for the total coal reserves of Japan Proper is about 18,400 million tons, of which only 35.7 per cent, or about 6,570 million tons, have been proved (240, 1940, p. 355). This may seem like a fairly large amount, especially when those of Korea and Formosa are added, but it must be realized that a large amount of what has been proved is not recoverable and that these reserves would be inadequate for more than a few decades of intensive industrial development even if a sufficient proportion were of good coking quality, which is not the case. The inadequacy of such coal reserves can best be realized by comparing Japan's present use of coal with what it might be in the near future as shown by the consumption in some of the other industrial countries. However, in making such comparisons, it should not be forgotten that, because of differences in climate, the domestic use of coal in Japan will probably always be considerably smaller than in most European countries and the United States.

The coal production of Japan Proper, which is also its approximate consumption, is not large as compared with other industrial countries.

It has been increasing quite rapidly in recent years, however, and certainly would have been expected to increase at an accelerated rate once her heavy industries were well started. Some idea of the increase that might be expected may be gained from what happened in the fifteen to twenty years preceding 1939: Japan's coal production almost doubled between 1921 and 1938 (286, 1929, p. 103; 1940–41, p. 134). Furthermore, 1937 plans called for raising production in Japan Proper to 79 million tons by 1941 (240, 1940, p. 355) and for increasing production in Korea and Formosa by an even larger proportion so that a total production of over 90 million tons within the Empire was planned

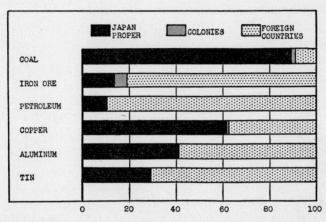

Fig. 4.—Percentage of selected minerals consumed by Japan, produced in Japan and her colonies, and imported from foreign countries, 1936 (Manchoukuo included with foreign countries). (Source: 240, 1940, p. 365; 403, p. 256.)

for by the time Japan launched her attack against us. The actual production is not known.

In addition to Empire production, the coal mined in Manchoukuo rose from about 8.6 million tons in 1931 and 1932 to 20 million tons in 1941, with still larger increases planned.

In 1936 about 10 per cent of Japan's coal was imported from Manchoukuo, China, and Indo-China. This is chiefly coal for metallurgical uses, of which Japan has little (240, 1940, p. 356). The plans made after the seizure of North China in 1937 for future imports of coal to Japan contemplated getting it chiefly from China, the coal of Manchoukuo being reserved for the heavy industries to be developed there.

There is no direct evidence regarding the success attained in pushing coal production in Japan to the new high levels planned for 1941, but there was indirect evidence in the expanding production in the heavy industries and in chemicals which consume a large part (about 40 per cent) of all the coal mined that its production was still increasing as late as 1939. Heavy industry and chemicals consumed 9,785,000 tons in 1934 and 16,602,000 tons in 1937 (240, 1940, p. 356). Although the production of chemicals does not seem to have increased much between 1937 and 1940 (first nine months) (286, 1940–41, p. 163), the production of iron, steel, etc., seems to have increased about 20 per cent in this period and would thus have demanded a considerable increase in coal. Production of electricity by steam was also increasing rapidly during these years.

Thus while it seems probable that coal production within the pre-1931 Empire of Japan can be temporarily increased to meet all her needs by trading steam coal for coking coal, it is clear that the lack of the latter was practically certain to cause uneasiness in the minds of the men who were ambitious to see Japan attain an industrial position of first importance. Besides, with production reaching 100 million or more tons annually, her proved reserves could scarcely be considered adequate for any great length of time, and yet coal is the mineral with which she seems most adequately endowed.

It is not surprising under these circumstances that the Japanese industrialists and militarists looked upon the coal reserves of Manchoukuo with a covetous eye. The Japanese had long been exploiting some of them and knew that they were both large and of good quality. They also had good reason to believe that further exploration would disclose new reserves. This proved to be the case, for by 1938 the more optimistic estimates of Manchoukuo's reserves had risen to about 20,000 million tons (see chap. v), and exploration was by no means complete.

The lack of large coal reserves in Japan Proper is even more serious than it would be in many other countries, because she has very little petroleum (see Fig. 5). The domestic production of petroleum in recent years has amounted to only about 10–12 per cent of consumption, and there is little prospect that this proportion will increase. Indeed, it is more likely to decline, for, in spite of rather intensive exploration, no oil fields of any importance have been found within the pre-1931 Empire. By 1940 her production of synthetic liquid fuel supplied an additional 15 per cent of her needs, so at that time she was producing with-

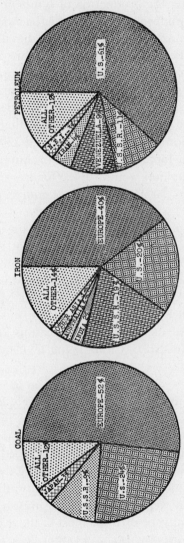

FIG. 5.—Proportion of the world production of coal, iron, and petroleum in selected areas, 1938. (Production of iron given in terms of mineral content.) (Data taken from C. K. Leith, J. W. Furness, and Cleona Lewis, *World Minerals and World Peace* [Washington, D.C.: Brookings Institution, 1943], pp. 34–36, 236–37.)

in the Empire and Manchoukuo somewhere between 25 and 30 per cent of the liquid fuel used, and the only real hope of becoming self-sufficing lay in increasing the production of synthetic fuel and in the increased distillation of oil from the shales of Manchoukuo. Such fuels are relatively expensive, and it is not to be wondered at that Japan's first great strike after Pearl Harbor was to secure the oil fields of Burma, the Netherlands East Indies, and British Borneo.

But, whatever Japan's intentions as to conquest may have been in 1937, she intended to use the coal supplies then under her control to decrease her dependence on imported liquid fuel. Plans were made to produce about 220 million gallons of gasoline and 230 million gallons of heavy oil from coal in Japan Proper by 1943. But even such an increase in domestic production would suffice for less than half her requirements (240, 1940, p. 360) and would, of course, greatly increase the use of coal.

Thus it appeared that if Japan were to continue the expansion of her industries for two or three decades at the rate of the 1930's, she would need 150–200 million tons of coal a year. At this rate her proved reserves in Japan Proper and in Korea and Formosa would be exhausted within that period. By 1937 even the coal reserves of Manchoukuo had begun to look small in the eyes of the ambitious Japanese ruling classes. This is without doubt one of the important reasons for the attack on China, the coal reserves of North China being by far the largest in all the East (see chap. xiv).

Japan is fortunate in the possession of a relatively large amount of water power, which has eased the fuel situation in the past and will help materially in the future. Estimates of the proportion of the potential water power of Japan Proper already developed vary from one-third to two-thirds, but, accepting even the lower figure, the future expansion of hydroelectric power would be far from sufficient to supply industrial power if Japan were to continue to industrialize as in the last twenty years. Coal must be used for most of the expansion of electric power. Korea and Formosa also have rather large water-power resources which are not yet developed, but the hydroelectric power of these colonies cannot be transmitted to Japan Proper.

The fuel situation in Japan may be summed up as follows: before the seizure of Manchoukuo it was not critical, except for liquid fuel, but it was far from satisfactory. The industrialists could see shortage ahead, but in the eyes of army and navy men the lack of liquid fuel was dangerous. After the seizure of Manchoukuo, the fuel situation, unless war came with some highly industrialized power like the United States before the liquefaction of coal was well developed, should have been much more satisfactory. Manchoukuo had large quantities of coal and oil shale, and some of this coal was of good quality for metallurgical purposes. The liquid fuel situation still remained highly unsatisfactory, and even the seizure of North China could not change this until the liquefaction of coal was undertaken on a large scale. Only the conquest of southeastern Asia promised a quick supply of liquid fuel adequate to the expanding demands of Japan's industrialists and military leaders.

COPPER

It was noted above that Japan possessed a considerable amount of copper. As long as she had only a small electrical industry and did not use much copper in her other metal industries, she could produce enough for her own use and some for export. However, as soon as she began to develop the copper-using industries, she became an importer of copper. Exports of copper practically ceased in 1920, and since that time imports have been increasing rather steadily, except in two or three depression years. The rather large imports after 1933 are no doubt due in part to the growth of the munitions industries, but the major factors have been the growing use of copper in the electrical industry at home and the increase in the export of goods in which copper is an important ingredient. In 1936 and 1937 the production of copper in Japan averaged about 91,000 tons, or about one-ninth of that of the United States (286, 1940–41, p. 143). The imports into Japan in those years averaged about 80,000 tons, or about one-third of those into the United States.

It can be seen from these data that until rather recently the use of copper in Japan was small and that even as late as 1936 and 1937 the per capita use was only a small fraction of that in the United States. But the United States and Japan were alike in that both were drawing a significant proportion of their total supplies from foreign countries and both could, if necessity demanded, increase home production temporarily to care for urgent needs. But this could be done only at a considerably increased cost. If Japan were to develop the copper-using industries until they were at all comparable to those of the United States, of Great Britain, or of Germany, she would steadily become more dependent on outside sources of supply.

In the production of copper, Korea and Formosa can contribute little. The copper they produce at present is largely a by-product of silver- and gold-mining and is almost negligible in amount. There are no known deposits of copper worth mining for their own sake (167, p. 70 and 108). Up to the present no important copper deposits have been found in Manchoukuo.

IRON ORE

In iron ore Japan Proper is extremely poor. Her deposits are widely scattered, of poor quality, and small in quantity. It is believed that they do not amount to more than 88 million tons—about what we are now using each year in the United States (240, 1940, p. 339). Production in Japan Proper has always been small and amounted to only about 683,000 tons in 1936, or about one-eighth of the ore used in that year. Korea sent to Japan about 267,000 tons, or about two-fifths of her production (403, p. 256). Japan and Korea together furnished less than one-fifth of all the ore used in Japan Proper in 1936. The greater part of the remaining four-fifths came from China (27 per cent), Malaya (36 per cent), and the Philippines (12 per cent).

In 1937, however, Korean production is said to have increased several fold in consequence of the opening-up of new fields, and shipments to Japan were reported to be about 1,500,000 tons (403, p. 370). The discovery of iron ore in northern Korea, estimated at over 1,000 million tons (167, p. 67), placed the pre-1931 Japanese Empire in position to supply its own needs for some time in the future if it proved economically usable. It should be noted, however, that even 1,000 million tons is not a large amount once heavy industry begins to develop. It would last us only about a dozen war years and perhaps from twenty to twenty-five normal years.

At the time of acquisition (1931) Manchoukuo was known to contain rather large amounts of low-grade ores. Since then discoveries of better ores have been large. The best of these are located in eastern Manchoukuo contiguous to the Korean discoveries just mentioned. They are also not far from what will be the largest water-power development in Manchoukuo and Korea. Thus the outlook of the post-1931 Japanese Empire as a producer of iron and steel was much improved over what it had been; the Japanese could scarcely expect their plea of lack of iron ore to gain much hearing after 1931. The granting of independence to Korea and the returning of Manchoukuo to China will again place Japan among the "have-nots" in iron ore, even more than in the past.

OTHER MINERALS

Japan has long been more than self-sufficient in the production of sulphur and sulphide iron ore. Recently new discoveries of sulphur have been made in Hokkaido which further strengthen her position. Since Korea also has large amounts of iron sulphides, Japan has had no worry about adequate supplies of this important material. She has become the second largest producer of sulfuric acid (403, p. 330), the United States being the first.

Although Japan Proper has no bauxite or other mineral from which aluminum can be made at the present time, Korea (167, p. 70; 403, p. 327) possesses rather large quantities of alunite and alunite shale, the exploitation of which has scarcely been begun. The use of these Korean resources might in time have made the Japanese Empire largely independent of outside sources of supply. Some of the South Pacific islands (Palau, Ponape, and Yap) under Japanese mandate are also said to have rather large laterite deposits, but these are of recent discovery and have not yet been exploited sufficiently to determine their worth (240, 1940, p. 569). Up to the present, Japan has relied largely on imports of bauxite from the Netherlands East Indies, the Federated Malay States, and Greece for her home manufactures of aluminum, but she has also imported a considerable amount of the metal from Canada, Switzerland, and Norway. The large increase in production of aluminum from about 14,000 tons in 1937 to 35,000 tons in 1940 (286, 1940–41, p. 149) would indicate that Japan was probably now making more use of Korean alunite, but there is no definite evidence on this point.

Here, again, the acquisition of Manchoukuo was of great value to the Japanese Empire. Alunite and alunite shales were found there in large quantities, and several plants for the production of aluminum were soon established but apparently did not begin actual production before 1935 (403, p. 455). Thus, while it appears that the Japanese Empire with Manchoukuo was probably self-sufficient in the raw materials of aluminum, these resources were all found in Korea, in the South Seas, or in Manchoukuo, all of which territories are to be severed from Japan.

The situation as regards magnesium within the Empire is about the same as for aluminum. There are no ore supplies of any importance in Japan Proper, but there are ample supplies of magnesite in Korea, estimated at 4,000 million tons or more, thus making it one of the world's great reservoirs. There also appear to be ample supplies in Manchoukuo. And, if it should prove feasible to produce magnesium from sea water in competition with production from magnesite, Japan's capacity to produce this metal would be limited only by the fuel available for power.

Likewise, Japan Proper is almost without supplies of graphite, but Korea has huge reserves and should, in the course of a few years, become one of the world's great suppliers.

Japan Proper has only a small supply of lead. She has been meeting less than 10 per cent of her needs by home production. In zinc she has been supplying 25–35 per cent of her needs, but her reserves are not large and are rather expensive to work. She imported both zinc and zinc concentrates. Korea has rather large reserves of both lead and zinc, but these are not yet exploited to any significant extent. No definite discoveries of these minerals have yet been made in Manchoukuo, but deposits are believed to be large (240, 1940, p. 763).

There is some tin in Japan, and before the war she was supplying about one-third of her needs (240, 1940, p. 352). But with the growth in the use of tin to be expected as industrialization increases, she became more and more dependent on foreign sources. Since there does not appear to be any significant amount of tin in the pre-1931 Empire, nor in Manchoukuo, the dismemberment of the Empire will make little change in this respect. Japan will then only be in the same position as the United States and Germany as regards her tin supply.

Since gold is of so little industrial importance, it is one of the ironies of fate that Japan seemed to have a fair abundance of it both in Japan Proper and in her colonies. She acquired still more with the seizure of Manchoukuo. With her departure from the gold standard in 1931 and with the rising price of gold in other lands, particularly in the United States, there was a great burst of activity in gold-mining after 1933. This relatively large gold production and our willingness to take gold in exchange for our shipments to Japan, will help to explain her ability to buy large quantities of scrap iron and petroleum products from us up to the time of our denunciation of our trade treaty. It is very profitable to mine gold with cheap labor as long as a "sucker" can be found to take it in trade for useful goods.

Of the more important alloy minerals, Japan Proper appears to have considerable amounts of chromium and manganese, although she may not be entirely self-sufficient. Korea had enough molybdenum and tungsten to render the pre-1931 Empire self-sufficient (403, p.

469). On the whole, it appears that the pre-1931 Empire was not worse off for alloys than most of the other industrial countries and, after the seizure of Manchoukuo, was probably better off than many of them.

Potash and phosphates for fertilizers are lacking in Japan Proper, and this has been a serious matter, since her agriculture is becoming increasingly dependent on commercial fertilizers for the maintenance of high yields. According to recent reports, both aluminum and potash are being obtained from the alunite deposits of Korea and additional resources of both potash and phosphates have been discovered in some of the Pacific islands under her mandate (403, p. 327). Production in these islands was being expanded rapidly just before 1941, and in conjunction with the large production of superphosphate of lime in Japan it seemed likely that the Empire's needs for these minerals would be met by its own resources.

The pre-1931 Japanese Empire, however, seems to have been quite lacking in natural nitrates. Present supplies of nitrates come primarily from synthetic manufactures and to a small extent, perhaps one-fifth, from imports (240, 1940, p. 392). The feasibility of adequate synthetic production is, of course, determined to a large extent by the abundance or scarcity of fuel.

JAPAN'S MINERAL OUTLOOK

The most important conclusion to be drawn from this brief survey of the mineral resources of the Japanese Empire is that Japan Proper has but meager mineral resources, while even the pre-1931 Empire would be hard put to it to maintain its pre-war rate of industrialization. Recent discoveries in Korea would have made the Empire somewhat less dependent on outside sources than it had been in the past, but it would still have been handicapped by inadequate fuel and iron ore unless the recent discoveries of iron in Korea are larger than estimated. If Japan Proper is forced to fall back on her own resources, her plight will be very serious indeed (see Fig. 4). The broader significance of all this for Japan's economy will be explored in somewhat more detail in chapters x and xi, but it should be noted here that if Japan is to develop her industry adequately to provide a better level of living for her people and if she is to do this without colonies, she can do it only through foreign trade; and, as we shall see, the difficulties she has encountered in attempting this in a world becoming more autarchic are very great indeed.

But in spite of the difficulties of industrialization in a country poor in raw materials there were in the decade before 1931 many Japanese who believed that the solution of Japan's economic problems lay in industrial development and foreign trade. The following quotations are typical of many that might be given.

In the *Japanese Yearbook* for 1927, Mr. Fujiwara, a prominent Japanese industrialist, "is reported to be of opinion that if properly developed, industrialized Japan can be expected to give work to 10 million more people. He admits that Japan is rather scantily favored in natural resources, but at the same time possesses in the near-by regions, in particular China and the South Seas, sufficient supply of raw materials which she can reship in finished form. Those districts are therefore ideal customers of Japan as regards both raw materials and finished goods. Mr. Fujiwara thinks that the only serious drawback handicapping the progress of Japanese industry is low efficiency of labor, mainly attributable to defective knowledge, skill, and exertion. He is of opinion that the defect, being artificial and not inherent, is surmountable, so that on the whole he is disinclined to be pessimistic as to the future of our industry. Increased output of manufactures demands their larger shipment to foreign market and greater consumption at home, and this point is well reflected in the customs returns and the chamber of commerce's reports" (242, 1927, Supp., p. 8).

Again, an important official of the Foreign Office, Marquis Komura, expressed the view that "Japan does not look to emigration to solve her population problem, but to a further industrialization of the country, so that this increase in the number of people in Japan will become not a reason for war but a means whereby international trade will be increased and the hope for a continued peace strengthened" (242, 1927, Supp., p. 9).

Many similar statements by prominent leaders showing a growing belief in the efficacy of industrialization and foreign trade to care for Japan's growing population might be quoted. It is, perhaps, significant that this attitude was quite prevalent before 1931, in the period when it appeared that the army was losing its power over the government and that the future of Japan was to be put in the keeping of her industrial oligarchs. The seizure of Manchoukuo by the Kwantung Army and "government by assassination" put an end to the attempts by the Japanese capitalists to work out the economic salvation of Japan solely by increased industrialization and commerce; they also helped to harden the hearts of Europeans against the trade of Japan when it became highly competitive after 1931, although there is very little in the trade war which ensued to suggest that Japan's trade expansion would have been more welcome in that part of the Orient controlled by Europeans if she had not invaded Manchoukuo. The attitude was rather: "If Japan can do what she is doing and import her raw materials, what will she not do if she has large supplies of her own?" The treatment of Japan's trade after 1931 was well calculated to make even the most ardent advocate of more industrialization as a solution of Japan's economic problems highly pessimistic (see chap. x) and thus to render her political control over more adequate mineral resources seem necessary to an increasing portion of her people who were familiar with these problems.

Chapter IX

JAPAN: MODERN INDUSTRIAL DEVELOPMENT

IT WAS only a little over seventy-five years ago (1868), with the restoration of the Emperor to the headship of the state, that Japan broke decisively with the traditional economy of the past and began to adopt the industrial economy of the West. Prior to that time Japanese industry was almost entirely a simple hand industry concerned with the needs of a local population. It was even more simple and local than our own economy two hundred years ago, because the Japanese people were then living even nearer to a mere subsistence level. Their needs were largely determined by custom and were stabilized at a level just sufficient to maintain life in the mass of the population. The Japanese were then living much as the mass of the Chinese do today, with an extremely narrow margin between their production and starvation—a margin which was not always maintained.

The leaders of the country, however, realized, even that early in their relations with the West, that Japan would become a vassal of the European states, certainly to as great an extent as China and probably even as much as India, if she were to remain as weak, economically, as they were. They saw that the Europeans hunting trade and resources were ready to exercise whatever political control was necessary to insure that trade. As a consequence, from the very beginning of Japan's entry into the sphere of the Western economy, she set herself resolutely to the task of becoming powerful enough economically to prevent her absorption into the European system as a colony, or semicolony, and she realized that this could be done only by developing a strong industry. This led to a nationally supported industrial development, and hence to a much more rapid development of machine industry in Japan than might have been expected by the interested observer of 1870.

GOVERNMENT PARTICIPATION IN INDUSTRY

Although there were wealthy families in feudal Japan, their wealth was locked up in land or in internal trade and was not readily available for the establishment of modern industry by private interests because corporate enterprise was unknown, and there was no way to assemble large amounts of private capital. Moreover, these families did not possess the knowledge and skill to undertake these new mechanized types of production with much hope of success. They were, however, able and willing to loan money to the government at good rates of interest. Thus it came about that modern industry first came to Japan by way of government ownership.

This was probably the only way in which modern types of industry could have been quickly established. Then, too, a quick and complete independence from the West could be achieved only by bringing in many foreign experts and technicians pending the time when Japanese sent abroad could acquire the training and experience essential to the efficient operation of machine industry and the establishment of adequate technical and trade education in Japan. The government was the only agency that could assume these costs, since such preparations for the development of modern industry could not be expected to yield any money return for some years.

By 1880 a number of the industries established by the government were going concerns, and some had shown the capacity to produce large profits. It was decided, therefore, that the time had come to turn these industries over to private ownership, and laws were enacted to this end. In the next dozen years most of the state factories were sold. The terms on which they were sold were extremely favorable to the purchasers both because the price was low and because there was comparatively little chance of other firms springing up to enter into effective competition with those to whom the state was selling.

The chief of the industries sold by the state between 1880 and 1893 were textiles, shipbuilding, cement, matches, gasworks, and brickyards, of which textiles were by far the most important. These industries, when sold, came into the control of three or four families which have since become almost fabulously wealthy and have been able to maintain rather tight control over a large proportion of Japanese industry down to the present. In recent years, however, they have had to share their pre-eminent position with a few parvenus who have been able to gain considerable power in spite of the many handicaps of a later start.

It should not be assumed, however, that the selling of these state enterprises to private interests meant that the state was no longer encouraging the development of industries which would make Japan powerful. From the beginning the state owned and operated many of the railways and by 1907 had bought the more important private lines at a huge price. It also developed the shops needed to maintain the railways. It built the first ironworks and arsenals, and it built the navy yards and organized the machine shops essential to the construction and maintenance of a strong navy.

The Sino-Japanese War of 1894–95, although fought largely with munitions bought from abroad, greatly strengthened the Japanese munitions industries. But this was a cheap war, and its successful issue enabled Japan to demand a large gold indemnity from China which proved extremely useful in furthering Japan's economic development. This indemnity was employed to establish her currency on the stable basis essential to the development of world trade and to undertake new industries which would strengthen both her economic and her military position.

The ironworks and arsenals planned in 1896 and established shortly thereafter, played an important part in equipping her army and navy for the Russo-Japanese War, although she still found it necessary to buy much heavy goods abroad.

The outcome of this war proved the wisdom of the policy of government enterprise and of generous government assistance to private enterprises. By following this course, Japan in about thirty years had ceased to be a weak feudal state which could easily have been conquered by any one of several European powers and had become one of the greater powers of the world. She alone of the oriental countries had been able to maintain a high degree of political and economic independence which was increased with the abolition of extra-territoriality in 1899, in part the result of her successful war with China, and which became complete with the gaining of tariff autonomy in 1911 shortly after her successful war with Russia. The lesson was obvious— to be independent, be strong; and to be strong, develop industry.

Before turning to the development of Japanese industry since 1870, we must emphasize again the relation between government and business in Japan following the period of early government enterprise and try to see this relation in its Japanese setting.

Although the establishment of industries by the government and their sale at reduced rates to the economic oligarchs, or vice versa, was the chief form of government aid in the early years of the modernization of Japanese industry, numerous other devices to aid industry were also employed. Some enterprises were subsidized (for example, shipping and the exploration for oil and minerals) and some were specially protected by tariffs (after tariff autonomy was gained in 1911); in some the government bought a considerable share of the stock on which it claimed no dividends until the stock in private hands had received dividends for several years at a sufficiently high rate to compensate fully for the *risk* taken; in some the government agreed that its stock should always receive a lower rate of dividends than the private stock. Finally, the government viewed with a lenient eye the monopolistic tendencies inherent in turning the management of the new economy over to a few powerful families. Such monopoly aided in the expansion of industry because it insured the rapid accumulation of capital in the hands of people who knew how to use it and where to find the technicians. Monopoly, or close trade associations, also contributed largely to the development of the foreign trade so badly needed by a country as poor as Japan in mineral resources.

Thus this close alliance between the state and industry, in which industry, including finance, seems to have been the senior partner, came to appear to the Japanese as the natural course of industrial development, and it certainly enabled Japanese capitalists to move rapidly and with confidence into any field which would yield profit or would contribute to the nation's economic strength.

The decade between the Russo-Japanese War and World War I saw a rather steady growth of Japanese industry, but World War I offered it a very unusual opportunity to expand because of the withdrawal of Europe, and later of the United States, from Eastern markets and the demand of the warring nations themselves for many kinds of goods needed for war or no longer made at home.

After the close of the first World War, Japanese industry had even become strong enough to challenge the power of the army in governmental affairs and during the 1920's seemed, for a time, to be in the ascendant. This growing dominance of the economic oligarchy was undoubtedly one of the most important elements in arousing the army to "government by assassination" by which, in the course of a few years, it gained large control of the government and hence an increasing, although by no means absolute, control over industry.

Too often this close co-operation between the Japanese government and industry is regarded by foreigners as a recent development intended solely to strengthen Japan's military power for aggression because such a close alliance had not been customary in the West, except in time of war, prior to the rise of totalitarian government in Italy and Germany. As we have seen, however, government assistance had its origin in the determination of the leaders of Japan not to accept a position of subservience to the Western powers and was adopted by Japan as a means of defending her independence and as a support to her industry in competition with that of other states with better-established industries.

INDUSTRIAL EXPANSION

As we have seen above (chap. viii), Japan Proper is but poorly endowed by nature with the raw materials essential to the development of industrial strength. This poverty in mineral resources will help to explain her relatively slow growth of heavy industry in spite of government aid. It will also help in understanding the anxiety of her army and navy men as well as her industrialists to secure empire sources of supply.

In 1870 Japan had almost no factories using mechanical power. She had to start from scratch. By 1905 there were 4,335 such factories employing almost 600,000 workers, and they had engines with a total of about 287,000 horsepower. This does not include the government factories, arsenals, navy yards, etc., which are credited with almost one-half as many workers and about 35 per cent of the horsepower of all private industry (242, 1907, pp. 383 and 401).

Thus in about thirty-five years Japanese industry had gone a long way from its hand-power status of 1870, although Japan was still far from being a great industrial country.

The interval between the Russo-Japanese War and World War I was a period of very rapid expansion in Japanese industry. The number of factories having mechanical power with five or more workers more than doubled in these nine years, while the number having only hand power rose by less than one-fourth. The horsepower employed in the former increased four and one-half times, and the number of workers rose to 854,000. The cotton goods produced more than trebled in volume, and the output of pig iron was doubled, although the total even then (outside government works) amounted to only a little over 332,000 tons. Steel production increased by four times but was still small (311,000 tons), the greater part of the supply still being imported. Electric generating capacity rose to 715,000 kilowatts in 1914, and coal production since 1905 more than doubled. Many new industries were also established at this time, and Japan, like the United States, found herself in position to profit largely by World War I.

Between 1914 and 1920 the number of factories having more than five workers and using mechanical power almost tripled, numbering over 30,000 on the latter date. The employees in such factories doubled in numbers, and the horsepower of the engines, motors, and other prime movers also doubled. During this period there was expansion in almost every line, but it was particularly rapid in metals and machinery and in chemicals. Textiles still constituted far the largest single industry in Japanese economy.

World War I not only gave Japan a chance to accumulate large reserves of capital because of her very profitable trade, but it also forced her to develop many new industries or to expand many incipient ones. She could not get machine tools abroad, so she had to begin making them; she could not buy textile equipment, so she made more of her own; she could not get access to chemicals and medicines, so she manufactured her own supplies.

One might enumerate many other lines in which the war gave Japan opportunity to develop industrial products she had previously purchased abroad, but it will suffice to say that she then acquired the experience as well as the capital needed to develop many new lines of industry. The paid-up capital and reserves of industrial companies more than quadrupled between 1914 and 1920, and although this does not mean that actual capital goods employed in manufacturing increased at the same rate, for prices had risen, yet it does mean a very rapid increase and a strong position for future growth. At the same time Japan's financial and commercial expansion maintained a like pace.

The decisive proof that World War I left Japan in position to proceed rapidly with all phases of industrialization and to expand her commerce is found in what happened in the next decade. The 30,000 factories of 1920 using mechanical power and having five or more employees became 51,000 by 1930. The horsepower they used increased from 2,619,000 to 8,551,000, or more than threefold. Rather strangely the total number of workers did not increase much even during the boom at the end of the 1920's and was somewhat smaller in 1930 than in 1920. This decline in number is probably due to the depression, which had also begun to affect Japan by 1930, but even in the boom year 1929 the number of workers was scarcely 100,000 larger than in 1920. The real explanation of this slow increase is probably to be found in the increased efficiency of industry as a whole, particularly in textiles and the heavy industries, and in the increased use of mechanical power to displace labor.

One might expect that this large increase in mechanical power used would be accompanied by an almost equally great increase in the production of coal; but this was not the case. The production of electricity by water power did, however, expand rapidly during this decade. In 1920 the total generating capacity of Japanese electrical plants was 1,377,000 kilowatts; this was more than tripled by 1930 (4,399,000 kw.), and, of this increase of over 3,000,000 kilowatts, almost 2,000,000 kilowatts were generated by water power. At that time Japan had developed only about one-third of her estimated water power.[1] Electric generating capacity further increased by over 50 per cent in the six years following 1930 and is estimated to have reached a total of about 8,000,000 kilowatts in 1940, with steam capacity growing faster than water power since 1930.

Evidence of the very rapid expansion of basic and heavy industry in the decade 1920–30 is also found in the production of iron and steel and machinery. The production of pig iron and steel, which was just under 600,000 tons for each in 1920, rose to 1,309,000 tons of pig iron and 2,116,000 tons of steel in 1930. The machinery industry in Japan amounted to very little before World War I, but it grew rapidly at that time. Although it could not continue a steady development at this pace, by 1926 it was in boom again and employed 273,000 workers (240, 1937, p. 564). It suffered heavily in the early years of the depression but had recovered to employ 367,000 workers in 1935 and to produce goods worth almost 1,462 million yen.

THE NEW INDUSTRIAL REVOLUTION

Between the end of World War I and 1930, Japanese industry passed through what may very properly be called a revolution. It not only moved into many entirely new lines of production—rayon and "staple" fiber, many new types of machinery and tools, and a greatly enlarged list of chemicals—but also expanded the productive capacity of most of its established industries; and it rationalized its plants so that they were far more efficient than in pre-war days. Finally, the Japanese industrialists had come to appreciate the value of industrial research and were supporting it on a large scale, with the result that they were developing methods of utilizing resources which had hitherto been useless because of inferior quality or high cost of conversion. In this connection it is said (403, p. 405) that the low-grade iron ores of Korea and Manchoukuo can now be treated economically and

[1] Estimated total available hydroelectric power which can be harnessed, 10,800,000 kilowatts (240, 1940, p. 385).

used in blast furnaces in competition with higher-grade ores. It is also claimed that the German methods of producing liquid fuel from coal had been improved upon and adapted to Japanese, Korean, and Manchoukuoan coals.

Fairly typical of what was happening throughout the nation at this time are the changes in the textile industry, Japan's leading industry. It was rationalized during the later 1920's so that it was in position to contribute largely to her industrial and trade expansion in the early 1930's. In 1926 the members of the Japan Cotton Spinners Association reported about 58,000 workers in their weaving mills, and they produced 1,277 million yards of cloth. Five years later the number of employees had fallen to about 29,000, or one-half, while the yardage of cloth rose to 1,405 million (468, p. 73). The rise in the output per operative in the cotton spinning mills was not so great as in weaving, but it, too, was large, showing a 47 per cent increase in five years (403, p. 649). Improvement in production per operative was much slower after 1931.

There is no evidence of as definite a character showing the improvement in other branches of textiles, but the increase in the output of rayon yarn from 5 million pounds in 1926 to 334 million in 1937 is evidence that Japanese rayon production must have been highly efficient, because Japan imported much of the pulp from which this yarn was made (240, 1940, p. 377) and yet by 1937 had become the world's largest producer of such yarn. Even more remarkable is the increase in "staple" fiber from nothing in 1931 to 375 million pounds in 1938. In this also Japan had become the world's largest producer by 1937. How her efficiency in textile production enabled her to compete in world markets will be shown in the following chapter.

There can be no doubt that Japan, like the United States, used much of her industrial and financial strength acquired during World War I to improve and expand her economic power during the following decade and to prepare for still further advance when the time was ripe. It is not necessary to give concrete details of increase in efficiency in most other lines as in textiles; very careful students have no doubt of the fact (403 and 6). In the metal trades and chemicals Allen finds convincing evidence of rapid improvement in the efficiency of Japanese labor in recent years in the opinions of engineers and other people with firsthand knowledge of what was happening (403, pp. 662-70). In coal-mining the output per worker can easily be measured, and the production per miner is known to have increased 50 per cent between 1928 and 1934.

But, while the efficiency of Japanese labor was growing rapidly, it must be noted that in most industries it was still far from attaining the efficiency of labor in the more advanced industrial countries of the West. It follows, therefore, that a considerable part of the ability of Japanese industrialists to compete with Western industrialists in world markets must come from the cheapness of their labor and from aid given them by the state in subsidies, in the form of tariffs as well as directly, and in the cartelization of many Japanese industries for foreign trade.

RECENT INDUSTRIAL EXPANSION

In recent years the complexity of Japan's industry has become so great and the volume so vast that it has become necessary to devise measures of production for industry as a whole and for the major

TABLE 11

INDICES OF INDUSTRIAL PRODUCTION, JAPAN, 1919–39

VOLUME OF PRODUCTION * (1928 = 100)				MANUFACTURING AND MINING INDUSTRIES † (1931–33 = 100)	
Year	Index	Year	Index	Year	Index
1919	65	1929	110	1931	91.1
1920	63	1930	109	1932	97.2
1921	62	1931	108	1933	112.5
1922	73	1932	124	1934	127.4
1923	77	1933	148	1935	141.0
1924	81	1934	166	1936	150.2
1925	85	1935	192	1937	169.7
1926	89	1936	212	1938	172.0
1927	95	1937	238	1939	180.6‡
1928	100				

* Source: 131, p. 76.
† Source: 240, p. 363.   ‡ Average of the first six months of 1939.

groups of industries. The outstanding feature of Japanese industrial production throughout the twenty-year period, illustrated by Table 11, is that it expanded rapidly and almost continuously with only a minor recession in 1930–31. It was approximately twice as great in 1932 as in 1919, and almost doubled again by 1937, according to the index for the longer period. According to the shorter index, the volume of production in manufacturing and mining almost doubled from 1931 to the first six months of 1939. No doubt a part of this recent increase is due to the preparation of Japan to attack, first, China and, later, the United Nations, but even this great expansion of industry for war would not have been possible had it not been for the fairly steady and rapid growth of all Japanese industry since World War I.

The data in Table 12 are of great interest as showing a rather steady trend since about 1926 toward a larger proportion of heavy industry and chemicals, the main sinews of war as well as of industrial strength.

TABLE 12*

PERCENTAGE OF THE VALUE OF ALL MANUFACTURES PRODUCED BY EACH OF THE
PRINCIPAL GROUPS OF MANUFACTURING INDUSTRIES, JAPAN, 1909–38

Year	Total†	Textiles	Metallics	Machines and Tools	Chemicals	Provisions
1938	100.0	20.3	23.8	19.4	17.6	9.1
1937	100.0	23.8	20.5	14.5	18.6	9.2
1936	100.0	27.5	17.3	13.1	17.9	10.1
1935	100.0	28.4	16.8	12.7	17.3	10.6
1934	100.0	31.0	15.5	11.5	16.1	11.1
1933	100.0	34.2	11.3	10.2	16.5	12.7
1932	100.0	34.0	9.9	9.1	15.9	14.8
1931	100.0	34.8	8.4	8.5	15.9	16.1
1930	100.0	34.2	8.8	10.3	15.5	15.9
1929	100.0	38.8	8.9	8.8	13.9	14.5
1928	100.0	39.5	7.6	8.7	12.9	15.7
1927	100.0	39.7	6.9	8.6	12.5	15.8
1926	100.0	41.4	6.4	7.8	11.6	16.0
1920	100.0	41.2	5.4	14.9	12.0	13.2
1914	100.0	46.1	3.6	8.2	13.1	16.3
1909	100.0	49.7	2.2	5.2	11.1	18.9

* Source: 403, 1940, p. 362; 328, pp. 552–53.
† Includes other industries except gas and electricity.

Textiles, while the most important single item (in value) in Japan's industrial production up to 1938, had been declining proportionally for some years. At the same time the metallic industries increased in importance quite rapidly, and by 1938 the value of their products exceeded that of textiles. In addition to machines and tools, the other rapidly growing group was chemicals; between 1926 and 1938 this group increased in value from 11.6 per cent of the total to 17.6 per cent. Ceramics, lumber and wood, and printing and book-binding lost in importance, but, as they always were minor groups, they may be passed over with the comment that their slow absolute increase was still probably sufficient to make possible an increasing per capita consumption of such goods. The manufacture of provisions (foodstuffs), however, declined so much proportionally and even absolutely in most years that it seems probable the per capita consumption of such goods may have declined when price rises and exports are taken into account.

Incomplete as this information on shifts in the types of production is, it is clear that a fundamental change has been taking place in the structure of Japanese industry—and that this change had been going on for some years, even before Japan seized Manchuria. Japanese industry had for some time been passing through an evolution not essentially different from that of Western countries. In the early days machine industry was largely occupied with providing clothing and food and the other daily necessities of the masses; it then began to sell some of these products abroad and also to provide its own people with the simpler types of metal goods, medicines, etc., which had previously been imported. Gradually it added more goods requiring more complex manufacturing processes and began to service the machines it was using in larger and larger numbers. From this it was only a step to beginning to build some of the simpler machines needed, and this, in turn, led to the building of more and more complicated machines, to the expansion of chemicals, and to a great variety of more highly processed goods.

This is exactly what has happened in every country in which modern industry has gained a foothold. Nor is it surprising that heavy industry developed rapidly in Japan in recent years (since World War I) once it was undertaken in earnest. Indeed, it would have been surprising if it had not. Since the Industrial Revolution first began, no people has been content to remain dependent on outside sources for its machines or for the major portion of its basic production longer than was absolutely necessary. Why should it be assumed unusual that Japan was not content to remain in this dependent condition?

HEAVY INDUSTRY AND THE MILITARY

As was pointed out above, Japan had severe natural handicaps to overcome in the development of heavy industry—the lack of iron and metallurgical coal, of petroleum, and the inadequacy of other important minerals, as well as the handicaps incident to the development of such machine industry in any backward country not completely in control of its own economic life. After World War I, Japan, like all the larger countries aspiring to an important position in world affairs, recognized the necessity of developing heavy industry and chemicals as a basic condition for maintaining her position in the modern world, to say nothing of strengthening it in relation to other great powers. It was her misfortune that she did not possess an adequate quantity of the basic raw materials at home and was compelled, therefore, either to import them or to annex territory in which they were found.

That she would develop heavy industry in sufficient amount to maintain her position vis-à-vis the other great powers by whatever means were necessary could be taken for granted in a world where the ability to apply force is the decisive factor in securing either political or economic concessions from the powers already in intrenched positions. Since the historic relation between government and industry in Japan was favorable to a rapid industrial development in any direction that seemed advantageous to the nation, limited in amount only by the nation's capacity to produce, it is not surprising that much of the capital accumulated by the economic oligarchy in recent years was devoted to the development of heavy industry and chemicals. In these lay military as well as industrial strength, and, with supreme power apparently falling into the hands of the economic oligarchs during the 1920's, they had no objection to the economic development taking a direction which would also give Japan greater military power. But it should be recognized that this growth of heavy industry and chemicals in Japan was also a normal growth for any country which had already progressed industrially as far as Japan had by 1925. There was nothing particularly sinister in it.

After 1931 the military had increasing influence on industrial development, but even until the "China Incident" in 1937 the influence of the military was not dominant in the industry of Japan Proper, and there is some question as to whether its control was ever dominant. It is perhaps unfortunate that any considerable industrial development inevitably increases a nation's military potential and is open to interpretation as a move in the "force" politics which now dominates the world. However, this being so, we should not overlook the interpretation which may be put on our own vast industrial potential by nations like Germany, Italy, and Japan.

Even if Japanese industrialists and financiers (largely the same men in Japan) were more ready to support military ventures than their counterparts in Europe in the nineteenth century, and there is little evidence that this was the case, they were not willing to see the military leaders embark upon a career of unlimited conquest entirely on their own. Undoubtedly they would have preferred small local actions which would strengthen their economic hold on particular areas but would not lead to a big war, since they knew this would almost inevitably lead to the increasing dominance of the military. The attitude of the economic oligarchy is shown best in the way it held aloof from the economic development of Manchoukuo for the first five or six years of Japanese occupation while the military authorities kept practically all economic affairs in their own hands. The single important exception was the South Manchuria Railway, which had long been committed to the development of this region and which could hold aloof from the army projects only at the risk of losing its already great investment and its dominant economic position.

After 1937, when the military relinquished much of its economic control and even offered concessions on extremely favorable terms to the capitalist interests, they showed more readiness to take hold of the development of the country; but by that time the war with China made it impossible to carry on as rapidly as the military desired, and North China was also offering golden opportunities (chap. v). The capitalist interests in Japan were probably favorable to political expansion just as long as they could control both the economic development of the territory acquired and keep the military authorities within bounds, but they certainly did not intend to have the terms on which they could develop Manchoukuo or any other conquest dictated to them by a military clique which seemed to favor state capitalism.

The reason for dwelling on these points is that there is a strong disposition in this country to think of all Japanese industrial development—certainly all that has taken place since World War I—as a carefully planned scheme to make Japan strong enough militarily to undertake the conquest of Eastern Asia and the Western Pacific. If this interpretation of Japan's industrial development is accepted, it seems to follow that stripping Japan of most of the industrial power she has developed in the last two decades will merely strip her of her power of aggression without doing any great harm to her *normal* development.

This view is fundamentally in error. The facts adduced above show that Japan's industrial development up to about 1931 was quite normal—that it was merely what was to be expected of any growing country thoroughly committed to the development of modern industry and striving to attain a stronger industrial and commercial position and that even up to 1937 much of the industrial expansion was only that to be expected of any country in Japan's stage of industrial development. Furthermore, it must not be forgotten that Japan's population grew by about seventeen million between 1920 and 1940, about two-thirds as much as our own, and that she had steadily developed more reliance on industry for the support of her people and the improvement of their living conditions. This is no different from what has happened in all modern industrial states, but, because of the lack of certain basic resources, Japan was more dependent on trade than the United States and certain other Western nations.

IF WE DESTROY JAPAN'S HEAVY INDUSTRY

Because of the great and increasing dependence of Japan on her industry and on the trade it generated to supply her with certain essential materials, her economy will be completely disrupted by any peace settlement which destroys her industrial plant or prevents her from sharing in world trade to as large an extent as in 1925–35. Any settlement which proposes to treat Japan as though nothing of economic importance had happened to her economy since 1910 or even since 1920 will be the occasion of a major catastrophe for Japan which may very well furnish the seed for another world cataclysm.

The Japan of 1931 was not the Japan of 1910, or even of 1920, any more than the United States of 1930 was the United States of 1900. By 1931 the economy of Formosa and Korea had been fully integrated into an imperial economy, and Japan was organized to take an important place in world trade.

To recognize these facts and to act upon them does not mean that Japanese conquests should be allowed to stand; it does not mean that even such great necessity as Japan has had and will have, when compared with that of the great European colonial powers, justifies conquest; but it does mean that a workable relationship between the great nations of the world is not to be found by denying that Japan has a right to proceed with the orderly development of her industry and trade.

To force Japan back to the industrial and economic status of 1900, or even to that of 1920, will arouse a bitterness and hatred in her people beside which their present attitudes toward Westerners will appear benevolent. If we do this, we must be prepared to be utterly ruthless in keeping the Japanese in subjection for two or three generations, either by our own military power or by helping China and other Asiatic countries to create military machines which will be strong enough to do the job.

Chapter X

JAPAN: FOREIGN TRADE

A S LATE as 1870 Japan had very little foreign trade of any kind. During the next ten years her exports about doubled, while imports increased only a little over 20 per cent, but both were still very small. They remained small until after 1890–91, although both more than doubled from 1880 to 1890. The war with China (1894–95) greatly stimulated Japan's trade with other countries. In 1900–1901 both exports and imports had grown to more than three times what they were in 1890–91 and totaled about 500 million yen, or more than ten times what they were in 1870. During all this period imports of goods into Japan exceeded exports except for an occasional year. Until after the Sino-Japanese War, therefore, Japan could be said to have been almost self-sufficient (Table 13).

During the thirty years 1870–1900 the character of Japan's foreign trade was about what would be expected from an industrially backward country which was compelled to practice near-free trade by the terms of its early treaties with the Western powers. In 1870 tea and silk products, raw silk predominating, accounted for almost two-thirds of Japan's total exports. These were agricultural products requiring a comparatively small amount of processing. In 1880 these same products were still predominant among exports, but important additions were fish and seaweed, camphor, and copper and coal. In the next twenty years, 1880–1900, silk held its own, but tea dropped into a minor position, while most of the other agricultural products and raw materials increased so that the same groups of products still accounted for almost four-fifths of all exports in 1900.

A country whose exports were largely agricultural products and raw materials, Japan imported chiefly manufactured goods. The only raw material of any importance imported in 1870 was raw cotton, which was only 3.3 per cent of all imports. In 1880 the situation was practically unaltered. By 1900, however, a definite change had set in—raw cotton constituted one-fifth of all the imports in that year, and iron goods, of which a considerable proportion was for use in construction, amounted to almost 10 per cent of the total. Manufactured cotton goods were no longer of much importance, but a large variety of manufactured goods still constituted the bulk of all imports.

After 1900 Japan's foreign trade increased rapidly. Both exports and imports about doubled between 1900 and 1910 and continued to increase in almost equal ratio up to the "China Incident" (1937). During the decade of World War I, from 1910–11 to 1920–21, Japan's foreign trade more than tripled in value. Rising prices probably account for much of this, but, when allowance is made for price changes, exports increased in volume by about 60 per cent and imports by

TABLE 13

AVERAGE ANNUAL VALUE OF EXPORT AND IMPORT
TRADE, JAPAN, 1870–1938

(In Millions of Yen)

Year	Total	Exports	Imports
1938 *................	5,353.0	2,690.0	2,663.0
1937 *................	6,958.0	3,175.0	3,783.0
1930–31 †.............	2,699.3	1,308.4	1,390.9
1920–21 †.............	3,575.8	1,600.6	1,975.2
1910–11 ‡.............	941.9	452.9	489.0
1900–1901 §...........	499.9	228.4	271.5
1890–91 §.............	140.4	68.1	72.3
1880–81 §.............	63.6	29.7	33.9
1870–71 §.............	44.1	16.3	27.8

* Source: 240, 1940, p. 450.
† Source: 233, 1937, p. 76.
‡ Source: 236, 1916, p. 86.
§ Source: 238, 1904, pp. 448–49.

about 90 per cent (Fig. 6). During the next decade, 1919–21 to 1929–31, the volume of trade again rose rapidly, exports by about 77 per cent and imports by almost 50 per cent, although their value declined (Table 13; Fig. 6).

The growing dependence of Japan on foreign trade is shown even better in the proportions of certain kinds of goods which were exported in recent years. In 1933 almost 58 per cent of all cotton textiles produced in Japan were exported, and from then on through 1938 exports of cotton goods averaged about 65 per cent of the country's total production. The export of silk fabrics was over 31 per cent of total production in 1933 and averaged over 34 per cent for the next four years. The exports of rayon fabric and mixtures amounted to as much as 81 per cent of all production in 1935, although they declined to only 31 per cent in 1938. The proportions of other textiles exported were much lower but were high enough at their peak to be of real importance to the Japanese economy. It would also appear that a rather large proportion of the Japanese production of bicycles and tires, electric-light bulbs, toys, rubber shoes, and light metal wares was exported, although no exact figures are available. In 1935 Japan's total industrial production was valued at 15,255 million yen and her total exports at 2,499 million yen. Thus 16 per cent was exported. By 1937

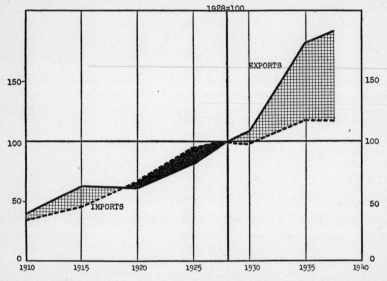

Fig. 6.—Volume of imports and exports of Japan, 1910–38 (three-year averages). (Source: 131, p. 76.)

this percentage had fallen to 14.9. In the United States the total exports amounted to only 6.9 per cent of the total exportable goods produced in 1935.[1]

The change in the character of Japan's foreign trade after 1900 is also proof of her increasing dependence on trade (Table 14). In 1903–4 Japan's exports consisted chiefly (47 per cent) of partly manufactured goods, raw silk and cotton yarn predominating. Wholly manufactured goods largely for consumption constituted almost 30 per cent of her exports, while raw materials and foodstuffs constituted about 9 and 12 per cent, respectively. Between 1903–4 and 1910–11

[1] This probably somewhat exaggerates the proportion of our total industrial production which was exported.

(1911 is the year in which Japan finally achieved complete tariff autonomy) there was not much change in these proportions, although the Russo-Japanese War had intervened. By 1920–21, however, there was a marked shift. Partly manufactured goods were no longer predominant. Wholly manufactured goods had risen to first place. Raw materials and foodstuffs had declined appreciably and were of decreasing

TABLE 14*

PERCENTAGE DISTRIBUTION OF JAPANESE FOREIGN TRADE BY CLASSES OF COMMODITIES
1903–37 (ANNUAL AVERAGE)

Year	Total	Foodstuffs	Raw Materials	Goods Partly Manufactured	Goods Wholly Manufactured	Miscellaneous
			Exports			
1936–37.......	100.0	7.7	4.4	26.2	58.9	2.8
1930–31.......	100.0	8.8	4.2	36.2	46.8	4.0
1926–27.......	100.0	7.2	6.9	43.0	41.7	1.2
1920–21.......	100.0	6.8	6.8	39.4	45.6	1.4
1917–18.......	100.0	10.7	5.2	41.6	40.4	2.1
1913–14.......	100.0	10.3	7.9	51.9	28.8	1.1
1910–11.......	100.0	11.4	8.9	48.4	30.3	1.0
1903–4........	100.0	11.8	9.2	47.0	29.6	2.4
			Imports			
1936–37.......	100.0	7.5	57.8	23.1	10.8	0.8
1930–31.......	100.0	13.2	54.5	15.0	16.2	1.1
1926–27.......	100.0	14.8	55.8	15.5	13.3	0.6
1920–21.......	100.0	11.2	50.4	21.0	16.7	0.8
1917–18.......	100.0	7.9	52.5	28.8	10.1	0.7
1913–14.......	100.0	15.0	51.5	16.8	16.0	0.7
1910–11.......	100.0	9.9	47.4	18.7	23.4	0.6
1903–4........	100.0	31.3	31.0	13.6	22.7	1.4

* Source: 1920–37, 233, 1937, p. 77; 1903–18, 496, pp. 5–6. These percentages may not be exactly comparable because it was necessary to use these two different sources to complete the series, but, even so, there is no doubt of the trend.

importance. As can be seen from Table 14, this trend, with some minor fluctuations, continued up to the attack on China. In 1936–37 the proportion of wholly manufactured goods had risen to about 59 per cent of all exports, the partly manufactured goods had fallen to 26 per cent, raw materials had declined to about 4.4 per cent, and foodstuffs were slightly above the level of 1920–21 (7.7 per cent).

The change in the character of imports during this period is equally marked and indicates a growing industrial maturity just as clearly as does the growth of industry described in the preceding chapter. Japan's imports of foodstuffs have fluctuated rather violently in the past, depending on the size of the home harvest. Thus in 1903–4 foodstuffs constituted over 31 per cent of all imports, while in 1910–11 the percentage dropped to 10. Such fluctuations considerably affect the proportions of other types of imports from year to year, but, even so, the data in Table 14 show conclusively that there has been a marked shift in imports from manufactured goods to raw materials. The former had declined from about 23 per cent in 1910–11 to about 11 per cent in 1936–37, while the latter rose from 47 to 58 per cent, with partly manufactured imports showing no definite change.

This brief description of the development of Japan's foreign trade shows clearly that it was becoming a more and more important factor in her economy, and Figure 6 shows that it had also been increasing very rapidly in volume even during the depression years. Japan was not only sending out a larger and larger volume of exports, but she was also capturing a larger share of the market in most of the Asiatic countries. Out of this situation grew many of the trade controls directed especially at reducing Japanese trade.

CONDITIONS FAVORING JAPAN'S RECENT TRADE EXPANSION

As already noted, the development of modern Japanese industry was very closely tied up with the government from its beginning. Some of the forms of this connection have already been described, but those which were particularly helpful in foreign trade may be mentioned again in passing.

Sometimes an industry was encouraged to form an association of producers, or of distributors, or of buyers of raw materials, or of exporters, or of all these, which was not only officially sanctioned but was given broad powers of control over the industry as a whole. Obviously a buying agency of this character had a great advantage in bargaining with a large number of independent sellers—for example, dealers in cotton, scattered all over the globe—or, if it were a selling agency, it could cut the costs of distributing the goods below the level likely to be attained by any given producer even if he were a large one. Such organizations could also help to enforce standards of quality and could allot export quotas to the several manufacturers; they could furnish much useful trade information, particularly to the smaller producers who could not afford elaborate selling organizations. The great size and monopolistic structure of these large organizations also enabled them in many cases to bypass the usual selling agencies in the customer countries and thus to establish a new system of distribution not burdened with the heavy costs and the traditional inertia of the existing system.

Actually the organization of trade associations, their operation, and their relation to the government were not so simple as the above statement may seem to imply. This relationship varied greatly from industry to industry, but there was a very effective working relationship which had not existed in the West since the days of the monopoly of the great trading companies. The advantage of this Japanese organization of industry lay in the military-like rapidity with which any industry and, indeed, all Japanese industry and trade could adjust itself to market conditions. Long before the Nazis had organized German business to force weaker countries to bow to their will in trade, the Japanese had many industrial and trade associations which were of help in dealing advantageously (to Japan) with the less efficiently organized businessmen of other lands. The Japanese, however, did not act as ruthlessly in forcing weaker countries to accept injurious terms of trade as did the Nazis, until after Japan had actually invaded Manchuria (1931) and China (1937).

It needs no close examination of the differences in business organization between Japan and the United States and Europe to show that the semimonopolistic character of much Japanese business and the semigovernmental authority granted to its trade associations gave Japanese business certain fundamental advantages, but many other factors were also of importance in the rapid development of Japanese foreign trade after about 1925.

Japan's advantage in being close to the Asiatic market needs only mention. Just as England had a natural advantage in trading with Europe and the East Coast of the United States, so Japan had a natural advantage in trading with East and South Asia.

The relative abundance and mobility of capital was another advantage. Japan had been accumulating capital quite rapidly ever since the outbreak of World War I, and its control was concentrated in so few hands that it was comparatively easy for Japanese industry to move into any chosen field quickly and in great force if it seemed wise to do so.

The rapid accumulation of capital was rendered easier by the abundance and docility of the labor supply. Japan's population had been growing so fast for several decades (see chap. vi) that about 400,000–450,000 more young workers (men and women) were entering the labor market each year than were leaving it by death or retirement (15, p. 192). The great majority of these had been raised on farms, and, since very few new farms were created after 1920, these young people were available for industrial work at near the low peasant standards of return to which they were accustomed. They had no opportunity, like European peasants during most of the nineteenth century when their numbers were growing rapidly, to emigrate to America or, indeed, of going anywhere else in any considerable numbers. They could stay on the farm, making at best a very meager living, or they could go into industry, where they did a little, but only a little, better. The latter was naturally the alternative chosen by a great many of them. As a consequence the home market for consumption goods did not expand as fast as it otherwise would, and the dominant capitalist group was able to turn a very large part of the surplus arising from more efficient industry into capital goods.

A fourth advantage lay in Japan's development of trained personnel. Ever since 1880, but particularly since 1914, Japan had been developing a relatively large group of trained engineers and managers and experienced workers on machines. Once a few thousands of experienced engineers and managers and a few hundred thousands of skilled industrial workers were available, the job of adding to these numbers became comparatively easy. In addition, the need for highly skilled workers decreased relatively as more and more machines became automatic. It is also clear now that industrial experience is cumulative and rather easily transferred not only from person to person but from industry to industry. By 1925–30, therefore, Japan had reached the point where the industrial personnel of the country which was needed, even for the rapid development of heavy industry and chemicals, could be increased about as fast as the demand for it.

Fifth, Japan had an understanding of oriental markets which most of the Western peoples had never troubled to acquire. She knew that most Orientals could not buy high-priced Western goods and that they must have cheaper cotton cloth, bicycles, electric lamps, shoes, and a hundred other items if they were to buy any such goods at all. Her businessmen saw that there was a new market with a very broad base to be opened up if cheap goods could be supplied. They understood this market because it was much like their home market, and they were equipped to supply it with the kinds of goods it could absorb.

Finally, Japan was also in an excellent position to trade with most oriental countries to their great mutual advantage. She needed iron ore, coking coal, tin, cotton, rubber, pulp for rayon and paper, the alloy minerals, petroleum and its products, bauxite, and a hundred other basic materials in which she herself was deficient; and these other countries, being still largely agricultural, needed Japan's cheap manufactured goods. The whole setup was favorable to the rapid expansion of Japanese trade in Asia.

As a consequence of these factors Japan found herself at the end of the 1920's in position to expand her industry as rapidly as she could dispose of the products and to produce many kinds of the consumption goods needed in Asia very cheaply (Table 15). The world depression, strange as it may seem, offered Japan just the opportunity she needed to sell cheap goods to oriental peoples. As a result of the great fall in the price and in the quantity of the raw materials exported, these peoples could no longer buy European goods at all, or only in very small amounts, for the prices of these manufactured goods remained close to pre-depression levels. Japan not only was ready to supply these peoples with textiles and other types of goods they had been buying, at lower prices than European goods had ever sold for, but was also ready to introduce new lines of goods not previously used by these peoples in any significant amount (bicycles, rubber shoes, electric lamps, etc.).

It was inevitable that any expansion of Japanese trade at a time of general depression would seem to cut into that of the established European traders to the full extent of this expansion; thus it was bound to bring down on the Japanese the wrath of the Europeans and the accusation that they were expanding their trade by "unfair" methods of competition. Newcomers with more efficient methods or who disregard established trade practices are always accused of "unfair" competition by those whose businesses they injure.

In this case it must always remain a matter of opinion how far the increase in the sale of Japanese goods in the colonial areas of Southeast Asia in the early 1930's was really due to "unfair" methods of trade, in any sense, except that they did not follow the pattern already set up and approved by Europeans. Furthermore, there must always be doubt how far the increased sale of Japanese goods amounted to a displacement of European and American goods and how far it was a real expansion of trade by tapping new and lower levels of purchasing power. There is some reason to believe that much of the Japanese goods really did reach levels of purchasers which would never have

TABLE 15*

PERCENTAGE DISTRIBUTION OF JAPAN'S EXPORTS BY CONTINENTS
AND SELECTED COUNTRIES, 1930–38

Country	1938	1937	1936	1935	1934	1933	1932	1931	1930
Asia....................	61.9	51.8	50.9	52.2	53.8	50.0	48.1	44.0	47.9
China†................	11.6	5.6	5.9	6.0	5.4	5.8	11.0	13.6	17.7
French Indo-China.......	0.1	0.1	0.2	0.2	0.1	0.2	0.2	0.1	0.2
British Malaya and Straits Settlements...........	1.8	2.2	2.3	2.0	2.9	2.5	1.8	1.7	1.8
British India...........	7.0	9.4	9.6	11.0	11.0	11.0	13.7	9.6	8.8
Netherlands East Indies...	3.9	6.3	4.8	5.7	7.3	8.5	7.1	5.5	4.5
Kwantung and Manchoukuo..................	31.7	19.3	18.5	17.1	18.6	16.3	9.6	5.7‡	5.9‡
Other..................	5.8	8.9	9.6	10.2	8.5	5.7	4.7	7.8	9.0
North America............	16.4	20.8	22.6	21.7	18.8	26.8	32.2	38.3	35.7
United States............	15.8	20.1	22.1	21.4	18.4	26.5	31.6	37.1	34.4
Other..................	0.6	0.7	0.5	0.3	0.4	0.3	0.6	1.2	1.3
Europe..................	9.7	11.2	11.4	10.5	10.5	9.8	8.9	9.1	8.7
Great Britain............	5.0	5.3	5.5	4.8	5.0	4.7	4.2	4.6	4.2
Germany...............	1.2	1.4	1.3	1.1	0.9	0.7	0.7	0.7	0.8
Other..................	3.5	4.5	4.6	4.6	4.6	4.4	4.0	3.8	3.7
South and Central America..	3.3	5.2	4.1	4.4	4.8	2.5	1.3	1.2	1.4
Oceania..................	3.6	3.4	3.6	3.8	3.7	2.8	3.4	2.3	2.4
Australia...............	2.6	2.3	2.6	3.0	3.0	2.8	2.6	1.6	1.7
New Zealand............	0.6	0.6	0.6	0.5	0.4	.....	0.2	0.2	0.2
Other..................	0.4	0.5	0.4	0.3	0.3	.....	0.6	0.5	0.5
Africa..................	5.1	7.6	7.3	7.3	8.4	7.4	6.1	5.1	3.9
Total.................	100.0	100.0	100.0	100.0	100.0	100.0	100.0	100.0	100.0

* Source: 240, 1934, p. 482; 240, 1940, p. 455.
† Exclusive of Manchuria, except in 1930 and 1931.
‡ Kwantung alone.

bought European goods because of their high price and, hence, that a considerable part of her trade expansion at this time was not gained at the expense of Europeans.[2]

[2] "Their [Japanese goods] low price, even when combined with low quality, appeals to populations with a purchasing power that is low at all times and has been further reduced in recent years by depression. In the case of a considerable range of imports there is reason to doubt whether, if the Japanese source of supply were eliminated, an approximately equivalent increase in imports from other countries would take place. . . . . One can only

JAPAN ENCOUNTERS TRADE WAR

Until the concurrence of the conditions briefly enumerated above, Japan had not been in position to challenge European trade in the Orient very effectively and did not know what real trade war was. She soon found out. She also found out that it was waged with political weapons as much as with economic weapons—by measures which were made possible only because a large part of South and East Asia was under the political control of Europe. The European colonial authorities regarded the use of their political control to maintain trade with the home country, or other Europeans, as justified by the fact that Japanese industry and commerce had long had a close tie-up with the government which gave it an "unfair" economic advantage. Thus the colonial authorities in their own view were only meeting political action with political action. The Japanese saw these discriminations against their trade as the consequence of political control of colonies and concluded that they could only be sure of their markets and the raw materials they needed if they, too, had political control over some of the areas which had the necessary raw materials.

It is not in order here to try to apportion the blame for the friction which arose between Japan and the several countries involved in trade disputes with her as the result of the increasing effectiveness of her economic competition. The fact is that the trade war with Japan which developed great intensity during the depression was merely one aspect of the interwar trend toward national or empire self-sufficiency which steadily narrowed the free trade area in the world.

In the effort to protect home industry, or to favor trade within an empire, or to insure access to strategic materials, many new forms of trade restriction were developed. Trade restrictions were no longer confined largely to tariffs and export duties. The great colonial powers generally claimed that these new restrictions were rendered necessary by the new forms of business organization which had sprung up in Italy, Japan, and Germany, that these new combinations of business and government for economic ends were so much more powerful and were so different from the private business enterprises developed under

---

conclude provisionally that Japanese industry, by reason of the low prices at which it can sell its products, has tapped new low levels of demand which Western manufacturers, with their higher production costs, have been unable, and continue to be unable, to satisfy" (G. E. Hubbard, assisted by Denzil Baring, *Eastern Industrialization and Its Effect on the West* [London: Oxford University Press, 1935], pp. 16–17; quoted by permission of the Oxford University Press).

laissez faire in the nineteenth century that the latter could not compete with them if "most favored nation" treatment were given to all peoples.

These new forms of economic nationalism need not be described here, for it can be assumed that we are all more or less familiar with the way in which Nazi Germany and, to a certain extent, Fascist Italy have used business cartels to further not only their economic advantage but to achieve political ends, and vice versa. It would appear that Japan was able to expand her foreign trade during the 1930's, in spite of these obstacles, largely because she was able to exploit new products and new markets faster than former products and former markets could be controlled. Here her military-like organization of business stood her in good stead.

The chief measures adopted to curb Japanese trade were preferential tariffs, bilateral trade treaties, and, closely related to these, reciprocity agreements, import quotas, special import duties levied on the goods of countries which had devalued their currencies more than that of the receiving country, and a variety of exchange control measures. It is obvious that any or all of these devices can be used to discriminate against the trade of any country if this is their object. Very few countries can completely balance their trade with other countries and yet get the goods they need; consequently, bilateral treaties and reciprocity agreements can easily be used to curb trade with a given country and encourage it with another. This is done chiefly by requiring a given amount of purchases of certain kinds of goods in return for the privilege of selling a given amount of other kinds of goods; or, in the case of reciprocity agreements, chiefly by so drawing the specifications that the given goods of only one country can be imported under the most favorable conditions or even by drawing the specifications so that they will completely exclude the competing goods of the countries whose trade is troublesome. Many such agreements were entered into in the effort to curb Japan's trade.

More important than bilateral agreements, however, were trade quotas. These could very easily be made to operate against Japan by picking those years for the calculation of quotas before Japan's trade with the given country had become important. This was done by British Malaya (316, pp. 150–51) and the Netherlands East Indies (109, p. 183). India also used a quota system but coupled it with a variation of the balancing agreement by which the permissible imports of cotton goods were increased in proportion to the increase in the exports of raw cotton to Japan (134, Part II, p. 119). India, like the rest of the British Empire, also gave tariff preferences to Empire goods.

Australia used preferential tariffs, import licenses, and quotas to restrict the import of certain types of Japanese goods, while trying to maintain exports to Japan of several times the value of her purchases from Japan (134, Part II, pp. 122–23). Quite naturally this effort was not successful for any length of time. Australia could not retain the trade advantages of being a member of the British Empire and at the same time sell her surplus food and wool in any considerable amounts on the Japanese market.

Most European countries and the United States relied chiefly on tariffs to curb imports in the interest of home industry, but we were not above juggling specifications in our reciprocity treaties to exclude Japanese goods (134, Part II, pp. 147–48). Both the United States and Great Britain also resorted occasionally to quotas which were generally arranged as gentlemen's agreements between trade organizations in the two countries rather than by the legal enactment of their governments (134, Part II, pp. 120–22).

Exchange restrictions were also used to control trade and became very widespread during the depression. Indeed, most countries instituted more or less rigid control over foreign exchange and thus were able to determine the direction, amount, and kind of trade. These measures were especially directed against Japan when imports from her became troublesome.

As a result of these restrictions on her trade, Japan found it increasingly difficult to sell abroad, although she did manage to maintain a steady growth in volume of exports through 1937. It was clear, however, that she was going to have further trouble in the future and that her trade would be less profitable. It was becoming more and more questionable whether she would be able to buy the raw materials she needed as her exports were subjected to more and more control in favor of European countries or in favor of home industry, as was increasingly the case in China and India.

TRADE RESTRICTIONS AND MILITARY EXPANSION

This situation was practically made to order for the expansionist group in Japan—the group which had already taken possession of Manchoukuo and which believed it the destiny of Japan to rule all of East Asia and the islands of the Pacific. They could maintain with much show of reason that Japan could not become a great industrial power if she did not have an empire within which to operate and that she dared not rely on foreign trade for her markets and raw materials. They could point to the unquestioned fact that, as she became economically strong and able to compete with the West, the Western countries used their political power at home and in their colonial areas to prevent her applying this economic strength to her own advantage.

In the same way that the great colonial powers regarded the not infrequent subsidizing of industry and transport by the Japanese government and the official sanction of a cartel-like organization of Japanese industry as an unfair use of political power to further economic ends, so the Japanese regarded the many discriminations against their trade as the "unfair" use of political power for the advantage of Western countries in their colonies. The obvious answer to the use of the power over colonies to control their trade was, according to the Japanese expansionists, to acquire colonies of their own whose economic life could be integrated into that of Japan as had already been done in Korea and Formosa and as was rapidly being done in Manchoukuo.

JAPANESE ENTERPRISE ABROAD

This growing precariousness of Japan's foreign trade was further aggravated by placing restrictions on her opportunity to develop the natural resources of the colonial East, and the Japanese had good reason to believe that these restrictions would be extended in any other part of the world if they showed an active interest in such development. The situation regarding the exploitation of natural resources in the Netherlands East Indies is described by Vandenbosch as follows:

"Licenses [for prospecting] are granted only to the following: Netherlanders, persons domiciled in the Netherlands or the East Indies, companies established in the Netherlands or the East Indies, or corporations whose managers or directors are citizens of the Netherlands or are domiciled in the East Indies and have full rights of domiciled persons, and who, if the latter, must at the same time reside in the East Indies or the Netherlands" (471, p. 256).

With many variations in the phrasing of laws and regulations and by many administrative devices not written Japan was excluded, or at least hindered, from sharing in the development of the colonial areas of South and East Asia on equal terms with the nationals of the colonial powers.

But even if there had been complete freedom to invest in and to develop the resources of the colonial East, this freedom would have been of minor advantage to Japan unless it were also accompanied by free, or relatively free, trade, as the following analysis will show.

Let us suppose a case in which Japanese capital produces some important raw material in a foreign country or colony under exactly the same legal regulations as any native producer of that country—for example, oil in California or Borneo. This Japanese company is just as free to sell its oil abroad or domestically as any United States company is. If it elects to export oil to Japan, what are the economic conditions under which it can do so, our basic assumption being that there is absolutely no legal control over this Japanese company which is not also applied to our own companies?

In the first place, it can be assumed that the costs of production of the Japanese company are about the same as those of companies owned by citizens of the United States. Hence the Japanese company cannot deliver oil to the tanker at a significantly lower price than any other company. If this cost is ninety cents a barrel, just to make the problem concrete, this amount must be paid out in American money, in wages, salaries, interest, transportation costs, repairs, materials, etc. Where is this money to come from? It will be assumed for the sake of simplicity that all the product of this company is sold to Japan. (The case would not be essentially altered if only a part of its product were exported.) This company can get the funds which are paid out for expenses only from those which are paid to Japan for goods she sells us, or from dollar exchange which she has acquired from some other country which has more dollars than she cares to spend in the United States and to which Japan in turn has sold more than she has bought, always including invisible items of trade such as shipping, insurance, new investment, interest on investment, etc.

Just because Japanese capital has come into the United States or into some colony and developed oil wells does not leave Japan free to secure this oil regardless of the amount and the balance of her trade with the United States and with the world at large. She is less restricted in importing goods whose production is financed by Japanese capital abroad than in importing goods produced by United States capital only to the extent of the net profits of the enterprise. If the terms under which her trade with other countries is conducted are such as to limit the volume of this trade arbitrarily, then she is by this much limited in the extent to which she can derive any advantage from Japanese-owned enterprise in foreign countries. In the long run, the costs of goods produced abroad and imported to Japan even though by Japanese companies must be met by exports into some country of goods produced, or services rendered, by Japan. There may be some advantage to Japan in the lower costs of imports produced by Japanese capital in the United States or elsewhere, but this cannot be great because we are assuming equal opportunity to both American and Japanese producers, and this means that their costs of production are determined by their efficiency and not by the mere fact that they are Japanese or American.

The freedom to engage in enterprise in foreign countries even where it exists and to buy at world prices in colonial markets cannot be considered equivalent to the possession of colonies giving a nation or an empire a large free trade territory, as long as we live in a world having unequal trade controls. There *is* an advantage in the possession of colonies, but it does not lie in the fact that the mother-country does not have to trade for colonial produce, because she does; it lies rather in the fact that she can control the terms of trade in her own favor, or in favor of the empire as a whole. She can even determine whether she will allow any trade at all with any given foreign country.

When a large number of countries and colonies raise trade barriers against any one country, as has actually happened to Japan, then that country will soon find itself in a position where it not only cannot derive any advantage from the ownership of productive enterprises in foreign countries but may even be unable to make any use at all of her existing enterprises abroad. This will happen when the country in which the investment lies adopts drastic export restrictions, as we did in scrap iron and oil, thus at one stroke wiping out the value of any Japanese enterprise which might have been dependent on such trade. Even more disastrous was the action of Australia in rescinding a permit to a Japanese company to develop iron mines after several million yen had been expended on the project and all arrangements were completed in Japan to use the ore thus secured. A similar agreement for the exploitation of iron mines in French Indo-China was in effect annulled by that government, after several million yen had been spent on development, by rescinding permission to export iron ore (130, 1938, p. 297).

Finally, as already noted, it simply is not true that the Japanese enjoyed the same right to exploit the raw materials of the European colonies in Asia as the nationals of the mother-countries or even of other European countries, although it is quite commonly assumed that this was the case and even vigorously asserted by many European defenders of their colonial system. Christian makes the definite statement that "the Government [Burma] has on several occasions refused permission for the Suzuki firm to engage in mining in the Shan States" (78, pp. 289–90). Leith states: "Japan also attempted to get control of the extensive iron-ore deposits on the island of Mindanao in the Philippines, but this was not permitted by the Philippine Government" (290, p. 178). Porter adds that "they [the Japanese] may belong to [Philippine] mining corporations as long as 60 per cent or more of the capital is subscribed by Filipino or American Interests" (130, 1940, p. 30). Regarding the Netherlands East Indies, Schumpeter says: "The Dutch have been reluctant to grant any further concessions to the Japanese even in the thinly settled and quite undeveloped outer islands of the Netherlands Indies" (403, p. 470).

The reasons for this reluctance to allow the Japanese equal rights of exploitation in the European-controlled colonies of South and East Asia may be perfectly sound from our point of view and may appear farsighted in view of what has happened since 1937, but from the point of view of the Japanese all such restrictions, when added to those on her trade, only deepened the conviction of the expansionists that Japan must have a large empire of her own within which she could control the terms of trade. They also made it easy for these expansionists to convince an increasing part of the public that conquest offered the only opportunity for acquiring the raw materials the country needed to continue her industrial expansion and improve her level of living.

JAPAN'S NEED FOR STABILITY IN FOREIGN TRADE CONDITIONS

From the standpoint of understanding Japan's precarious economic situation during the years immediately preceding the outbreak of World War II, the important point to realize is that even if she had had full right to establish enterprises in the colonies of foreign countries and in the countries themselves, this would not have assured her a steady flow of raw materials for her industries even during peacetime, trade restrictions being what they were. Japan needed assurance that the terms of foreign trade would not be suddenly changed to her disadvantage as well as assurance that her foreign enterprises would not be shut down just when she had come to rely on the materials she was producing. Such assurance was entirely lacking, and, as has been shown above, this situation could not be expected to improve (from Japan's point of view) in the immediate future. Is it any wonder that many Japanese came to believe that the actual political control of the lands having the resources they needed was indispensable?

Of course, while these conditions help to explain, they do not justify Japan's attack on Manchuria and China and her subsequent attempt to take over all the colonial areas in South and East Asia. But it is a plain fact that Japan has become increasingly dependent on foreign trade for the maintenance of her people even at their present low level of living, and to deprive her of this trade is to condemn the Japanese people to mere subsistence or, not improbably, to condemn some millions of them to starvation. It is not surprising, then, that many Japanese could be convinced quite easily that conquest offered the only possible way out.

It is sometimes said that the poverty of the Japanese people was due to the fact that the capitalist class in Japan did not justly divide the gains from increased industrial efficiency and larger trade with the peasants and workers, that, if it had done so, the level of living of the masses would have been higher and the country would have been less dependent on foreign trade than she is. The reply must be that Japan grows no cotton and has no land to spare for it; she must, therefore, trade for it; that Japan has no iron ore, or at least no significant quantity; and this, too, she must purchase abroad; that Japan has insufficient coking coal, copper, lead, zinc, bauxite, and magnesite; and all these must be bought abroad with goods Japan has manufactured, since she has only insignificant amounts of other raw materials to trade for them. Likewise Japan must get most of her salt, her fertilizer materials, and even the 15 per cent deficit in her rice and most of her sugar abroad. She may trade sulphur and a certain amount of bunker and domestic coal for some of these much-needed products, but she, like Great Britain, must rely chiefly on manufactures for foreign trade. Without a large foreign trade in such goods, Japan would become one of the poorest of even the oriental countries.

Chapter XI

JAPAN: ECONOMIC FUTURE

I T HAS been quite generally assumed by Americans that the victory of the United Nations will result in the breakup of the Japanese Empire, that Formosa and Manchoukuo will be returned to China, and that Korea will be given her independence. In this respect the Cairo Declaration gave expression only to a very generally accepted belief. The future of the European colonies in the Far East was less clearly envisaged prior to this declaration. The one thing certain was that these colonies would not be left in the hands of Japan.

The Cairo Conference, having confirmed these surmises regarding the intentions of the three big nations with respect to the area of postwar Japan, and by implication having shown that there will be no change in the status of colonies of South and East Asia, it becomes necessary to consider the economic future of Japan in the light of these developments if we would assay the chances for peace in the Pacific. The future apparently being planned for the European colonies will be discussed in chapter xix.

Even with Korea and Formosa as integral parts of the Japanese Empire, this empire could scarcely be said to possess more than a very modest economic base of natural resources. After the seizure of Manchoukuo the situation was significantly changed; both the variety and the quantity of mineral resources were fairly adequate for the next few decades. In addition, further exploration within this enlarged empire seemed likely to uncover new reserves and thus increase their adequacy as the basis for continued industrialization. Because of the importance of her colonies (Korea and Formosa) and of Manchoukuo in her economy, it will be well to contrast very briefly the economic situation of Japan with and without her colonies and Manchoukuo as shown by the data given above, if we are to discuss her economic future realistically.

JAPAN WITH COLONIES

The future growth of population in Japan Proper as outlined in chapter vi—suggesting an increase from a little over 73 million in 1940 to 85–95 million by about 1970—was predicated on the assumption that the pre-1931 Japanese Empire would continue to function as a political and economic unit. It was further shown in the chapter on agriculture that Japan had been steadily growing more dependent on the rice, the sugar, the bananas, the pineapples, and, to a minor extent, the animal products coming from Korea and Formosa. These colonies supplied over 16 per cent of her rice in recent years, almost all of her sugar, bananas, and pineapples, as well as a small amount but an increasing proportion of her meat and eggs. These agricultural products had come to be counted on just as much as the products of Japan herself. They also came in at relatively low prices because of the efficient manner in which the Chinese (Formosans) and Koreans were exploited by the large corporations of Japan and the complete control of their trade by Japan.

That the continuation of the existing system of colonial exploitation in the pre-1931 Empire did not seem capable of assuring Japan Proper a satisfactory food supply in the future, in view of the probable increase in population, was one of the reasons advanced for the seizure of Manchoukuo. Japan's population was growing by almost a million a year, and supplying this increase with food would have required a very rapid expansion in agricultural production in both Korea and Formosa even if there had been no increase in the populations of these colonies to use a growing proportion of their own agricultural produce. As a matter of fact, however, the population of these colonies was increasing even faster than that of Japan and had not yet shown a proved tendency to a lower birth rate as did Japan. As a consequence it was highly optimistic to assume that the Japanese Empire as it was before the seizure of Manchoukuo could long continue to supply itself with food even at the meager level of the past.

The more realistic view was that if Japan did not tap new sources of supply, by trade or conquest, her food standards would deteriorate seriously before the birth rate fell sufficiently to reduce her population growth to the pace of the growth in the food supply of the Empire. Moreover, in the pre-1931 Japanese Empire any significant expansion of industry involved importing larger and larger amounts of raw materials from foreign countries. This is shown clearly by the increase in raw-material imports during Japan's economic boom after 1931. Finally, it was becoming increasingly clear that great difficulties would be encountered in expanding trade to the extent needed to continue her industrial development.

JAPAN WITH MANCHOUKUO

The acquisition of Manchoukuo in 1931 improved Japan's situation appreciably both agriculturally and industrially by bringing a large and rich territory completely under the control of the Japanese economy. On the agricultural side Manchoukuo had large areas which had not yet been tilled, and much of the tilled land could be made to produce larger crops by the use of better farm practices and a more liberal dosage of fertilizers. The Japanese also believed that the distress due to overpopulation in agricultural Japan could be greatly relieved by migration to Manchoukuo and made plans to move a million Japanese families into this region by 1956 (chap. v). When it is added that Manchoukuo was also known to contain large mineral resources, it can readily be understood that many Japanese looked upon its acquisition as solving Japan's most urgent economic problems for some decades to come.

Therefore, on the basis of the area controlled politically by Japan after 1931 the outlook for the future was reasonably good. There seemed to be no valid reason why Japan should not continue to industrialize at a fairly rapid rate and to care for her probable future population in a better manner than in the past. How fast her colonial *subjects* would be allowed to share in these improvements was another question. Japan did not treat the Koreans and Chinese as equals any more than the British, the Dutch, the French, and the Americans treated their colonial peoples as equals. Apparently she shared the general belief prevailing before World War I that it is quite proper for the master-power to take from a colony the major part of the surplus produced there because of the more efficient use of its resources under more experienced direction.

In this respect there has been little to choose between European and Japanese exploitation until quite recently; for, although we quite commonly assume that the Japanese have been more ruthless exploiters than Europeans, there is no clear proof that the Javanese under Dutch rule or the Malays under British rule lived appreciably better than the Koreans under Japanese rule. This is not an argument for allowing Japan to retain her colonies; rather it is an argument against the whole colonial system (see chap. xix).

However, the important point for our discussion is that, after 1931, Japan's economic outlook was much improved. The acquisition of Manchoukuo had added large agricultural and mineral resources and in time would have added large markets within the imperial customs boundaries. For Japan, Manchoukuo constituted an addition which might be likened to adding all the territory west of the Mississippi River to a United States which had previously consisted only of territory east of that river. A Japanese Empire consisting of Japan Proper, Korea, Formosa, and Manchoukuo was in position to proceed with an enlarged industrial program which promised well for the future. The Japanese could no longer plead unusual need as the basis for territorial expansion with anything like the plausibility that they could before 1931. Even the restrictions on Japanese trade imposed by other countries became far less serious when Manchoukuo was considered a part of the Empire (see chap. x). Finally, Japan's strategic position vis-à-vis the Soviet Union was greatly strengthened by the conquest of Manchoukuo, which had cost her very little in men or wealth.

JAPAN WITHOUT COLONIES

Without her colonies Japan will be forced at once to rely on rather large food imports from outside the yen bloc, although they may still come from Korea, Formosa, and Manchoukuo. This will inevitably raise the cost of rice and sugar and bean products to Japan Proper— to the Japan envisaged by the Cairo Declaration—in terms of the quantity of manufactured goods that will exchange for a given amount of these food products, and will create new and difficult problems of foreign trade. Japan Proper simply cannot supply her people with food from home resources without very considerably reducing their level of living, for she cannot intensify her home agricultural production significantly without reducing the product per worker.

If Japan Proper is forced to rely entirely on her own food supplies and on such imports as she can buy from foreign countries, to say nothing of additional restrictions likely to be imposed on her trade after the war, we shall probably witness wholesale starvation of the population in bad years and even in good years such a lowering of standards of nutrition that Japan will no longer be able to maintain the moderate death rate which has recently prevailed. It does not seem possible that Japan Proper can find the means to trade for the food she will need once she is driven back, economically, into her own islands and is forced to rely solely on her own very limited resources for the production of goods for trade. There is not one word in the Cairo Declaration to indicate that the greater freedom of trade envisaged in the Atlantic Charter is to be extended to Japan in the postwar world.

From the standpoint of the Japanese, therefore, and also from a humanitarian standpoint, a complete severance of the close economic relations of Japan and her former colonies can be regarded only as a catastrophe of the first order, a fatal blow to Japan not only politically —that we could contemplate with equanimity—but also economically and in terms of human life. The immediate effect, as just indicated, will be to create a serious problem of mere survival for some millions of Japanese. The longer-time economic effect will be to place Japan at a great disadvantage in what we have hoped would be a world-wide movement toward better living conditions and toward the easing of the economic stresses *which are a potent factor in causing war*.

It will be said that a nation does not need colonies to assure itself food and the raw materials for industrial development and that these can be secured through trade and on the same terms by the nations without colonies as by those holding colonies. In a *free-trade* world this would *tend* to be the case. But, as has been shown above, this is an increasingly autarchic world in which Japan's trade was discriminated against more and more as her industry expanded and as she sought new markets for her low-priced manufactures.

The older industrial nations had no intention of allowing Japan to take their trade or even to open up new markets for cheap goods in the territories they controlled; nor did the less industrialized nations interested in developing home industry—the Latin-American countries and China, for example—intend to allow Japanese goods to come in at the expense of their "infant" industries. These are facts. They cannot be ignored. They render absurd the claim, generally made by the nationals of the European powers having large colonial possessions, that no nation needs colonies to assure itself an adequate supply of raw materials and food—that trade can take the place of colonies. The actual conditions of foreign trade being what they were in the inter-war world, one must agree with the Japanese that such assertions are the product of either ignorance or hypocrisy. Japan could not assure herself adequate food and raw materials without colonies in the world as organized in the period 1920–39.

If Japan cannot sell her textiles and bicycles and brass goods, etc., to Malaya, she cannot buy tin and rubber and iron ore; if she cannot sell cotton and rayon goods and toys and light bulbs, etc., to India, she cannot buy raw cotton and hemp and pig iron from her. One might continue this enumeration indefinitely, but there is no need. The fact is that Japan was facing a critical situation in which her entire economy was seriously threatened because of trade barriers being erected against her all over the world. She needed an area within which she could control the terms of trade. It was not and it will not be sufficient that she *was* free to buy raw materials in the sense that there was no legal barrier to her purchase of them until war became imminent. Obviously she could buy very little of any kind of goods abroad unless she was also free to sell, and this she was not.

This is a fact about which there can be no dispute. More and more, Japan found herself in the position where she could only carry on trade, outside her Empire, on terms which were decidedly disadvantageous to her as compared with other industrial countries. It is idle to talk about freedom to buy when there is not also freedom to sell. The full meaning of the Cairo Declaration for Japan can be realized only if we keep in mind the economic situation outlined above.

THE CAIRO DECLARATION

A peace based on the Cairo Declaration as it stands will enable the imperialistic elements of Japan to say with truth: "We told you so; the Western powers are determined to destroy us! They intend to starve us while they continue to hold the vast resources of the East in reserve for their own enrichment. Our only sin was our weakness. Let us see to it that next time we do not commit this sin!"

If this is what we really intend, we must certainly expect that such a statement will render a huge and ruthless military establishment necessary to maintain the peace. Any people will hold together tighter if they believe they are to be destroyed by the peace imposed on them as surely as by war. A people without hope will become a desperate people. We must recognize this.

It is possible, of course, that the Japanese attitude of fighting to the last soldier on the approaches to Japan, regardless of the chances of victory, had no connection with the harsh sentence implied in the Cairo Declaration, for we know too little about Japanese psychology to interpret such conduct with assurance; but we should make every effort to convince the Japanese people that they can hope for an endurable future, and one which will improve in the course of time, if they are willing to co-operate with the other peoples of the world in establishing peace. If this does not gain any response, we shall at least have done our part in offering honorable terms to a beaten foe and can proceed with the harsh measures necessary to assure our safety with fewer qualms of conscience.

We want to be sure, however, that the dreary implications of the Cairo Declaration are necessary and that such a peace is not being made merely in the interest of European and American traders who thereby hope to wipe out Japanese competition in our day, that we were not fighting for trade rather than to build a world in which all men can be free from fear and want and compulsion. It is certainly not in the interest of the common man anywhere to see Japan crushed, her people starved, and her levels of living driven down to those of China or India, to a bare subsistence, unless it is absolutely necessary, and the evidence to this effect is not yet convincing.

If as common people we concur in the decision that Japan should be deprived of her colonies, it is not because we believe that the Japanese should be made the servants of the victors, but because we believe the colonial system is iniquitous. If we want to wipe out Japan's military power now and render her impotent in the future, it is in the belief that, by so doing, we can begin building "a brave new world" in which all peoples and races can have *their place* but not *a place* dependent on the military power they can exercise.

If it is believed that a Japan without colonies and with little foreign trade will be a weak Japan and therefore not dangerous, we must realize that this will be true only if we leave the Japanese a reasonable hope of a better future, or as long as the military victors have the will, as well as the power, to starve them and keep them in complete subjection. How long we will have to keep the Japanese in subjection by force if we deprive them of hope for the future no one can say; but it will certainly be a long time, decades rather than years, and we in the United States must ask ourselves how long we will be willing to keep a large military establishment in the Pacific and spend several hundreds of millions annually on our Asiatic military police alone.

Will we be willing to keep them there for a generation, or two generations, until China becomes strong enough to police Japan as we think she should be policed? Will we even do it for as long as ten years? One may be permitted to doubt it. Will England or the Soviet Union do this policing after a few years if we are not willing to keep it up? It is hardly likely. England will have her hands full policing her share of the continent of Europe and the colonies. She can hardly take on the job of keeping Japan disarmed. The Soviet Union will also have her hands full elsewhere for the time being and may decide that her interests will be served best by fortifying her western frontier and allowing Japan to expand to the islands of the Pacific as a foil to the growing strength of China. Moreover, she can only undertake the policing of Japan at the expense of foregoing a large measure of the internal development she has set her heart on, and this she is not likely to do. Will Australia and New Zealand do it? They can be counted out except for minor help. Together they have fewer than 9 million people and their rate of natural increase is rapidly approaching zero (see chap. iv). Besides, they have shown no disposition in the past to take any effective steps to increase immigration so that they might build up a population of 25–30 million, which is the smallest that will enable them to put up a good defense of their own territory a generation or two hence (see chap. iv). As for China she cannot be expected to become a foil to Japan in time to prevent her making another try for the domination of East Asia, unless we are willing to assist China far more in her economic development than now seems probable. Besides China, whatever the reason may be, now seems rather lukewarm to the whole idea of completely crushing Japan and keeping her from further industrial development.

Furthermore, we are too likely to forget that it took Germany at the longest only six years to prepare for this war, and, with the experience gained since 1937, it would probably take Japan but little longer to prepare for the next war once she put all her energies into it. Every war must be fought largely with goods currently produced, so the best preparation for war up to a comparatively short time before its outbreak is the development of an industrial system which can be converted quickly to the making of armaments. This conversion can be effected quite rapidly, as we have proved. Only constant and close police supervision of the industry of a country and sufficient power to stop such conversion in its early stages will keep a determined people from preparing for war in a comparatively short time. The Soviet Union passed through an industrial revolution between 1929 and 1941 which required eight or ten times as long in England and five or six times as long in the United States even when we could profit by England's vast experience.

In view of the relatively short time that a nation really determined to develop its industry and to expand war production needs to accomplish this end, even when there are heavy handicaps, we must recognize that if we tire of policing Japan in a few years and if China is not in position to take over the job, Japan could become strong enough within a decade or a little more to start another war which would undoubtedly spread over the whole world. If she is stripped of her colonies and her numbers have been reduced by 5 or 10 millions through hardship, she will be weakened but she will not be rendered harmless.

What I am saying is that either we must find some way by which the Japanese can continue to industrialize on a scale sufficient to insure themselves a rising level of living and thus prove to them that progress and security do not depend on conquest, or we must, by force, keep them so weak that they cannot make war. If we do not do either of these, we must be prepared to fight Japan again as soon as she has somewhat recovered from her defeat. A Japan without colonies and also prevented from developing a large foreign trade will be a desperate Japan, and a desperate nation, like a desperate individual, is always dangerous because it cannot lose. If we decide that Japan is to be kept too weak to start a war, the only effective way to accomplish this is to keep her people living at a mere subsistence level such as prevails in most other parts of the East, to destroy her industry, and thus to prevent the production of any surplus which could be used for war. But we must not forget that such a peace will require ruthless enforcement for several decades at least.

SOME ELEMENTS OF A JUST PEACE

If we reject this essentially Nazi plan of ruthless subjection and strive for peace through justice, we must undertake to organize the economic life of the world in such a way that Japan can secure the raw materials she needs to insure herself a slow but steady economic improvement. But, if we do this, we must also make certain for at least a generation that this increasing economic power will not be used to prepare the more quickly for another attempt to dominate South and East Asia. It seems reasonable to suppose that a people actually improving its level of living and finding larger opportunity opening to it will be less likely to risk all in another war than one that is harshly ground down by the victors and then suddenly released from all control. But in the very nature of the case we cannot be sure that even a relatively long supervision of Japan's economy coupled with stern but just treatment will turn her from the paths of conquest.

It seems not unlikely that there will also have to be a revolution within Japan which will not only overthrow the present military leaders and the financial oligarchy but will also entirely eliminate the emperor and the doctrines based on belief in his divinity and the divinity of the Japanese people, before we can expect their wholehearted cooperation in the establishment of a world order in which they will not claim a privileged position (269). But even with such a revolution behind them it is doubtful if the Japanese can be rendered harmless for long if we deprive them of all hope of an improving future.

On the other hand, if we organize the economy of the world so that the possession of an empire will not be necessary to insure really free access to raw materials and food, we can at least cherish a rational hope that national aggrandizement will cease to be worth fighting for. When there is a more just distribution of the world's resources, it will be harder to convince the people that they have anything to gain by going to war. I recognize that the economic motive is not the only one that leads people to aggressive military action, but I believe that it is so predominating a motive that even a Hitler would have made little headway in inspiring his *Herrenvolk* to bloody conquest if he had not promised his assistants that they would become a dominant economic class in an enlarged Reich and had not held the lure of a better living before all his people.

But while I believe that the economic motive is the dominant motive in urging a people to aggressive action and while there is reason to believe that relatively free trade would help to relieve many of the economic stresses and strains developing in countries like Japan, Germany, and Italy, we must not forget that as long as population is increasing rapidly in Japan, or in other oriental countries, we are facing a dynamic, changing situation which must be taken into account in trying to remove the causes of war. Either we must make a peace in which it is possible for Japan to support a growing population at improving levels of living for the next two or three decades or we must be prepared for another outburst within a short time after we relax the vigilance of our police control over her economy.

It will be said that what is advocated here is a "soft" peace, and, as such, it will be rejected by many who believe in a "hard" peace—in the destruction of Japan. But it is not a question of a "soft" or a "hard" peace for Japan. It is rather a question of a wise peace, a workable peace, a peace that has a real chance to endure. We come back, then, to the proposition that it is never wise to render a people so desperate that they prefer death to submission. The advocates of a "hard" peace are making exactly the same mistake the Germans and the Japanese made in dealing with their conquered peoples: leaving them only a choice between complete subservience and opposition to the death.

I believe that our people want a peace which will settle our troubles with Japan in the course of time and not one which will drive her to desperate measures as soon as our vigilance is relaxed. It should be a stern peace, but it should not deprive the Japanese of hope for the future; it should be a peace which will make the Japanese people feel their responsibility for the trouble their leaders have brought on the world but not a peace which makes them feel that the conqueror is being merely vindictive. I maintain that this kind of peace is not "soft" but wise and workable, that it is necessary if we are to have time to erect and try out a world organization which can deal with international frictions before they lead to armed conflict.

Chapter XII

CHINA: POPULATION AND AGRICULTURE

THE intimate relationship that obtains between population and means of subsistence for any given people is, perhaps, nowhere more clearly illustrated than in China. For that reason it seems both appropriate and advantageous to discuss China's population and her agriculture together. The discussion will be limited primarily to the eighteen provinces of China Proper, since Manchuria and some of the neighboring provinces have already been dealt with (chap. v).

This area, which is usually thought of as "China," contains about 1.4 million square miles and comprises about one-third the entire territory of the Chinese Empire. It is somewhat less than half the size of the United States, whereas the total Chinese Empire is about one-half larger. China, thus limited, extends only as far north as Minneapolis–St. Paul, but its southern boundary reaches about three degrees within the tropics, as far south as Cuba. About half of this area lies south of the latitude of 30°.

China has a monsoon climate. Its rains come with the summer winds from the Pacific and provide more than half of China, or almost all of the area south of about 32°, with adequate rainfall to insure crops in most years. North of this area, the rainfall rapidly diminishes toward the west, and much of northwestern China has less than 20 inches annually; it is somewhat comparable to the "dust-bowl" area of the United States. In this part of China the rainfall is too low for large crops and intensive cultivation and often fails so completely that famine is frequent (46, p. 109). In winter, cold dry winds blow toward the coast from the high plateaus of central Asia so that even tropical China may be quite cool during the winter months, and frost may reach as far south as the Tropic of Cancer.

China is a mountainous country with a relatively small amount of tillable land. There are a number of plains of moderate size, but combined they do not compare in extent with our Middle West prairie regions (46, p. 93). As a consequence of this rough topography with relatively small plains areas and river valleys, not a great deal of the tillable area of China, except in parts of the north and west, is suitable for cultivation in the extensive manner characteristic of American agriculture. This would be true even if the chief crops in the center and south, including almost two-thirds of China, were such as to lend themselves readily to extensive tillage. But the need to keep rice fields flooded during the greater part of the growing season puts serious obstacles in the way of mechanized agriculture in a hilly and mountainous country.

The mountainous character of China also increases the difficulty of building lines of transportation and communication and has retarded her economic development in modern times. Primarily, however, China has not had the capital to build adequate railways, roads, airlines, or telegraph and telephone lines, nor has she had, during the last forty years at least, the political stability to insure the safety of investments in these fields.

THE SIZE OF THE POPULATION

Any discussion of the population of China must be prefaced by saying that little is *known* about it. There has never been a census as we ordinarily use that term, nor has any reliable register been maintained either by the local governments or by the central government within the past century. The so-called "censuses" are at most merely the sum of the guesses of local officials, and usually they cover only a part of the country. Any more or less official figure for China's population must therefore be treated as a guess. This does not mean, however, that one "census" is as good as another; a critical evaluation of these "censuses" may result in a better guess than any one "census."

I myself am one of those who believe that many, if not most, of the guesses as to China's population in recent years have been too high. A most careful review of the material covering this point has been made by Professor Willcox (486, pp. 511–40), who concludes that the evidence available does not justify an estimate of over 350 million in the Chinese Empire in 1937. Of these, about 320–25 million lived in China Proper. This figure, although more than 100 million less than that most commonly used by the Chinese today and now adopted by the majority of Westerners, in many respects seems more reasonable to me than the larger figures. On the basis of study and observations made with this definite purpose in mind, I am convinced that we in the West are likely to hold exaggerated notions of both the density and the size of China's population. We have been too much influenced in our notions of China's ability to support population by widely circulated descriptions of the intensity of her agriculture (257) and by oft-repeated statements regarding the "limitless" riches of the country.

It is not surprising that, when Westerners first see Chinese agriculture, they are much impressed with the great amount of labor bestowed on a small amount of land and with the number of people an acre of good land thus intensively tilled will feed, since the Chinese use practically all their grain for human food and very little for livestock. Nor is it surprising that the calculations of the size of the population made on the basis of density of population, size of the country, average size of family, and area tilled—all of which involve estimates and assumptions which cannot be validated except for small areas—often lead to estimates of population greatly in excess of that accepted by Professor Willcox.

My own opinion is that such calculations, while of interest, are of less value in arriving at reasonable conclusions than a critical appraisal of "censuses" such as Professor Willcox has made. I am, however, disposed to accept Dr. Willcox's 350 million for the Empire as the figure for China Proper and to add about 50 million for the remainder of the Empire (including Manchoukuo), but I would want to hyphenate these figures and *guess* that China's population is somewhere between 325–75 million and that the Empire's population is 375–425 million. These figures seem to me as good as we can hope to arrive at until more reliable data are available. The simple fact is that we do not know what China's population is within very large limits and that any figure used may well be in error by many millions. Table 16 will show how some of the current *guesses* of China's population vary.

But I would like to emphasize the fact that the argument advanced in this book is not affected, whether China has a population of 350 million, or 400 million, or even of 450 million or more. The population is huge in any event, and, in making calculations for illustrative purposes, the round figures of 350 million for China Proper and 400 million for the Empire will be used. Should these figures turn out to be much too small, when China actually comes to count heads, the argument will only be strengthened.

BIRTH AND DEATH RATES

Of more importance to our purposes than the exact size of China's population, or even than precise birth rates and death rates, is a judgment as to the reasonable limits of her potential rate of growth. A variety of evidence is available on this point, and, although none of it is satisfactory, it is not altogether useless in trying to get a general view of the population situation in China and in evaluating future growth in broad terms.

The largest Chinese group for which fairly reliable data on births and deaths are available is that in Formosa (see chap. vi). In 1934–37 the average annual recorded birth rate in Formosa was 45.6 per 1,000 and the death rate 20.7. Since the recorded birth rate in Formosa is undoubtedly somewhat deficient, the actual figure may well be three

TABLE 16

ESTIMATES OF THE POPULATION
OF THE CHINESE EMPIRE

Authority for Estimate	Year	Population (in Millions)
Willcox *	1937	350
Ministry of Interior †	1940	450
Chang-hung Chen ‡	1930	480
D. K. Lieu §	1930	470–80
M. T. Z. Tyan §	1930	463
Warren H. Chen §	1930	445
Maritime Customs §	1930	444‖
Ministry of Interior §	1931	474
Post Office ¶	1926	485

* Source: 486, p. 528.

† Source: 72, 1937–43, p. 2.

‡ Source: 70, October, 1933, p. 326.

§ Source: 91, p. 19.

‖ Eighteen provinces and Manchuria.

¶ Source: 73, 1931–32, p. 2. Does not include Mongolia and Tibet.

or four points higher; the death rate may also be several points too low; but there can be no reasonable doubt that it has fallen greatly during the last three or four decades, which have brought better living conditions and a stable government.

A second source of data is Dr. Buck's study of land utilization in China Proper, which gives the birth rate in 1929–31 as 38.3 (46, p. 383) and the death rate as 27.1 (46, p. 387). The conditions under which these figures were gathered made it inevitable that the proportion of omissions should be rather high and that those for deaths would probably be greater than those for births. Besides, the population involved was less than one-tenth of the Chinese population of Formosa although scattered over many parts of China, so all that can reasonably be concluded from these data is that the birth rate in the area surveyed was certainly well over 40, while the death rate was well over 30, probably nearer 40.

Thus there is not a great difference in the birth rates of the Chinese provided by these two sources, but there is a large, though unknown, difference in their death rates. The far higher death rate in China found in Dr. Buck's study, increased largely to allow for omission, appears to me highly reasonable in view of the utter lack of any health service in these communities.

In an intensive study of population movements in a Chinese community in the Yangtze delta (Kiangyin) carried out under the direction of the writer over a four-year period, the recorded birth rate was 45.1, the death rate 38.7, and the infant mortality rate 240.9 (445). These birth and death rates are known to be too low, particularly the death rate, since there was greater reluctance to report deaths than births (it was only by most persistent visiting that what is believed to be a "fair" degree of accuracy was attained), and if the death rate was more defective than the birth rate, then the rate of natural increase found (6.4) may well have been two or three points too high.

In the Ting Hsien health area (67, January, 1936, and 46, p. 387) the birth rate for a population of about 14,000 in 1933 and 1934 averaged 39.6. The death rate was 29.2 in 1933 but fell to 23.8 in 1934, only to rise to 29.1 in 1935 in an area several times as large, about four-fifths of which was included for the first time in the registration area. Thus, in comparison with Buck's study, the Kiangyin area showed significantly higher birth and death rates and the Ting Hsien area showed slightly higher rates, except for the death rate in the year 1934 (which took place in an area in which health work was then fairly well established).

If the preceding investigation does not enable us to say with any precision what China's birth and death rates are, it is of some use in helping us to fix rather broad limits within which they almost certainly fall. It seems reasonably certain that the birth rate in China is not under 40, and my *belief* is that it will average at least as high as that recorded for Formosa (45.6) and possibly even higher. The data on the death rate are even less consistent than those on the birth rate but seem to justify the statement that the death rate probably seldom falls below 35 and then only under conditions quite exceptional in China, such as in a small area where there is some health work or in a "good" year when the harvest is abundant and epidemic disease is mild. Furthermore, the death rate in China is highly variable from year to year and from place to place, as is shown in all the studies referred to (Table 17). This violent fluctuation, much more violent than the fluctuation in birth rates, is probably characteristic of all populations which, like that of China, have practically no health service and live close to the subsistence level even in "good" years.

TABLE 17*

BIRTHS AND DEATHS BY SEX, CRUDE BIRTH AND DEATH RATES, AND
NATURAL INCREASE IN HSIAO CHI, KIANGYIN, KIANGSU, CHINA
SEPTEMBER, 1931, TO AUGUST, 1935

YEAR	BIRTHS		DEATHS		BIRTH RATE†			DEATH RATE‡			NATU-RAL IN-CREASE§
	Male	Fe-male	Male	Fe-male	Both Sexes	Male	Fe-male	Both Sexes	Male	Fe-male	
1931–35......	2,039	1,825	1,735	1,579	45.1	45.0	45.3	38.7	38.3	39.2	6.4
1934–35......	572	440	277	225	48.0	51.1	44.6	23.8	24.8	22.8	24.2
1933–34......	428	420	552	549	40.0	38.2	42.1	52.0	49.3	55.0	−12.0
1932–33......	487	460	398	378	44.1	43.0	45.3	36.1	35.2	37.2	8.0
1931–32......	552	505	508	427	48.3	47.8	49.0	42.8	44.0	41.4	5.5

* Source: 445, p. 70.

† Number of births per 1,000 of total midyear population.

‡ Number of deaths per 1,000 of total midyear population.

§ Birth rate minus death rate.

With this brief review of Chinese birth rates and death rates, we have some basis for judging of probable future growth as well as of probable growth during the last thirty to forty years.

CONDITIONS DETERMINING CHINA'S POPULATION GROWTH

The conditions that make for a low death rate everywhere have been referred to as "favorable living conditions." Among any people of high birth rate, population growth becomes more rapid as the level of living rises, because this quickly reduces the death rate (see chaps. i and ii). With this in mind, I have done my best to to find out whether the Chinese level of living had been improving over the last three or four decades. Since definite data are entirely lacking, I was forced to resort to personal inquiry while in the country. In pursuing these inquiries, I did not find anyone—either a foreigner who had lived long in China or an older native, either one who had traveled much or one who had remained at home—who would unhesitatingly say that the living conditions of any significant portion of the people he knew had changed appreciably within his memory. I also made a special point of inquiring about sanitary conditions, health service, and food supply, all of which would be likely to affect the death rate. I was unable to get anyone to say that living conditions, and in particular sanitary conditions, had improved during the last four or five decades for any but a tiny fraction of the people he knew, although I was frequently told that the well-to-do portion of the Chinese population in the treaty ports (not the more crowded population of the typically native quarters) was better off as regards sanitation.

On the other hand, many older persons believed that living conditions had considerably deteriorated during this period, especially since the fall of the Manchus and the complete breakdown of civil order in many regions. When due allowance was made for the tendency of older people to deplore present evils, it seemed to me that the only reasonable conclusion permitted by these inquiries was that there had been no significant improvement in living conditions, in sanitary practice, or in civil stability among the great mass of the Chinese people in recent decades. If this conclusion is correct, there is no reason to believe that there has been any appreciable decline in the death rate in recent decades which would have resulted in a growth of population comparable to that taking place in many other parts of the East (see chaps. vi–xi, xv–xvi, and xvii–xix).

POSSIBLE FUTURE GROWTH

Whatever the population is, whatever the birth and death rate, it is of far greater importance from the standpoint of our discussion here to understand the potentialities of population growth in China and the conditions under which these potentialities may become actual. The basic point for our argument is the simple statement which no one will dispute—that China has a huge population, almost certainly not less than 350 million and possibly in excess of 450 million. A second statement which no one at all familiar with living conditions in China will doubt is that the possibility of growth for several decades to come will be measured by the extent of the control achieved over the death rate, since the birth rate will remain high and will vary within rather narrow limits. The rate of growth for some decades to come might, therefore, easily equal and might well exceed that of Europe after

1800, if a strong, unified China were in a position, now that the war is over, to improve public health, to establish irrigation projects, to extend the tilled area by mechanized farming in regions of light rainfall, to build railroads and roads, and to industrialize. All of these improvements are confidently expected to come rather quickly, both by many Chinese and by many foreigners. A natural increase of only 10 per 1,000 per year in a population of 350 million would mean an increase of over 36.5 million in a decade, while a natural increase of 15 per cent in a decade, such as prevailed in India (excluding Burma) during the decade 1931–41, would raise this to about 56 million. An increase of about 25 per 1,000 per year, such as now prevails among the Chinese in Formosa, would raise the numerical increase to about 98 million.

It must not be forgotten that in China we are dealing with numbers so much greater than those in the West that we are likely to underestimate potential future growth. For China to add to her numbers in a single decade as many people as there are in France, or in the United Kingdom, or even in Germany would not require a rate of increase greater than that which has prevailed in many parts of Europe for relatively long periods during the nineteenth century and significantly less than that in much of the New World during that time.

It is not fantastic to contemplate such a population growth in China in the light of what we have already found happening in the Japanese Empire and what we shall find below regarding the actual population growth in Southeast Asia during the last several decades. We must face the fact that China will almost certainly grow by 40–60 million in each decade as soon as a few relatively simple economic and political changes are made.

How long can China care for such increases in numbers? How is she to feed, clothe, and shelter such numbers, even at the present subsistence level, twenty or thirty years hence when the first easy economic gains have been achieved? How is she to provide the higher level of living which her leaders are now urging, and which the people themselves will one day demand, if toward the end of the century her population is growing 50–70 million in each decade? Finally, how will such a growth affect the politics and the economy of the rest of the world?

Intelligent consideration of these questions cannot be undertaken without at least some inquiry into the agricultural conditions and possibilities in China.

CHINA'S AGRICULTURE

The climatic and topographic factors mentioned at the start of this chapter make it appear highly probable that the limits imposed on cultivation by natural conditions have been more nearly reached in China Proper than in Europe and certainly than in North America. With only about 25 per cent of her land now being tilled, China has far less opportunity for agricultural expansion than most Western lands would have with the same proportion of tilled land. There is, for example, relatively much more rough land in China than in the United States. There is also a vast "dust bowl" in Northwest China, where crop failures are frequent and famines follow regularly.

The fact that Dr. Buck estimates the cultivated area of China at about 340,000 square miles or only one-fourth of the total area of China Proper seems to me to justify the common belief that little more is tillable under existing agricultural conditions in spite of the great need for more land.

In addition, the topography is least favorable to tillage in those parts of the country where the rainfall is most abundant and most certain, while in the north and west, where the topography is somewhat more favorable, rainfall is deficient and undependable. As a result, China is far from being the naturally rich agricultural area we are likely to associate with a dense population and an intensive use of land. Indeed, the good land must be used very intensively because there is so little of it. It should also be remembered that rice culture is almost, of necessity, an intensive hand culture in China, where there has been no chance to develop large fields with the use of modern machinery as in Louisiana, Texas, California, and a few of the more recently developed rice areas of Southeast Asia.

It may also be noted here that, although rice is far and away the most important crop in China, there is a considerable area in North China, perhaps one-third of the total, where the rainfall and climate are much better for the growing of wheat, soybeans, and kaoliang than of rice. Moreover, throughout most of central China the winter crop on two-crop land is chiefly wheat. The Chinese, at least in the northern half of the country, are not a rice-eating people to anything like the same extent as the Japanese or most of the peoples of Southeast Asia. But where natural conditions are suitable for rice-growing it is always the chief crop, and, since practically all of it is used for human food, it will support a relatively dense population.

EXTENSION OF THE CULTIVATED AREA

No complete land survey has ever been made in China, and it is not possible to say what area might be added to that already cultivated if modern methods of extensive cultivation were put into use in the wheat region and if large irrigation works were undertaken where feasible. The diversification of crops and better farm practice might also make it possible to use more of the rough and sloping land for root crops and for orchards (nuts and fruits). Many men familiar with Chinese agriculture believe that the wheat area might be considerably extended by the use of modern machinery just as our wheat area was expanded by the use of better machinery from about 1900 to 1930; but the risks would be similar to those in our "dust bowl," and the crop failures would almost certainly be more frequent than in most of the present wheat region. As in much of the area of the United States where the rainfall is below 20 inches, only irrigation from large storage reservoirs will insure good crops every year.

In the rice region where the fields must be level enough to be flooded several inches deep during most of the growing season the possible extension is certain to be small, for in a large part of this area the rainfall is not sufficient or is too irregular to keep the fields flooded as in the delta areas of Burma, Thailand, and Indo-China, and water must be pumped, usually by human power, from streams, canals, and ponds. The tremendous effort involved in this process can be understood once one knows that to flood one acre 4 inches requires over 100,000 gallons of water if there is no wastage. With the primitive pumps at the farmers' disposal, it is quite impossible to raise rice in fields more than a few feet above the level of the canals and streams from which water is pumped.

More scientific and larger-scale irrigation works with storage reservoirs would undoubtedly add some land to the rice area at higher levels than can now be reached, but not a great deal new rice acreage should be expected from this source. In the rice area new irrigation works would probably do more to intensify culture on the present rice lands than to add new lands, while in the north it would probably increase both the area and the intensity of use of land for wheat, beans, and kaoliang rather than add to the area in rice. However, until the government is strong enough to undertake reclamation on a vast scale —and the prospect for this is not bright—there will be little new irrigated land for any purpose.

Little can be said at present about the possibilities of extending the tilled area in the thinly settled provinces of Southwest China because not much is known about the quality of the forest soils or the extent of the fairly level lands. These provinces are largely in forest now. Their climate is tropical or subtropical, with abundant rainfall, but they are very mountainous. It would seem that at most this region could furnish homes to the possible overflow from the more densely settled provinces to the east and the north for only a few years.

The greater hope for the increase of the agricultural area in China Proper in the near future probably lies in the growing of crops in the rice area which do not need irrigation and can, therefore, be grown on rolling or hilly land—for example, corn, Irish and sweet potatoes, vegetables, and tree crops of fruit and nuts. But if these hills are used, great care must be taken to use contour terraces to prevent erosion; already many, perhaps most, of China's hillsides that might be described as gently rolling have been denuded of their natural forest cover and have been so eroded that they are almost useless for agriculture.

The more complete use of the land already in farms offers another opportunity to extend the cultivated area. No one can study the countryside in China and Japan without being convinced that the Japanese make much better use of the nooks and corners of their fields and of the land around their homes than do the Chinese, who could add considerably to their vegetable and fruit crops by more complete use of these small "patches." The food to be gained in this way may seem inconsiderable to us, but to a people living at near-subsistence level such a small addition would be of much importance. Furthermore, with an increase in variety, particularly in fruits and nuts, the diet should be far more satisfactory from the standpoint of nutrition.

Estimates of the new lands suitable for settlement within the Chinese Empire but outside China Proper are also extremely unsatisfactory, but such lands are generally believed to be considerable. As we have seen (chap. v), there is still much land suitable for agriculture in Manchoukuo, and the adjoining areas (in what is generally called Mongolia) are also believed to have much agricultural land which is now used only for pasture. As evidence of unused land in Manchuria one may cite the large land-settlement schemes of the Japanese, who planned to settle 1,000,000 families there in twenty years (1936–56).

As to the possibilities in the far northwest, outside China Proper, one must remain skeptical until more evidence is available, although many Chinese are convinced that there is much good agricultural land in this region.

Altogether these new areas of settlement within the Empire may well provide for several tens of millions more people at present levels of living (256, pp. 89 and 98 n.); but, since Manchoukuo can probably supply most of its own future settlers, only a few of these tens of millions would come from China Proper.

Even if it is assumed that the new areas available for settlement within the Chinese Empire could accommodate one-fourth to one-third as many people as China Proper now has—a highly optimistic assumption—it would be unfortunate if these new areas were to be fully settled within the next three or four decades. It would seem much more desirable to postpone the use of these open spaces until the Chinese had learned something of the relation between the use of land, the growth of population, and the level of living. Unless the Chinese begin to control their population growth before they settle these new lands, it will merely mean another 75–100 million Chinese living at the same near-subsistence level with no hope of further new settlement within the Empire.

CROP IMPROVEMENT

The greatest increase in the food supply of China within the next few decades will probably come through general improvement in agricultural practice: better tillage, better varieties of crops, and more scientific fertility practices. It is through such methods that Japan has done most to increase her agricultural production, and there is good reason to believe that China can do likewise. At present the Chinese use very little commercial fertilizer, depending largely on their livestock and human excrement for their fertilizer, and farm practices in general remain about what they have been for ages past.

An ancient civilization like China develops many farming customs which are very difficult to alter. It is hard for an Occidental to realize how completely custom dominates the thinking and conduct of the Chinese farmer; only the spread of education among the young will break down the obstacles to better farming found in age-old customs, and this will take time. There are evidences of changes here and there, but to us they seem almost incredibly slow. The war may have lent some impetus to change, but China must have a much improved system of transportation and communication and a far more extensive educational system before any rapid change in agricultural practices can be expected.

Likewise the improvement of crop varieties, which has done so much to increase yields in the West, proceeds very slowly in China. In the first place, plant breeding has as yet received comparatively little attention. But even when varieties have been developed which are more resistant to disease and insects, which have better-feeding root systems and thus very definitely give better yields, their use spreads but slowly. I was much impressed by the slow, uphill struggle of the agricultural specialists to get better cotton seed used in one of the more progressive areas of Chekiang Province. They had demonstration plots showing the greater immunity of the new variety to damage by both insects and disease, the advantages in a sturdier stem and in more uniform ripening, and, most important of all, the greater weight of both seed and lint. But the farmers were very slow to accept the new seed. Not only does custom prescribe the planting of the same crop that has been raised in times past but it raises fears of the new and the untried which are greater than the hope of gains even in the face of actual demonstration. Moreover, communication with farmers, few of whom read, is slow and difficult, and new crops and varieties long remain unknown.

Extensive education in agriculture undertaken by a politically and economically strong government would undoubtedly increase the speed of beneficial changes.

It has been estimated by those who know Chinese agriculture well that increases of 50 per cent and even more in the yields of the more important crops are quite possible if the better varieties of these crops already developed come into general use. But where we take years to change to hybrid corn, the Chinese may take decades to adopt a new rice: they have not yet begun the educational spadework in agriculture which we began with the establishment of our agricultural colleges about eighty years ago. Undoubtedly much of the scientific work in agriculture done in Japan, in the Netherlands East Indies, in the Philippines, in India, and elsewhere in the Orient, can be rather easily adapted to conditions in China, but China must tackle her political and educational problems with vigor before she can take full advantage of the researches already available.

AGRICULTURAL IMPROVEMENT AND POPULATION GROWTH

The great danger, from the standpoint of a Westerner interested in seeing China achieve a better level of living, is that improvements in

Chinese agriculture will take place so slowly that they will only serve to increase the population without raising the level of living. This often does happen among the most poverty-stricken peoples (see chap. ii). Any increase in food reduces the death rate and thus raises the rate of natural increase, and very quickly the food available per capita tends to decline to about what it was before the increase in production took place. This happens so imperceptibly, so automatically, that the people themselves generally do not realize it, and thus have no clear choice between better living with little or no increase in numbers and the same low level with larger numbers. The larger numbers come *naturally* with the lower death rate following some easing of the struggle for subsistence because the birth rate remains at its customary level.

This is the usual result when people live as the Chinese are now living and when they take no thought for the adjustment of their numbers to their means of livelihood. In thinking of the relation of the improvement of agriculture and population growth in China, we must not forget the picture of population growth drawn earlier in this chapter.

MIGRATION AND POPULATION GROWTH

Migration might also have a pronounced effect on China's population growth—an effect that we will only mention here but will return to in the chapter on migration and population pressure.

If the Chinese had several Manchurias to which they could move freely and cheaply, securing land without cost or at a very low cost as in the settlement of the United States, then we might expect an almost immediate improvement in the level of living for both old and new communities. There can be no reasonable doubt that, under these conditions, the Chinese would expand rapidly into any new area to which they could gain ready access and where agricultural conditions were reasonably familiar. They have proved good pioneers in Manchuria and Mongolia, in the north, and in a number of places in the tropics. But it should be made clear that the amount of migration from China would have to be large and continuous for many years in order to establish a better level of living. It seems doubtful now that any such vast migration can be managed in time to prevent the population at home from increasing during the next three or four decades about as fast as improvements in agriculture can be introduced (see chap. xx).

In arriving at this conclusion, the probable effects of industrialization on the level of living are not being overlooked. But the speed with which industrialization can effect improvements is often exaggerated by the nationals of industrially backward countries. Furthermore, they seem to attribute all the improvements in level of living in the West to industrialization, to overlook the fact that the West had an abundance of land for settlement at the same time that industrialization was proceeding rapidly. It remains to be seen whether any crowded people having a very low level of living and without a relative abundance of land at its disposal can improve its level of living except very slowly when forced to rely to a large extent on the growth of machine industry (see chap. xiii).

FORESTRY IN RELATION TO AGRICULTURE

No Westerner can possibly fail to be impressed by the absence of forests and woods in most of northern, central, and southeastern China. The existence of woods in villages, around temples, and sometimes in graveyards only accentuates the general barrenness of the hills and the rough lands.

In North China the hills and mountains not only lack trees but more often than not seem to lack all vegetation. On the other hand, grasses and bushes cover most of the treeless hills in southern and central China because the rainfall is more abundant and the growing season longer. The more important forest areas in China Proper are in the far west and in the southwest, although there are many small areas all over China in which good forestry practice has maintained the steady yield of forests (300). In general, the parts still having good forests are regions of sparse population where there has been no great pressure of numbers on these resources, or regions, as in western Szechuan, where the forests have not been readily accessible to the dense populations of the plains (151). There are still large forests in Manchoukuo.

In the more densely settled areas, however, the hills either are bare or produce only an annual crop of weeds, grass, and bushes. This annual cover is gathered for fuel by the people in the valleys and near-by towns and cities, or is burned in the hope that the ash will be washed down to fertilize the fields in the valleys (a most wasteful process). This denudation of the hills has gone on for so long that a large proportion of them are already eroded to bare rock, and many others will grow only the most scanty crop of weeds or grass. It has not only reduced the total production of fuel and lumber from the hills but has increased the volume and the speed of the run-off of water and thus led to a vast amount of soil erosion and to more frequent and severe floods. The last link in this chain of evils is the destruction of much valuable valley land and the silting-up of rivers, canals, and reservoirs.

How long it would take China to reforest a large part of her rough, untillable land cannot be told, but it will be a long and difficult task. The habit of denuding the neighboring hills for fuel is an ancient one and can be broken only by providing a better and cheaper fuel (coal) and by establishing a police strong enough to protect new plantings from the annual depredations of the people. Only a strong government thoroughly familiar with local habits and customs can achieve these goals.

Over much of the country, from central China south, it might not take long to develop a fairly good forest cover again if the people could be kept from plundering, for bamboo grows rapidly, and the replanting might well be started with some such useful and quick-growing plant. Moreover, bamboo can be used for many, possibly most, of the purposes for which we use timber. A small amount of reforestation is already being undertaken (151, p. 25), but a vigorous forestry policy looking to the covering of China's hills with grasses and trees is essential not only to the development of many kinds of industry in the future but also to the maintenance and extension of her agriculture and water power (300, p. 141).

No country in the world stands in such great need of increased forest resources. It does not seem an exaggeration to say that the very maintenance of Chinese agriculture, to say nothing of reclaiming many areas formerly used, depends upon the development of scientific forestry practice over a large part of China; only thus can China be assured of a reasonably full use of her agricultural resources.

Chapter XIII

CHINA: MINERAL RESOURCES AND INDUSTRY[1]

NOT many years ago it was quite the usual thing to speak of China as a land of "vast," or indeed of "limitless," resources. To an American this generally meant vast new lands to be settled, great forests to be felled, and huge stores of coal and iron and copper and oil and of most other useful minerals to be exploited. It was natural for Westerners to think of China, because of her size, as a greater United States, with vast new areas to be settled in Manchuria and with mineral resources which staggered the imagination. Travelers quite generally brought back reports of iron furnaces operating in all parts of the country, of frequently encountered oil seepages, of copper, tin, and tungsten mines scattered over much of southern China, and of great wealth and luxury in the larger cities. With these resources China seemed a land of almost limitless possibilities, since she also had a huge population of industrious people who could cheaply turn her raw materials into usable goods once the use of modern machinery was begun.

We have already seen that, while China's agricultural resources are by no means as completely exploited as are those of Japan, they are, nevertheless, very definitely limited; also that her forest resources are comparatively small and that in the areas bordering North China, even with Manchoukuo, the opportunity for pioneer settlement within the Empire is rather limited when her vast population is taken into account. Unfortunately, more recent and more scientific exploration leads to the conclusion that China's mineral resources are also far smaller than was formerly thought.

MINERAL RESOURCES

Although there is much difference of opinion regarding the size of the coal reserves of China, there is general agreement that they are large and that they are sufficiently varied in quality to meet all her fuel needs for a long time to come. The estimates made vary from a low of about 40,000 million tons to twenty or thirty times this amount

[1] Excluding Manchoukuo, discussed separately in chap. v.

(22, p. 51), with 250,000 million tons emerging as a not improbable figure for China apart from Manchoukuo, which has 20,000 million tons more according to late Japanese estimates (135, p. 27). China's coal reserves are widely, although not uniformly, distributed (22, p. 49) so that no part of the country is without fairly easy access to coal. However, the coals best suited to metallurgical uses are concentrated in the northern half of the country, where the best iron reserves are also found.

It can be said with reasonable assurance, therefore, that China's industrial development in the next several generations will not be seriously limited by lack of coal or by the shortage of particular varieties of coal. Indeed, China has in her coal supplies a trade weapon of much potency in dealing with other oriental countries, Japan in particular, because Japan badly needs Chinese coal for her metal industries.

Some years ago China's petroleum resources were believed to be very great because numerous seepages were found in widely separated areas. Then there was a period lasting almost to the present when they seemed to be quite negligible save for the oil shales of Manchoukuo and Shensi, which are by no means large. However, in the *China Handbook* (72, 1943) rather large claims are made for new fields recently discovered in northwestern China, and fourteen wells are said to be producing. The *Austral-Asiatic Bulletin* also speaks of large untapped oil deposits in the northwest (16, Suppl. December–January, 1940–41, p. 8). In view of past disappointments, however, it would be well to reserve judgment on the value of these new discoveries until more development work has been done. Several years ago Mr. W. B. Heroy, an oil geologist (22), believed that the geological structure of China was such as to hold little hope that any considerable amount of oil would be found in areas which had not yet been fully explored.

It appears probable, at the moment, that China must depend largely on outside sources for her liquid fuels until such time as the liquefaction of coal can be carried out on a commercial scale. Because of her large coal reserves, the lack of petroleum may prove far less a handicap in her future industrial development than would have been supposed a few years ago—but if China is forced to use such manufactured fuels while Western countries use petroleum, she will labor under a severe handicap as regards the cost of certain types of transportation.

Considering her vast area, China has comparatively little water power, although her total resources are not inconsiderable. Estimates vary from about 20 million horsepower (353, March, 1942, p. 50) to about twice that amount, with practically none developed. Any large development of these resources, to be economically sound, must take place in connection with large irrigation and flood-control projects, and the prospect that these will be undertaken in the near future is far from bright. However, this comparative lack of water power will be a far less serious handicap to China than it would be to a country with scanty coal supplies and, therefore, with relatively costly steam power.

In contrast to her relative abundance of coal, China is poor in iron. Bain, in his review of the evidence, quotes Tegengren, with apparent approval, as follows:

"China can no longer be regarded as a storehouse of inexhaustible future reserves of iron ore, to be drawn upon when the supplies of other countries are beginning to give out. On the contrary, her iron ore resources must be termed very modest, or even scant, when her potentialities of industrial development are taken into consideration, and the strictest economy would be indispensable to guard against future unpleasant contingencies. By way of illustration it may be pointed out that the total quantity of iron ore (both actual and potential) represented by the figures above would be consumed by the iron industry of the United States within less than nine years" (22, pp. 94–95).

The figures referred to in this quotation show that, of the 396 million tons of "actual" ore reserves in China, 295 million are in or near Manchuria and that, of the 556 million tons of "potential" reserves, 477 million are in or near Manchuria. This leaves only about 180 million tons of ore with an iron content of about 100 million tons in China outside those in or near Manchuria, an amount which we would use up at our present rate of production in less than two years.

Recently some new discoveries have been made, and one late estimate (129, XXXV [1939], 97) of China's iron ore, not including Manchoukuo's, comes to 323 million tons; on the other hand, the China Handbook for 1943 (72, p. 484) gives total reserves, including Manchuria, as only 1,694 million tons. But even if the highest estimates of all authorities are accepted (including Manchoukuo), Bain's conclusion certainly holds good:

"The evidence would seem to be conclusive that there is no warrant in present knowledge for the expectation that China will be able to supply iron ore that will contribute to the world's exportable surplus to any considerable degree or even that China can support for any long period a domestic industry consuming steel per capita at a rate comparable to those in Western countries" (22, pp. 103–4).

There is, of course, always the possibility that, in a country no more thoroughly explored than China, large new deposits of high-grade iron ore will be found, but I was told by Chinese geologists who had for years been searching for minerals that the net effect of their work up to 1931 had been to reduce previous estimates of these resources, particularly in coal, iron, and petroleum. The present prospect is, then, that China cannot have a large iron and steel industry for a long period based on her own ores even when Manchuria is included. These ores are relatively small in quantity, rather poor in quality, and too widely scattered over the country to permit of large-scale, efficient production in more than a few places. It seems reasonably certain that her heavy industry must be rather short-lived and weak unless larger outside sources of cheap ore or pig iron are found. The known sources now available in the Orient are not large, although it is possible that considerable amounts of ore might be brought from the Philippines and the Netherlands East Indies for some years and that rather large amounts of pig iron might be secured from India as her iron industry grows and as transportation is improved.

Of other minerals of economic importance, China seems to have only two or three in such abundance that she can be said to have an adequate supply for her own use and possibly some for export.

Before 1937 she produced a considerable part of the world's antimony, and it is believed that the reserves, estimated at from 1.5 (22, p. 184) to 2.7 million tons of metal (72, p. 490), are sufficient to enable her to retain this market for many years, although there is evidence that Mexico and Bolivia are already displacing China in the American market (390, p. 271). But since the world was using only about 30,000–40,000 tons of antimony annually before the war, of which China supplied about half (461, 1940, p. 721), even at the price of fifteen to twenty cents a pound the total value was not large. China's future exports of antimony will not pay for much iron and steel and copper and oil.

China has also supplied a large part of the world's tungsten and, with reserves of perhaps a million tons of high-grade ore (323, p. 115), seems likely to continue to do so for some time. But here again the total amount used in the world is small so that China's 10,000–12,000 tons in normal times—almost 20,000 in 1937—will not go far in helping her to pay for imports, although tungsten is several times as valuable as antimony.

There appears to be sufficient bauxite or alunite in the northeastern part of China (Shantung), and also in Manchuria, to supply China's needs for many years at a rate of use that would have been considered normal before World War II. How adequate it will prove if used to displace iron to any considerable extent is much more doubtful. The *China Handbook* (72, 1943, p. 491) indicates that large new reserves have been found in both the northwest (Kansu) and the southwest (Yunnan), but, since these have not been proved, it will be well to reserve final judgment for the present. It appears probable that China with Manchoukuo is fairly well supplied with bauxite and with alumina shale, which can also be used for the manufacture of aluminum, although the cost of production is higher.

Several discoveries of copper have been reported recently in western and southwestern China, but the estimates of reserves are not very reliable. The *China Handbook* (72, p. 488) gives these at about 2.6 million tons of pure copper, or a little over one year's supply for the world. Up to the present, China's copper production has been almost negligible, perhaps 1,000 tons in 1940 (135, p. 5). About all that can be said at present is that China's copper will probably not go far in the development of an important electrical industry. In the United States we use from three-fourths of a million to a million tons in a normal year.

China does not seem to have any significant amount of sulphur or pyrites. Any considerable development of chemical industries would require the importation of large amounts.

If it proves feasible in the postwar world to produce magnesium from sea water rather than from magnesite, as seems not unlikely, then the cost of power along the coast would be the decisive factor in China's production. In this respect China, with her abundant coal supply, some of it near the coast, would not appear to be at any special disadvantage as compared with most other countries.

Of other important minerals—manganese, mercury, lead, zinc, silver, nickel, molybdenum, gold, etc.—China appears to have some of most of them but in such small amounts that she will have to rely largely on imports, except possibly for manganese. This seems to be true also of phosphates, potash, and nitrates for fertilizers, although here again her abundant coal supply may make it possible to provide synthetic nitrates at a fairly low cost.

INADEQUACY OF CHINA'S MINERAL RESOURCES

One must conclude that China's industrial development over a long period will be heavily handicapped by the lack of many important minerals, particularly by her small resources of high-quality iron and copper, and hence that she will be forced to rely heavily on imports from abroad for many types of goods essential to further industrial development and to the improvement of standards of living. It does not follow from such a conclusion that, other conditions being favorable, China cannot go ahead rather rapidly in the immediate future in the development of certain industries, but it does mean that the development of other industries will be handicapped for a long time or even indefinitely. Of course, new processes may make hitherto unusable resources usable and may cheapen the use of low-grade resources, as seems to be happening with low-grade iron ores in Manchoukuo; but the use of such resources generally involves the building of a more complex industrial plant which is more costly to operate. Substitutes for other minerals which now appear to be lacking may also be found (e.g., for copper), but it should be recognized that the lack of adequate mineral resources of good quality is a severe handicap to industrial development because it renders the balancing of a nation's foreign trade account more difficult than would otherwise be the case.

In building and equipping her railways, in shipbuilding, in developing motor transport and farm machinery, and in establishing all manner of new industries, China will for some time be rather heavily handicapped as compared with Western Europe, Russia, or the United States by reason of high-cost steel. She simply has not the good mineral resources to make cheap production possible even though she may be able to build the plants within a few years. She must plan to pick up the manufacture of much of her iron and steel at later stages of processing and to devote a larger portion of her industry to the production of light consumption goods than has been customary in the West. Moreover, for a few years China must import pig iron and steel from the United States or India and copper from Chile or Africa, and to do so she must sell us her agricultural and mineral raw minerals and her industrial products. The lack of good basic raw materials will certainly complicate all China's postwar economic problems, particularly her foreign trade.

INDUSTRIAL BACKWARDNESS

As is generally known, China's industrial development has lagged far behind that of Japan and even India. But how far it has lagged and how utterly different it is from that of the West is extremely difficult for most of us to realize. In wandering about in any Chinese city, except in the more Westernized parts of the treaty ports, one can see even now the same type of hand industry being carried on in the home and factory as is associated with the Middle Ages in Europe. Since that time Europe has passed through a series of industrial and agricultural, as well as political, revolutions, while China has changed but little except in parts of the treaty ports and is only now feeling many of the impulses which stirred Western Europe two centuries or more ago.

In China today spinning and weaving, the most extensive of all industries, are still carried on chiefly by hand labor in the home; it is estimated that 80 per cent of all cloth is woven on hand looms in the cottages of the peasants or by the village weavers (200, p. 196), and much of the yarn used is still made by hand. The next most important industries are the making of household utensils and farm tools, and these, too, are largely made either at home by the family for its own use or in small household factories whose market is entirely in the neighborhood. Almost no machinery is used in their manufacture, except that which is homemade and operated by hand.

Most lumber is still sawed by hand; much of the heavy transportation, except immediately on the rivers, canals, and the few railroads, is by wheelbarrow or the carrying-stick, both handmade. In fact, almost everything the Chinese consume or use is produced by such primitive methods at a tremendous cost in terms of human labor. As yet only a few modern factories, chiefly in the treaty ports, use power machinery, and their total production is scarcely more than a drop in the bucket of China's total production whether we place her population at 350 million or at 450 million.

The reasons for this lag in the use of power machines can be stated briefly.

In the first place, for a century or more China has had no strong central government like that of Japan which could take the lead in industrial development, as entrepreneur, as supplier of capital, and as guarantor of peace and order within the country. The risk in industry and trade becomes prohibitive when every local authority or war lord can levy taxes as he pleases without being able to insure protection in return; a strong, stable central government with a definite fiscal and industrial policy is a first prerequisite to the development of modern industry on any significant scale, whether that industry be state or private. Since extra-territoriality has been relinquished by the foreign powers, this will be more true than ever, for there are now no "havens of refuge" in the foreign concessions to provide protection and equitable government to developing industry.

In the second place, China's semicolonial status, although nominally a sovereign power, deprived her of tariff autonomy until 1929. Thus she had had only a few years in which to foster "infant" industry by the use of tariffs, even if the Nanking government (Kuomintang) had had an industrial policy and had had the power, the will, and the money to embark on the industrial development of the country. The Western powers and Japan have been far more interested in keeping China in a colonial status—as a supplier of raw materials and a market for manufactures—than in seeing her develop her industry. They did not want her to become more self-sufficient economically because this would almost certainly result in the development of industries which would cut into their markets and in time would also give her the strength to throw off the control of outside powers. Witness the importance of Japan's industrial strength in keeping her from becoming a colonial appendage of Europe.

In the third place, there was comparatively little native capital available for the development of large-scale enterprise—for example, the building of rail transportation and ports or the establishment of factories using expensive machinery. Besides, such capital as there was in the country could not be readily mobilized because the structure of Chinese society was not conducive to the organization of joint-stock enterprises managed solely in the interest of economic efficiency. Business could not easily be shifted from a family basis, with all the inefficiencies inherent in a strong nepotism, to a more broadly co-operative basis in which family ties count for little. Large blocks of capital probably could not have been assembled even if they had been available. In addition, foreign capital was afraid to venture much outside the treaty ports, and, when it did, it made such demands both as to returns and as to supervision of the enterprise that the Chinese nationalists did not care to yield the political control which was involved.

In the fourth place, there were few Chinese trained in the management of business, in the organization of industrial processes, and in the operation of machines, and again there was no strong central government to undertake large-scale training both at home and abroad as the Japanese government had done. There were also many social handicaps to be overcome, "cakes of custom" to be shattered, before such training could be made effective in Chinese life. The stigma attached to working with the hands by those who were not actually forced to do so, and the loss of "face" involved in engaging in any occupation or task which was not traditional in the family, were handicaps of great weight and could not be thrown off in a moment even by Western-trained men. They found the family too strong to be ignored.

There was also just as complete a lack of workers skilled in the use and the upkeep of machines. No matter how skilled the worker might be at any kind of hand work, he was generally quite helpless in using machines. Thus only the simplest types of work could be undertaken until machine habits had been developed in a considerable body of workers. Here, again, the lack of a strong government which could establish trade schools and bring in foreign instructors was a heavy handicap. The lack of government-subsidized or government-owned factories in which the key men could be brought in from abroad to train young workers likewise made the development of a class of skilled workers and foremen very slow. Modern industry is as dependent on these skilled workers as it is on the trained engineer and manager, so it is not surprising that the development of modern industry in China was slow and that most of what there was took place in the treaty ports and was owned and managed by foreigners.

THE DEVELOPMENT OF SELECTED INDUSTRIES

In China, as in most other countries, the first important development in machine industry was in textiles. But since Chinese textiles had to compete not only with those from the well-organized industry of Western countries but also with those of Japan, and since, until 1929, China could impose only a nominal tariff on such imports, the textile industry did not expand as rapidly as might have been expected. Although China had a practically unlimited and very cheap labor supply and grew her own cotton, the growth of cotton mills was slow during the period from the establishment of the first mill in 1890 to World War I (200, p. 188).

In 1913 there were only twenty-eight mills with 1,210,000 spindles and a few thousand looms. During this period the mills were largely engaged in spinning, the yarn being sold chiefly to local hand weavers. Between 1913 and 1925 the number of mills increased almost fourfold, the number of spindles about threefold, and the number of looms at an even faster rate. This was the heyday of the modern Chinese cotton industry, for the European nations were entirely out of the market for several years, and Japan could not keep up with the demand.

TABLE 18*

COMPARISON OF JAPANESE-OPERATED MILL IN TSINGTAO (AMONG THE MORE EFFICIENT MILLS IN CHINA) WITH A SIMILAR MILL IN JAPAN, 1940

	SPINNING		WEAVING	
	Tsingtao	Japan	Tsingtao	Japan
Working hours per shift..........	11.5	8.0	11.5	8.0
Production per shift ("momme" per hour).......................	5.5	6.9	47.4 yd.	60.0 yd.
Average wage per shift in yen.....	0.59	0.85	0.59	0.85
Average wage per shift in dollars†..	0.14	0.20	0.14	0.20

* Source: 32, pp. 38–39.

† Yen converted to dollars at an exchange of 0.2344. Owing to the drastic depreciation in the value of the yen starting in 1932, these wages are much lower in dollars than in 1930, when the yen was worth about fifty cents.

Since 1925 the rate of growth has been much slower and an increasing proportion of the production seems to have taken place in the Japanese-owned mills, especially since 1930. It appears that the Chinese-owned mills cannot compete in efficiency with Japanese-owned mills and were progressively being put out of business, particularly in the larger treaty ports (Table 18). As a result, most new Chinese-owned mills are being built in smaller places where they will depend largely on nearness to raw material and a local market to offset the greater efficiency of the workers in Japanese-owned mills (32, p. 63).

With the growth of the cotton industry in China after 1913 the imports of yarn began to decline, and after 1920 the exports mounted rapidly (200, p. 191). At the same time the imports of cotton cloth began to decline and the exports to increase. By 1934 the exports of cloth were almost equal to the imports. But it should be noted that, although the manufacture of cotton cloth by machinery has made rapid progress since 1913, it has by no means displaced hand manufacture, particularly in weaving. As noted above, it is estimated that about four-fifths (200, p. 196) of the cotton goods used in China were still made on hand looms shortly before the outbreak of the war with Japan.

Although the manufacture of cotton is the outstanding example of the development of modern industry in China, it is, unfortunately, not a purely Chinese industry—about 40 per cent of the spindles and over half of the looms are foreign-owned, chiefly by the Japanese—and cannot supply very clear evidence of the ability of the Chinese to develop their own industry under the conditions that prevailed up to about the time of the attack by Japan. The fact that after 1930 the Chinese-owned cotton mills increasingly got into financial difficulty because of their low efficiency and were selling out to the Japanese at a rather rapid rate, when war necessitated their closing, was very discouraging, to say the least. The Chinese still have to prove that they are prepared to meet the competition of other industrial nations in the Orient even in this, one of the simplest processes of machine production.

Iron and steel are so essential to all modern development that a description of the effort to establish this industry in China will be highly instructive in attempting to arrive at some notion of the difficulties of industrialization in postwar China.

Bain (22, pp. 104–5) gives the annual capacity in 1920 of relatively modern blast furnaces in China as about 900,000 tons. However, in 1922 it appears that actual production was not in excess of 180,000–200,000 tons. This included the production of Manchuria as well as of China Proper. In 1928 the total production (including Manchuria) is given as about 434,000 tons, of which 244,000 tons were in Manchuria under Japanese management, 179,000 in the small native furnaces in China Proper, and only a little over 10,000 in the larger furnaces. The *China Yearbook* (73, 1936, p. 335) gives the production of pig iron in 1934 in the more modern furnaces of China Proper as only 21,000 tons, with 135,000 from the small native furnaces and about 445,000 tons in Manchuria. I cite this almost complete disappearance of iron production in the modern blast furnaces of China Proper to show the inability of the Chinese, under the conditions that prevailed between the end of World War I and the attack by Japan in 1937, to build up an iron industry.

Since 1936 the government has definitely undertaken to encourage the establishment of basic industries and the development of power, but under war conditions it has had an uphill job and has accomplished little. In describing the progress since the removal of the government to Chungking, the *China Handbook* (72, 1943, p. 443) speaks of thirty-ton blast furnaces as large and ten-ton Bessemer furnaces as though they were the largest in operation, and it gives no figures for production, merely saying that private ironworks produced about 2.3 times as much in 1941 and 5.5 times as much in 1942, as in 1940.

A recent book dealing with industry in "Free China" speaks of making 100,000 tons of pig iron in 1940 and of increasing the production several fold in the near future (151, pp. 44 and 46). Assuming that this has been done and that steel output is proceeding apace with pig iron, China's production of iron and steel is yet almost negligible and is all taking place in such small units that the cost is certain to be very high. Even for those few kinds of steel that can be made in small furnaces and mills this is the case, while most shapes for industrial use cannot be made at all except in modern large mills. It seems, therefore, that even though under present conditions of high prices and subsidies a growing iron and steel industry is being built up, it is unlikely to attain any significant size or to endure unless the basic economic obstacles to industrialization enumerated above are removed.

TRANSPORTATION

The lack of good cheap transportation is, as we have already noted, one of the great obstacles to the industrialization of China. Obviously, all the difficulties of securing capital for industry will be encountered in raising capital for railways and steamship lines. Likewise the deficiencies of Chinese management manifested in the cotton and steel mills are quite likely to crop up in managing railways, steamship lines, etc. But, because good transportation is so fundamental to the development of all modern industry, the improvement of her transport must be one of the first undertakings in postwar China.

To stress the urgency of developing better transport in China does not mean, however, that China needs to develop a network of railways comparable to those of Western Europe or the United States before she can begin her industrial expansion. The development of the automobile has rendered this unnecessary. What China needs in railways is a well-planned system of trunk lines reaching all important cities and regions, but not a network of branch lines like that in Europe. In the second place, she should plan for the more complete use of her rivers and canals and coastal transport. In the third place, she should build an elaborate system of highways as feeders to both the rail system and water transport and for local passenger and freight service. These highways should reach every small city and market town in the country.

What Japan has already done, or at least has got well started, in Manchuria might easily furnish a pattern for all of China. A relatively few thousand miles of railways (perhaps 50,000–75,000) plus a few thousand miles of canal, river, and coastal routes, and, finally, a great mileage of roads with traffic capacity adjusted to the local needs— perhaps not over 20–25 per cent of these would need to be built for heavy traffic—would provide an adequate transportation basis for China's modern industrial development for some years.

SOCIAL OBSTACLES TO INDUSTRIALIZATION

Under the conditions that have prevailed in the past the Chinese have not shown the adaptability needed to make them efficient managers and workers in modern factories. The source of China's industrial weakness is only in part in those handicaps discussed above (lack of capital, lack of a competent technical staff and skilled labor, uncertainty of the taxes and other governmental exactions to which industry may be subjected, and lack of a stable social order); it is also to be found in certain social and psychological handicaps which may be even harder to overcome than these economic obstacles.

We cannot expect too much of Chinese industry until the people have come to value more highly those qualities which make for efficiency in economic enterprise than those which gave them status in their society as now constituted. A deep loyalty to the family, making the practice of nepotism a matter of the first importance, the saving of "face," making the acknowledgment of mistakes extremely embarrassing, the maintenance of those habits and customs associated with belonging to an upper class which need not work with its hands, and the observance of all the traditions inculcated by the ethics of the great leaders of the past, may make a fine gentleman according to common consent and may even be conducive to an equanimity of spirit exciting envy among other peoples, but they are not good qualities in the manager of a business enterprise which must compete with other enterprises on the basis of efficiency.

The Chinese cannot retain all these qualities which gave them status in a pre-industrial society and at the same time succeed in their economic competition with peoples whose values revolve around the goal of economic efficiency. The Chinese lack of efficiency in modern industry is not a matter of inherent ability at all; it is merely a matter of social values which may be changed once it seems worth while to do so, albeit the change will probably come more slowly than we may think desirable.

However, we should not overlook the fact that until the Chinese can compete with other peoples in their management of factories and commercial enterprises and in the quantity and quality of the work they turn out, they can scarcely expect to make rapid progress in the development of modern industry; nor will shutting themselves within a tariff wall as high or even higher than that of Hawley-Smoot, of sad memory, insure the rapid development of home industry. It is the failure to face these facts that is responsible in large measure for the slow development of industry in China. This is not to forget that the Great Powers held China in a semicolonial status until quite recently and must bear a heavy share of the responsibility for her lack of industrial progress, but she must herself recognize that the advantages of efficient industry cannot be had without giving up many of the values highly prized by a relatively static society.

This analysis will help us to understand why all China (outside of Tientsin) had only 245 factories employing more than thirty workers in 1913 and only about eight times as many in 1930 (200, p. 188); why nearly all the iron ore she mined was sent to Japan along with the coking coal to smelt it; why foreign shipping dominated both her river traffic and her coastal trade. China's rate of progress in industrialization in the future will depend in considerable degree on how deeply the Chinese themselves desire such progress and how ready they now are to pay the price. The price may not be worth paying, but it must be paid or China will remain weak and poor and consequently more or less at the mercy of the stronger powers, politically and economically. The great plans now being made for the future (135) must be studied in the light of these difficulties.

The failure of the Chinese to build a textile industry able to compete with foreign-owned textile plants and their inability to maintain their iron and steel industry at the level of 1920—to which must be added that of their cigarette industry to compete with foreign-owned factories—are pointed out not to belittle their positive efforts or because there is reason to believe in any inherent lack of capacity in the Chinese to build efficient industry, but because these are real cases in which the Chinese have tried to develop industry and have not been able to surmount the difficulties they have encountered. It is dangerous to ignore these failures or to gloss them over. It will not conduce to world peace to assume that now China is ready to go ahead with industrialization at a rapid rate and that she will become strong enough in a decade or two to be a satisfactory foil to Japanese ambitions in the East. Nor is it likely to prove any kindness to China to assume that she can proceed to develop a modern economy without a revolution in her social, economic, and political life.

If China fails to measure up to the large expectations of her industrial growth entertained by many younger Chinese because of failure to recognize the need for making fundamental changes in her social order, it is not at all improbable that there will again arise strong pressure to put her back into the semicolonial status she has occupied almost since the beginning of her contact with the West. Any determined effort to do this would almost certainly involve us in another world war because of the scramble of the powers for "spheres of influence." Furthermore, in this third world war it is not unlikely that we would find Japan championing, far more effectively than now, *the freedom of Asia* against the West and being supported more actively by the countries she has so recently tried to dominate.

This matter of the industrial future of China is of such importance that it merits further treatment in connection with the discussion in the following chapter of her whole economic future.

Chapter XIV

CHINA: ECONOMIC FUTURE

UNDER this heading we shall consider chiefly the outlook for improvement in the level of living of the mass of the Chinese people. By "improvement" is understood more adequate food, clothing, and shelter, the gradual development of an effective health service, the expansion of opportunities for education, and the furnishing of an increasing variety of goods and services which will contribute to a healthier and less poverty-stricken life. The idea "level of living" as used here is, then, chiefly economic, and it is assumed that an improvement has been made when per capita increase in the goods and services just mentioned has taken place.

THE NEED FOR GREATER PER CAPITA PRODUCTIVITY

There is only one sure way to secure the larger meed of economic goods and services which are essential to better living in China, and that is to make man's labor more productive, although we should not ignore the fact that a more just division of product between landlord and tenant would be very beneficial to a large proportion of the peasants. Likewise the myriad other inequities of the Chinese social system if corrected would help many individuals. But in a country as poverty-stricken as China there cannot be enough of anything to insure decent living to the masses of the people until the productivity of labor is greatly increased.

We have already mentioned some of the possibilities of getting increased agricultural production in China, but this discussion was confined largely to the ways of producing a larger total product. If the Chinese are to live better, there must be a larger per capita product to divide, and this can come only if the whole system of agriculture and industry is revolutionized to make the farmer's and industrial worker's labor more productive. Farms must be increased in size (at present there is only about .43 acre of tilled land per person) and consolidated into units large enough to permit the use of improved machinery and to employ the farmer a larger portion of the year; the farmer must also have access to the credit needed to stock and operate an efficient farm unit and on terms which do not make him the virtual slave of the moneylender; research into better crops and farm practices must be established, and a system for the dissemination of its results must be organized.

As long as the Chinese peasant can scarcely produce enough to keep body and soul together, even when he owns his land, there is little hope of better living from the improvement of the distribution of his present product. He must produce more for a given amount of labor and work a longer year. The same is true also of the weaver and the spinner and the blacksmith and the other workers at nonagricultural tasks. They must have better tools and machines and a more efficient organization before they can produce much beyond the bare necessities of life.

JOBS FOR DISPLACED FARMERS

Supposing that the productivity of the agricultural worker can be increased, what, then, is to become of the farmers displaced by the increase in the size of the farm, by the use of more machinery, and by the adoption of more efficient farm practices? Obviously there are only two things they can do: they must go into some kind of industrial or commercial occupation or move onto new land. It seems highly doubtful that a people depending on a rice culture to the extent that the Chinese do can ever reduce their agricultural population to the 20 per cent that is approached in the United States and Australia and still have an abundance of food. But in the light of the studies of Buck and in view of what has actually happened in Japan, it would not appear unlikely that the proportion of the population engaged in agriculture could be reduced from 80–85 per cent to 40–45 per cent, or even somewhat lower, and yet produce enough so that every person could have a more satisfactory diet, better clothes, and a better house than at present, while the community supported a fairly efficient health service.

Such a displacement of population can, of course, take place only if a considerable part of the people no longer needed on the land can be employed in making goods for the farmers and themselves. This means a relatively high degree of industrialization as compared with what now exists. In the course of time China will become increasingly industrialized, but this change cannot come rapidly, and it is not at all certain that it will result in increasing the per capita product available anything like as much as in the West during the past century. In other words, it appears very doubtful whether more productive jobs can be found during the next few decades for all the Chinese who must have such work if agricultural improvement goes forward with fair speed.

In the first place, the agricultural revolution referred to above as essential to increased per capita productivity on the farms will be far more difficult to achieve than is commonly believed because of the very abundance of people and their high potential rate of increase. Supposing that larger farm units with better equipment could be provided almost overnight, could the gains in per capita productivity thus achieved be maintained indefinitely? From our knowledge of the processes of population growth in a country like China we have already remarked quite positively that farmers with twice the product the Chinese have been accustomed to would have lower death rates almost at once and that before long they would have about as much manpower per acre as they had before they obtained their larger farms and adopted more efficient farm practices. It might take a generation or more for the agricultural population to revert to its former labor-land ratio, but it would almost certainly revert unless some other employment, either in industry or on new land, were found for perhaps a half of the children raised by the Chinese farm family under these improved conditions. That the settlement on new land can absorb any large proportion of the children not needed on farms is also extremely unlikely, for China, as we have seen, does not have vast areas of good unused land such as were available to Europeans and their children throughout the nineteenth century.

Therefore, if China is to improve the level of living of her people, she must find a place for the surplus children of her farmers in non-agricultural tasks, particularly in manufacturing, trade, and the service jobs. But, unfortunately, even an increase in general productive efficiency, unless it comes about through settlement on new cheap land, is no guaranty of immediate and permanent improvement in the level of living. There is always the danger that most or even all of the increased per capita product both in agriculture and in industry will be taken by the landlord or employer because of the prevailing habits and customs of the community and the scarcity of new land. This danger is especially great where population is dense and most of it is living at a subsistence level.

I would repeat again that only a revolution in Chinese agriculture can make the farmer more productive, and only the provision of some other kind of work for a considerable part of his children, perhaps half or more, can keep him more productive, since there is insufficient new land under Chinese control on which to settle the children not needed at home. Under these conditions the development of nonagricultural industry must be extremely rapid to absorb the increase of population on the farms which will result from any substantial improvement in the living conditions of the peasants.

CHINA'S MALTHUSIAN DILEMMA

This race between increasing per capita productivity and population growth is the real Malthusian dilemma, and China is caught on its horns. As shown in chapter xii, China is now experiencing the high death rate consequent upon having more children born than can be provided for under the present conditions of production. Probably China can temporarily, and to a limited extent, reduce the hardships of life and hence her death rate by reorganizing her agriculture and by building up her industry; however, we should not expect too much in the near future from industry alone or from agriculture and industry combined in a country already having a dense population and where the birth rate approaches the physiological maximum. Chinese industry would have to expand at a much more rapid rate than is probable to offer any real relief to the mass of her people during the next few decades, while permanent relief can come only after the country has learned to control its birth rate. All desired improvement in manner of living can easily be nullified during the next few decades by the more rapid increase of population.

We must think of China as having a strong tendency to increase in numbers for the next several decades and discuss possibilities of improvement with this in mind.

MANCHOUKUO AND FORMOSA IN THE CHINESE ECONOMY

What China will recover in the way of industry in the former treaty ports can be a matter only of guesswork. The safest guess would seem to be that all factories and equipment of any importance have been destroyed or very badly damaged during the war and that what survives is greatly deteriorated. In Manchuria at the time of the Japanese capitulation the damage to industry apparently was not serious but that now taking place as the consequence of civil war is very great. It is possible that such Manchurian industry as survives when peace finally comes might be made immediately useful to China by striking a bargain with the Japanese management for its operation until the Chinese have acquired the know-how. The situation is practically the same as regards the transportation system.

Such a deal might provide a significant proportion of the steel needed to build her railways, to set up again the steel industry in central China, to establish other heavy industries, to assist in the development of her mines, to start her in shipbuilding, and to provide materials for many light-metal industries. But fully as important as the immediate acquirement of the goods these Manchurian industries might produce would be the acquiring of efficient management and technical services for certain types of heavy industry until such time as China could train her own managers. It will not be easy to make such a dual Chinese-Japanese management work effectively even if the factories can be saved, but after seeing how the party managers and the technical managers in Soviet factories did get a fair measure of production in spite of all handicaps, one is prepared to believe that a Chinese political manager with powers defined by his own government and a Japanese technical management answerable to him could get fair production out of any Japanese plants that may survive in Manchuria.

Such industry would provide the nucleus for a training program for managers, technicians, and skilled laborers. This would be far cheaper than sending the same number of students abroad or importing the needed managers and skilled workmen from abroad. Besides, the Japanese have already worked out many of the problems of training Chinese labor better than either the Chinese or other foreigners. Their cotton mills in China, admittedly, got more work out of the Chinese than either the Chinese or the British.

Another great gain would accrue to the Chinese from a deal whereby the Japanese management of the railways could be retained until the Chinese were prepared to take over without serious damage to either service or equipment. Even before Japan took over Manchuria there was no comparison in the efficiency of the service on the South Manchuria Railway and on the Chinese railways, as anyone who has used both will readily testify. Here again, China would acquire a great school for training workers if she could come to some understanding with the Japanese management. To acquire the Manchurian railways in operating condition would be worth so much to China that she could even afford to allow a significant interest to remain in the hands of the management. There probably is little chance that any such arrangement can be effected, but it would seem worth trying, and others of the United Nations should not discourage it.

Even assuming that Manchurian industry is destroyed and has to be entirely rebuilt, however, the relation of Manchuria to Japan in the postwar world should be somewhat different for some time from that of any other part of China. Manchuria has long depended on its exports of beans and wheat and coal and timber to Japan for the exchange to buy much of her manufactured goods. More recently her industries have sent iron and steel and aluminum and other manufactured or semimanufactured products to Japan in considerable amounts. The complete disruption of this close economic relation would be very hard on both Manchuria and Japan. It would be of great mutual advantage to China and Japan to maintain this close relation for some time while gradually shifting the balance of Manchurian trade and industry to China as she becomes able to absorb more and more of Manchurian production.

As was said above, Formosa is far more completely assimilated into Japanese economy than Manchoukuo. Japan has become heavily dependent on Formosa's rice and sugar, pineapples and bananas. It would be cruel as well as unwise to sever these ties at once, whether by the use of tariffs or as the result of strict military control of Formosa by China. The economic ties of Japan and Formosa should be loosened only as China can absorb Formosa's products and as Japan is able to find new sources of supply.

This is only economic common sense, and it would be of no greater benefit to Japan than to Formosa and China. No matter how we in this country may feel about it now, China is bound to have close economic relations with Japan in the postwar world unless Japan is driven back into an almost complete agricultural economy. We would be wise to recognize the inevitable if Japan is allowed to retain any significant amount of industry, and to encourage relations between them which will be to their mutual advantage even though such arrangements may decrease our sales to China to some slight extent. China has to live as a close neighbor of Japan; she will derive great benefit from cultivating close economic relations with Japan, and we should not fight against the inevitable simply because we hate Japan.

If China fails to recognize that Manchuria and Formosa must be allowed to retain special economic relations with Japan for sometime after they become a part of China politically, she will not only weaken them and herself economically but will stand a good chance of encouraging separatist political movements which would weaken her as a world power. Neither China nor her powerful allies must allow their hatred of Japan, or their vindictiveness, to lead them into a situation where they make her an even more bitter enemy and at the same time create divisions among the Chinese which can be exploited by Japan. This would be extremely shortsighted.

China's control of her returned possessions—Manchuria and Formosa—may well determine the future of Sino-Japanese relations for some decades and may also greatly affect China's economic future. It may even determine whether we shall have war between them again in the not distant future. For these reasons the way in which China's control of Manchuria and Formosa is exercised in the postwar period cannot be a matter of indifference to us.

THE NEED FOR LOANS AND THE LIMITATIONS THEY IMPOSE

No matter what China may be able to salvage from Japan's industrial and transportation works in Manchuria and Formosa, and no matter what reparations in the form of industrial equipment she may get from Japan, she will still be in great need of equipment and loans from abroad and of technical assistance in her postwar industrialization. Now that Europeans have given up their special privileges in China, it is a good time for the great nations of the world to establish a new policy in making loans to all industrially backward peoples. If all such loans were to be made through and under the supervision of the Economic and Social Commission of the United Nations Organization, it would do away with the scramble of the powers for concessions and spheres of influence which has been so closely associated with the making of foreign loans in the past. Once foreign loans cease to be used to secure special political and economic privileges for the loaning country, China, or any other country, can accept them without the constant dread of having given important hostages to an enemy.

The first loans to China should probably be for the purpose of improving her transportation. Her basic transportation needs will require some billions of dollars, much of which will have to be borrowed if these needs are to be met within the next two decades. Until China has reasonably good transport facilities, it is not certain that her central government will be able to put down local "war lords" and to unite the nation. In other words a reasonably adequate system of transport by rail, water, highway, and air is essential strategically, not only vis-à-vis foreign enemies but for the unification and industrialization of China.

Heavy industry as well as transportation will necessitate large foreign borrowing, and before China begins to borrow certain very fundamental decisions should be made—decisions which will determine whether China is to move in the direction of full national independence or remain in a semicolonial condition. As said above, loans to China by private interests representing a single power should not be allowed in the future. But even under United Nations' control loans might come from either private or public funds and might be made either to the Chinese government or to private interests, so they might be used to determine the future form of China's economy: whether it will be primarily a state economy or a private economy.

At the present time it is difficult to see how private interests in China can command the confidence of lenders to a degree likely to insure the amounts of capital needed for large enterprises. For the reasons already noted regarding the difficulties of industrialization the Chinese are not likely to be in position to give adequate security for large loans in their private capacity and the government is not likely to allow them to contract loans if they involve the danger of foreign political control. It seems probable, therefore, that the Chinese government will have to be the chief, if not the sole, borrower, or will have to become the guarantor of all loans made to private interests. Thus China may well be compelled by force of circumstances and probably much against the wishes of both the Chinese leaders and the foreign lenders to become the owner of, and for the time being at least the final authority over, most of her mines, heavy industry, railways, steamship lines, and other large-scale enterprises.

This does not mean that the enterprises which the government establishes must always remain state enterprises or that the government need enter into all types of industry. But if the need to industrialize rapidly is urgent because the political independence of the country is felt to be at stake, then state capitalism may grow rapidly once a strong central government is well established. The Kuomintang leaders would clearly prefer to follow a laissez faire policy in which the state assumed few economic responsibilities—but there may not be time.

Obviously, China will also have urgent need to increase her foreign trade to enable her to buy the raw materials, the manufactured goods and machinery, and to hire the foreign experts she will need for developing industry and building a transport system. Her problem of foreign trade is not essentially different from that of all other countries, except that she possibly has less to trade of the goods which are in wide demand elsewhere than some of the others. She has only a few hand-manufactured goods and small amounts of raw materials like tungsten and antimony, of which the amounts used in the world are quite small, to trade for iron, machinery, etc. Her chief agricultural exports—silk, tea, cotton, tung oil—are not great enough to pay even the debt service on steel mills, railroad equipment, automobiles, textile machinery, and the other essential capital goods she will need. Besides, any increased surplus of agricultural products used for foreign trade will involve great additional hardships on the mass of the people unless per capita production can be increased at the same time.

Since the latter can be accomplished only by a strong government acting energetically in the common interest, it raises again the question of the role of the government in the future development of China. Will it assume economic as well as political leadership, or will it stand aloof from economic matters after the approved pattern in the West and be content with a slow development of industry?

In order to make consideration of this topic as realistic as possible, certain definite assumptions will be made. They are (a) that political unity and stability will be achieved shortly; (b) that the transportation system will be vigorously expanded by this government; (c) that industrialization will go forward rapidly, perhaps as rapidly as in Japan after 1905, probably by the government guaranty of foreign loans; (d) that agriculture will be extended and improved at a fairly rapid pace through active governmental assistance; and (e) that all these advances will continue for the next forty to fifty years. What will then be the living conditions in China? Of course, this question cannot be answered with assurance, but some enlightening considerations can be adduced.

The first measurable effect on population of such a development as assumed here will be an improvement in general health with a marked lowering of the death rate. The basis for this statement is what has happened in most of the West, in Japan, in India, and in other parts of South and East Asia (see chaps. vi, xv, xvii, and xviii). An increase of population of 10 per cent in each decade would be a very conservative estimate of the increase likely to follow such improvements in living; it is more likely to reach 15 per cent. Just to make easy figuring we will use 400 million as the population of the Chinese Empire, including Manchoukuo.

Assuming a 10 per cent increase in each decade, a population of 400 million in 1940 would become about 585 million in 1980. At a rate of increase of 15 per cent in a decade (which is approximately that of India for the years 1931–41 and less than the rate of the Philippines), China would have approximately 700 million by 1980. Fantastic! Perhaps, but this growth is taking place elsewhere in Asia, and a small measure of the favorable conditions assumed above are just the conditions which are bringing it about.

I have said "favorable conditions assumed," but most Chinese who talk about these matters would say that I have underestimated their resources and have made too much of both the economic and the psychological difficulties in the way of agricultural and industrial development. If this is so, then the probable increase in population is also underrated, because if there is faster improvement in the level of living than assumed, there will also be a greater drop in the death rate. Let us not forget that the Japanese figures for the Chinese in Formosa show a rate of increase not of 10 per cent in a decade, nor even of 15 per cent, but of about *25 per cent*, and that as yet there is no sign of any decrease in the birth rate, while the death rate is still falling.

Can the increase in per capita productivity go on fast enough during the next forty to fifty years to care for such an increase in numbers at a substantially higher level of living? The answer must be "No"! Therefore, it will not be any kindness to help China improve her agriculture and develop her industry merely to find that by the end of the century she has twice her present population existing at the level of living now prevailing. From the standpoint both of the welfare of the Chinese people and of our own position in the future when China has a greatly increased population and enough industry to make her a formidable military power, help to China in modernizing her economy *should be made contingent on the willingness of the Chinese leaders to show their people the need for voluntary control of population growth.*

There is not room in the world for the numbers that will naturally come if we teach all the "backward" industrial peoples how to reduce their death rates but do not at the same time show them the necessity of reducing their birth rates and how this can be done. Even with the most earnest efforts to teach these peoples how to control births they will grow rapidly once modern sanitation supported by a more productive industry and agriculture helps them to reduce their death rates. This is inevitable. Consequently, we must consider not only all possible means which can be made available for the care of this inevitable increase—the improvement of agriculture, the expansion of industry and emigration—but also the means of acquainting them with the control of their birth rates.

Chapter XV

INDIA: POPULATION AND AGRICULTURE

STRICTLY speaking, India is not a part of the Pacific Region with which we are chiefly concerned here, but in many ways it is, of course, very closely related to South and East Asia. In addition, India is such an excellent example of some of the general principles of population growth on which the thesis of this book rests that it would be a serious omission not to support these principles directly and concretely by Indian data.

India[1] lies between 8° and 37° north latitude, and, although the greater part, in area, lies north of the Tropic of Cancer, it can very properly be thought of as a tropical country. The total area of India (not including Burma, for which see chap. xviii) is a little over one-half that of the United States and only a little greater than China Proper. India, like China, depends largely on monsoon rains which fall chiefly from June to September, inclusive. Coming with the southwest winds from the Arabian Sea and with the south winds from the Bay of Bengal, the east and west coats of the peninsula get a very heavy rainfall as does also the great Ganges Plain. The only regions in India which ordinarily do not get much rain during the southwest monsoon are parts of the peninsular plateau and northwestern India.

Since India is much less mountainous than China, it has a much larger proportion of tillable land within the area of rainfall sufficient to support agriculture. It also appears to have a larger area which can be irrigated by the water flowing from the high mountains lying to the north. Since a larger part of India than of China is tropical, the winter dry season does not prevent the growth of crops to the same extent, so second crops on the same land are a more important source of food in India than in China. But it should be noted that India, like China, is so dependent on the monsoon rains that any failure has most serious effects—just how serious will be brought out in the discussion of population growth and of Indian agriculture.

[1] From our standpoint there will be no need to distinguish with care between British territory (860,000 square miles) and native states (711,000 square miles) or to emphasize the racial and religious differences in the population of the different parts of India. This is unnecessary because no attempt will be made to survey those problems which do not arise out of the nature of population growth and the general character of Indian economy.

THE GROWTH OF INDIA'S POPULATION

The first census of India was taken in 1872, and the population enumerated at that time was a little over 203 million. The territory since included in the censuses and the improvement in methods lead to the conclusion that the real population of the territory now called India was at that time actually about 256 million (Table 19), or approximately 25 per cent greater than that then enumerated. Starting with this number as the real population of India in 1872, the data in columns 5 and 6 give the real growth and rate of growth since that time.[2]

TABLE 19

POPULATION GROWTH OF INDIA (EXCLUDING BURMA), 1872–1941

(In Thousands)

| YEAR | CENSUS POPULA- TION (1) | INTERCENSAL INCREASE | | | | | POPULA- TION (USING REAL INCREASE) (7) |
| | | Total (2) | Inclu- sion of New Terri- tory (3) | Improve- ment of Method (4) | Real Increase | | |
					Num- ber (5)	Per Cent (6)	
1941.............	388,988	50,817	....	....	50,817	15.0	388,988
1931.............	338,171	32,441	....	....	32,441	10.6	338,171
1921.............	305,730	2,689	....	....	2,689	0.9	305,730
1911.............	303,041	19,171	1,740	....	17,431	6.1	303,041
1901.............	283,870	4,277	1,434	200	2,643	0.9	285,610
1891.............	279,593	29,433	2,650	3,100	23,683	9.5	282,967
1881.............	250,160	46,745	33,139	10,700	2,906	1.4	259,284
1872.............	203,415	....	....	....	....	......	256,378

It may be said in passing that India has had a strong and stable government during all this time and that this experienced administration should have been able to take reasonably accurate censuses after experience with two or three, so there is no reason to doubt the substantial accuracy of the count from 1891 onward and the corrections of earlier counts by the census authorities.

The most striking feature of the rates of increase (col. 6) during this entire period is that until 1921–41 there have never been two successive decades in which the rate of growth was even approximately the same. In the first six census periods the growth was alternately low and moderately high, but in the seventh period, 1931–41, it moved to a new

[2] Although Burma was administered as a part of India until 1937, it is not included in this discussion at any point.

high level (15 per cent) following a fairly high level (10 per cent). This pattern is striking because it is so different from that of most of the West after census-taking began. There the rate of increase was fairly consistent decade after decade, although, as shown above (chap. i), there were some fairly large and rapid variations in certain European countries down to the middle of the nineteenth century.

LIMITING FACTORS IN INDIA'S POPULATION GROWTH

The reasons for these rather violent fluctuations since 1872, from 0.9 per cent in 1911–21 to almost seventeen times that rate in 1931–41, are not difficult to find. With the information at our disposal now, we can say with assurance that shortage of food and a heavier than usual incidence of disease will account for the low rates of increase, while just the opposite conditions—good crops and a lower incidence of disease—explain the higher increases.

It is quite generally recognized that the great famine of 1878 killed many millions directly and caused widespread epidemics, wiping out the increase in numbers that would otherwise have occurred during this decade. No one can read some of the descriptions of this famine without being greatly impressed with the way in which severe and widespread famine not only leads to actual starvation but breaks down the very structure of community life and spreads disease over great areas. Furthermore, the excess of deaths from disease is by no means confined to the famine area. The mass migration of people in search of food spreads it to areas where otherwise there would have been no more than a normal amount.

Another factor of very great importance in determining the effect of any famine on population growth is the availability of transportation to move food into the stricken area, because it seldom happens that there is a starvation dearth over all of any large region like India. India had no railroads before 1853 and by 1870 had only 4,255 miles of lines, and the mileage was growing slowly. Thus while she had begun to remove the transportation obstacles to feeding the stricken population of inland areas, they were still formidable in 1878. As a matter of fact, the famine of 1878–79 gave great impetus to railroad-building in India.

In the decade 1881–91 India suffered no great catastrophe, and the population grew by 9.1 per cent. But in the following decade famine struck again, and the rate of growth was only 0.9 per cent. By this time the railroad system had further expanded, but even so it was impossible to prevent an appalling loss of life because of the widespread failure of crops and the ensuing disease. Many millions of people starved, while many more millions were weakened by hunger and became an easy prey to epidemic diseases. In the decade 1901–11 the population growth rose to 6.1 per cent, about two-thirds of what it had been in the "good" decade 1881–91. During this decade northern and western India suffered heavily from the plague, but the rest of the country, containing about two-thirds of the population, seems to have experienced no unusual check to growth.

It is in the decade 1911–21 that we find the best-known example of the effect of disease on population growth in a country in which health agencies are few and are still relatively ineffective. While we in the West thought of the influenza epidemic (1918–19) as an awful scourge, it wrought almost no devastation here compared with its ravages in India. In the United States, for example, the excess of deaths due to influenza amounted to about 500,000. With the same incidence India should have had only about 1.5 million deaths. The lowest figure ever given is about 8.5 million, or five to six times the rate in the United States (207, I, Part I, 13–14). But this figure is known to be highly deficient in two respects: it includes only a little over three-fourths of the population of India and "there is a difference of nearly 4 millions between the census figures [1921] and the deduced population, a considerable proportion of which must be due to omissions of influenza deaths" (207, I, Part I, 13–18). When these deficiencies in reporting influenza deaths are taken into account, we must assume that a minimum of 15 million persons died of this disease in India in 1918 and 1919, and it is quite possible that the number was several million more.

The terrific ravages of influenza during this decade are further shown by a comparison of India's population growth in this decade with that of the preceding and succeeding decades. In 1901–11 the growth amounted to 17.4 million, although there was, as already noted, a severe epidemic of plague in the north and the west. In the decade 1921–31, when there were no unusual epidemics or severe crop shortages, the growth was 32.5 million. The average growth for these two decades was about 25.0 million. This would seem a reasonable growth to have expected in the absence of famines and epidemics of unusual severity in the decade 1911–21, although it would indicate less favorable conditions in these respects than the census estimate indicated prior to late 1918. It makes allowance for a moderate amount of plague and cholera and for some mild crop shortages and yet is almost nine times the actual increase—2.7 million.

These effects of the influenza epidemic of 1918–19 are not outlined with the intent of fixing precisely the death toll but rather to show how epidemics have quite recently affected the growth of population in a country like India. We are not justified in assuming that such a visitation will never again occur there, although the steady, if slow, progress of health work renders this less and less likely.

The reader will not have failed to note that in the population growth of India the death rates are the decisive factor. When crops are good and epidemics are confined to the usual local and almost annual epidemics of typhoid, cholera, dysentery, smallpox, and malaria, then population grows with moderate rapidity, for the death rate falls well below the birth rate. On the other hand, famine and unusual epidemics reduce population growth in direct proportion to their severity and extent chiefly because they raise the death rate, although they also tend to reduce the birth rate in due course.

The effects of epidemics and famine on Indian population growth are now less direct and severe than in many other lands because India has a fairly adequate railway system supplemented by a moderately good highway system, and because she also has a strong government which can organize famine relief and maintain a fair health service. But although they appear to be of diminishing importance, they cannot be dismissed as a factor in India's future. Famine has struck several times in recent years, and, in fact, some part of India seems to be always on the border of a famine. This is not particularly surprising when we look at the population increase in the twenty years 1921–41— about 83 million, or almost two-thirds as much as the total population of the United States.

BIRTH AND DEATH RATES

Unfortunately, we do not have accurate data for either birth rates or death rates, although both are presumably registered in about three-fourths of India. There are still such large omissions that we must use them cautiously. When an attempt is made to calculate the population growth during a decade by subtracting deaths from births, the result is not accurate. The provinces of British India which had vital registration in 1921 had a census population of 230 million. In 1931 they had a population of 253 million, a gain of a little over 23.1 million, or just in excess of 10 per cent; but when vital statistics—births minus deaths—were used to calculate the decennial increase, it amounted to only 19.2 million.

There was some migration during this decade, but the migration gain in one province is believed to cancel the loss in another, so migration may be neglected without significantly affecting the results. Leaving migration out of account, it would be necessary to add 3.9 million births, or 4.9 per cent, to the 80,246,000 recorded births during the decade to raise the increase to that actually taking place according to the census. This assumes the essential accuracy of recorded deaths and makes no allowance for deaths among the additional births just mentioned. Thus there can be no reasonable doubt that over 5 per cent more births than deaths must have been missed in registration. Five or 6 per cent may be considered a measure of the relatively greater nonregistration of births than of deaths at this time, but this does not add much to our knowledge of actual birth and death rates if there are also large omissions in the registration of deaths.

Many estimates and calculations have been made in the effort to arrive at a reliable estimate of the deficiencies in registration, but all of them with which I am familiar involve assumptions which still leave them in the realm of estimates. Most of them are, nevertheless, an improvement on the recorded rates. Using the 1911 census, Mr. Acland estimated that the recorded births were deficient by 7–8 per 1,000 and deaths by somewhat less. The average birth rate according to this estimate was 43–44 and the death rate was 39–40. If the birth rate for 1901–11 given in Table 20 is increased by 8, it becomes 46, and if the death rate is increased by 7, it rises to 41. But this difference is not quite enough to account for the growth of the population between 1901 and 1911, which was 6.1 per cent. I would be disposed to believe that the birth rate should be raised even more to secure the proper difference—to 47, let us say. This opinion is based chiefly on later studies which point to the likelihood that deficiencies of registration are even greater (207, I, Part I, 15) and on the opinions of Indian students. Mr. Chand holds that deficiencies in the registration of births amount to about one-third of those recorded and of deaths to about 30 per cent of those recorded (60, p. 98). If these rates of deficiency are applied to the recorded rates since 1911, the columns marked "Estimated" (Table 20) are secured, and the high rates thus obtained are not improbable in a country like India.

It is true that in two out of the four decades they give natural increases which are so far out of line with the census results (see Table 19) that they cannot be accepted. Thus, while the rate of population increase was 0.9 per cent in the decade 1911–21, the natural increase thus arrived at would give over six times this increase. Since this was the decade when influenza killed such a huge number and registration was badly disrupted, we can assume that the registration of deaths was unusually deficient during the latter part of this decade.

In the next decade, 1921–31, the estimated natural increase is also too high. Here, too, the most reasonable assumption in my opinion is that the deficiency in the recorded death rate is greater than estimated,

TABLE 20*

BIRTH AND DEATH RATE OF INDIA PER MILLE SINCE 1885

YEAR	BIRTH RATE		DEATH RATE		NATURAL INCREASE	
	Recorded	Estimated †	Recorded	Estimated †	Recorded	Estimated
1931–35.......	35	46.7	24	31.2	11	15.5
1921–31.......	35	46.7	26	33.8	9	12.9
1911–21.......	37	49.3	34	44.2	3	5.1
1901–11.......	38	50.7	34	44.2	4	6.5
1890–01.......	34	....	31	....	....	....
1885–90.......	36	....	26	....	....	....

* Source: 60, p. 99. Permission granted by George Allen & Unwin.

† Recorded birth rate raised by 33 per cent and death rate by 30 per cent (90, p. 98).

for I can find no evidence anywhere of a downward trend in the birth rate. The variations in the birth rate are only such as might readily occur from year to year in any population living close to subsistence level as in India. In the decade just passed, 1931–41, the estimated rates give only a little higher rate of natural increase than actually took place (15 per cent). Again I would emphasize that we do not *know* birth rates and death rates in India, but we do know that the recorded rates are highly deficient both from numerous small sample investigations (207, I, Part I, 14, and 313, pp. 50–52) and from the studies of actuaries on the age composition of the population, and we do know the rate of population growth with reasonable accuracy.

Hence we are justified in concluding (*a*) that the birth rate in India is somewhere between 45 and 50; (*b*) that the birth rate shows no definite downward trend, the variations from year to year being quite within what may be considered *normal* for such a high birth rate; and (c) that the death rate is still very high but does show a definite downward trend and during this past decade probably reached a new low level of between 30 and 35 per 1,000. Such conclusions may appear undesirably vague, but they must remain so for the present—and they are just as valuable, in trying to look ahead to India's future population growth, which is of prime interest to our discussion here, as if they were more precise.[3]

INDIA'S FUTURE GROWTH

As a result of investigating India's population growth since census-taking began and interpreting it in the light of our knowledge of population growth elsewhere, we can arrive at some useful conclusions regarding India's probable future growth. This seems likely to be determined for some time to come, as it has been in the past, by the incidence of the forces governing the death rates—disease and hunger and possibly war—since it is highly probable that the birth rate will show no significant downward trend for several decades. This is not to say that India's birth rate will not decline in the course of time. It probably will follow much the same course manifested in the West during the nineteenth century, particularly during the latter half, and in Japan during the past few years, but the exact length of time needed by India to pass through the different stages of growth described in chapters i and ii cannot be foretold. Certainly most Indian writers on population would be surprised if such a change took place in appreciably less than four or five decades, as would I.

Indeed, there are some changes in Indian customs which might result from industrialization that would temporarily raise the birth rate. The relaxation of the rather strict taboo upon the remarriage of widows might well increase the proportion of married women in the population who are still young enough to contribute significantly to the birth rate, since there is always a large surplus of males in India. In 1931 there were almost three million widows in India over fifteen and under thirty years of age, and they constituted over 6 per cent of all women of these ages. The remarriage of an increasing proportion of these might easily offset for two or three decades a slow decline in the number of births per 1,000 married women. The migration of some

[3] Dr. Kingsley Davis, in "Demographic Fact and Policy in India" (*Milbank Memorial Fund Quarterly*), gives greater precision to India's birth rates and death rates than I have felt justified in doing. The rates he has calculated, however, in no way affect the general conclusions expressed above regarding the size or the trend of these rates in India (99).

millions of young people from the agricultural villages to the cities is almost certain to have a profound effect on such customs, but it will almost as certainly and as quickly weaken the religious taboos which might retard the spread of contraception. Thus, although there is no good reason why the reproductive behavior of the Indians should be essentially different from that of other peoples who have moved into cities and gone into industrial work, I believe that it will be several decades before contraception effectively reduces the birth rate. In the meantime it will continue to be the level of the death rate which will actually determine population growth.

We cannot, however, be even moderately certain that the relatively low death rate of the past decade will prevail for another ten years. India's health service is very feeble compared with that in Japan, in Europe, and in North America. She has a comparatively small agricultural surplus above her annual needs, and the extension of her tilled area, particularly her irrigated area, will not be so easy in the future as it has been in the past. Finally, it is extremely doubtful whether industrialization can proceed at a pace which will absorb any significant proportion of the almost sixty-million increase she will have between 1941 and 1951 if she continues to grow as during the past decade.

Because of these uncertainties all one can do is to say that if India increases in each of the next four decades as in the past decade (15 per cent), she will have a population of 680 million in 1981. This is not a prediction but a probability; how probable depends upon the difficulties India will encounter in extending her agricultural area and in building new industries to provide for feeding and clothing such an increase even at the present low standards. Such a rate of increase for several decades has been common in the West during the last hundred and fifty years, and Japan has had a rate of 11–14 per cent most of the time since 1880. A natural increase of 15 per cent in a decade is so common that it is safe to say that it will be the pressure of India's population on its food supply and her ability to control disease which will determine her growth during the next four or five decades. Changes in her birth rate will be of very minor significance during this time.

INDIA'S AGRICULTURE

As compared with China, there is a great deal of information about India's agriculture, although from the standpoint of exact data about tillable land, acreage, and production of crops, this information is still highly deficient. In the first place, there is often no clear distinction made between data for British India and for the Native States. In the second place, for some crops only data for British India are given, while for others data for both areas are given, and for still others the data are for British India and a part only of the Native States. The result is that there is much confusion and some contradiction in the data not only from different sources but even from the same source in different years. We can make no effort to straighten out this confusion, but we will use the most reliable data that can be found. Since 1937 the situation as regards comparison with past years has been further complicated by the separation of Burma, containing approximately 150 million acres, from British India. In the discussion here, as in that of population, Burma is not included with India.

India is overwhelmingly an agricultural country. In 1931, 89 per cent of the population lived in small villages and was classed as rural (208, I, Part I, 60). In 1941 this proportion had only fallen to 87 per cent (208a, I, 57 and 72). In 1931 the proportion of the population supported by agriculture was approximately 80 per cent, while 71 per cent of the workers were engaged directly in agriculture (208, I, Part I, 266; and 130, 1943, p. 19). There had been no significant change in the proportion of agriculturists between 1921 and 1931. Whether there was such a change between 1931 and 1941 cannot be told at this time.

It is apparent from these facts that any appreciable improvement in the living conditions of Indians in the near future must come in large part from the increased productivity of agriculture. Until there is such an increase in productivity, there can be little increase in the part of the population engaged in nonagricultural tasks, since the market for such goods must come largely from the increased purchasing power of the agricultural population. In 1931 not quite 10 per cent of all workers were reported as engaged in industry, which is a little less than that in 1921 (10.7 per cent). This decline between 1921 and 1931 may be real or it may be due to the depression in the latter years, but clearly any increase during the decade could not have been large.

In any event, no one will dispute the statement that the welfare of the people of India in the immediate future as in the recent past depends primarily on what happens in agriculture. If per capita agricultural productivity increases, Indian life will be somewhat improved; otherwise improvement will be so slow as to be almost inappreciable.

In the more distant future, after a decade or two, the development of industry may pick up speed and may exert a more obvious influence on the course of life (see chap. xvi).

THE YIELD OF THE LAND

In India, as in all the warmer parts of Asia, the chief crop is rice. It occupies about 70–75 million acres, about one-fifth to one-fourth of the total crop area. The other chief crops are: wheat, about 35 million acres; the millets and sorghums, about 40–45 million acres; pulses (legumes), about 40–45 million acres; other food grains (barley, corn, etc.), about 40 million acres; cotton, about 24 million acres; oilseeds and groundnuts, 20–25 million acres; jute, about 2 million acres; sugar cane, about 3.5 million acres; with tea, tobacco, fruit, and a variety of lesser crops to make a total crop area of about 280–300 million acres, of which all but 45–50 million acres are food crops. These 45–50 million acres may be classed as industrial crops, chiefly fibers (cotton, jute, and hemp) and oilseeds (sesame, rape, linseed, groundnuts, etc.).

In any given year one-fifth to one-sixth as much land lies fallow as is put in crops, and, of the total tilled land, about 50 million acres are irrigated (204, 1934–35, p. 80).

When one turns to an examination of agricultural production, the most striking fact is the low acreage yield of rice as compared with China and Japan, particularly Japan, and the relatively low yields of other crops (wheat, barley, corn, sugar cane) as compared with many large growers of these crops (see Table 21).

Clearly there is room for much improvement in the yields of most of India's important crops. If Indian agriculture were extensive and highly mechanized like that of the United States, Canada, and Australia, these low acreage yields of cereals would not be a serious handicap to a high level of living, but this is not the case. India's agriculture is still largely a hand agriculture like that of China, although there is one pair of bullocks to about each 10 acres of tilled land (331, I, 139). Moreover, on farms averaging only 4.5 acres for each owner and tenant cultivator and only 2.9 acres for each "agriculturist," there is little chance to "mechanize" agriculture (208, I, Part I, 288–89). The most that can be hoped for along this line is the provision of somewhat better plows and cultivators for use with oxen and better hoes and sickles, etc., for hand tillage.

More co-operation within the village might also make possible the use of modern harvesting machinery, but better machinery of any kind which means the use of less labor for a given amount of product will be of little benefit to the Indian people as a mass unless new land can be brought into cultivation fast enough to provide farms for the laborers thus displaced or unless nonagricultural industries can expand their employment fast enough to provide them with jobs. This latter

TABLE 21*

CROP YIELDS IN INDIA AND OTHER COUNTRIES, 1938–41

(Pounds per Acre)

CROP AND COUNTRY	1940–41	1939–40	1938–39	AVERAGE	
				Years	Amount
Rough rice:					
British India†	1,017	1,168	1,098	1938–41	1,094
Burma	1,423	1,305	1,437	1938–41	1,388
Korea	....	1,940	2,428	1938–40	2,184
Netherlands Indies‡	....	1,509	1,365	1938–40	1,437
Indo-China	....	....	1,059	1938–39	1,059
Japan	3,204	3,608	3,415	1938–41	3,409
China	....	....	....	1921–25	2,283
Wheat:					
British India	710	630	676	1938–41	672
Japan	1,923	2,010	1,528	1938–41	1,820
United States	911	843	800	1938–41	851
Netherlands	....	2,997	3,071	1938–40	3,034
United Kingdom	....	2,096	2,283	1938–40	2,190
China	....	....	....	1921–25	863
Barley:					
British India§	....	....	751	1938–39	751
Japan	2,012	2,087	1,628	1938–41	1,909
United States	1,111	1,043	1,155	1938–41	1,103
China	....	....	....	1921–25	1,004

* Source: 286 except for China, where data are taken from 46, p. 204. Quintals per hectare converted to pounds per acre by multiplying by 89.215.

† Not including several Native States.

‡ Java and Madura.

§ Excluding Native States.

point will not be discussed here (see chap. xvi), but it may be said that for the immediate future the expansion of machine industry seems likely to displace far more hand artisans (weavers, potters, black-smiths, brass workers, etc.) than it can employ in its new works. There are many Indians, and others, who believe that this is already taking place.

FUTURE POSSIBILITIES

With regard to the opportunity to settle on new land, not a great deal seems to be known. Sir Bryce Burt makes the statement: "Of the remaining area [the area not now in crops] we have 170 million acres classed as culturable waste but much of this has never been under cultivation and its agricultural value is highly problematical" (331, I, 126). This is not the total of tillable land not now in use, because it does not include estimates for a considerable part of the Native States, perhaps as much as 45–50 per cent, for which there is no survey; but it does include Burma, which has about one-fourth the area of the Native States—200 million acres. All in all, the amount of "culturable waste" in the whole of India might be 200–250 million acres. Since about 340–350 million acres are now under tillage (including fallow), this would add somewhere from 60 to 70 per cent to the tilled area. It is reasonably certain, however, that this new land is mostly of inferior quality and that much of it would need irrigation to insure regular production. The slow extension of the agricultural area in the last two decades is regarded by many people as proof of the difficulty of making a living on these new lands.

Thus while the area of tilled land can be considerably extended, the new land cannot be expected to yield even the present small crops. It will probably be more valuable for pasture than for crops, but even its use in this way would constitute an important addition to India's food supply for that part of the population that will eat meat and also to the animal power on farms, for it would increase the feed supply. Where this new land can be irrigated, it would be of great value, but I have not been able to find any statement of how much of it might be irrigated. The inference is that no appreciable portion can be flooded for rice. Therefore, we must conclude that this "culturable waste" is not expected to make anything like a proportional contribution to Indian agricultural production.

On the other hand, there is a large body of opinion to the effect that better tillage, increase in the use of fertilizer, the extension of seeding with better and more disease-resistant varieties of the chief crops, and the increase in the proportion of irrigated land, although they have already increased the efficiency of agricultural labor appreciably, have only begun to operate. This point of view is well summed up by Mukerjee in the following quotation:

"The only remedy for this desperate situation [the crowding of population on food supply] will be to increase the yield from the land already under cultivation. Much has already been done in this direction with the help of canal irrigation. . . . . The yields also have been increased enormously with the introduction of improved seed by the Agricultural Department. Much, however, remains to be done and it is safe to say that, with better seed and more efficient cultivation, the yield from crops in India could be increased by from 30 to 50 per cent according to the locality. Thus as the pressure of the population on the land increases, the value of these great irrigation works constructed in the past will become more and more apparent" (331, I, 167).

The data on crop yields given above certainly indicate that there is much room for improvement in Indian agriculture. There seems to be almost universal agreement by writers that this is so, but it also seems to be agreed that this improvement will be slow and that it will almost certainly require several decades to achieve large results. One cannot help asking, therefore, whether even the great agricultural advances which are possible can keep the food supply ahead of the needs of the population when it increases by 10–15 per cent in a decade as it has since 1921. Before discussing this point, it will be well to mention briefly the place of livestock in Indian agriculture.

India, unlike most other Asiatic countries, has a great number of cattle and sheep, perhaps as many as 275–300 million head altogether. Of these, cattle and buffaloes account for about 200 million, and sheep and goats for most of the remainder. Nearly all Indian livestock is of distinctly inferior quality. As work animals most of the bullocks and buffaloes are too small and too weak to make a good job of tillage possible. The unconscious policy of the Indian cultivator seems to have been to produce as many cattle as possible regardless of the feed available and of the deterioriation in size and stamina due to prolonged inbreeding.

As milk producers the cows are equally poor. The quantity of milk produced is very small for the same reasons that the draft animals are small and weak—lack of feed and poor breeding. Since for religious reasons the Hindus do not eat beef, these cattle add very little (milk) directly to the food supply of two-thirds to three-fourths of the people. India is the world's largest producer of inferior hides and skins, but she would be better off with a much smaller livestock population if at the same time the quality of the animals both for draft and for milk could be improved. Of course, any change in religious beliefs which would sanction the eating of beef would add considerably to the food supply, but such a change is hardly to be anticipated within the foreseeable future.

INDIA'S LEVEL OF LIVING

There is a great deal of discussion in India as to whether the changes that have taken place in Indian agriculture have done anything to improve the level of living of the mass of the people, and whether anything is to be expected from further improvements along these lines. These arguments frequently rely on more or less dubious statistical materials to show that there has been or has not been any significant increase either in the food available or in the per capita income and, hence, in the level of living of the people. After reading many of these arguments, I have been forced to conclude that no case has been proved, since the data are so incomplete and so lacking in consistency that they do not clearly support either view. On the whole, the evidence *tends* to support the view that there has been some improvement in the level of living for a not insignificant portion of the people.

The chief reasons for the belief that there has been some improvement are not found in the statistics of income and production but in those of population growth and in certain nonstatistical evidences of increased welfare. The best proof that a somewhat better level of living has prevailed for some time past is the steady and fairly rapid increase of population since 1921. Why has there been no serious famine in recent years, with the possible exception of that in 1943–44? Why has there been no virulent outbreak of plague or cholera or other disease since 1919? Why has the death rate remained at a level well below what it was before that time? There must be reasons for these improvements, and they are most likely to be found in the better level of living of a significant part of the population and in the increasing effectiveness of health services. The indisputable fact is that the means were being found somewhere to spend more for health and agricultural research and new irrigation and the better transportation needed to abolish local food shortages and to extend market areas. These undertakings are the best proof available that the margin between starvation and production is a little wider than it was formerly and that, even though the level of living is almost incredibly low, it is not quite as low, on the average, as it was.

The great amount of discussion of India's economic problems by Indians also indicates that a fairly large and rapidly growing body of

Indians have already tasted the benefits derived from a more efficient economy and better health conditions and believe that these benefits can be greatly increased and extended if proper political and economic measures are taken. My own opinion is that the outcry against the terrible poverty of the country arises from the increased awareness of the possibilities of improvement due to having already had a little improvement and not from the actual deterioration of economic conditions. It is always thus when a people or class has for generations or even for centuries remained at a very low level of living with almost no change in customs or conditions of life. Once the level of living shows a little improvement, from whatever source or motive it may come, the leaders of the people soon see new vistas ahead and begin to demand participation in better living for themselves and for their followers.

To me, therefore, the awakening of India to the opportunities for improvement and the willingness of a growing class to fight for them are the best proofs that many of her people have already enjoyed some small measure of better living. At least their leaders assume the masses will understand what is meant when they are told how they are being abused by foreign masters and local Shylocks. The ferment created by a small measure of better living has begun to work, and conditions which were accepted with almost complete passivity a few decades ago are no longer acceptable.

THE RACE BETWEEN AGRICULTURAL PRODUCTION AND POPULATION

When we try to peer into the future to discern how improvement of agriculture is likely to affect the level of living during the next few decades, it is hard to see how the improvements already noted as under way can be expected to raise the general level of living more than a little. Admittedly there is but little surplus food produced at the present time even in good years; in years not so good, as in 1943, there is famine in the stricken areas. Besides, in recent years India has become an importer of food, particularly of rice from Burma, which she pays for largely by exports of cotton, jute, and oilseeds or from oil pressed from these seeds.

If we accept the more optimistic guesses that India can increase her tilled area by about 60 per cent, we must still make reservations regarding the fertility of this new land. It is hardly likely that it will yield more than one-half to two-thirds as much as the land now in tillage. Thus a guess regarding the increase in the food supply to be expected from this source would be one-fifth to one-fourth.

Again, if we are optimistic and assume that the improvements in agriculture will add 50 per cent to yields, it would appear that India might increase her food supply by 75–80 per cent. This is probably too generous an estimate, but, accepting it for the moment, what does it promise for India's future? The increase in food production must go ahead at an accelerated pace, at 20–25 per cent or even more each decade, if India is to have a rising level of living and is to continue her present rate of population growth—15 per cent. Can such agricultural improvement reasonably be expected to take place regularly for the four or five decades which are a minimum before we can rationally hope for any decrease in the birth rate.

The answer appears to be, "No!" The Indian farmer is reluctant to adopt new practices and new crops, the landlord system and the credit structure are vicious in the extreme, and the farm laborer is truly ground to a subsistence level. Progress will be slow in spite of all the efforts of any government. Furthermore, as mentioned above, the progress of manufacturing will depend chiefly on an increase in the per capita purchasing power of the agricultural population. If the latter is rapid, then the former should be correspondingly rapid; but, since it is doubtful whether the rate of future agricultural progress can equal that of the past, it is equally doubtful that industry can do much more than give employment to about the same proportion of the people it now does. And unless both agriculture and industry increase their productivity faster than ever before, they cannot even support the present rate of population growth, to say nothing of raising the level of living for the mass of the people.

Even if both agriculture and industry double their total production in the next four decades, does this mean any very considerable improvement in the level of living for the masses of the people? I think not, because population will almost if not altogether keep pace, with the result that there will be but a small per capita increase in consumption. At the rate of increase of 15 per cent in ten years, the rate actually prevailing 1931–41, India will have a population of 680 million in 1981, or 75 per cent above that of 1941. This would leave only one-fourth of a doubled production for better living. And if India's economic situation improves at a faster rate than in the past, there is good reason to believe that her population also will grow at a faster rate for at least four or five decades, bringing it to about 800 million in 1981.

Such a growth of population is more probable in the near future with a rapid improvement in economic conditions than is the rapid decline of the birth rate, which is the only thing that can check it effectively. When one asks whether the lot of the masses of the people in India will be any better in 1981, even with the rapid progress assumed above, if there are somewhere between 680 and 800 million persons, the answer must almost certainly be that it will be little or no better, possibly even worse. The great increase in production will be consumed in keeping increased numbers of people alive at about the level of living now prevailing. Furthermore, the danger of real catastrophe will be increased as the limit of agricultural production is approached. A great famine may take off tens of millions instead of merely millions, and the disease which would accompany it will also take its tens of millions.

The improvement of India's agriculture, even at the most rapid rate feasible, cannot do much to improve the level of living unless at the same time the Indian people take measures to reduce the birth rate. I have little doubt that they will voluntarily reduce the birth rate in the course of time, but that they can or will do so in time to insure any significant improvement in living even if a large increase in productivity is achieved during the next three or four decades is highly doubtful. What is more likely is that the increase in productivity will go forward more slowly and that population will just about keep pace with it for several decades, the level of living rising only a little in the meantime. As the level of living rises and as people move to the cities to enter industry, the birth rate will gradually come under control. It is to be hoped that, when it comes under voluntary control, there will still be room for progress in agriculture and industry which will accrue to the advantage of the individual and family because it is no longer needed to care for the mere increase in numbers. We will return to this point after examining India's mineral resources and opportunities for industrial development.

Chapter XVI

INDIA: MINERAL RESOURCES, INDUSTRY
AND ECONOMIC OUTLOOK

INDIA is more richly endowed with minerals than any other country in South and East Asia. But she is a large country and should be compared with China rather than with Japan or other smaller lands; if India were divided into a number of smaller states, most of them, like Japan, would be seriously lacking in important minerals.

The estimates of coal reserves in India vary greatly, from about 36,000 million tons (450, No. 816, p. 4) to more than twice that amount (331, II, 74, and 30, p. 226 n.). These reserves are small as compared with China's, but from the standpoint of the development of industry in India during the next few decades even the lower estimate need not arouse concern. At the present rate of mining—25–28 million tons annually—36,000 million tons would last several centuries, and, even with a greatly increased consumption, coal should not be a seriously limiting factor in Indian industry within the ensuing century or more. The fact that the better coal, particularly the better metallurgical coal, of which the total amount is not great, lies in a relatively small area to the west of Calcutta may make it difficult to develop basic industry in other parts of the country but should not greatly retard the development of the country as a whole. Heavy basic industry should not be greatly handicapped by this concentration of coal reserves, because the better iron ore is also found in the same region.

Very little petroleum is produced in India at present, and, so far as is known, there are but small reserves: a little in the northeast in Assam near the Burma border, and still less in the west, in Punjab and Baluchistan. Even when Burma was a part of India (before 1937), imports of oil almost equaled native production. The country is favorably located, however, to import oil from both the Netherlands East Indies and Arabia as well as from Burma.

The hydroelectric resources of India are said to be considerable, estimates varying from about 27 million horsepower (130, 1942, p. 71) to 39 million. Not over 3 per cent of this has been developed, nearly all the electricity in India now being produced by steam power. The development of hydroelectric power should be of very considerable assistance in the expansion of Indian industry, since much of it can be developed in regions which lack coal. However, it is said that hydroelectric development will be quite expensive, since large storage reservoirs must be built for most projects on account of the highly seasonal (monsoon) rainfall.

Altogether, India apparently possesses an abundance of power in the form of both coal and water power to support a considerable industrial development. The lack of petroleum places her at a disadvantage, for the time being at least, in the development of airplane and automobile transport; but, when most fuel for internal-combustion engines comes from the liquefaction of coal, she should suffer no disadvantage as compared with most other countries.

India also possesses rather large quantities of high-grade iron ore, much larger than those of any other country of South and East Asia. They allegedly amount to at least 3,000 million tons of 60–69 per cent iron content (69, p. 413, and 30). Other authorities liken these reserves to those of the Lake Superior region in the United States both in amount and in quality (290, p. 97), while one popular pamphlet says they are estimated as high as 20,000 million tons (132, p. 37) for which I can find no verification.

Here, as in the case of coal, there is no need to accept the larger figure in order to conclude that for several decades and probably for several generations India will have an abundance of good iron ore to meet all her needs and can even count on trading iron and steel for some of the other minerals and goods she may need to import. If the larger estimate (20,000 million tons) should prove correct, then India could be classed as one of the few countries of the world which could reasonably expect a long-continued development of heavy industry.

In other minerals, too, India is very well off. Her bauxite deposits are large, estimated at 250 million tons, much of which is of high grade. This makes her one of the greatest potential suppliers of bauxite in the world. Present production, however, is quite small, and the first actual production of aluminum took place either late in 1941 or in early 1942 (211, September 15, 1940, p. 214). It is expected that production will soon amount to 5,000 tons annually (165, pp. 193–94).

Manganese deposits are likewise large (22, p. 81), and India has for some time supplied about one-fourth to one-third of the world's needs (331, II, 80), Russia being the principal source. No official estimate of manganese reserves has been found, but all authorities seem to take it for granted that they are adequate both to meet India's own needs for a long time to come and to enable her to export considerable quantities to other lands.

Other minerals of which India possesses ample reserves are mica, chromite, ilmenite, molybdenum, salt, tungsten, and materials for cement, glass, refractories, and abrasives. The more important minerals which seem to be lacking or at least the supplies of which seem inadequate for any large industrial development, although all are found, are sulphur, copper, tin, nickel, lead, zinc, graphite, phosphates, and potash.

Thus it can be said that India is quite well endowed with the basic mineral and power resources needed for the development of modern industry, and those which she lacks should not be difficult to secure from other Asiatic countries in exchange for heavy goods; sulphur from Japan, nickel, tin, lead, zinc, and oil from Burma, the Netherlands East Indies, and Arabia; and small amounts of alloy minerals from China, the Philippines, and other near-by regions.

INDUSTRY IN INDIA

The Indian writers on the economy and industry of the country almost without exception stress the slow development of machine production and then proceed to explain the reasons for this slow progress. In the first place, it should be said that India's industrial progress only appears slow when the comparison is with the Soviet Union or with Japan. When the comparison is with China, the countries of South and East Asia, or even with many Western lands, India appears to have made fairly rapid progress.

Like all of Asia, until the last six to eight decades, Indian industry was a hand industry with almost no machine or implement more complicated than the hand loom, the blacksmith's forge, or the ironmakers' primitive furnaces which used charcoal for the smelting of local ores. In making cotton cloth, the seed was first picked from the cotton by hand, then the thread was spun by hand, and the cloth was woven on a hand-operated loom. The small amount of iron used, after being smelted in a small charcoal furnace a few pounds at each heating, was then worked up by the local smith or foundry into the simple tools and utensils commonly in use in the village. Occasionally, the local artisans made articles which were taken to the bazaars of the neighboring cities, but for the most part each community produced only what it needed for itself, and it produced most of this from local materials. For all but a few articles of high value, used only by the wealthy and the nobles, the cost of transport of most goods outside the locality of production was prohibitive.

Even in the early days of European occupation, though, India exported some very fine goods. The names of some of our fine cottons (Madras) came from the exports of these provinces to Europe. Indian brassware and jewels were much valued in the West, and Indian tea came into wide use. Like the Chinese and Japanese, the Indians showed a high degree of artistry and skill in the design and execution of a variety of goods, but all these were handmade and so costly in terms of labor that only a very very small part of the population could ever afford to use or to own them. The goods in common use were the rather rough and crude product of local workers who were compelled to produce for utility only and with as small an expenditure of labor as possible.

In India, as elsewhere in the East before the middle of the nineteenth century, there were no really large cities because there was no way to supply them with food at a moderate price or to transport to and from them the goods they might have used and made up into articles of commerce. If we remember that this was the case and that modern steam transport had very little influence on Indian economy before about 1860–70, we will not be much surprised that machine production has seemed to most Indians to proceed very slowly. A look at what has actually happened in machine production and transportation in the last six or seven decades will show what has been accomplished in modern industrial organization.

The total number of persons employed in factories[1] in 1941 was 2,156,000 (230, February, 1944, p. 234). In 1938 only 1,738,000 were so employed, an increase of 24 per cent in three years, which may be attributed largely to war work. There is no way to tell what proportion these factory workers constitute of all persons engaged in industry, since the 1941 census data on occupations are not available. A total of 15,352,000 persons were reported as engaged in industry in 1931, and, if this number has increased in proportion to the total population (which is probable since the proportion of "agriculturists" seems to have remained about stationary for some time), the industrial workers would number about 17,655,000 in 1941, and the workers in mod- ·

[1] A factory is an enterprise employing ten or more persons, most of whom, but not all, use power-driven machinery.

ern factories would constitute about 12.2 per cent of all industrial workers. This is not an inconsiderable proportion, but it shows clearly that the great majority of industrial workers still ply their trades by hand in the traditional manner.

But to the workers in factories must be added railroad workers, miners, a certain proportion of those engaged in road and water transport, in certain nonfactory industries such as building, and some of those in shops employing less than ten persons, if we would get a fairly adequate notion of the proportion of nonagricultural workers who use modern power-driven tools and machines. The railroads and mines employ about 1,100,000 workers (1941), but there is no way to estimate, even this roughly, how many other workers employ power in their tasks. A close enough guess would be that, out of perhaps 20 million workers in industry and transport in 1941, 3.0–3.5 million were working more or less with some kind of power-driven tools and machinery, possibly 15–18 per cent of all such workers. This may seem like a small proportion, but it is certainly much larger than in China and most of the other lands of South and East Asia. How important machine production has become in India can be seen from the actual growth of the leading industries using power.

DEVELOPMENT OF SELECTED INDUSTRIES

The most developed of India's modern industries is textiles. The number of workers in all branches of the textile industry in establishments having more than ten employees was 953,000 in 1941—44 per per cent of the total of 2,156,000 employees in such establishments (230, February, 1944, p. 234). Of these workers, about two-thirds are engaged in the various branches of the cotton industry and somewhat under one-third in jute. The small remainder are employed in factories producing silks and woolens (331, II, 31).

In 1941–42 the factory production of cotton cloth amounted to about 4,500 million yards, from about 200,000 looms, as compared with about 2,000 million yards from 2 million hand looms (483, p. 53). These are very interesting figures, for, unless the number of nonfactory workers in the cotton industry fell greatly between 1931 and 1941, they constituted about four-fifths of all cotton textile workers and yet they produced only about three-tenths of the cloth. And even this ratio underestimates the relative productivity of machine and handwork because a large part of the yarn used by the hand looms was made by workers in modern factories.

The cotton industry has been developing rapidly in India during the last thirty years from about 5.8 million spindles and 85,000 looms in 1913 to a little over 10 million spindles and over 200,000 looms in 1941. The result is that India is rapidly becoming self-sufficient in the production of cotton goods, and her imports have already been tremendously reduced.

Jute manufacture constitutes the other important branch of Indian textiles. India has a virtual monopoly of jute production in the world. Prior to World War I, she exported a large proportion of her jute as raw material to be made into burlap and bags in Scotland, England, and the United States. In recent years more and more has been manufactured in India. At the outbreak of World War II, India had over 100 jute mills with about 1.25 million spindles and 60,000 looms employing about 300,000 workers. In 1938–39 jute manufactures constituted 16.2 per cent, in value, of all her exports, and raw jute amounted to 8.2 per cent (483, p. 56). Thus jute, raw and manufactured, was far and away the most important of her exports, raw cotton being only about two-thirds as large. Since the war it appears that an even larger proportion of the jute crop is being manufactured in India.

India has also made rapid progress in the production of refined sugar in recent years and now supplies practically all her own needs. In 1931–32 she had 31 sugar mills producing a little less than 160,000 tons, but by the outbreak of World War II she had over 150 mills producing about 1.25 million tons, and her imports had dropped from over one million tons to a few thousand (331, II, 40–41).

In some respects the most important industrial advance made in India in the last three decades is in the production of iron and steel. Before 1911 the only iron and steel produced domestically, aside from the small native furnaces each of which turned out only a few tons a year, was from the furnaces of the Bengal Iron and Steel Company and amounted to 35,000–40,000 tons a year. The greater part of India's needs was supplied by imports, chiefly from the United Kingdom. Since 1911, when the Tata Iron and Steel Company began producing, there has been a fairly rapid increase in production (331, II, 37–39): by 1941 pig-iron production was supposed to have reached 2 million tons and steel production about 1.25 million tons (321, p. 221), these amounts apparently increased still further under the pressure of war needs. Before World War II, India exported a considerable proportion of the pig iron produced but was still importing about 300,000 tons of steel which she was not then equipped to produce (69, pp. 415–16).

This rapid expansion of India's iron and steel industry was greatly aided by tariff protection, but there was hope that, as the industry grew and the management and workers became more experienced, there would be no need of protection (331, II, 39). The recent formation of two new iron and steel companies testifies to the belief held by many Indians and some British that iron and steel can be made profitably in India with the present protection and, if the above statement is correct, that this protection will not be needed for long.

There has been, however, no parallel development of the heavy machine and tool industries. Before World War II, India imported a large part of her machinery, locomotives, railway rolling stock, machine tools, and much other heavy goods. "A glance at the figures regarding imports of manufactured articles made almost entirely from minerals gives point to this remark. An average quantity of well over Rs. 360,000,000 [about $130 million] worth of such materials is annually imported. . . . . The predominance of imports of what are mainly iron and steel articles is striking" (331, II, 69).

This situation is evidently being changed under the stress of war shortages (211). India is now making tools and machinery never made there before; she is also using these tools to make many new kinds of goods which were previously imported. The development going on in her iron and steel industry in many ways seems analogous to what happened in Japan during World War I. If anything, it is even more rapid and, because of India's good natural resources, seems more likely to continue without break, although postwar developments probably will depend largely on the adequacy and the will of the governmental organization to carry forward war enterprises.

Although no other Indian industries rank in importance with textiles and iron and steel, a number have been started and have assuredly been greatly stimulated by the war. Among those which already had shown a significant development before World War II were paper, glass, cement, pottery, tanning, rubber, and chemicals. The numbers employed in such work were so small that India could scarcely be said to possess modern industries in any of these lines except cement, but the experience gained must have been considerable to judge by progress since 1939. Although no definite figures can be given for chemicals, the impression conveyed is that good headway has been made both in the production of heavy chemicals (sulphuric acid, caustic soda, ammonia, chlorine, etc.) and in that of drugs and medicinal supplies; also in the production of glassware, particularly optical glass, in the manufacture of cutlery and many kinds of light hardware, well as as in that of actual war supplies. The production of aluminum from India's large bauxite resources has also been started on a small scale.

In addition, it appears that many thousands of Indian civilians are being given industrial training, and some hundreds of thousands in the army are gaining experience in the assembling, operation, and repair of machinery, which will stand them in good stead if and when India's industries need more skilled workers. Thus one of the serious obstacles to rapid postwar industrial development is being overcome—but this is only one of the many difficulties in the way of India's rapid manufacturing development, and war work does not by any means give all of the training needed by a balanced peacetime economy.

OBSTACLES TO THE DEVELOPMENT OF INDUSTRY

There is a widely held belief in Western Europe and America that there is some peculiar mechanical aptitude among our people, the lack of which in large measure accounts for industrial backwardness in other parts of the world. Anyone who has been interested in the development of industry and has visited some of the "backward" countries can tell a multitude of stories about the ineptitudes of these peoples in the use of machinery. The basic assumption underlying such stories is generally that the industrial backwardness of these peoples is a consequence of their *natural* lack of the aptitudes which made us so successful in machine operation and in factory organization.

It may seem needless to point out that our present knowledge of the nature of heredity does not justify the belief that the failure to operate a machine successfully, or to improve its construction, or to develop new processes of production, or to display managerial competence, are racial or national traits. There are individuals everywhere who do not fit well into a machine economy, but such ineptitudes as those just noted are far more likely to arise from a lack of training and experience than from an inherent lack of capacity in any race or nation. Since many still seem to feel that some races are inherently deficient in these qualities, it may be well to call attention to a few facts which contradict this view.

The war has shown us that, although the Russians may not yet get as much production from a given factory as some other peoples, they were getting enough both in quantity and quality to fight the greatest military actions in history quite successfully, even when due allowance is made for lend-lease. Certainly there can no longer be any convincing talk about the ineptitude of the Russians in the use of machines or about their inability to organize for efficient operations on a large scale. Indeed, the organization of their service of supplies was one of the outstanding marvels of the war; it rivaled that of the Germans, who have always been considered organizers par excellence.

Nor do we any longer doubt the ability of the Japanese to build good machines and to use them well, although they may not be quite equal to our best. They had many better machines than we had at the outset of the war, and they introduced many new ones of excellent quality. It may be that they were largely copies of the machines developed by other peoples, but in such matters—matters of invention—it is perfectly natural for any people in the early stages of industrialization to copy the patterns of older, better-established industries abroad. Our own history shows plenty of such examples: imitation is by no means rare, nor does it prove any inherent mechanical deficiency. Finally, can anyone doubt that if we had made such a conquest as the Japanese made in the year following Pearl Harbor, we would have hailed it as a marvel of American organization and as proof of superior mechanical efficiency?

Again, it was only a few years ago that the iron and steel masters of Great Britain said unhesitatingly that India could never make iron and steel to compete with the West because her people lacked the qualities needed for this job. But with no more, if as much, tariff protection as we in the United States had when steel was an infant industry, India has begun to make iron and steel in considerable quantity and is gradually building an export market in competition with the West. There now remains no doubt that she can increase her production in this field at any time there is demand and at moderate costs. In addition, the data given above show very clearly that Indian industry is making headway along many lines and that the needed skills are being acquired as opportunity offers. Besides, enough of this industry is being managed by Indians to prove beyond doubt that, when they have the experience and the desire, they can do a good organizational job.

It is high time to recognize that the industrial dominance of Western Europe and North America during the last hundred and fifty years was a historical accident and that it did not and does not rest on any unique capacity to do the jobs of a machine economy better than any other people once they have had the training and experience that we have had and the national will to develop their industry becomes strong. Of course, this does not mean that the path of industrial development will be the same in these "backward" countries as in the West, or that it will be easy for them to change over from a hand economy to a machine economy—but the lack of trained personnel must not be confused with an inherent lack in national or racial character which will make the development of modern industry impossible. The obstacles to this development are social and economic rather than racial or hereditary.

Although the Indians and the Chinese, and all other "backward" peoples, may and probably will become expert in machine production and proficient in the management of industry, it takes time to acquire this experience, and India and China are going to suffer from the lack of trained men for several decades at least. Just how long they will be handicapped in this respect will depend on many factors, but that technical training can be acquired rather quickly both Japan and Russia had shown before the war. It seems to depend on how urgent the need is and whether the state and/or some powerful group of industrialists will undertake to provide the opportunity for training.

It is not improbable that the whole civilization of India may be less favorable to the rapid development of the attitudes of mind essential to the successful operation of modern industry than was that of the Soviet Union or even that of Japan. Such a break with the past as is involved in working effectively at modern industry is not easy to accomplish anywhere, and the "cake of custom" is thick and tough in India. To the extent that religious beliefs, the caste system, the seclusion of women, the general attitude of passivity, the contempt for work with the hands, and many other social attitudes make the Indians disdain participation in modern industrial activity more than was the case among Western peoples, to that extent they will retard Indian industrial development. These difficulties may prove just as stubborn to overcome as some of the more material and tangible factors retarding industrial expansion, because they are due to differences in civilization, in the values and motives which control behavior. No people can be expected to work hard and steadily at jobs which do not have any meaning to them or which do not yield the returns which they value.

Another difficulty is that India is a tropical country in which ma-

laria and many parasitic diseases are very widespread. One consequence of this is that a large proportion of the people are weak and lack
the energy we temperate-zone peoples are accustomed to expect from
practically everyone in the population. This will aggravate the problem of securing, training, and maintaining an adequate personnel for
modern industry; but this is a health problem and should not be confused with the problem that would arise if it were a hereditary characteristic. It is possible, of course, that all tropical peoples will show a
lack of energy as compared with the peoples living in temperate zones,
but we cannot say so with any semblance of justification until their

TABLE 22*

INDUSTRIALISTS' PLAN FOR INDIAN RECONSTRUCTION

(Expenditure of Thirty Billion Dollars
Spread over Fifteen Years)

Project	Amount (In Millions)
Basic industries (includes power, engineering, and chemical)	$10,440
Consumer goods industries	3,000
Agriculture	3,720
Communication	2,820
Education	1,470
Health	1,350
Housing	6,600

* Source: *Manchester Guardian Weekly*, January 28, 1944,
p. 54. Converted at the rate of one rupee = 30 cents.

health conditions have approximated those of the Western peoples for
several decades.

Thus, while I would not for a moment deny that it will be difficult
for India to develop an adequate industrial personnel and that it will
take some years, possibly several decades, there is no reason at all to
assume that it cannot be done and done rather quickly if the country
organizes industrial education and training as was done in the Soviet
Union and to a lesser extent in Japan. It is likely to take India (or
China) longer to train such a personnel because of the greater social
obstacles imposed by her civilization—perhaps two to four decades
depending on the urgency of the need and the vigor with which such
a program is pursued. But if such a program of industrialization and
improvement as is contemplated (see Table 22) is carried out with
energy and foresight, there would seem to be no good reason to doubt
that the personnel to operate it can be trained in the time allotted.

India will, of course, encounter the other obstacles delaying industrialization and social betterment common to all "backward" lands. Since they are common to all such peoples and have been noted at some length in the discussion of China's future, they need only be enumerated here. First, the lack of capital will certainly cause delay. If India gains her independence without disruption of her governmental control or appreciable lessening of its efficiency, she should be able to borrow abroad sooner and on better terms than China; but if she remains a colony and the development of her industry is controlled by Great Britain to the same extent as in the past, her industrialization will probably be slow.

Second, the lack of markets for a greatly increased industrial product will prove a very formidable obstacle. Here the situation is not greatly different from that in China, except that India should be able to expand her export of iron and steel rather rapidly and will not have to find foreign exchange for these materials when she uses them at home. As we saw in the preceding chapter, the slow increase in per capita productivity in agriculture will be a prime factor in retarding the rapid expansion of industrial productivity. It may be overcome to a certain extent if the state buys great quantities of industrial goods for capital uses, but there is little prospect that private enterprise will be in position to make immediate use of great quantities of capital goods.

The displacement of hand workers by the development of the factory production of consumption goods will also have a retarding effect on the growth of the domestic market. In the opinion of many well-informed people, India is already suffering in this respect. For example, the result of increasing the textile workers in factories by perhaps 300,000–400,000 would be to displace seven to ten times as many hand workers. Since the total number of workers in modern factories did not much exceed 2 million in 1941, only a small proportion of the textile workers who have already been displaced could have gone into machine industries, and most of them must have gone into other types of inefficient hand work or gone on the land. It would appear very doubtful, therefore, whether the domestic market in India for consumption goods of new kinds can be expanded fast enough to absorb the workers displaced by machine industry making the customary articles of use, to say nothing of the great increase of workers now taking place year by year. The real hope of a rapid expansion of the domestic market for machine-made goods lies in the absorption of a large amount of capital goods by new and expanding factories, by additional transport equipment, etc., rather than in the rapid expansion of consumption among the masses.

Finally, attention should be called to the part played by the extension and the mechanization of agriculture in the expansion of the domestic market for industrial goods in the West and the virtual absence of similar factors in India and in China. The accessibility of vast areas of good new land by making possible a large per capita increase in agricultural productivity opened up a domestic market for industrial goods far faster and far greater than India can expect. As we have seen, she has not the land to make this possible. For this reason peoples like the Indians and Chinese and Japanese must depend more largely on the rapid accumulation of industrial capital as a market for their factory goods than did the West.

FUTURE LIVING CONDITIONS

There seems to be no hope at this time that India can so expand her markets, either domestic or foreign, that she can offer industrial jobs at improving rates of pay to the increase of workers which is now taking place year by year. Although I believe this opinion is justified by the considerations adduced above, it also rests on several assumptions which should be explicitly stated. They are (a) that India will remain in fact a colony for some time to come, perhaps two or three decades, even though some concessions to home rule will be made; (b) that during this period of colonial tenure the system of economy that has prevailed in the past, which for want of a better term I will call *colonial laissez faire*, will continue; (c) that, at best, there will be only a slow relaxation of the trade restrictions which now fetter the entire world; (d) that Indians will not be allowed to settle in any considerable numbers either on the tropical islands south and east of Asia—Madagascar, New Guinea, Borneo—or in the thinly settled tropics of Africa; and, finally, (e) that India will continue to have a strong, stable central government.

At present there are insufficient signs of basic changes to justify assuming that India's agriculture and industry will develop under more favorable conditions than those assumed here, however much we may desire to see the rosy dreams of prosperity through speedy industrialization and agricultural improvement come true. And then, again, it is one thing to provide a better living for a population of 400 million (389 million in 1941) which is not growing and quite another to provide this for such a population growing at 10–15 per cent each decade. As shown above, the only thing which will prevent a continued growth at this rate, amounting to 5 million or more a year, will be a rising death rate due to a deterioration of living conditions. Any improvement in economic conditions will raise the rate of increase by further lowering the death rate, since there is no prospect of any significant decline in the birth rate for at least three to four decades.

Thus the task facing agriculture and industry in India is not only to raise the level of living for 400 million people but also to provide for an additional population of 50–70 million each ten years, until such time as the Indians bring their birth rate under control. But the world's experience in the last hundred and fifty years shows that the decline of the birth rate is associated closely with industrial and commercial development in cities and requires several decades at best. This is a universal experience, and there is no reason to think that the process will be different in India. India may not need as long a time to gain control over her birth rate as was required in England, the United States, or even Japan, but such a change in reproduction cannot be effected in a few years in a poverty-stricken agricultural country. We must think in terms of a few decades at least, and we must not forget that the conditions favorable to the spread of the practice of birth control are also favorable to the further control of deaths. Even after there is clear evidence of a decline in the birth rate, as in Japan during the 1920's, the rate of increase may continue at the same high level for some years.

Finally, then, we must conclude that India's population will continue to grow fairly rapidly unless her economic conditions deteriorate; that her level of living will, at best, rise slowly because of the scarcity of land and the slowness of industrial development; that, in spite of heavy handicaps, her industrial strength will increase considerably in the course of the next three or four decades; and that her per capita income will probably increase a little, but the feeling of need for better health service, for better food and more of it, for better housing, for more land to till, for more industrial products, etc., will increase more rapidly. Now the question facing us is: Under these conditions will India remain a docile colony or even a docile independent nation once home rule is achieved? Or will she cast covetous eyes at thinly inhabited Madagascar and New Guinea and the almost equally unused areas of tropical Africa? At the oil of Sumatra and Burma? At the tin of the Netherlands East Indies? Once her people have enjoyed some of the good things produced by a more efficient economy, will they be content with small "doses" when their leaders show them how they can acquire larger doses by taking the colonies of other peoples and exploiting their resources?

I do not *know* the answer to these questions, but I do not think we can assume that any people will quietly acquiesce in a division of the resources of the world which it believes unjust when it is fully aware of the situation and when it has the power to make a bid for them and has, in its eyes, a fighting chance of success. If we want to avoid future wars for colonies, we must abolish colonies and make the world's resources available to all peoples.

Even this, however, will not remove unequal population pressure arising out of differential population growth. The more just distribution of the world's resources (first those of the unused areas) will help for a time to reduce unequal population pressures, as will freer trade, but in the long run all peoples must control their numbers so that they will not periodically feel the urge to expand beyond their existing boundaries. Only for a short time can we help India to care for her "teeming millions" by the more complete use of the resources in the thinly settled regions of the earth. The only permanent solution is for her to take measures of her own to reduce the *teeming* of her millions.

Chapter XVII

THE COLONIES OF SOUTHEAST ASIA. I

BURMA, Malaya, French Indo-China, the Netherlands East Indies, and the Philippines are the main colonies of this region. Thailand, though not a colony, also belongs in this group because her economy is essentially colonial and she has not been an entirely free agent politically. All these colonies have many features in common, and since for our purposes the likenesses are more fundamental than the differences, they can be stressed to good advantage.

All Southeast Asia is tropical, and the great mass of the people, like those of India and southern China, live in a very simple and, to us, primitive manner. Most of the housing is for protection from the rain and the sun rather than for warmth. It is very simple and cheap in construction, being made entirely of local forest and plant products. For most families the house consists of a single room.

Clothing is about as simple as housing. There are, of course, many variations, but it consists in the main of a cotton garment or two, or a simple wrapping (sarong). In spite of this, textiles commonly constitute the largest single item of import, and the native textile industry, hand spinning and weaving, is the largest home industry (although it is on the decline in most of the region since handwork cannot compete with the machine-made textiles of Europe and Japan). Shoes are not much worn in this region and where used are generally made at home of plaited straw (a cheap rubber slipper, chiefly made in Japan, is slowly coming into use).

Throughout the area the staple of diet is rice, even more than in Japan, China, and India. Many vegetables and fruits are also grown, and sugar cane is a common crop. With few exceptions most villages are self-sufficing in food production, and most families supply their own needs. On the whole, native agriculture is a small-scale family enterprise carried on chiefly by hand work, and the family produces very little beyond its own needs. In the entire region agriculture employs 70–80 per cent of the people, the higher figure probably being more representative than the lower. The agricultural population almost without exception lives in small villages and goes out to work on the surrounding fields. Native industry is also located chiefly in these small villages and consists principally of spinning and weaving, the making of agricultural tools and household utensils, the processing (hulling) of rice, the pressing of oil, and a few other types of work essential to village life. As we shall see, the development of commercial agriculture is changing this situation to some extent, but for most of the people life is still very simple, with the villages supplying nearly all their own needs.

The high rainfall in this region and the necessity of keeping rice plots flooded during the growing season raise certain health problems. Malaria is widespread and is quite commonly regarded as the chief cause of death. The constant wading in the mud of the rice fields also makes infestation by certain parasites almost universal, and in the absence of definite and sustained public health efforts the so-called "filth" diseases—typhoid, dysentery, and cholera—claim a heavy toll of lives almost every year in nearly all villages. Smallpox, too, is always present, and its control also depends on the public health service. In the absence of public health service, as in the past, death rates must have been very high and when coupled with the general insecurity of life, owing to the very desultory policing which preceded European control, must have about equaled the birth rates so that there was little increase of population. Where there was an increase, it was quite irregular, depending on the severity of disease, famine, and war losses at any given time.

In very broad outline these living conditions, though now modified in certain respects, still prevail in much of the area. The chief modifications have come as the result of the colonial status of these lands.

THE NETHERLANDS EAST INDIES

The Netherlands East Indies constitute the greatest colonial area of South and East Asia, with the exception of India, and are also perhaps the best managed of these colonies. They comprise a group of islands, some thousands in number, lying off the south and southeast coasts of Asia, athwart the Equator and with about two-thirds of their 735,000 square miles in the Southern Hemisphere. From west to east they extend from Sumatra almost 3,000 miles to the middle of New Guinea. The two largest islands in this group—New Guinea, with about 310,000 square miles, and Borneo, with about 290,000 square miles—are divided between the Dutch and the British (including Australia), and what will be said later of the Dutch portion of Borneo applies with almost equal force to the British portion. Since New Guinea has already been treated as a part of Oceania (see chap. iii), the discussion here will be confined to the other islands. The other large islands in this colony are Sumatra, with about 164,000 square miles; Celebes, with 73,000; and Java, with 51,000 (339, 1934, p. 2). These five large islands, including Borneo and New Guinea, have a total area of about 880,000 square miles, of which about 650,000 are controlled by the Dutch.

Although Java, with which Madura is generally included, is considerably the smallest of these five islands, it is much the most important. It contains about 70 per cent of the population of the Netherlands East Indies; it is the seat of government; and, before the depression, it supplied almost one-half of the exports (in value) and took almost two-thirds of the imports. After 1930 its proportion of exports declined, but it still continued to take the major part of the imports. It is the only part of the colony which has been intensively developed.

POPULATION OF JAVA AND THE OUTER PROVINCES

The Dutch have had a foothold in this region for about three hundred years, but the period with which we are concerned here may be said to have begun in 1816, when, at the close of the Napoleonic Wars, these islands were given back to the Dutch. At that time Java was supposed to have a population of about 4.5 million (471, p. 14), which was almost wholly native. No estimate is available for the population of the "Outer Provinces" at that time (the Outer Provinces include all the remainder of the Netherlands East Indies), but there is no good reason to suppose that the present great disparity in numbers existed then. It was only after 1816 that conditions changed in Java, while they remained until about 1910 much as they had been in the Outer Provinces. By 1930 the native population of Java had grown to almost 40.9 million, and the total population, including Europeans (193,000), Chinese (582,000), and other Asiatics (52,000), amounted to 41,718,000 (339, 1934, p. 12). However, these figures give a somewhat misleading impression of the number of Europeans, for "the European population is divided into two groups: the Europeans and the Eurasians, generally called Indo-Europeans. There are no official statistics on the percentage in each group, since the Eurasians are legally assimilated to the Europeans, but the percentage of the latter [Eurasians] is high, probably as high as 80 per cent" (471, p. 7). In addition, a number of Japanese (4,000 in 1930) and natives (about 5,300 in 1930) are "legally" Europeans and are included in the number given above. When account is taken of these facts, it is probable that the number of persons of pure European blood in 1930 was in the neighborhood of only 40,000.

By 1940 the total population of Java was estimated at 49–50 million (471, p. 1) and that of the entire Netherlands East Indies at about 70–

TABLE 23

POPULATION OF THE NETHERLANDS EAST INDIES BY RACIAL GROUPS, 1920–40

RACIAL GROUP	POPULATION (IN THOUSANDS)			PERCENTAGE 1930 POPULATION WAS OF 1920	PERCENTAGE OF THE TOTAL POPULATION	
	1940*	1930	1920		1930	1920
Total						
Natives.............	68,168	59,138	48,304	122.4	97.4	97.9
Europeans...........	277	240	170	141.7	0.4	0.4
Chinese.............	1,422	1,233	810	152.3	2.0	1.6
Other Asiatics.......	133	116	67	172.8	0.2	0.1
Total..........	70,000	60,727	49,351	123.0	100.0	100.0
Java and Madura Only						
Natives.............	47,126	40,891	34,433	118.8	98.0	98.4
Europeans...........	241	193	135	142.3	0.5	0.4
Chinese.............	673	582	....	....	1.4	....
Other Asiatics.......	48	52	415	152.8	.1	1.2
Total..........	48,088	41,718	34,984	119.2	100.0	100.0

* Estimated on basis of 1930 distribution, assuming a 1940 mid-year population of 70,000,000 for the Netherlands East Indies and 48,088,000 for Java and Madura.

71 million. This estimate of 20–21 million in the Outer Provinces may seem somewhat low, but the important point is that they were very thinly settled, averaging not over 35 persons per square mile, as compared with about 950 per square mile in Java and Madura, and probably were not increasing as rapidly in numbers as the latter.

In 1930 the several racial groups in the Netherlands East Indies were quite differently distributed in Java and in the Outer Provinces (Table 23). The Europeans were more heavily concentrated in Java than even the natives, while over half the Chinese were in the Outer

Provinces. This would seem to indicate a more hardy pioneering spirit among the Chinese than among the Europeans, for Java is no longer a pioneer area, while the Outer Provinces are, except in a few places.

It should be noted at this point that the native population of Java, as of all the islands except New Guinea and some small neighboring islands, is Malayan. It is the same stock as the native population of the Malay Peninsula and the Philippine Islands. There is also a strong, perhaps predominant, Malayan strain in the Japanese. But the problem of central interest to us is rather the great increase in the population of Java since 1816 and the more recent growth of numbers in the Outer Provinces, because in this we find one of the inevitable dilemmas which arise when the colonial system operates effectively. It will be necessary, therefore, to go into the history of population growth in the Netherlands East Indies, and particularly since 1900, by which time the population of Java was already becoming dense.

There can be little doubt that the population of Java, estimated at 4,500,000 in 1815, began to grow almost at once following the re-establishment of Dutch rule in 1816. This statement will hold even if we suppose that the growth to over 11,750,000 in 1858 is due in considerable measure to the extension of the area covered by the estimates and to their increasing reliability.

In the early years following 1816 the chief factor contributing to the population growth of Java was undoubtedly the pacification of the island. At first the Dutch controlled only a few coastal regions, but they gradually extended their control into the hinterland, putting an end to the wars between native states and tribes. This alone provided an important favorable condition for population growth which was made still more favorable as the policing of the fringe of settlement became more efficient, making it safe for the surplus people of a village to move out to neighboring unoccupied lands. Later the building of roads and irrigation works and the introduction of some sanitary measures continued to increase the chances of life and thus to encourage population growth.

Unfortunately, vital statistics are of little help in proving that it is the lowering of the death rate which has been the significant factor in the growth of Java's population. In the first place, such data are entirely lacking until quite recently, and those for recent years are almost certainly highly defective. This is always the case when the registration of births and deaths is first undertaken. Registered births of

27–28 per 1,000 during the 1930's and deaths of 17–18 (134, Part I, p. 6, and 339, 1934, p. 60) are certainly defective, possibly by as much as 50 per cent or more. The growth of population shown by the census between 1920 and 1930 indicates that the difference between birth rates and death rates averaged about 17 per 1,000 during that decade, while the difference between the registered birth rate and death rate during the 1930's would give a natural increase of only 10–11 per 1,000. The rate of natural increase may have been higher during the 1920's than during the 1930's, but people familiar with the situation in Java do not seem to think so. Hence it seems more reasonable to assume that the registration of births and deaths is highly defective, with that of births being relatively more defective than that of deaths, as is generally the case, and to assume birth rates and death rates which will yield a natural increase of 16–17 per 1,000—i.e., a birth rate of 40–45 per 1,000, possibly even higher, and a death rate of 25–30 with a probability that it is higher rather than lower.

To the "historical" factors favorable to Java's population growth must be added the great natural fertility of the island and the favorable rainfall which make it possible for a considerable part of the tilled area to produce two rice crops annually (three for some of it when under good irrigation) and the relatively large area of new land which has been available for cultivation but which is now practically exhausted. The greater fertility of Java's soil than of that of the other large islands in the Netherlands East Indies is explained chiefly by its more recent volcanic origin, allowing a rapid disintegration of its soils which makes an abundance of plant food available. But although this superior soil fertility as well as the possibility of adding rapidly to tilled land have existed for ages, they did not open the way for population growth until after the Dutch had undertaken a vigorous and, in recent decades, an enlightened program of colonial development.

Until about thirty years ago it was almost exclusively the system of estate agriculture for export that made possible a stable and efficient government, the building of roads, railroads, harbors, and good shipping services, the development of a public health organization and the other services which have contributed so largely to the lower death rate. In the last thirty years, but particularly since World War I, the exploitation of minerals, tin, oil, and, to a minor extent, coal and the development of native commercial agriculture have contributed more and more to the surplus needed to maintain and enlarge these older services and to extend the educational system which had been badly neglected before about 1929. It is probably true that the part of this surplus, arising from good colonial management, which was used for these services was so used because only in this way could the exploitation of agriculture and minerals be made profitable both to the governing country and to the men engaged directly in such enterprises, but this does not alter the fact that, being so used, this surplus had a profound effect on Java's population growth. The sad part of the whole situation is that, with possibly eight times as many people in 1940 as in 1840, there is no convincing evidence that all this efficient colonial exploitation which has raised the level of living enough to insure a lower death rate can maintain even the present low level. The term "level of living" is used here to include the decrease in the death rate, the greater freedom from certain epidemic diseases, and a modicum of schooling as well as "subsistence" in the narrowest sense. The lowering of the death rate is in itself proof of a certain amount of improvement in the level of living.

The irony of the situation is that the colonial exploitation of Java lies at the base of its Malthusian dilemma today—the growing danger of famine and its accompanying disease and disorder—which is disturbing conscientious administrators and students more and more each year. The easy ways of producing more food on the island which have been employed in the past (the extension of the tilled area, the increase of irrigation, and the use of better varieties of crops) are now almost exhausted, but the "artificial" organization for reducing the death rate (health service, transportation which can relieve local crop shortages, stable civil government, etc.) remains. Finally, there is no evidence of any reduction in the birth rate. For the next few decades, then, it appears that the staving-off of disaster depends on the ability of the Dutch colonial authorities (assuming the continuance of their control) to settle large numbers of Javanese in the Outer Provinces and to use a considerable part of the increase of population in the exploitation of mineral resources and in industrial development.

RELIEF FOR JAVA

The widespread belief that a decrease in per capita production in Java is more likely than an increase and that before long this will lead to an increase in the death rate has led to much anxiety on the part of the colonial authorities. What is to be done? Four measures are generally advocated: the extension of the area of cultivation, the intensification of cultivation and improvement of the varieties of the more important crops, the encouragement of migration, and the development of industry. It is of great significance that while a fifth answer might seem the most obvious of all—reduction of the birth rate—it is not advanced seriously as an immediate possibility by anyone familiar with Java's problems. This is probably because it seems to be so far outside the realm of the practicable for several decades that there is no use discussing it at the present time. Since the other solutions will be discussed later in connection with Java's agriculture and industry, we will pass at once to the question of migration.

In recent years the migration of large numbers of Javanese to the Outer Provinces, where they can settle on new lands and raise the crops with which they are familiar, seems to be attracting most attention as a measure for the relief of population pressure in Java. The importance the Dutch authorities attach to migration is shown chiefly by the very active interest they have taken in it since about 1930. Before that time the government could scarcely be said to have encouraged migration actively. Migration from Java had consisted largely of coolies going out to work temporarily on the commercial plantations of Sumatra and to a minor degree on those of Borneo and Celebes. The number involved was quite large, but, since most of them did not take their families with them and returned to Java at the expiration of their contracts, this movement did little to relieve the pressure in Java.

When the government first undertook to put Javanese colonists on the land in the Outer Provinces, its attempts were both expensive and ineffectual. In general, it contemplated the settling of Javanese families on the land as individual families and ignored the fact that the village is far more the social unit among the Javanese than in the West. The family was given only financial help when it needed even more the moral support and co-operation of a village group. By 1930 not more than 800,000 Javanese were living in the Outer Provinces (471, p. 267), and a large part of these were coolie laborers who were only temporarily abroad. During the depression of the 1930's over 150,000 Javanese were sent back from Sumatra alone. Broek (42) gives the number of agricultural colonists in the Outer Provinces in 1930 as only a little over 40,000.

During the depression the population problem of Java became increasingly acute because of the shrinkage in world markets for colonial produce. As a consequence of urgent need, the scheme of settling Javanese in the Outer Provinces was revived and revised. Group settlement was adopted, and the prospective emigrants were carefully selected, were given "shots" to protect them from certain common diseases like dysentery, typhoid, and cholera, and were sent out at the time of the year when they could immediately earn their way by assisting colonists already established with their harvest, thus earning enough to keep them until work on their own land brought in returns. This new scheme had not had long to prove its worth before the war intervened, but it seemed to be succeeding admirably. The number of colonists, which was only 7,000 in 1932 (42, p. 23), about doubled by 1936 (471, p. 267), mounted to over 45,000 in 1939, and is supposed to have exceeded 60,000 in 1941. The cost, land being free, was reduced from about 300 guilders (42, p. 23) per family under the old system to about 45 under the new. Irrigation costs are not included in either case.

Perhaps the chief fault to be found with this resettlement scheme as operating just before the Japanese invasion was the small amount of land allotted to each family—not quite a hectare (2.4 acres).[1] This is not enough to insure any substantial increase in per capita production; but the Dutch authorities seemed to be learning rapidly about the needs of settlers, and it does not seem unreasonable to hope that, when they have a chance to resume resettlement work, they will provide enough land for each family to insure it a chance to improve its level of living.

The 60,000 emigrants of 1941 may not seem of much importance in view of an annual increase in population in Java amounting to about 650,000 between 1920 and 1930 and probably averaging 700,000 or more during the 1930's; but a movement of this kind, when it is sound and the need is real, is cumulative and gathers momentum once it is started. All large free migrations of modern times—not forced migrations like those of the Greeks from Asia Minor and the replacement of the Poles in western Poland by Germans after 1939—have started in a small way with the movement of a few people who then let their friends and relatives know the opportunities open to them and encouraged them to come to the new country. It appears that such a movement may have been in the making in the Netherlands East Indies, with Java as the center of emigration, when the war put an end to it tem-

[1] Information contained in a personal letter from Dr. Karl J. Pelzer, whose book, *Pioneer Settlement in the Asiatic Tropics* ("American Geographical Society Publications," No. 29), did not appear in time to be included in the Bibliography.

porarily. Since there is no question of an abundance of good rice land in the Outer Provinces or of difficulties due to settlement in a different national jurisdiction or among people of a different race, or even of the dampening effect of having to settle among strangers, it would seem that this movement has a good chance to attain large proportions when peace is established and a competent government familiar with the needs of Java is again in power. The stage would seem to be set, therefore, to give migration, as a solution of Java's population problem, a real trial if political conditions are such as to permit it.

TABLE 24

POPULATION AND DENSITY OF THE NETHERLANDS EAST INDIES

ISLANDS	AREA (IN SQUARE MILES)	POPULATION (IN THOUSANDS)			DENSITY PER SQUARE MILE	
		1940*	1930	1920	1940	1930
Java and Madura...	51,034	48,088	41,718	34,984	942	818
Sumatra..........	164,154	8,850	7,678	5,852	54	47
Borneo............	208,294	2,500	2,169	1,626	12	10
Celebes...........	72,989	4,878	4,232	3,108	67	58
Bangka and Billiton..	6,477	321	279	223	50	43
Timor.............	24,450	1,910	1,657	1,147	78	68
Riouw............	12,235	344	298	223	28	24
Bali and Lombok....	3,973	2,078	1,803	1,565	523	454
Amboina and Ternate	191,684	1,030	893	623	5	5
Total..........	735,297	70,000	60,727	49,351	95	83
Outer Provinces.....	684,262	21,911	19,009	14,367	32	28

* Estimated on basis of 1930 distribution, assuming a 1940 mid-year population of 70,000,000.

Although there is room for a large increase in numbers in most of the Outer Provinces (see Table 24), a word of caution should be sounded. While Java is about thirty times as densely peopled as the Outer Provinces taken as a whole, it should not be assumed that the Outer Provinces can support a population of 900 or more per square mile even at the Javanese level of living. When the differences between Java and the Outer Provinces are taken into account, however, there is no reasonable doubt of the capacity of the latter to absorb the increase of Java for some years to come, even if New Guinea is left out of account. The element of doubt rests in the ability of the colonial authorities to develop an organization capable of handling the vast number of emigrants who must leave Java.

JAVA'S AGRICULTURE

Up to the present the increase in Java's population has been supported by an almost equally rapid increase in tilled land, of which a considerable part is irrigated, by some improvement in crop yields, and by an extension of commercial agriculture the product of which could be exchanged for more rice than could have been grown in Java with the same amount of labor. There seems to be no doubt, however, that these means are no longer adequate to insure the customary mode of living to the population to be expected in the near future while im-

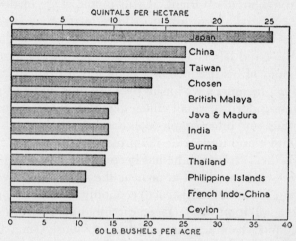

FIG. 7.—Comparative levels of rice yields in countries of monsoon Asia, cleaned rice, average 1930–31 to 1934–35. (Reproduced from V. D. Wickizer and M. K. Bennett, *The Rice Economy of Monsoon Asia* [Stanford University: Stanford University, Food Research Institute, 1941]. Used by permission of the Food Research Institute.)

provement in level of living is not given serious consideration. The area that can be added to the tilled area in Java is estimated at only 750,000 acres (42, p. 19), and most of this will certainly be less fertile than the average of that now in use. The irrigated area cannot be extended substantially without building very expensive reservoirs, and the means for this are not at present available. The improvement of rice yields offers considerably more promise, for Java's yield is scarcely one-half that of Japan (484, p. 60), but this will involve expensive irrigation and intensive fertilization, which are both beyond the means of the Javanese peasant (Fig. 7). For these reasons there is serious doubt that the yields of Javanese agriculture can be increased sufficiently fast in the immediate future to care for the increase in numbers even for another decade at present levels. Indeed, there are many who think that the Javanese level of living is either static or already on the decline (42, p. 18; 471, p. 266; and 33, pp. 160 and 165). It appears that the extension of the agricultural area and the improvements in agricultural practice in Java during the last three or four decades have scarcely kept pace with the growth of population; hence per capita income appears to have changed little if any during this time.

What part do "estate" and "native" agriculture play in the life of the Netherlands East Indies, particularly Java? "Native" agriculture here, as throughout the Orient, is still in the stage of development which characterized almost all agriculture in the days preceding the Industrial Revolution: it is almost entirely a subsistence agriculture carried out by hand labor. The farmer does not expect to sell any significant amount of his produce or to buy much from the townsman. He grows what he must have for his own use plus that needed to meet his taxes and support the small village population which supplies him with hoes, flails, and other simple tools and household goods he cannot make for himself and to provide the professional services (chiefly religious and medical) to which he has become accustomed. Under such a regime he has always lived at or near the subsistence level.

This system of native (subsistence) economy, in which 80 per cent or more of the population was engaged directly in agriculture, was what the Dutch found when they went to Java. Obviously, such a system offered little profit to the colonial power. There was very little surplus which the trader could take, and there was an equally small market for the goods he might import. It was necessary to induce the native to produce spices, or tea, or coffees, or some other product desired in Europe and to pay him for his production in beads, or cloth, or hoes, or some other kind of simple goods in common use.

"Estate" agriculture came into being to assure the production of the desired export crops. Sugar, coffee, tea, and, after a time, rubber, coconuts, cinchona, kapok, and a number of other crops were grown on "estates," the natives taking almost no part in such production on their own account. Thus a dual system of agriculture grew up. One, the native, was merely a continuance of one that had long been followed, with improvements in irrigation and culture hastened by the aid given by the colonial authorities; the other, the "estate," produced for commerce and yielded a new surplus beyond the subsistence of the people employed. Although a considerable portion of the "estate" produce was traded for subsistence—rice, or beans, or clothing formerly made locally—some of it also went to pay returns on the investment in estates by foreigners, the salaries of managers, the cost of the government, and other services leading to the improvement of living conditions among the people. Thus the surplus production arising from the better management of their economy and their government by the Dutch was not all drained off to Holland even in the days of forced labor on estates under the "culture" system which prevailed before about 1860.

In the course of time, however, under colonial control, even native culture came to be involved to a small but increasing extent in production for commerce. In 1929 products raised by natives on their own account constituted 18 per cent of the value of all agricultural exports from Java, the remainder coming from estates (339, 1934, pp. 242–43). In the Outer Provinces, on the other hand, where commercial agriculture has been the basis of most of the agricultural expansion since 1900, native products constituted 59 per cent of the value of all such exports. In the colony as a whole native products constituted 36.5 per cent of all agricultural exports in value in 1929, and in 1938 the percentage rose to 39.6; thus it is clear that the native has become increasingly involved in commercial agriculture, particularly in the Outer Provinces, where population is relatively sparse but land is plentiful.

In the end we find that the ability of the Netherlands East Indies to support their probable increase in population in the next few decades depends upon the amount of migration from Java to the Outer Provinces. There is land in abundance, and the prospect for emigration from Java is relatively good, so the agricultural outlook is far more encouraging than in China and India.

MINERAL RESOURCES

The coal resources of the Netherlands East Indies, while not of the first magnitude, are still considerable, probably about 700 million tons (22, pp. 74–75), and should be sufficient to support as much industry as the islands are likely to develop in the foreseeable future. Most of this coal is not usable for metallurgical purposes, but if there is some coking coal in Borneo (as is claimed), the Netherlands East Indies would seem to be better situated to develop a modest iron and steel industry than most other countries in this region. But, even if not suitable for use in the metal industries, this coal is satisfactory for producing power, and, since none of it is needed for home heating, which demands a large part of all our own coal, it should go much further in supporting industry than a similar amount in a temperate climate.

These islands also contain the largest known oil reserves in South and East Asia. Before the Japanese invasion their annual production had mounted to over eight million tons, of which about four-fifths was refined and exported. The producing wells are located chiefly in Sumatra and Borneo, and the reserves in these islands are generally assumed to be large, although no recent estimate of their size is available. A 1920 estimate gave them at over three billion barrels (8, May, 1920, p. 123), which would not be a large amount for a highly developed industrial country but would be sufficient to supply the needs of the Indies for some time to come, to assist materially in their industrialization, and to provide a considerable export balance. New discoveries are considered quite probable, too, but production has mounted rapidly; and there is danger that, with increasing exports, the Netherlands East Indies will be denuded of their best oil before their own industry is in position to make much use of it (130, 1939, p. 131). It is of interest that, although there is a serious problem of finding work for the natives of Java, the large oil companies exploiting the resources of Sumatra and Borneo use chiefly Chinese labor (405, p. 44).

As to iron ore, Leith, Furness, and Lewis (290) place the Netherlands and her possessions in Class D, which is to say that the supply is of little practical value under present conditions. While this may be the case when the entire Dutch Empire is considered, it seems a little too low a rating when only the Netherlands East Indies are under consideration. Celebes alone is said to have 1,400 million tons (452, p. 179), and Brouwer (43) speaks of about 400 million tons or more in Straits Laut and neighboring Borneo, which, as far as one can judge, does not include 117 million tons recently discovered on Palau Laut (130, 1940, pp. 167–68). In addition, it appears that there is some ore on Sumatra (22, p. 114). Much of this ore is not of a quality which can be used economically at present and heretofore the distance from coking coal has also been a drawback. Recently, however, it has been claimed (130, 1940, p. 167) that there is some coking coal in southeastern Borneo not far from Straits Laut and that some of the ore there is usable.

The situation is not altogether clear from the information available, but it would appear that the possibility of making iron in southeastern Borneo or on some of the neighboring islands is not so hopeless as was formerly thought. If some way of utilizing their inferior ores can be found which is not too expensive, as the Japanese claim to have done in Manchoukuo, the Netherlands East Indies might not only become self-sufficing in iron and steel but be able to export considerable amounts for some years, in view of the large amounts of rather low-grade ore in their reserves.

The Netherlands East Indies is already a very large producer of tin and contains some of the largest known reserves, enough for export as well as for domestic use. The larger part of the ore is sent abroad for smelting, although this situation was being changed just before the war. In the tin mines and smelters, as in the oil fields and coal mines, a large part of the labor is furnished by Chinese contract labor.

The discovery of bauxite is rather recent, and the deposits on islands off the coast of Sumatra are estimated at about 20 million tons containing 50 per cent alumina (130, 1939, p. 145). This constitutes a very important supply, and its exploitation was being vigorously pushed just before the invasion. The export in 1939 amounted to almost 250,000 tons (323, p. 209) and definite plans were made in 1941 to produce aluminum in Sumatra. Here, again, the Netherlands East Indies possesses resources not only adequate to their own needs for some decades but sufficient to permit of considerable exports.

Other minerals of which the colonies possess small amounts are gold, silver, nickel, and sulphur. But the reserves of these do not appear to be large, and they would do little to further industrialization.

On the whole, the Netherlands East Indies can hardly be called "very rich" in minerals (405, p. 42)—but this does not mean that they do not have resources adequate to supply their own needs for coal, oil, tin, aluminum, and possibly for iron, for some decades to come, even though these needs expand quite rapidly. And it is probably not unreasonable to regard the present known reserves of minerals as a minimum, since there are vast areas which have not yet been carefully explored. Indeed, none of the Outer Provinces, with the possible exception of Sumatra, has yet been searched with any care.

INDUSTRY

Prior to the depression of the 1930's the industry of the Netherlands East Indies which used power machinery was confined largely to the processing of agricultural products for market—sugar and rubber—to the operation of mines, to the reduction of some of the tin ore for shipment, to the production and refining of petroleum, to the production of electricity, and to the operation and maintenance of the transportation system. In other words, power-driven machinery was used chiefly in those types of work which were concerned with the production and handling of the raw materials intended for export. There were some exceptions to this highly exclusive use of power machinery in the exploitative interest of the Westerners, but they were incidental and would not of themselves have called forth the establishment of modern industrial works.

Most of the wants of the natives were supplied by a primitive hand industry which was but little changed from what it had been for ages past, with one or two exceptions. The native textile industry, for example, had been almost destroyed by the import of cloth from Europe, and the simple tools used in agriculture as well as the household utensils formerly made entirely by hand in the village were more and more being imported. But, even so, native village industry using only hand power still supplied far the greater part of the needs of the natives.

It is not possible, with the data available, to indicate with any precision the relative importance of these two types of industry—"foreign" (or "Western") and "native"—either by the number of workers employed in them or by the value of their products. However, one important exception was the group of workers engaged in the preparation of the produce of the islands for shipment abroad. These workers for the most part used modern power-driven machinery, and some idea of their place in the life of the colony can be gained from these figures:

In the 1930 census over 2.2 million persons were classified as employed in industry (339, 1934, pp. 136–39). In 1936 an official estimate placed the number of workers in "large factories" at about 120,-000, while the number of full-time handicraft workers was given as 1,535,000 (405, p. 82). Thus the total in 1936 (1,655,000) was considerably smaller than that given in the census of 1930. This difference is probably due in part to the depressed conditions in 1936 which would bear very heavily on the workers in "Western" industry, but the larger part of the difference is probably due to a different classification being used in the census from that followed in making the estimate just referred to. The census undoubtedly included many women who gave only a part of their time to domestic handicrafts, while the estimate for 1936 did not take account of such workers; and workers in "large" factories are not inclusive of all workers in factories using power machinery. But we are unquestionably justified in saying that, even up to 1936, modern factory industry employed very few people as compared with the traditional handicrafts, and, as we shall see in a moment, the official movement for the greater industrialization of the Netherlands East Indies which began during the depression had already had some effect by 1936.

By 1939 another official estimate placed the number of workers in industries using mechanical power at 300,000 (42, p. 81). There is no official estimate of handicraft workers to join with this, but estimates of wages and salaries paid in the mechanical and handicraft shops led Broek (42, p. 81) to believe that twice as many persons were employed in the latter as in the former, since the former have a relatively high proportion of technicians and skilled workers, many of them Europeans, drawing good wages and salaries, while the latter have only poorly paid native workers. In view of this situation, Broek's estimate that handicraft workers are twice as numerous as workers in factories using mechanical power seems very conservative. In any event, even in 1939 in spite of the active encouragement of industry in the Netherlands East Indies since about 1930, it seems highly improbable that as many as one-fourth of all industrial workers were found in factories using mechanical power.

There is nothing surprising in this small development of machine industry in the Netherlands East Indies. It was the natural result of the policies pursued by the Dutch and, one may add, by the other colonial powers in South and East Asia. The Netherlands East Indies, in spite of the growing power of the idea of trusteeship in the Dutch masters, were valued chiefly as a source of raw materials to be traded to the more industrialized countries, and consequently they had to be kept as a market for the manufactured goods of these countries, with Holland handling as much of the trade as possible and supplying her fair share of their manufactured imports.

In this connection, however, it should be said that from 1860 to 1933 trade with the Netherlands East Indies had been open to all countries on practically equal terms. Not since 1860 has Holland ever furnished more than about one-third of their imports and by the end of the 1920's was supplying only about one-fifth of them, according to official figures (339, 1934, p. 280). Likewise Holland's share of the exports of the Netherlands East Indies has been declining as their exports—rubber, tin, sugar, oil, cinchona, etc.—came into large demand by other countries. The economic stake of Holland in the Netherlands East Indies has increasingly become that of an investor in the production of raw materials and a trader in both exports and imports.

But, in spite of this liberal trade policy in the Netherlands East Indies, it was not to the advantage of the Dutch to build up industry there which would render it impossible for other nations as well as for themselves to sell their goods in this market. Clearly they could not expect to profit by the export of large quantities of raw materials if the islands did not buy large amounts of manufactured goods from the peoples who wanted their rubber, tin, oil, etc. It is inevitable that any area treated primarily as a source of raw materials will find its industrial development neglected, if not actively opposed, by the country which controls its production of raw materials and profits by sending it manufactured goods.

The general industrial situation in the Netherlands East Indies prior to the depression of the 1930's was, then, what was to be expected in any colony where the foreigner comes in as an exploiter rather than as a settler—backward—and was kept this way because it best suited the dominant interests of the colonial power. With the coming of the depression, however, a new situation arose. The very great dependence of the Netherlands East Indies on world markets which had been developed in consequence of the exploitation of their raw materials made their economy highly susceptible to the fluctuations in the world demand for rubber, tin, sugar, oil, and many other minor products. It is estimated that half of the 1.2 million plantation workers of 1929 were unemployed by 1933, many workers in the processing industries were also thrown out of work, and a large proportion of the native producers of rubber, kapok, and coconuts was left with a greatly diminished market and was forced to sell at prices which were ruinous. The situation became desperate, and the government was forced to take positive relief measures which would result in making the Netherlands East Indies more nearly self-sufficing than they had been since World War I. In addition to turning land from commercial agricultural production to food production (270), the government began to encourage local industry to produce goods which had been imported. Partly because the establishment of industry in a new area is made more difficult by the pursuit of a free-trade policy, and partly to preserve the smaller market that remained to their European customers, the Netherlands East Indies authorities also abandoned free trade in 1933.

The encouragement of industry after 1930 consisted in various forms of assistance to small-scale native industries, the training of workers, the standardizing of goods, the provision of better credit facilities, and aid in marketing their products (405, p. 58, and 184,

p. 87). These were the first measures because employment in small-scale native industry largely carried on by hand labor seemed to promise the most effective unemployment relief and also the quickest way to an adequate supply of many kinds of goods which could no longer be imported.

The raising of tariffs and the use of the quota system for imports from 1933 onward also encouraged the establishment of *Western* factories. The textile industry (not batik), which had been almost destroyed by the import of cheap cloth, was revived. The chief evidence of this change is found in the import of yarn, which amounted to only 6,414 tons in 1931 but rose to 21,323 tons in 1939. The native production of European-style cigars and cigarettes rose many fold (from a value of a million florins in 1933 to 14.2 million in 1939). Other "native" manufactures which were encouraged were plaited goods, furniture, leather, light-metal goods, and bricks and tiles.

The "Western" industries encouraged consisted largely of light consumption industries such as soap and vegetable oils, electrical goods, cigarettes, brewing, and canned foodstuffs; and several factories were established for industries not so light, such as automobile assembly plants, a tire factory, and a number of machine and metal-working shops. Practically all these Western factories were financed by private European or American capital, although some Chinese also took part in this development. Another field in which there was considerable expansion was in the generation of electricity. Here a rather large amount of state capital was invested, and by 1937 the state, that is, the government, was also actively assisting small-scale native industry with loans, although the amounts involved were quite small.

To understand the activity of the government in this whole industrialization program, we must remember that it was no stranger to the operation of economic enterprise. It had long operated many estates and had a virtual monopoly in the exploitation of the teak forests of East Java; it also operated tin and coal mines, the railways and salt-works, and it participated in many other enterprises, such as oil and bauxite and nickel mining (42, p. 33). It was, therefore, well prepared to assume the active direction of new and more extensive enterprise when it became necessary to reorganize the economy of the colony to provide greater self-sufficiency. Until the war in Europe, however, the influence of the government over the economy of the colony was manifested in the extension of its control over industry rather than by increase in its direct ownership and operation. Its aim was to ease the shock of the depression, and in this it had a fair measure of success. But, in doing this, the Netherlands East Indies almost inevitably developed a measure of self-sufficiency in textiles, in tobacco, in soap, in tires and tubes, in electrical supplies, in manufactured food products, in furniture, and in certain other goods, which was quite incompatible with their status as a colony furnishing raw materials to Western industry. That this development was not planned but was merely a by-product of the necessity of finding work for those left stranded by the depression and of the measures taken to prevent the Japanese from monopolizing the market for manufactured goods does not alter the fact that the Netherlands East Indies were becoming more self-sufficing than was consistent with imperialist ideas of the function of a colony.

The result of the several measures taken to encourage home industry during the depression was that at the outbreak of the war in Europe the government of the Netherlands East Indies, as well as many men financially interested in the economy of the colony, found a growing industry which it was to their advantage to maintain and enlarge. The fact that, with recovery in the West and the increased demand for rubber and tin in particular, some of the most urgent need for this industry disappeared did not greatly alter the attitude of the interests that stood to profit by this new development.

But while there was some slackening of the industrial drive as recovery progressed in the West before 1939, the war in Europe renewed and enhanced its vigor. Not only did the war almost at once disrupt many of the customary business relations with Europe, but it also led to a considerable further migration of capital, Dutch capital in particular, to the Netherlands East Indies and also to the migration of some of the capitalists. Thus the war both tended to decrease the lingering reluctance to develop home industry in the Indies, since goods from Europe could not be had, and at the same time provided a new source of capital for local enterprise. The isolation of the colonies from Holland and Europe was an important stimulant of local industrial enterprise, but it was also strongly reinforced by the growing conviction that Japan had plans of her own for the Netherlands East Indies which could be thwarted only by the development of strong local industry. It became increasingly clear that if Japan moved against the Netherlands East Indies, they had to depend largely on their own power of defense and on such aid as they might obtain from Australia and the United States. The British navy could no longer be counted on for the defense of the Dutch Empire. Although there was then neither time nor means to achieve any considerable industrial development which would be useful in defense of the Indies, the government moved vigorously to do what it could. It laid plans for the smelting of scrap iron and the fabrication of the steel thus produced, for new hydroelectric development to provide power for small plants, for the establishment of a chemical industry, for an aluminum plant, and for many other industries useful not only for defense but also for increasing the self-sufficiency of the colony (405, pp. 84–85; 323, pp. 215–18; and 42, pp. 84–85).

While this wartime development may be regarded as unusual and while some of it is undoubtedly unsound economically, there can be little doubt that it will profoundly affect the life of the colony in the future, both politically and economically. It does not require prophetic powers to see that the experience of the colonial administration in providing employment during the depression, in encouraging local industry, in attempting to build defense strength, and, above all, in carrying on independently in a time of great stress, will alter greatly the whole outlook of the colony and its place in the Dutch Empire and in world economy. If at the same time the Europeans, chiefly Dutch, residing in the Netherlands East Indies definitely throw in their lot with the Indonesians and make the islands their home instead of keeping their faces turned to Europe as a place to return to when they have made their "pile"—and there is some indication that this is happening (270, p. 344)—there can be little doubt that the industrial development started during the depression and intensified after 1939 will bear fruit in the postwar period. That some of the Dutch also believe this will be the case is shown clearly in the following quotation.

"The program of industrialization to be followed by the Netherlands Government in later years, consequently, may be summarized as follows:

"1. Rapid expansion of elementary education.

"2. General and individual increase in agricultural production, with resulting increase in the purchasing power of the native farmer.

"3. Gradual absorption of native farmers into small-scale industries, operated by and for the Indonesians.

"4. Organization of small-scale industrial workers into production centers with finishing and sales divisions.

"5. Development of factories organized by Westerners, as well as by Indonesian entrepreneurs.

"The encouragement and development of Indonesian leadership to attain the fifth stage of industrialization have been, and will again become, after the war, an integral part of the Indies Government policy, and it is the general hope that more and more Indonesians will be able to take over the larger factories and to derive the benefits of a well-balanced relationship with local consumption, as well as with local customs. Such an industry could then become a real and vital part of this new development in the Indonesian way of life" (270, p. 391).

In the light of what has happened during the last fifteen years, it is difficult to believe that the Netherlands East Indies will ever return fully to either the political or the economic status they occupied before 1933.

CAN INDUSTRY SUPPLY ENOUGH JOBS?

Now we have a basis for answering a little more adequately the question: Can industrial development in the Netherlands East Indies proceed fast enough to care for the probable increase in population in Java, which cannot be cared for by agricultural migration, until such time as the urbanized industrial population will begin to reduce its birth rate? Of course, this question cannot be answered categorically. The increase of population in Java at the time of Japanese occupation was probably 700,000, or somewhat more, annually. There is no reason to hope that the annual rate of natural increase, which is now 15–18 per 1,000, will become any smaller in the next several decades even with fairly rapid industrialization unless the level of living deteriorates sufficiently to cause a rise in the death rate. On the other hand, with the better living conditions which would probably ensue upon a general increase in productive efficiency, a still higher rate of natural increase, perhaps as high as in the Philippines (see chap. xviii), would be expected because of the further lowering of the death rate. Hence the Netherlands East Indies may soon be called upon to provide for even more than 700,000 additional persons each year. Since agricultural resettlement can probably provide for a considerable proportion of this increase within a few years, the burden falling on industry will be proportionally far less than in China and India.

Until rather recently the facts did not seem to justify the belief that industrial development was likely to do much to relieve the hardships which would accompany the continued increase of Java's population. The pace of industrialization seemed too slow to permit of hope that it could absorb any considerable portion of the expected increase and the colonization in the Outer Provinces had been a practical failure.

THE COLONIES OF SOUTHEAST ASIA. I

However, the more active and the better-informed participation of the government in colonization and in industrial development since 1933 and intensified after 1939 seem to have changed the outlook significantly. With the large amount of good land available for settlement (even if New Guinea is left out of account), with the available mineral resources, and with the will to use these to support the growth of the native population instead of so exclusively for the benefit of the mother country and her exploiting sons, there is reason to hope that the urgency of Java's population problem can be postponed for the next few decades. It will not be easy to do this, but it does not seem as nearly impossible as it did some years ago, largely because of the changed attitude of the government. A permanent solution of Java's problem of population pressure is, of course, a different matter. This can be achieved only by the control of population growth to keep pace with the intelligent use of resources for the benefit of the natives.

Chapter XVIII

THE COLONIES OF SOUTHEAST ASIA. II

THE PHILIPPINES, INDO-CHINA, BURMA, MALAYA, AND THAILAND

THE Philippines consist of a group of about seven thousand islands with a total area of approximately 115,000 square miles. The thirteen largest islands, each of which contains over 400 square miles, also contain almost fifteen million persons, or 92 per cent of the 1939 population (364, II, 42). The Philippine Islands are wholly tropical. Manila, the capital, is about 600 miles southeast of Hong Kong, and the northern tip of Luzon—the main island—is only about 300 miles from southern Formosa. One small island, Y'ami, is only 35 miles from Formosa. Like the Netherlands East Indies, they are an integral part of Southeast Asia.

POPULATION OF THE PHILIPPINES

The estimates of population since 1800 show a somewhat variable but rather rapid growth (364) during most of the time. If the estimates preceding the first census after United States' occupation are accepted, the population grew from a little over 1.5 in 1800 to 7.6 million in 1903, or by about fivefold during this century. It has more than doubled since 1903, and in 1939 was over ten times as large (16 million) as in 1800. Even under what we in the United States have ordinarily thought of as "Spanish misrule," the population grew as rapidly as did the population of Java between 1816 and 1900 under Dutch rule. Only toward the end of Spanish control, 1877–97, did the rate of growth average as low as 5–7 per 1,000 per year. Between 1903 and 1939 the population growth has averaged about 21 per 1,000 per year. Prior to American occupation the chief contribution of the Spanish to population growth in the Philippines was the establishment of law and order in a large part of the islands. When the United States added health measures, education, and colonial agriculture for export, the growth of population was stimulated just as it was in Java by similar developments.

The average annual rate of population growth in the Philippines given above was calculated from the census rather than from the

birth rates and death rates (286, 1940–41), because the latter indicate a
natural increase of only about 15–16 per 1,000, whereas the censuses,
which are generally considered reliable, show that it must have been
about one-third higher. The recorded birth rate, which is about 32,
and the recorded death rate, which is 16–17, must both be highly deficient. In order to get a rate of natural increase which will accord with
the census enumerations, it is necessary to assume that the birth rate
in the Philippines is at least 40–42 per 1,000 if the death rate is 18–20,
a low death rate for such a people in their present stage of development. The alternative is to assume that the 1939 census is much more
accurate and complete than the 1918 census and the 1918 census more
accurate than that of 1903, so that the difference between the natural
increase of 15–16 shown by birth rates and death rates and 21 shown
by the censuses is due chiefly to better enumeration.

My own opinion, arrived at from long study of such matters as well as
from personal observation, is that the omissions of registration are
likely to be greater than those of the census and that a natural increase averaging about 20–21 per 1,000 has characterized the Philippine population for the last thirty years or more. It was probably
somewhat lower in the first decade of our occupation and somewhat
higher in recent years. But whether we accept a natural increase of
15 or 20 makes little difference in our important conclusion, which
is that the population of the Philippines is now (and has been for
several decades at least) growing at a rate probably somewhat greater
than that of most Western countries during much of the nineteenth
century.

The density of population in the Philippines (140 per square mile)
is far below that of Java—less than one-sixth as great—but the Philippines as a whole are far less fertile, probably more like Sumatra and
Borneo (see Table 24). Moreover, there are large differences in density
between the several islands; for example, the small island of Bantayan
has a density of 640 per square mile, and Cebu, the ninth in size, has a
density of over 550, but Luzon, the main island, has only a little over
180, and Mindanao, second in size, has only 50.

At present the population problem of the Philippines is not one of
lack of land but of better distribution of people on the land. Much
thought is being given to organizing a large and steady migration from
the more densely settled islands and provinces to those which still have
an abundance of land. In this respect the population problem in certain provinces of the Philippines resembles that of Java in relation to

the remainder of the Netherlands East Indies. For two or three decades to come the Philippines should be able to find land for their probable increase in numbers by organizing an efficient migration service. They had already begun this when war intervened.

In the Philippines, as in Java, there is as yet no clear evidence of any decline in the birth rate, although the wider education of the people may already have encouraged some small decline in certain classes. Moreover, there are differences in social conditions between the Filipinos and the people of the Netherlands East Indies which may work faster in this direction:

First, the great majority of the Filipinos are Christians (Catholics), while the Malays of the Netherlands East Indies are predominantly Moslems; in the West, Christians have not found it inconsistent with their religious beliefs to control their birth rates. We have little evidence regarding the attitude Moslems will take in this matter as they come within the influence of Western industry and city life, but I for one find it difficult to believe that their attitude toward uncontrolled fertility will differ much from that of people in the West if, and when, they are subjected to the same general urban, industrial, and educational influences which make a lower birth rate appear desirable to us.

Second, public education is much more advanced in the Philippines than in the Netherlands East Indies and is now under the control of the Filipinos themselves. Thus they are better prepared to understand the relation between population growth and welfare than the people of the Netherlands East Indies.

Third, the awareness of the difficulties arising as a consequence of rapid population growth is far more widespread among native Filipino leaders than among native leaders in the Netherlands East Indies. This is an inevitable consequence of the definite policy of the United States regarding Philippine independence. If the Filipinos were to be independent, they had to have native leaders, while in a colony which is expected to remain a colony native leaders are at least a nuisance, if not a serious danger.

Nevertheless, with the evidence now at our disposal, it is only reasonable to expect a continued rapid increase of the Filipino population for at least two or three decades.

AGRICULTURE OF THE PHILIPPINES

The agriculture of these islands is characterized by a greater dependence on commercial crops than even that of the Netherlands East

Indies. The export crops, chiefly sugar, coconuts, hemp, and tobacco, occupy about one-half as much land as those grown almost entirely for food and exceed the food crops in value (370, p. 147). The area under crops is about 11 million acres, less than one-sixth of the total area and only a little over one-fourth of the land classified as arable (370, p. 60), so there can be little doubt that there is room for considerable expansion of Philippine agriculture. But this expansion has been slow because of the lack of any definite policy of agricultural resettlement on the part of the American authorities earlier and by the commonwealth government until the last two or three years before the Japanese invasion.

The high proportion of Philippine crops grown for export, largely to the United States because of the absence of tariff barriers, made the islands very dependent on economic conditions in this country. When we bought their products at good prices, they were relatively prosperous; but when we did not buy them or bought them at low prices, they suffered heavily. This great dependence on the free market of the United States also promises ill for Philippine economy after independence, since they will no longer enjoy the full tariff advantage. Many measures are being taken to lessen the economic shock to Philippine agriculture certain to come as the consequence of independence, but suffice it to note that preferential treatment of Philippine products in the American market for a few years was being planned, that the development of domestic industry was expected to absorb some of the labor not needed for export crops as well as to furnish much of the goods heretofore imported, and that the export of Philippine minerals was expected to pay for some of the imports which their agricultural exports would no longer buy.

But while there is no doubt that the Philippines have enough arable land to care for their increase in population for several decades, it will not be easy to organize the use of this land as rapidly as needed. The system of large landholdings has resulted in about one-half of the farmers being tenants in spite of an abundance of unused land. The development of roads has done little to open new areas, and the commonwealth government lacks the means even if it has the will to open up new free land rapidly. With the coming of complete independence, the settlement of new areas may be and probably will be much accelerated, but whether it will proceed fast enough to alter the position of tenants substantially remains open to question. The landlords, who are powerful both economically and politically, will oppose any such rapid opening of new lands as will result in the loss of their tenants to these new lands and will also oppose the development of industry if it seriously threatens to compete with them for labor.

The only agency able to drive vigorously for the better use of Philippine agricultural resources is the government, and there is not yet any clear indication that it is prepared to assume this responsibility. The landlord class still dominates the government. And even if the government is willing to encourage a large redistribution of population, there is real danger that the gaining of independence may result in such a serious economic setback that conditions favoring the continued rapid growth of population will deteriorate. We will be in a better position to judge these future possibilities after we have examined the mineral resources of the islands.

MINERAL RESOURCES OF THE PHILIPPINES

The Philippines' mineral resources are not large as compared with those of the Netherlands East Indies. They possess only two or three minerals in sufficient quantities to be of much assistance in the development of industry or by the export of which they can pay for essential imports.

They possess but little coal: one estimate of their reserves is 60 million tons (129, 1940, p. 38). Even this seems somewhat optimistic, and besides none of this coal is suitable for metallurgical purposes. So if the Filipinos are ever to build an iron industry, it will be necessary to import practically the entire fuel supply. Already about seven-eighths of all coal (323, p. 233) used on the railways and in the production of electrical power is imported because Philippine coal is of poor quality and expensive to mine.

While there are some indications of the presence of oil in the islands, and much money and effort have been expended in prospecting and drilling, no commercial production has been achieved, and it now appears doubtful that there is any significant amount to be expected.

Thus the Philippines appear very poorly supplied with fuel. Since the volume of water power is also small, this shortage of fuel constitutes a severe handicap in the development of machine industry.

The reserves of iron ore are perhaps the most important of all the minerals the islands possess. The ores now being exploited come from small deposits of high grade which will soon be exhausted at the rate of mining prevailing in 1940. In that year over 1.36 million tons were mined, most of it being sent to Japan. The total known deposits of iron actually exploitable now probably do not exceed 10–12 million tons, but there is one large deposit of lower-grade ore on the island of Mindanao estimated at between 500 and 1,000 million tons. This will prove of great value if and when efficient methods of using such ore are developed.

The gold mined in the Philippines constituted over 85 per cent of the value of all minerals mined in 1936–40 (323, p. 234). It helps materially in maintaining favorable foreign trade balances, but of course it can contribute to the industrial strength of the islands only as long as the United States continues to take it in payment for goods sold.

The Philippines do possess the largest known single deposit of chrome—10–11 million tons (323, p. 233)—and mining had attained fairly large proportions by 1940 (about 200,000 tons annually). All of it was exported, the United States taking over 80 per cent and Japan most of the remainder (370, p. 149). There is also some manganese, amount unknown, but most of it is not of high grade. About 55,000–60,000 tons were mined in 1940. Prior to 1940 Japan got the major portion; after that the United States took most of it (370, p. 149, and 323, p. 230).

The production of copper concentrates reached almost 9,000 tons in 1940 (370, p. 149, and 323, p. 234). Exports of copper went chiefly to Japan. No estimate of reserves of copper is available, but they do not seem to be large. Lead and zinc, like copper, are chiefly by-products of gold mining and smelting, and the known resources are not large. Asbestos, molybdenum, and platinum are also found, but, as far as is known, the deposits are small and of little industrial significance.

It is possible, of course, that the Philippines have much larger mineral resources than those indicated above. But with our present knowledge the implication not infrequently made that mining and metallurgical exports will take the place of agricultural exports when independence comes seems highly optimistic (370, p. 72, and 323, p. 234). Their high-quality iron ore is already well on the road to exhaustion, and the total known chrome supply at pre-war prices would sell for less than a single year's exports of agricultural products. Only gold, the value of which averaged almost $30 million annually in 1936–40, would seem to exist in quantities large enough to play an important part in balancing foreign accounts. One must conclude that the mineral resources of the Philippines cannot play a very important part in their future economic development.

INDUSTRY IN THE PHILIPPINES

As soon as it was decided that the Philippines would have their independence, it was realized that their products would no longer enjoy a price differential due to sale within the tariff wall of the United States. This meant the disruption of their entire economy. It was in preparation for this severance of both political and economic ties that the Philippine leaders began to talk about self-sufficiency and industrialization and to lay plans to achieve these ends. It is not minimizing their accomplishment to say that up to the outbreak of war in 1941 little had been achieved. Some promising beginnings, however, had been made.

Prior to the granting of independence most of the industries established had to do either with the processing of agricultural products or with mining. Little interest was manifested in industries to supply the consumption needs of the Filipinos. On the other hand, Americans to a much greater extent than either the Dutch or the British did allow the natives to share in the economic development of the colony. Filipinos did own a substantial share in the sugar industry, estimated at 45 per cent of the capital invested in sugar mills (405, p. 94). They had a much smaller share in the coconut industries, about 7 or 8 per cent; but in the cordage industry they owned about 41 per cent of the spindle capacity, and they held a substantial interest in the tobacco industry. In mining, the Filipino interest is also said to be substantial, while in lumbering it amounted to about 25 per cent.

The native was not crowded out of Western types of enterprise in the Philippines to anything like the same extent as in most other colonies. His leaders were therefore in much better position to undertake an industrial development intended to make the country self-sufficient.

It was soon realized by these leaders that if independence were not to lead to grave economic disaster, they must plan quickly and with determination for the future and that a large part of this planning must be done by the government, for there was no other organization competent to plan or to execute plans. In 1935 President Quezon stated the position of the government as follows:

"I am not in favor of the Government engaging directly in business enterprises that could well be left in the hands of private individuals, except as to some public utilities. However, if no private capital is available or willing to undertake the establishment of an industry which may be considered necessary and urgent for purposes of national defense, to provide the national economy with an indispensable requirement, or to promote the public welfare the Government should, alone or in cooperation with private capital, establish and operate that industry. . . . . The creation of this National Economic Council answers an urgent national need and formally commits this Government to a definite economic policy. We don't believe in the economic philosophy of *laissez-faire*. We favor government leadership in productive activities. We believe in planning the national economy" (405, pp. 113–14).

As a matter of fact, it was necessary for the government to become the entrepreneur, the banker, and the co-ordinator of the whole industrialization movement if fairly rapid progress was to be made; but it has not excluded the participation of private interests in the schemes it has undertaken. With the reconstruction required now, it would appear that even more leadership will devolve on the government.

About all that can be said concerning this industrialization movement up to the outbreak of war is that some industries already established have been given new life by it. The cement industry, largely government-owned, is being expanded. Such "light" industries as cigars and cigarettes, rattan furniture, candy, and soap, privately owned, are also being encouraged to expand. The main industrial drive, however, seems to be in the preparation of food products and the manufacture of textiles, the government furnishing both plans and capital. In the case of textiles the aim is not to displace native hand industry but to supplement it and perhaps to furnish it with better materials. An effort is also being made to provide adequate electric power for the light consumption industries which private enterprise is being encouraged to establish—clothing, rubber shoes, pottery, building materials, breweries, etc.

It is not surprising that industrialization has proceeded slowly and scarcely promises to take up a great deal of the slack likely to come with independence. The natives in any colony have comparatively little opportunity to accumulate capital or to develop economic and technical leadership. Moreover, in view of the many political and economic uncertainties arising from the rapid transition of a colony into an independent nation, there was bound to be much confusion, and different classes and factions were certain to work at cross-purposes.

If the Filipinos had had a longer time between the definite promise of independence and complete autonomy, perhaps twenty years instead of ten, and if they had gone about preparing for independence with the same vigor they displayed between 1934 and 1941, they would undoubtedly have been able to develop more domestic industry and plan more thoroughgoing agricultural adjustments to ease the inevitable shock. There certainly is no good reason to think that the obstacles to the establishment of consumption industries in the Philippines are insuperable, nor is there reason to think that cotton, kapok, additional rice, meat, dairy products, and other goods, primarily agricultural, which now constitute about one-fourth of all imports, could not be produced at home by using some of the land now devoted to export crops and by employing some of the displaced agricultural labor in mills and factories. But to do all this takes careful national planning, a relatively large amount of capital, a trained and experienced personnel, and a strong agricultural settlement and extension service, all of which are still inadequate.

In conclusion it seems safe to assume that the population of the Philippines will continue to grow at about the rate of the last thirty years for at least that long in the future unless some widespread catastrophe lowers the level of living to the point where the death rate will rise sufficiently to reduce the natural increase. It also appears that there is land enough to provide for such an increase if it is well used and if at the same time industry is carried forward at a reasonable pace. But another doubling of population in the next thirty-five years or thereabouts will leave the Philippines in an entirely different situation from the present one as regards caring for a fairly rapidly growing population.

FRENCH INDO-CHINA

French Indo-China, lying to the south of China with a long coast line facing the Pacific (South China Sea), covers an area almost two and one-half times as large as the Philippines—about 285,000 square miles. It is entirely tropical, and its crops are dependent on the monsoon rains of the summer months as in all of Southeast Asia. It contains rather large mountainous areas, but it also has large river deltas which are ideal for the growing of rice.

In 1936 the colony had a population of about 23 million. At the rate of increase (somewhat over 7 per cent in five years) which had prevailed since 1921, the population in 1941 would have increased to about 24.7 million (134, Part I, p. 44). Except for unusual catastrophes, such a rate can be expected to continue for some time. Any widespread improvement in living conditions and in public health service would undoubtedly raise the rate of growth well above the present level.

As in the Philippines and the Netherlands East Indies, the population problem of Indo-China at present arises from the unequal distribution of the population over the land rather than from too great numbers in the country as a whole. The people of Indo-China are heavily concentrated in the great alluvial plains near the sea where the land is rich and where the flooding of the rice fields, largely as a consequence of the heavy rainfall, makes irrigation unnecessary. But even in these alluvial lands the density varies from about 600 or fewer per square mile in the rice lands of Cochin China in the south to about three times this number in the rice lands of Annam and Tonkin farther north. A redistribution of population more in accordance with the agricultural opportunities available would enable French Indo-China to support its probable increase of population at the present level of living for several decades, quite possibly at a higher level.

At present only about 15 per cent of the land is utilized at all, and not much more than half of this is cultivated (chiefly rice). The "rice area" alone is estimated at about 20,000 square miles (134, Part I, p. 3) and would support about 36 million persons if all of it had the same density per square mile as the rice land in Tonkin. This would leave over 90 per cent of the land for other uses, and there is little reason to doubt that a considerable part of this could be used for nonirrigated crops.

The mineral resources of Indo-China are relatively more abundant than those of the Philippines but can scarcely be called "great" or "rich" according to Western standards.

A large body of anthracite coal, estimated at about 20,000 million tons, exists in the colony. This is suitable for power purposes but does not seem suitable for most metallurgical uses. About three-fourths of the 2.5 million tons mined annually before the war were exported, chiefly to Japan (286, 1941–42, p. 141). There is also some lignite, but this seems to be of little value at the present time, and no estimate of reserves is available.

There is also some iron ore, but no estimate of reserves seems to have been made. Actual production did not begin until recently, about 1936, and has never exceeded 75,000 tons in any year (286, 1941–42, p. 145). Practically all of this ore was exported to Japan. From what is known now it does not appear that Indo-China has enough ore to support more than a small iron industry even if its coal could be used for smelting.

The country has some rich tin deposits, but they, too, appear to be quite small; so far production (metal content) has never much exceeded 1,500 tons (405, p. 16) in any one year. It also possesses some manganese, antimony, tungsten, zinc, graphite, phosphates, gold, lead, and silver, but in quantities that do not appear to be large enough to be of much importance in the future economic development of the country.

At present practically all the minerals produced are exported, and it seems likely that this will continue to be the case for some time. The one important local industry based on native mineral resources is cement-making. The materials for this appear abundant, and the colony not only supplies her own needs but exports a considerable proportion of the product.

Indo-China, like all other colonial areas in this region, has little modern industry—having been exploited chiefly as a source of raw materials and a market for manufactured goods. But, in spite of this, and possibly because of France's colonial policy which restricts the trade of her colonies with other countries by making them a more integral part of the French economy than does that of the British and Dutch, Indo-China has retained her handicraft industries more intact than most of the colonies in this region. A few modern factories for the making of textiles, sugar, soap, matches, paper, and some other light consumption goods have been established, but industrial development is small in comparison with the needs of the people. Care has been taken to see that the industries established should not interfere seriously with the trade in French manufactures.

It is not likely that French Indo-China can develop any considerable amount of basic heavy industry because of her lack of coking coal and iron. Her future industrial development must be based chiefly on the use of her own agricultural products in the consumption industries. In this field she might well produce her own cotton and rayon, coconut oil or other oils for soap and margarine, rubber for domestic use, matches, and such canned foods as she needs. Already she supplies her own sugar and is beginning to distill alcohol from rice, which is her principal crop. She exports about 1.5 million tons of rice annually, thus being one of the three great rice-exporting areas of the world, Burma and Thailand being the others. But she will no doubt have to continue to import most of her iron and steel, her machinery, and her petroleum, and pay for them with her rice, her corn, her rubber, and her tin.

In brief, Indo-China can probably support a considerably larger population at a better level of living if she seriously undertakes the development of her consumption industries, the expansion of her agricultural area through a large redistribution of her population, and the improvement of agricultural practices.

BURMA

Burma, like French Indo-China, is a tropical country lying south of China in the Indo-Chinese peninsula. It is rather mountainous but has large alluvial plains around the mouths of its more important rivers, which are among the best rice lands in the world. It is a British colony which until 1937 was administered as part of India. Since that time it has been a separate crown colony.

The population of Burma has grown quite rapidly in recent decades. The census of 1901 gave a population of 10.5 million, which had grown to 14.7 million by 1931, a gain of almost 40 per cent in thirty years, or an average of 12 per cent in each decade. If this rate continued to 1941, the population at that time would have been about 16.4 million. The same factors which we have seen operating to decrease the death rate in the Netherlands East Indies and the Philippines have been at work here—internal order has been maintained, a health service of sorts established, some improvement in agricultural practices, particularly in rice culture, has been attained, and the exploitation of mineral resources has gone forward rapidly. As a consequence the growth of population, although not quite so rapid as in some of the other areas, has nevertheless been substantial and is probably just well started.

The most serious population problem of Burma in the near future is not one of numbers or even of distribution but, as will be shown in a moment, one arising out of her rapid exploitation as a colony. The expansion of her rice culture and the exploitation of her oil and minerals have resulted in the immigration of considerable numbers of Indians and Chinese, because of the unwillingness of the natives to work steadily at these jobs. Consequently, a race problem of serious proportions is developing. As is generally the case, race antagonisms are aggravated by the fact that a large measure of control over economic resources has also been lost, chiefly to the British but in an increasing measure to the Indians and Chinese. The better-educated Burmese are well aware of what has been happening and, as we saw during the early years of the war, showed no love for their British masters, whom they held responsible for the ills which they had only begun to realize. But the common people do not see this far and are venting their resentment directly on the Indians and Chinese, who as middlemen and money-lenders and landlords exploit the natives in many ways which are extremely irritating. There have been some serious race riots in recent years, and the prospect is that they will grow both in numbers and in violence if a larger measure of economic control is not returned to the Burmese.

Burma contains about 262,000 square miles, of which only about 11 per cent, or 18 million acres, are cultivated. Since it is estimated that an additional 50–60 million acres can be tilled, it can be seen that there is room for a rather large expansion of her agriculture. Rice is the chief crop and occupies about two-thirds of the total tilled area; this is about two and one-half times the area devoted to it in 1890. Because of this rapid growth in production, Burma is now the leading rice exporter in the world, exporting about 3.5 million tons a year (78, p. 106), an amount greater than that of Thailand and French Indo-China combined. Since the best rice lands are already in cultivation and since the population is growing quite rapidly, it is not expected that Burmese exports of rice will increase in the future; indeed, they are much more likely to decline.

Sesame, the oil of which is exported, occupies about 1.4 million acres and peanuts a somewhat smaller area, while cotton, lac, tobacco, and rubber are also exported in small amounts. The export of forest products, chiefly teakwood, is large, the forest area being generally estimated at a half or more of the total area (418), perhaps 130,000 square miles. The other chief crops raised for domestic use are sugar cane, millet and forage, fruits, coffee, and tea. The methods of cultivation are generally quite primitive. Most of the work is done by hand or by very primitive plows pulled by water buffaloes, although steel plows are quite common in the rice areas, and a few large plantations even use tractors and power-drawn implements.

On the whole, the agriculture of Burma is better than that of the other countries of the Indo-Chinese peninsula (Thailand, French Indo-China, and Malaya), and the Burmese allegedly enjoy a considerably higher level of life.

With a large amount of tillable land still available and with about three-fifths of her rice being exported, there is no reason to anticipate any serious difficulty in caring for the probable growth of population during the next several decades (78, p. 106). Some writers, however, believe that the practicable limit of rice cultivation has been reached and that the future increase of population beyond what the present rice production will support must depend chiefly on bringing new non-rice land into use and on the improvement of crop production on the land now in use by better agricultural practice.

Burma is rather well favored with mineral resources but is seriously lacking in two of the most essential minerals of modern industry. There is some iron ore in the country, quantity unknown, but it appears to be of low grade and is probably not usable under present conditions. Her coal is in the form of lignite and thus is not suitable for the development of the metallurgical industries even if she possessed the other minerals. It might very well be used for power, however, as it seems to be moderately abundant.

Burma has rather large reserves of oil which are being rapidly exploited. Her proportion of the world production of oil, however, is only 0.4–0.5 of 1 per cent, although she is the fourteenth country in rank (78, p. 140). Practically all the oil not used in the country is sent to India, and, until the invasion by Japan, Burmese refineries were supplying a considerable part of the high-grade aviation gasoline used by the British in the East.

Burma is also a large producer of tungsten, in normal times furnishing about 17–20 per cent of the world's supply and holding second place as a producer. After China ceased to export tungsten, Burma became the leading exporter of this metal for several years, production amounting to over 12,000 tons in 1939. Her reserves are said to amount to over 650,000 tons.

There are also considerable amounts of tin, lead, zinc, and silver and some copper and nickel in the country, but in the absence of coal and iron it is probable that most of her minerals, with as little refining as is required to keep the cost of transport low, will be exported to steel-producing countries. At present the export of these minerals is of material aid in the purchase of steel, machinery, and other manufactured goods, although the export of rice is far and away the most important item in Burmese trade.

Burma and India have a large trade with each other. India is more developed industrially and can supply textiles, iron and steel, coal, and some machinery, while she needs Burma's rice, tin, oil, timber, and alloy minerals. Japan imports some raw cotton and some minerals from Burma and sends her a considerable amount of cotton manufactures, but her trade is small when compared with that of India.

Aside from the exploitation of minerals—oil, lead, zinc, copper, tin, and tungsten—there is comparatively little modern industry in Burma (413, p. 78). There are, of course, some modern rice mills, sawmills, sugar mills, cotton gins, and oil mills employed in the processing of agricultural products for export, but except for a small amount of textiles most of the actual manufactures consumed by the Burmese are the traditional handmade goods produced in the small villages where about 90 per cent of the people live.

Then, too, nearly all the modern factories, oil wells, refineries, and smelters are owned by foreigners. Even the rice mills belong chiefly to foreigners. The Burmese share here is higher (30 per cent) than in other "factories," but even so it is only a little larger than that of the Indians and Chinese combined. The total number of workers in factories just exceeded 100,000 in 1926–28 but fell after that and was only a little over 86,000 in 1938.

Burmese industry is, if anything, even more completely dominated by the British than that of the Netherlands East Indies by the Dutch. The British completely dominated the export and import trade and had the largest share in the processing of agricultural products. They were, however, having increasing competition from the Indians in the processing enterprises and in the trade between India and Burma. The Burmese share in the exploitation of this country has consisted largely in being allowed to work at the more poorly paid jobs in "factories" and in growing the rice, cotton, oil seeds, etc., for the foreign traders and processors.

This last statement is much resented by the colonial authorities, who point to the health service they have established, the educational system they have inaugurated, the improved transportation they have built, and, above all, to the tranquil civil conditions they have enforced, as proof of their humanitarian interest in the natives and also as evidence that European exploitation has raised the general level of living. It is true that these conditions have been brought about since and during British control, and they are not to be ignored, but they were established in the first instance primarily because they were essential to the profitable exploitation of the colony and to the comfort and health of the Europeans, not because of consideration for the native. More recently humanitarian considerations have played a larger part in introducing further improvements.

BRITISH MALAYA

Not all the area to which this name is customarily applied—the Federated Malay States and the Unfederated Malay States—is a colony when political niceties are observed, but for all practical purposes it constitutes a British colony and will so be treated here. North Borneo, which is administered by the government of the Straits Settlements, need not enter into the discussion, because what was said about the Dutch portion of Borneo applies equally to the British portion (80,-000 square miles).

Malaya thus understood consists chiefly of the lower portion of the Malay peninsula and Singapore and extends from the Equator to 6° 30′ north latitude. There are also a number of islands some of which are of fair size (Penang), but they need not be noted separately. The area of Malaya seems a little uncertain, estimates varying from about 50,000 to about 53,000 square miles (438, p. 1; 134, Part I, p. 141; and 316, p. 2).

As a consequence of the rapid development of export agriculture, the expansion of tin mining, and the large entrepôt trade of Singapore, the population of the colony has grown very rapidly, from about 2.7 million in 1911 (316, p. 25) to an estimated 5.4 million in 1939 (323, p. 178), thus doubling in twenty-eight years. Unlike the population of the other colonies in this region, though, a significant part of this increase has come from migration and not from the excess of births over deaths in the native population. The Malay population, which constituted about 51 per cent of the total in 1911 (316, p. 25) and numbered about 1,360,000, was estimated at only about 42 per cent in 1939 and numbered about 2,260,000 (323, p. 178), an increase of about two-thirds. The Chinese now outnumber the Malays and constitute over 43 per cent of the total, while the Indians are about one-third as numerous as the Malays and constitute about 14 per cent of the total. In 1931 the European population was a little less than 18,000, or a little over 0.4 per cent, and in 1939 it was estimated at about 30,000, not quite 0.6 per cent.

Here, as in the other colonies, the exploitation of resources could not be made highly profitable until the death rates of the working population were lowered, and this in turn raised the natural increase among both the imported workers and the native Malays. There is now a fairly high natural increase in both groups which will continue for several decades unless something happens to destroy the health services, the communications, and the good internal order established by the British. This may have happened during the Japanese occupation, but presumably the re-establishment of British control will restore the conditions which made rapid population growth possible.

The chief reason for the extremely rapid growth of the non-Malayan population—140 per cent in twenty-eight years—is found in the rapid increase of rubber and vegetable-oil production and in the expansion of tin mining and smelting. Since the Malays of this area did not take as kindly to plantation work as those of Java and the Philippines, it was necessary to import Chinese and Indians if the planting of rubber- and oil-bearing trees and the production of other commercial crops were to go forward as rapidly as the British desired, and if the tin resources were to be exploited in a few years. Since the Indians and Chinese were indentured when first introduced into the colony in considerable numbers, most of them did not bring their wives and families with them. In the course of time, however, many of them have settled in Malaya, and in 1931 (last census) about 31 per cent of the Chinese were native-born as opposed to only 22 per cent in 1921. The corresponding figures for the Indians are 21 and 12 per cent, respectively.

At the present time less than one-fifth of the total area of Malaya is in crops; the remaining four-fifths is forest. Of the 5–6 million acres in crops (134, Part I, p. 141), over 3.3 million were planted in rubber in 1937 (316, p. 212). When the acreage of the other export crops is added—pineapples, coconuts, palm kernels, etc.—the total amounts to about three-fifths of all the land tilled. This is a larger proportion in export crops than in any of the other colonies of South and East Asia. The result is that British Malaya is even more dependent on world economic conditions than the Netherlands East Indies or the Philippines. But while the agriculture of Malaya is highly commercialized, there is still a relative abundance of land so that there should be no difficulty in caring for the probable growth of population for some decades, although the colony even now imports a considerable proportion of its rice.

The Chinese and to a minor degree the Indians have now acquired a rather large stake in the exploitation of the resources of Malaya and in the operation of its public services. The native Malays, on the other hand, have not yet become much involved either in commercial (export) agriculture or in the exploitation of minerals, although they have some small rubber holdings (316, p. 192). In general, it may be said that the Malays live quite apart from the whole *modernization* movement. Of the total area in rubber in 1937, almost 54 per cent consisted of Asiatic holdings, chiefly Chinese. At that time there were over 350,000 Indian and Chinese laborers on the estates. The Chinese stake in rubber production is large and is next to that of the British in size. That of the Indians is far from insignificant, however. The only group having no significant stake in rubber is the native Malay population, for whom the colony is now being "held in trust."

The Chinese also constitute an important entrepreneur element in the tin industry, but their share has been diminishing rather rapidly. It fell from 80 per cent in 1912 to 34 per cent in 1935. The volume of production in Chinese-owned mines also declined but not in like measure because of the increase in total tin mined. Since most of the laborers (316, p. 239) both in the mines (77.6 per cent in 1937) and in the smelters (78 per cent of all factory workers) are Chinese, they have a very great interest in the tin industry. On the other hand, Chinese laborers on the estates are greatly outnumbered by Indians, although in 1937 this was the largest single group of Chinese workers, numbering almost 76,000 and constituting over 21 per cent of all estate laborers (316, p. 239).

As already noted, the Chinese and Indians are more closely associated with the commercial exploitation of Malaya than with settlement on the land, although many have established their homes there. As long as Malaya is exploited as a colony, this situation will change little, since Malayan labor is not sufficient in numbers or docile enough to carry on production in a manner profitable to the foreign entrepreneurs. And even if something should seriously and permanently interfere with the production of rubber and tin and thus induce a decline in the Chinese and Indian populations, it is not certain that the Malays will ever again constitute the majority of the population in Malaya.

The country is already saddled with an even more serious racial problem than is Burma, largely as a result of the European's haste to make money out of tin and rubber. Because the Chinese, and to a minor extent the Indians, come into contact with the natives and the imported workers chiefly when they are pawnbrokers, moneylenders, middlemen, and mine and estate owners, they have abundant opportunity to exploit them in many ways. Only the most constant vigilance by the British government prevents the unmerciful abuse of both native and foreign workers by the Chinese and Indians. There is in the making a bitter racial conflict in which the Chinese will probably be the chief objects of hatred, since they come in much closer contact with the natives than the British and take advantage of them in so many small but extremely irritating ways. The Indians will also share this dislike because many of them engage in the same practices.

Then, too, there are many causes of irritation between Chinese and Indians. It requires no particular foresight to predict that the Chinese and the Indians will in the future be looked upon as the "hated foreigner" far more than the British. But it should not be forgotten that the basic cause of this whole situation is the European effort to make quick money out of the resources of Malaya.

Malaya's mineral resources cannot be looked upon as of much significance, because of the possibility of their early exhaustion. There is a small amount of rather low-grade coal; it is used in power plants and in the smelting of tin but does not seem likely to be of much importance in the industrial development of the country. There is also some iron, but the amount is not large as far as is now known, estimates varying from about 8 million tons (22, p. 116) to about twice that amount (130, 1939, p. 67). The average annual production in 1936–39 was over 1.7 million tons (461, 1940, p. 552), a rate at which the mines would be exhausted in ten years or less. The ore is of good quality and was mined by Japanese companies, which exported it to Japan.

The importance of tin mining and smelting to the economy of Malaya has already been mentioned. It is said that at full production Malaya could probably produce about 100,000 tons a year—and that at this rate its tin resources would be exhausted in about ten years. It has never produced this much in any year, but it has produced over 75,000 tons several times, and if this rate were kept up resources would last only thirteen to fourteen years. Thus tin can scarcely be regarded as a permanent source of income.

The amount of bauxite mined in Malaya rose from almost nothing in 1936 to over 90,000 tons in 1939—all of it going to Japan (461, 1940, p. 646). Since there appears to be no estimate of reserves, it is impossible to say how important they might be in the future development of the country. About 30,000 tons of manganese were being mined annually before the invasion, but again there appears to be no estimate of reserves so no statement of their significance in the future economy of the country can be made. But since manganese goes to steel-making centers, it will probably be exported from Malaya as raw material.

While Malaya contains some phosphates, which have largely gone to Japan, the reserves are said to be small (461, 1940, p. 1281). They are not likely to be of much value even in Malayan agriculture, to say nothing of allowing significant exports over a period of years. For five years before 1940 the average amount of tungsten mined was about 1,300–1,400 tons, but the one small deposit appeared to have been about exhausted, and only 500 tons were produced in 1940 (461, 1940, p. 623).

Up to 1941 the modern industry of Malaya was confined largely to the processing of raw materials, rubber, coconuts, pineapples, and tin, and to those services needed to keep the exploitative machinery in working order, ship repairs, machine shops, auto repairs, and the other services which must be performed on the spot. There is very little factory production for consumption in the colony, nor has there been any effort by the governing authorities to get consumption industries started as in the Netherlands East Indies and the Philippines. Up to the time of the Japanese invasion Malaya had been developed solely as a producer of raw materials and a consumer of manufactured goods to be brought in by the exploiters, hence, industrial development was taboo.

For the future, however, there would seem to be no reason why Malaya should not establish the same type of consumption industries as have been started in, and as are planned for, the Netherlands East Indies and the Philippines. They will undoubtedly be owned and controlled by foreigners, chiefly British and Chinese, but this cannot be helped now as the Malays constitute only a little over two-fifths of the population and are quite without the capital, experience, and education to proceed with industry, while the British and Chinese possess all these qualifications.

Unfortunately, the small mineral resources of Malaya do not give much hope that any significant development of basic industry can take place there. Tin smelting was important before the invasion but is unlikely to recover after the war because the Dutch had been more and more smelting their own tin, and it is not at all certain that Thailand, French Indo-China, Burma, and even more distant countries will continue to send their tin to the smelters of Malaya. The future industry of Malaya is therefore likely to be confined largely to the further process-

ing of local products for local use—using rubber for shoes, making coconut oil into soap and margarine, manufacturing cotton, extending
the trade in pineapple products, and manufacturing other light consumption goods.

Since only about one-fifth of the land in Malaya is now tilled, a considerable increase in agricultural production can be anticipated, and
there is no reason to doubt the ability of Malaya to support a considerably larger population than at present on higher levels of living. But
Malaya is small and does not have either the agricultural or the industrial possibilities of some of the other colonies.

THAILAND

Although Thailand remained nominally independent up to the time
of the Japanese invasion, it was actually in the position of a colony
controlled by the British. It fits naturally into any discussion of the colonies of Southeast Asia.

Thailand is also tropical and contains approximately 200,000 square
miles. The census of 1937 gave the population as 14.5 million (271, p.
22). This represents a gain of over 3 million, or 28.3 per cent, since
1929. These figures, if correct, would mean an increase of about 32 per
1,000 per year since 1929—a rate so high that it seems improbable in
view of the rather small amount of health work being carried on and
the simple, not to say primitive, conditions of life of most of the people.
It is far more reasonable to assume that the count of population in
1937 was a considerable improvement over 1929 just as that one was
over earlier censuses, and that the rate of increase was significantly less
than 32 per 1,000. Indeed, such a rate, in the absence of large immigration, is so high as to arouse skepticism in the mind of any demographer even moderately familiar with living conditions in these tropical
areas and with their lack of efficient health service. Thailand's natural
increase is probably about like that of Malaya or the Netherlands
East Indies, which is fairly rapid but far below this level.

The population of Thailand is largely native but includes a considerable Chinese element, perhaps as many as 800,000 or 1,000,000 Chinese citizens (271, p. 22, and 91, p. 506) and twice that number with
some degree of Chinese parentage. It also has a Malay element estimated at about 400,000 (441, p. 13). Racially the natives of Thailand
are closely related to the southwestern Chinese, but, with the growth of
nationalistic sentiment in the past twenty years, they have come to feel
quite distinct from the Chinese, who retain their language, customs,

and loyalty to things Chinese. Another strong element in producing this feeling of difference from the Chinese is undoubtedly the fact that the latter are largely middlemen and moneylenders and, as such, take advantage of the Thai peasants and arouse their ill-will. The number of Chinese engaged in trade is not known, but they are believed to constitute a majority of the 357,000 persons listed by the 1937 census as engaged in trade. Moreover, wherever steady labor is required, as in the tin mines, on the plantations, and in factories, the Chinese are preponderant because they will work regularly, while the people of Thailand are not accustomed to steady labor and as yet do not take to it kindly.

Thailand is still almost wholly an agricultural country. It is estimated that about 80 per cent of the people are on the land (139, November, 1940, p. 190) and that about another 8 per cent are engaged in fishing (441, p. 608). The cultivation of rice is greatly predominant, 90–95 per cent of all tilled land being devoted to it (30, p. 272, and 91, p. 509). Most of the cultivated land is in the valleys and alluvial plains, where it can be kept flooded by the heavy rainfall. The total production of rice is placed at about 5 million tons, of which one-third or more is ordinarily exported, constituting about 70 per cent of all exports (420, p. 319, and 91, p. 510). Thailand also exports about 40,000 tons of rubber.

As far as is known at the present time, Thailand has no mineral resources of any importance except tin. This is being exploited quite rapidly, exports of tin amounting to about 17,000 tons in 1939 (30, p. 272). These were very helpful in paying for her imports as well as in supporting the various services of the government, and, together with her exports of rice and rubber, they furnished the economic basis for the small degree of modernization that has taken place within the country.

The few nonagricultural products used by the mass of the people, aside from cloth, come largely from the part-time cottage industries typical of a simple agricultural people. There are, of course, rice mills for handling the export crop and sawmills for teak and the simple mills essential to preparing rubber for shipment, but there is little else that might be classed as "modern industry," that is, using power-driven machinery. The government has established some factories and made some effort to acquire control over mines and transportation and even over certain types of distribution (oil). In spite of these efforts, however, Thailand is still in a colonial status, exporting raw materials and rice and importing manufactures, and her trade is largely in the hands of foreigners. The political and economic helplessness usually accompanying this status was somewhat mitigated by her ability to play off Japan against Great Britain in granting certain economic concessions, but this did not bring much relief, because Thailand was not in position to expand her industry and her public services without a large measure of foreign aid. Since any substantial aid to economic development would rapidly lead to greater independence, it was not forthcoming.

Because there are no coal or iron deposits of any importance, Thailand cannot hope to develop any heavy basic industries in the foreseeable future. The best she can hope for is to develop the light consumption industries in fields where there is already a market and where she can produce the necessary raw materials, like cotton and jute and sugar cane, rubber and vegetable oils.

With an area of about 200,000 square miles, of which only about 10 per cent is cultivated (441, p. 369) and that very inefficiently, Thailand would seem to possess adequate land both to extend the area of present crops and to plant such new crops as would be needed to increase her economic independence—cotton, tobacco, silk, fruit, forage crops, etc. It would appear, therefore, that Thailand, like all the colonial areas of Southeast Asia (except India), has plenty of land to care for her population growth during the next few decades, and that significant improvement in agricultural yields is feasible—for example, the yield of rice is only 12.1 bushels per acre (441, p. 360), about one-third the average for Japan (484, p. 60). But even though Thailand still has a fairly large margin of safety, with a continuance of the current rate of population increase, probably 15–20 per 1,000, she will have twice her present population within four or five decades and will then face the same "Malthusian dilemma" as all these other colonial areas if, in the meantime, she takes no steps to reduce her birth rate.

Chapter XIX

THE COLONIAL SYSTEM IN SOUTH
AND EAST ASIA

AT THIS point we must attempt to evaluate the colonial system in terms of human welfare and world peace, since there is much reason to think that it is one of the strongly aggravating causes of modern wars and may become even more dangerous in the future. Certainly the talk of the need for colonies has figured prominently in the outpourings of the militarists of Germany, Italy, and Japan. The determination to keep their colonial empires is also certain to be decisive in the attitudes of the Western European powers toward the structure of the peace.

In the colonies of South and East Asia the number of bona fide white settlers is negligible. The white man is generally a bird of passage spending a few years there, as few as he possibly can, while he accumulates enough to retire on in the form of either profits of business enterprise or a pension which will support him in the manner fitting to his superior station. For benefits conferred on the natives during twenty or so years he claims the right to live at a high European level for the rest of his days. Furthermore, he has no doubt that the interests of the natives can best be served by preserving the system which has enabled him to exploit the cheap labor of the East.

At the present time the maintenance of these colonies, like all those which are not areas of European settlement, is justified largely on the basis of the benefits which are conferred on the natives by European control. The justification of European control as contrasted with Japanese control is that the natives are treated more humanely, are less ruthlessly exploited, and are being better prepared for self-government than they would be under the Japanese. Even as between European nations it is common to find the assertion made by the British and the Dutch that the Germans are not fit to hold colonies because they do not adequately respect the rights of the natives.

It is significant that today one does not often find a frank statement of the economic advantages to be derived from colonies advanced as a reason for holding them, nor does one often find a statement of the political prestige deriving from colonial power given as a reason for retaining this power. Mr. Churchill's statement, "I did not become the king's first minister to preside at the liquidation of the British Empire," shocked many people in this country because it seemed to put the political prestige of the British Empire ahead of the rights of the colonial peoples, ahead of the basic interests of the democracies in the achievement of peace, and even ahead of justice itself. But he merely put in blunt words the values everyone at all conversant with colonial enterprise recognizes as actually operative. It is the advantages which are believed to flow from the possession of colonies, whether psychological, economic, or political, that account for the maintenance of the system.

The many claims of trusteeship and of benefits conferred on the natives as the justification for holding colonies have never contained more than half the truth—the other half, unexpressed, being that *it is to our advantage economically and/or politically to hold colonies, and therefore we hold them and will hold them as long as we are able.* The belief that the governing country did derive economic benefit from colonies and that national power and prestige were strengthened by their possession were and are powerful factors in determining national policies and will continue to be as long as this system exists. This is not to impugn the integrity of the apologists for colonies or to deny that many conscientious colonial administrators have done much to advance the interests of the natives, particularly during the last thirty or forty years; but it is to recognize that, when native interests have definitely come into conflict with imperial interests and with the interests of the dominant economic classes at home, these latter interests have usually prevailed. Before pursuing these more general considerations further, let us examine some of the ways in which the colonial system actually operates.

ADVANTAGES OF THE COLONIAL SYSTEM TO THE COLONY

Undoubtedly judgment regarding the advantages or disadvantages accruing to natives from the control of the colonies of Southeast Asia by European countries will frequently, if not always, turn on the point of view adopted; that is, upon the values which we attach to certain social and economic institutions and activities. But we should not forget that the natives also have their scales of values, which may be quite different from ours.

To the European and American mind the maintenance of internal order is one of the great benefits, if not the greatest, conferred on these backward peoples by European colonial control. In general, this has been achieved in all colonies where any serious effort has been made at economic development. Good examples of the maintenance of internal tranquillity are India and Java. In the days before their colonial status was well established there were numerous states and tribal groups which were at war with one another much of the time. There is little doubt that these petty wars took a heavy toll in human life. They involved a large part of the population and not only resulted in much direct loss of life but so disturbed the regular conduct of agriculture, industry, and trade that famine and disease were always present in many regions, adding their toll to that of war. Almost the only internal disturbances in the European colonies in the East in recent years have been minor quarrels between tribal groups in the less developed areas, and even these small tribal wars have almost certainly been rendered less deadly and occur far less frequently than formerly. This maintenance of internal order is perhaps the most basic of all the blessings conferred on these "backward" peoples by their colonial status. Without it none of the other benefits could have been achieved. It must be noted, however, that not all "backward" peoples appreciate internal tranquillity to the same extent as ourselves.

From the standpoint of the European, the improvement in economic and health conditions, resulting in a lower death rate, is an undoubted advantage. The differences between India, the Netherlands East Indies, and the Philippines, on the one hand, and China, on the other, are often cited as showing how European control benefits the natives in this respect. As shown above (chap. vi), Korea and Formosa should be added to the list of colonies which now have lower death rates than they could reasonably be expected to have had they remained parts of the Chinese Empire or had they become independent as a result of the Sino-Japanese War of 1894–95.

There is little doubt that there is essential truth in this claim that colonial control has been instrumental in reducing the death rate in most of these South and East Asia colonies. No one who knows the facts and has observed the living conditions would be disposed to deny that the death rate is lower now in these colonial areas than in China, in which outside control has been only partial and local.

A third benefit claimed for colonial control is the security from external aggression guaranteed by the colonial relation to a strong power. On the whole, this colonial system, once all the *backward* areas were transformed into colonies, did furnish a high degree of security against outside attack, but by no means has it worked perfectly. One need only mention the transfer of colonies that took place as a consequence of the Spanish-American War and World War I to show that large colonies have changed hands quite recently. But it remained for World War II to take large military operations into the colonies themselves and thus to explode the belief that colonial status insured or can insure freedom from external aggression. Strong powers fought for years in the colonies for the control of the raw materials and the economic developments already achieved as well as for the political prestige and the economic strength that it was hoped they would confer in the future. At present there is no guaranty in colonial status against aggression.

A fourth "blessing" brought by colonial government is the development of transportation. It is obvious that trade, using this term in a broad sense, cannot expand much without cheap and efficient transportation. The very name "colonial produce" has come to mean rather bulky agricultural products which are of low unit value. If they are to enter into world commerce, they must be carried long distances at low rates per ton. Moreover, the maintenance of internal order was and is, in part, dependent on being able to get troops to the right place at the right time. Before the latter third of the nineteenth century, ships furnished practically all the transport for colonial goods in South and East Asia. Hence the establishment of shipping both for foreign and for coastwise service was one of the first endeavors of all colonial powers. Roads of a sort were also built to make possible communication between ports and the nearer hinterland, but it was not until railroads came into use that a rapid development of the resources of colonies became possible.

It is not surprising in view of the fundamental role of transportation in colonial exploitation that a considerable part of the investment of European capital in colonies went into transportation facilities. Only as transport became adequate and cheap was it profitable to engage in rubber, sugar, and coconut planting and in the production of minerals and oil for world commerce. But though the provision of adequate transportation was undertaken primarily as a business measure to insure the movement of colonial produce homeward and the movement of manufactures outward, it had another effect which certainly was not anticipated at first. For the first time in the history of South and East Asia it became possible, other conditions being favorable, to move large food supplies into famine-stricken areas without using up most of the relief supplies in the process. Thus better transportation made it possible to eliminate the worst effects of famine and the disease which almost always accompanies it. But, of course, the colonial government had to be strong and internal order had to be maintained before this was possible.

In this connection the Indian authorities frequently point to the fact that the great Indian famine of 1876–78 showed the need for more and better rail transport and hastened railroad building in India, particularly by the government. Better transportation must then be considered as another of the important benefits conferred on the more backward countries which were taken in charge by the strong powers and developed as colonies.

A fifth advantage claimed for European control is the more efficient exploitation of the colonies' agricultural and mineral resources, thus increasing their wealth. One may cite here the introduction of many new commercial crops and their efficient production on large plantations, which in turn led to a great increase in the trade and the wealth of the colonies. One at once thinks of rubber, sugar, jute, cotton, coconuts, kapok, spices, groundnuts, coffee, tea, quinine (cinchona), and a number of lesser crops. Some of these crops were entirely new to Southeast Asia, and the cultivation and preparation of some of the others were greatly improved under the guidance of the colonial authorities. There can be no doubt that, on the whole, the economic status of these colonial areas has been significantly improved since their exploitation was begun by the great powers.

Finally, it is frequently claimed that the establishment of educational facilities in conjunction with their broader economic activity is preparing the native populations for participation in a world order at a much faster rate than would otherwise be the case, although it is quite generally admitted that education is still woefully inadequate. The colonial administrator claims with pride that many natives are being trained to take over the work of government and to manage business concerns, so that in the course of time the European can withdraw from the colonies without producing chaos such as he found when he took them over.

It should not be inferred from these comments, however, that all European colonies have received the same treatment or that only European colonies have received these benefits from their subjection to an outside governing power. We can very truthfully claim to have done as well in the Philippines in most respects as any of the European powers, and, in addition, to have provided a more adequate system of education calculated to lead to the abrogation of colonial status in a short time. The most conspicuous way in which we have fallen short of enlightened colonial practice in the Philippines, in view of our declared intention to give them their independence at an early date, is in the virtual monopolization of their trade by means of our tariff policy, somewhat after the manner of the French and the Japanese, rather than in following the more liberal British and Dutch practice, prior to the great depression, of allowing free or almost free trade in their colonies.

In addition, honesty compels us to recognize that Japanese colonies have been managed in much the same way as European colonies and that practically all the benefits that accrue to natives in European colonies have also been achieved by the natives in Japanese colonies. It is quite common to assume that the Japanese have generally been much more oppressive and brutal than the Europeans.

ADVANTAGES OF THE COLONIAL SYSTEM TO THE HOLDING POWER

In this process of introducing stable government and Western economy to colonies, care has been taken to see that the economic cream of the trade has gone to the Europeans, whether in the form of profits on trade, on industrial enterprise, and on agriculture or in the form of salaries and pensions to managers and officials. Until quite recently, indeed, the entire purpose of the system was frankly admitted to be the enhancement of the political and economic power of the governing country. Furthermore, there was almost no question in the minds of most people who thought about the colonial system at all that it did contribute to national strength both politically and economically. It is only in recent decades that the advantage of the possession of colonies to the holding power has been questioned and that the possessors of colonies have felt called upon to justify their position before the world by the development of the doctrine that they are merely trustees for the natives, or partners, albeit senior partners, in a common enterprise, and are not owners in perpetuity (179, pp. 1–7).

World War I brought to a head the doubts many people had had regarding the economic advantages of possessing colonies, and some even began to question the political advantages. More and more people were disposed to distinguish between the advantages derived from colonies by certain classes and groups of individuals in the governing country and those accruing to the nation as a whole. Those who calculated the net profit accruing to the nation from trade with a particular colony and who set against this the cost of protecting that colony (the navy and army establishment and the elaborate foreign service needed for diplomatic jockeying with other powers) came out with figures which proved to their own satisfaction that colonies did not pay the nation, although they might be highly profitable to certain classes of traders and manufacturers who dealt in colonial products and to the diplomats who carried on the political maneuvers (82). My own opinion is that they made their point and were justified in saying that the citizenry of the colonial power paid a high price for the national prestige thus acquired, that the profits of colonial enterprise did go largely to a small business and official group, while the costs of being a colonial power were paid by all the taxpayers of this power.

However, the advantage in the possession of colonies through assuring supplies of food and raw materials to the colonial power under all conditions, even though the price to her manufacturers is a world price, should not be overlooked—as it seems to me has been done in these calculations. Experience has shown that the flow of colonial produce to the nonpossessing countries is highly precarious under the political and economic conditions which have prevailed hitherto (see chap. x). An assured supply of essential materials may be fully as important to the economic welfare of a nation as a cheap supply. It has been quite commonly assumed that the possession of colonies furnished this assurance; but the steady flow of colonial produce from South and East Asia to Europe during the last century has actually been assured by the preponderant power of the British navy, that is, by the benign use of Britain's military power and not by the mere possession of colonies. This worked well as long as there was no very keen competition for colonial trade, but, as we have seen, it broke down completely in recent years. Control of the conditions of trade with colonies was certain to become increasingly distasteful if it came to be used more and more for the benefit of the possessing power, as is claimed by Japan and Germany and even by the United States on occasion, although, considering their own monopolization of colonial trade, the United States and Japan had scant reason to make such charges.

The military and therefore the political strength of any particular power at a given time may be greater with colonies than without colonies. Indeed, this seems to admit of little doubt because the mere possession of colonies has generally made it necessary to devote a larger proportion of the nation's income to the military establishment and to the foreign service than would have been spent on them if there had been no colonies. But it can be argued with much reason that Great Britain's vast political power has been due rather to the great expenditures on her navy made necessary by her colonies than to the economic advantages she derived from them. It can further be argued that the means for maintaining her naval establishment were not derived directly from the profits of colonial trade but came in large measure from the pockets of the mass of British people, and hence that her colonies were primarily of advantage to the dominant economic classes directly concerned in colonial enterprise. There can be little doubt, on the other hand, that national prestige has been much enhanced in the past century or two by the mere possession of large colonies.

EFFECTS OF THE COLONIAL SYSTEM ON NONCOLONIAL POWERS

The benign use of British sea power to insure the relatively unhindered movement of goods, from and to colonies as well as between nations, when coupled with the fact that the manufacturers of the noncolonial powers could buy colonial produce as cheaply as those of the colonial powers, has again and again been cited to "prove" that Germany, Italy, and Japan did not need colonies. It is said that they suffered no disadvantage because of this lack, since they were quite free to buy in world markets at world prices and could move these goods where and when they wanted without hindrance from the colonial powers. There would be a large measure of truth in this position if free trade were the rule in the world and if military crises, or the fear of them, were eliminated through some effective political and economic organization of the world. But certainly no one will claim that these conditions have prevailed in recent decades and particularly in the inter-war period 1919–39.

As has been shown above (chap. x), it is little comfort to a nation to be able to sail the seas freely and to be able to buy rubber, tin, cotton, or iron on a world market at world prices if the goods which must be sold to pay for these raw materials are refused entrance by country after country; or if negotiations to develop needed resources in colonial areas belonging to other countries are either refused outright or are made subject to such delaying tactics that they are given up in despair; or if arrangements already entered into for the exploitation of raw materials are canceled after much money and effort have been spent in actual development. All these things happened to Japan in the pre-war years and certainly were not calculated to allay the fear of the Japanese that they might at some future time find their economic life throttled by the unpredictable actions of other powers which controlled large colonial resources.

Although I am disposed to doubt that the powers possessing large colonies gain any substantial economic advantage from such possession in the long run, I am not convinced that the arguments by the peoples possessing colonies, to the effect that colonies really do not give their possessor an economic advantage, are wholly sincere. The chief reason for this doubt is that not one of the large colonial powers has ever made any official proposal whereby all colonial areas might be internationalized and actually thrown open to equal exploitation by all nations under rules generally agreed upon as adequate to safeguard the rights of the natives. It is hard to accept the argument that it would be of no advantage to Japan or Germany to possess colonies in the light of the tenacity with which the possessing powers generally hold on to them, manifestly believing that they do obtain substantial advantage of some kind from their possessions. If this tenacity derives largely, or entirely, from considerations of national or imperial prestige, it will naturally be regarded with little respect by the nonpossessing powers or even by the powers, large or small, which themselves have no colonial ambitions; if it derives from the belief that only the present colonial powers are fit to govern "backward" peoples, it will be accorded as little credit for sincerity by all other peoples.

Finally, if the tenacity with which the possessing powers hold on to their colonies arises primarily from the belief in their sacred trusteeship for the natives, it is hard to accept this argument as entirely sincere in view of their unwillingness to intrust this guardianship to some international organization and particularly in view of the many ways in which the trusteeship argument is used to prevent the nonpossessing nations from equal access to colonial resources. The profession of lofty motives of native welfare as reasons for the denial of equal access to resources to all peoples, while these same motives do not deter the possessors from active exploitation of limited resources, is bound to be suspected. This is inevitable.

All the arguments that colonial produce is available to all peoples at a uniform price will not convince the non-possessing powers of the justice of the present system in which the possessing powers are able to determine the conditions of trade as they see fit, any more than the "benefits" conferred on the natives appear to have convinced them of the essential justice of the system. Of the attitude of the Japanese and Germans toward the colonial setup as it existed before 1939 there has been no doubt for some years. The attitude of the colonials themselves has not always been so clear, but their reaction to Japanese invasion leaves little room for doubt as to what they thought of it. They may admit their preference of European control to Japanese control now, but they are showing clearly that they are not reconciled to continued European control.

SOME WEAKNESSES OF THE COLONIAL SYSTEM

Whatever explanation may be advanced for the apathy, to use the mildest term possible, of the colonial peoples in South and East Asia in the face of a change of "masters," it now seems impossible for anyone to doubt that the Europeans had completely failed to develop any significant sentiment of loyalty in their "subjects." Well-authenticated facts show that the overwhelming feeling of the natives was one of indifference to a change of colonial masters. Furthermore, it appears that, where indifference was discarded for partisanship, the anti-European forces (not the pro-Japanese) have been stronger and more active than the pro-European. If it is said that the lack of arms and military training explain the failure of the native peoples to defend themselves and their European masters, the answer is that the European was afraid to arm these peoples and train them in the defense of their country. In other words, the Europeans themselves seem to have had serious doubts whether natives trained in the use of the weapons of modern war would not use their new power to depose their European masters instead of in defense only of their colonial status. They seem to have been quite justified in harboring such doubts. Clearly the native was not convinced that the European colonial system as he knew it conferred any "benefits" on him which were worth fighting for. Rather he was convinced that this system did impose restrictions worth fighting against.

It seems that the *benefits* enumerated above are regarded as benefits chiefly by the Europeans. The native in most instances can see no reason to be grateful to his foreign master for such changes as came with colonial status. Those who had become involved in the production of colonial goods—sugar, rubber, coconuts, hemp, tin, oil, etc.—had lost much of the security of their former status as members of a village community, while those still living the village life of old were unaware of any economic advantage arising from colonial status. The former were without any resources whatever, unless they could go back to their relatives still living on farms, when they lost their jobs in the mines, on the plantations, and in the sugar mills because of fluctuations in economic activity in the world represented by the European. Moreover, the agriculturists who supplied the simple needs of these workers, and had thus become partially dependent on the sale of crops, in turn lost their small markets when work was slack. The damaging repercussions of economic fluctuations in the West on the colonies of the East introduced elements of insecurity which may well have seemed as harmful to the natives as the lack of internal order seemed to the European several decades ago. Thus neither the development of scientific plantation agriculture nor the exploitation of mineral resources, which were a sign of progress to the European, necessarily appeared as a clear gain to the people in the colonies who were directly involved, while the great masses who lived practically self-sufficing lives in their village communities had little reason either to support or to oppose European control.

If it is pointed out to the colonials that the oil, the tin, the rubber, etc., which they have supplied to the world are of very great benefit to it, the question of the better informed will be, "Of benefit to whom? Why should our resources be drained off and taken to enrich the West?" The average small cultivator would simply wonder what it was all about and blame the "master" for his troubles even though they were the same troubles he had had for ages past. Again I say that the apathy of the natives in the European colonies of South and East Asia when there was a prospect of a change in masters is the best proof that they felt no obligation to or love for their European masters. We may believe that they would be worse off under the new masters, but we can at least understand why they were not much concerned over the change. A master is a master, and he takes what he wants, leaving only the necessities to the native and not always enough of them.

Even the lowering of the death rate, which we regard as a great boon, does not necessarily appear so to an Easterner, who does not place the same value on life that we do, except in time of war. I have elsewhere expressed the opinion that the decline in the death rate seems to me to argue strongly for the view that most of these peoples have experienced a slightly improved level of living. But there are many who do believe that this has not been the case and that, at best, the improvement has been so small that the mass of the people is not aware of it. If this is true, it is almost certain that they will blame their masters for the hardships they feel but will be far less likely to credit them with the small improvements achieved and of which they are probably unconscious. The simple fact is that most natives, if they ever think of this matter at all, have no compelling reason to consider the way in which their death rates have been affected by their colonial status as of any real benefit. And obviously they cannot be expected to feel grateful for something they scarcely know they have received and which may seem of doubtful advantage if they do know about it.

Finally, a different attitude of a colonial people toward a change of masters as affected by their outlook on the future is clearly shown by the Filipinos. We need not make extravagant claims for our colonial administration there to clinch the point that a significant number of Filipinos did take a different attitude toward the defense of their homeland than did the Javanese, the Burmese, the Malayans, and others. The fact that the Philippine Army put up a good fight against the Japanese in view of their meager and inferior equipment stands out in sharp contrast to the indifference of the natives in Java, Malaya, and Burma. For all our mistakes in the past a considerable body of Filipinos saw that they were fighting for themselves, not for the Americans, and fought with a will. They knew that they were soon to become completely self-governing and that if they became subject to Japan they would lose this new freedom the taste of which they were already beginning to savor.

Moreover, we did not fear to arm the Filipinos because, once a definite arrangement had been made abolishing their colonial status, we knew that they were not likely to use their arms to oust us from the islands. We had nothing to lose nor had they anything to gain by turning their growing military power against us. This situation made it possible for us to co-operate with the Filipinos in the defense of their land to the extent of our joint ability. Likewise, the "underground" movement among the Filipinos appears to have been well organized and was of great value in driving Japan from the islands.

Now, all that has been said above about the failure of the European colonial system applies equally to the Japanese colonies. They have also failed to secure the loyalty of their colonial peoples—the Koreans and Formosans—but there is no evidence that their failure is significantly greater than that of the Europeans. Nor is there convincing evidence that the Japanese have exploited their colonials more mercilessly than the Europeans, although we quite commonly assume that this is the case.

It is of the essence of the colonial system as it now operates to use cheap (subsistence) labor largely under the direction of men from the homeland to produce raw materials and food for the more industrially developed governing country. The governing country discourages, passively if not actively, the industrialization of the colony because this will result, at least temporarily, in cutting down exports and probably in producing a rise in the cost of the raw materials it produces. Thus a well-balanced economy in the colony means that it will not long remain of much advantage to the particular groups of the governing country which have profited most by its exploitation in the past. The freedom of the colony to lay tariffs and to determine the conditions of exploitation by nonnatives would also tend to put all foreigners on the same footing in the economic race. This is one very important reason, perhaps the chief reason, why the ruling classes of colonial powers do not want to change the status of their colonies by granting them a greater measure of self-government, to say nothing of actively assisting them in the development of economic and political independence.

In other words, the colonial system as it now operates provides a high degree of monopoly control of large populations and areas to the governing groups of the colonial powers, and they are very reluctant, as monopolists always are, to share their power and their perquisites either with the natives or with foreigners. Both the educated natives and the foreigners desiring rights of exploitation in the colonies of other countries are well aware of this monopolistic position of the governing power and are much irritated by the "unfair" advantages which it confers. The more intelligent natives in particular also feel a frustration in not being able to compete with the nationals of the governing power on equal terms. This leads to a high degree of irresponsibility both in talk and in action, as we shall see in a moment.

One very ironical element in the colonial situation today is that by its very nature it keeps the colony militarily weak. Military power, even the power to defend one's country, depends not only on the existence of abundant manpower but also on the possession of industry, particularly of heavy industry. The colonial system, however, purposely keeps the colony industrially weak and therefore militarily weak, as we have had abundant opportunity to see. This situation poses a real dilemma to the colonial powers. If the colonies are allowed to industrialize, they are lost as colonies, and if they do not industrialize, they are likely to be taken by some aggressor. There is apparently no way in which colonies can be made strong enough to defend themselves and still be kept subject.

In the light of the facts now available it is no exaggeration to say that the colonial system in the East is bankrupt. The possessors of colonies were unable to defend them in 1941 and will be even less able to do so in the future if they continue to consider them as "possessions" and rely on their own national power or on an alliance between the possessing nations only. The Dutch, and only to a lesser degree the French, have for a long time relied on British sea power to protect their colonies. Even the United States never forgot that Great Britain had a powerful navy devoted to the preservation of the status quo. The emerging fact is that only the United States and the Soviet Union, of all the great powers with interests in the Pacific, will be able to defend colonial "possessions" there in the near future. We do not want colonies, although we may want strategic bases. Just what the Soviet Union wants we are in no position to say. Will an effective international organization long support the present colonial system? The prospect is that any effective postwar organization will not be truly international but rather an alliance between the four or five strongest of the United Nations. Such an alliance can undoubtedly maintain the status quo as regards colonies as long as it endures. But history shows that such war-born alliances do not last long, and it requires but little imagination to enable anyone to conjure up almost innumerable causes of friction within it in addition to those that have already come into the open.

It is worse than futile—it is dangerous—to ignore the differences of opinion regarding colonies which exist between the United States and the great European colonial powers or to suppose that the Soviet Union will continue to manifest indifference to colonies and spheres of influence among the "backward" peoples of the western Pacific if and when these colonies are used to prevent the development of her "vital" interests. The disposition made of the Pacific colonies is, therefore, one of the basic elements in the peace structure. This system was the outgrowth of a period of *differential* population growth and *differential* economic development which made it possible for a few of the more industrially and commercially advanced nations to conquer and hold "possessions" in South and East Asia because they were expanding peoples and had no well-armed opposition. These nations are no longer expanding, and their industrial power is being matched by that of new powers which now have expanding populations. As long as colonies are treated as national "possessions" to be exploited chiefly in the interest of the possessor, these new nations increasing in numbers and in industrial power are going to demand, and some of them will be ready to fight for, "possessions" of their own just as Germany and Japan have fought. Only the abolition of the colonial system and the preparation of the present colonial peoples to take part in a world organization guaranteeing equal status to all peoples can prevent the recurrence of such efforts to secure "possessions." When the balance of population and of industrial power and hence of military strength shifts, then the attempt by the growing nation or nations to take colonies from those becoming relatively weaker is inevitable as long as *force*, either that of single nations or of an alliance of nations, is relied on to hold possessions.

But the dangers of the colonial system are not confined to the attempts of growing powers to wrest them from the possessing powers as the balance of population and industrial strength shifts; they are also to be found in the growing population and industrial strength of the colonies themselves. Will we remain neutral or support Great Britain when India revolts, as revolt she will if not given a more equal status in the family of nations? Are we going to support Holland and France now that their colonies demand the freedom we have recently granted the Philippines? What becomes of an alliance when such problems arise and decision must be made?

THE FUTURE CONTROL OF "BACKWARD" AREAS

The only fairly sure way to prevent the repeated efforts of the growing powers to acquire colonies and to avoid embroilment in colonial revolts is to abolish the system by which any nation "possesses" other lands and peoples, to treat all peoples as equals in a world organization, and to provide that in so far as the exploitation of the thinly settled areas of the world is to be allowed to others than the natives it should be open on equal terms to all peoples. No particular area should be allotted to any nation. Colonies, "spheres of influence," "reserved areas," and other special privileges should have no place in a system devised for the future use of the earth's resources by all of its people. The principles which should govern the exploitation of the lands occupied by the weaker peoples not yet able to look after themselves are few and relatively simple.

The first is that all peoples should be treated as equals. This does not mean that all peoples are equally capable of self-government now, nor that the mere living in a land gives right to full possession and control of all its resources. For instance, a few hundred thousand natives in New Guinea need not be guaranteed complete control of this great island in order to be treated as equals. They will have to be treated as wards, as children, for some time. Our children are our equals even though we find it necessary to exercise a large measure of control over them for several years. It is being treated as inferiors, as having no rights, except those granted by the condescending exploiters, which must be done away with. We must recognize that there is no *Herrenvolk* and cease to act this role when we come in contact with these still undeveloped peoples. This applies to all the contacts of Western Europeans with Asiatic peoples, and it must be a first principle in planning for the future of colonial peoples.

Second, the guaranty of freedom for development of resources in the present colonial areas should come from an international organization and not from a particular nation or the alliance of a few nations. The present colonial peoples, like the rest of us, must come to look to an international organization for their guaranties of peace and freedom, for if this war does not issue, in the course of a decade or two, in a true international organization which has more power and prestige in world affairs than any one nation or empire, or the war-born alliance which must of necessity launch it, there is little chance that colonial areas, or indeed, any other people can be guaranteed freedom. Any alliance of several great powers if it endures for even a decade will certainly operate largely in the interest of its members and by log-rolling will divide the entire world into "spheres of influence" in which each of these larger powers will be dominant until one or two of them feel strong enough to take over the others and enlarge their colonial "possessions" by a third world war. If we cannot learn to think internationally about colonies, there is little hope that we can avoid future wars over them.

Third, the colonies should be aided in the development of a better-balanced economy in order to decrease their dependence on cheap exports and in order to increase their productive capacity. As long as they depend on plantation agriculture and mining for their exports, they can never have even a moderately stable economy. Furthermore, reasonable equality of bargaining power between the more *advanced* industrial peoples and the *backward* agricultural peoples is quite impossible if one may judge from the history of our economic development in the West since the Industrial Revolution. Areas which are primarily agricultural and produce chiefly raw materials have never been able to trade on reasonably just terms with more developed industrial areas, even within national boundaries.

In the fourth place, the unused or little used areas of the earth should be regarded not as the property of any one nation or even of the natives but as common property to be used for the benefit of those who need them. This means that Chinese and Indians and Japanese must be accorded rights in the use of the world's unused resources as well as those peoples who happened to be fortunate enough to seize them at some earlier date. In the long run this principle will probably have to be applied to the resources of nations as well as to those of colonies, but except in a few cases (see chap. xxii) this can probably be postponed for several decades so that we will have time to become accustomed to this idea. In the case of colonies the matter is much more urgent, for the existence of unused resources is a constant temptation to those peoples growing in power and numbers who stand in great need of them.

POPULATION CONTROL

International control over the colonial areas of the earth may temporarily remove some of the conditions which make colonies a tempting prey to growing nations, but there will long be differentials in population growth and in pressure on resources which will make conquest seem desirable to ruling cliques and will make it relatively easy for them to sell the idea of a war of necessity to their peoples if population continues to grow without control.

Thus the long-time success of any international organization in removing colonies as sources of armed conflict must be dependent in large measure on the control of population growth, not only in the colonies but in all industrially backward lands. Even the most rapid conceivable expansion of the economy of these colonial areas cannot do much to ease the population pressures now developing in Asia and in some of the colonies themselves if birth rates are not brought under control. The more successful any government in these colonial lands is in organizing health service and in increasing economic efficiency, the sooner will these peoples face the problem of how to care for their rapidly increasing numbers. This is the Malthusian dilemma of all colonialism.

As matters now stand, the encouragement of any practice which will reduce the birth rate and of any changes in economy which will result in substantially raising the level of living is fundamentally inconsistent with primary colonial aims—*cheap* labor to produce *cheap* raw materials and the maintenance of markets for certain minimum amounts of manufactured goods. Only an international organization which is first and foremost interested in colonies as a part of the world organization can be expected to encourage the control of population growth in the interest of higher levels of living among these colonial peoples and to point out its need among other industrially backward peoples.

It must not be forgotten that with the continuance of customary colonial administration most of these colonies have only a few decades ahead of them in which their present increase in population can be cared for by the mere expansion of their agricultural areas even if they are reserved entirely for the natives. The probable exceptions are the Netherlands East Indies and the Australian "sphere of influence" in which the ratio of people to usable land is very low and is likely to remain so for some time. But if there should be any considerable migration from the more crowded countries—India, China, Japan—the tillable land even in these colonies would not last long (see chap. xx).

Fortunately, the mere expansion of tilled land is not the only resource available to care for a growing population in these colonies. Industrialization is important in the solution of population problems not only because it increases the productivity of labor but also, and probably more so, because it actively encourages the fairly rapid development of those modes of living which lead to the control of the birth rate. This has been our experience in the West, and the same development has been going on in Japan for some years. It seems reasonable to assume that this same voluntary control over the birth rate will take place in these colonial areas as their economy becomes more industrialized and urbanized. But there can be no assurance that this control over the birth rate will come fast enough to hold population growth in these "backward" areas within limits which will permit of the rather rapid and continuous economic improvement which is the best guaranty of effective population control.

These peoples of South and East Asia when considered as a single group do not have the large areas of untilled lands which we had in the West in 1800 or the vast mineral resources. There is, therefore, urgent need to make them acquainted with the relations between economic resources, low death rates, the increase of population, and the level of living and also to assist them in securing the knowledge and the means to control their population growth when they are convinced of the need of doing so.

The use of colonial areas in the future, as well as the industrial and agricultural development of semicolonial areas like China, presents serious population problems to the entire world. Justice and decency demand that these areas be assisted in the development of a more productive and a more balanced economy which can be achieved only by the establishment of industry and the more complete use of all their natural resources for their own benefit. Since this type of development also presents the only way known at present by which a people will come fairly quickly to a voluntary control of the birth rate which will most surely ease the pressure of numbers on resources, it is also the most sensible way the low-birth-rate countries can take to assure the continuance and improvement of their own standards of life.

Experience shows, however, that such development causes the death rate to fall for some decades before the new economic and social structure leads the people to control births, so there is a period during which population increases rapidly. This period may be quite long, as it was in England (1750–1910), or shorter, as seems likely in Japan (1870–1935). If there is abundance of land and minerals in relation to the size of the population which is in a position to use them, as was the case in Western Europe and its settlements in 1800, and in the Soviet Union today, then the rapid increase in population for a century or even more need not seriously interfere with a great rise in the level of living. But it may be characterized by an almost stationary level of living if this increase in population takes place in an area already crowded and with only a relatively small amount of new land available, as is happening in India and will probably soon happen in China and in the colonial areas of South and East Asia.

This situation poses a real dilemma. We cannot be certain that there is a way out, but it would seem only good common sense to make the best use we can of the unused resources of the world in colonies to try to find a way. It cannot be done under the present colonial system.

POSSESSIONS OR INTERNATIONAL WARDS

If the colonial system is continued with only minor modifications and the doctrine of trusteeship for the natives continues to be used as an excuse for not allowing the Indians, the Chinese, or the Japanese to settle and develop the unused areas of South and East Asia (and Africa), what will be the attitudes of these people three or four decades from now toward the colonial powers, when with several hundred millions more people they have reached the limit of their resources and have achieved but little improvement in living?

The answer is obvious. It will be the same answer Japan made in

1931 when she began her active period of aggression. If force is the sole determiner of the right of access to the unused resources of colonies, then force will be used by any people when it feels that it needs these resources and believes itself strong enough to challenge the power of the nation or nations holding them. Whatever the situation might actually have been as regards the advantages they would derive from the possession of colonies, Japan and Germany and Italy believed they would be better off with them than without them. They also believed that they would never get equal access to the world's resources until they acquired new territory to exploit in the national interest and that only force would enable them to secure this equal access. There was no world organization which would enable them to share the resources of colonial areas by peaceful means.

.This is by no means the whole story of Axis aggression, but to deny that the drive for colonies and for areas that could be exploited as colonies was a potent factor in the situation is to ignore some very obvious facts. If conditions remain as they were, if the colonial system as it has operated is not abolished, if such exploitation of present colonial areas as is consistent with an enlightened conception of native rights is not made free to all peoples, they will remain a sore in international relations and will continue to fester and poison them in the future much as in the past.

The determined policing of Japan for the next few decades may prevent the recurrence of aggressive action on her part as long as such policing lasts. But we must recognize that Japan's aggression was not the consequence of something inherently evil in the nature of the Japanese. It was rather the consequence of the political, social, and, above all, economic organization of the world including that of Japan herself. If, in developing a new economic basis for international organization we do not remove the existing colonial system with its inevitable differentials in access to resources, colonies will remain fair game for any ravenous animal on the prowl.

In the modern world colonies can be retained only by force, and, when the force relations of nations change, a struggle for the exploitable areas, that is, the colonies, is inevitable. This is the basic reason for urging the abolition of the national ownership of colonies and the establishment of an international organization for the protection and guidance of the weak, backward peoples who are not yet prepared to take their place as full equals in a world society. This would be implementing the doctrine of trusteeship in a truly effective manner because it would remove the power from any given nation or empire to reserve rights over these weaker peoples for itself to the disadvantage of the colonials or of any other people.

The establishment of a world organization which had as one of its functions the supervision of the present colonial areas would not necessitate the abolition of pre-war administrations of the several colonies immediately but would result in making them responsible, not to a colonial office of the possessing power, but to an "international commission for the 'backward' peoples." It would be a catastrophe to the colonial peoples themselves to lose the experienced colonial administrators of these colonies, but the policies they were to carry out should be determined by an international organization and not by any particular country. This is the only way to avoid the selfish exploitation of colonial areas. Even the policy of the Dutch in allowing other countries to participate in the exploitation of the Indies, which has been very liberal according to existing practice, has resulted in retaining a large proportion of the colonial enterprise in Dutch hands and in complaints, even by other Western peoples, that they have not been treated fairly, while the educated Indonesians complain bitterly that natives have no part in the whole scheme of exploitation save as hewers of wood and drawers of water.

Any change in the colonial system such as that suggested here will inevitably result in the gradual decrease of Western influence in the East and in the increase of the ties between the present colonial areas and also between them and the independent countries of Asia. This is desirable and should not occasion any heartburning among people who really believe in the democratic doctrine of the equal status of all peoples. It will, of course, be deplored by those accustomed to receiving the deference demanded by masters and the larger incomes arising from the unequal trade of colonial produce for manufactured goods. But these colonial peoples are Eastern rather than Western in culture and will undoubtedly be far better content to become partners in a new Asiatic regional bloc than to remain the subjects, however well treated they may be, of a Western power.

Furthermore, being raised from a colonial status to one of tutelage to a world organization with the definite assurance of self-government at an early date is certain to hasten the development both of a competent native administrative class and of widespread responsibility among the people at large. Certainly the only way these "backward" peoples can really learn the responsibilities of citizenship in the world of today is by securing and exercising the rights, privileges, and responsibilities of world citizenship as rapidly as possible and thus being removed from the exploitable class—the weak, the ignorant, and the provincial.

The abolition of the colonial system will not, of course, solve the economic problems connected with the too rapid growth of population, nor will it solve the political problems that are an inevitable accompaniment of becoming a part of a larger and more complex world order. People can learn to govern themselves only by trying to do it, and the primary functions of a world organization for the assistance of the "backward" peoples would be to help them govern themselves and to improve their economy. It would plan to use the natives in the government as fast as possible and to train them in the operation of a more efficient economy. At the same time it would educate them not in a narrow and violent nationalism, such as has swept the Western world this last century and seems to be developing now in the East, but as partners in a world order. In giving such training to these backward peoples, it is to be hoped that we "advanced" peoples would also learn better what it means to be partners in a world order. We may have as much to learn as these backward peoples—possibly more— because we have to unlearn some of the habits of thought which we have acquired as a result of our individualistic nationalism, and we unlearn them slowly, as two great wars have shown. If, on the other hand, from the very beginning of their life as national entities these colonial peoples could also learn to accept world responsibility, it would be a great aid in developing a world order which would make effectively for peace.

Chapter XX

MIGRATION AND POPULATION PRESSURE
IN SOUTH AND EAST ASIA

W E KNOW that three countries in South and East Asia already have large populations in relation to their agricultural potentialities and their mineral resources: India, China, and Japan. There are also certain portions of other countries and colonies which are densely peopled—Java, some parts of the Philippines, and several delta areas suitable for rice culture in the Indo-Chinese peninsula. But except for India, China, and Japan, the other countries of Southeast Asia, considered either individually or in the aggregate, do not have so dense a population in relation to tillable land that there need be any great concern over their ability to support their growth in numbers during the next three or four decades if they actively undertake some internal redistribution of their people.

The migration scheme being developed in the Netherlands East Indies during the last few years preceding the Japanese invasion might, with modifications suited to the peculiar needs of each of these colonial areas, except India, go a long way to prevent any general increase of population pressure during the next few decades. However, one very important modification in the migration scheme of the Netherlands East Indies should be given careful consideration in undertaking the redistribution of population within these countries.

There should be a determined effort to enlarge the average size of the farms on which settlement is being made so that the total production of the family could be considerably increased as more efficient agricultural practices and better implements come into use. The present scheme in the Netherlands East Indies is to allot a little less than 2.5 acres to a family, approximately what the average Javanese farmer now has. This will tend to fix the size of farm in new areas at near the subsistence level and will make it very difficult to introduce better tillage implements and the diversification of crops which will certainly be among the most efficacious means of raising the level of living in the future. This shortcoming seems to have been avoided in the Philippine land-settlement scheme: the amount of land being allotted to a settler is large enough to permit of desirable expansion in the future, although it may be more than he can till effectively under present conditions.

But in spite of the shortcomings of the present scheme for the redistribution of population in the Netherlands East Indies, and in spite of the lack of any active effort to encourage redistribution in most of them, the fact remains that Burma, Thailand, French Indo-China, the Netherlands East Indies, the Philippines, and Malaya have sufficient land not now in use or so little used as to make a significant redistribution of population possible, a movement which could be made large enough year by year to care for the increase in numbers which seems likely to occur within the next three or four decades in the more crowded areas of these colonies. It is true that some of them have relatively more tillable land than others and that some of them have better opportunity to develop industry because of better and larger mineral resources, but, by and large, these countries can take care of their increase in population at home for some time yet and can, at the same time, increase their per capita production both in agriculture and in industry, thus opening the way to a substantial improvement in their levels of living, which in most of them are already higher than in China and India.

Any substantial improvement in the level of living in these countries will, however, almost certainly increase their rate of population growth, which is already fairly rapid, and thus will hasten the time when the ratio of population to tillable land will be much less favorable than it now is, if no control of population growth is developed. It would not be in the least surprising if the colonial populations of Southeast Asia, excepting India, doubled before the end of the century. Land for this appears to be available within all the colonies, except India, and mineral resources, while not large according to our standards, are sufficient to permit of a significant amount of industry when they are considered as a whole, although the development of heavy industry on a large scale is not to be anticipated. The manufacture of consumption goods on a much larger scale, using native products for raw materials, seems quite feasible.

Even if population should double by 1980 to 1990, there is reason to think that these increased numbers can be supported at a better level than now prevails. By the end of this century, however, the situation is likely to be greatly changed. The Netherlands East Indies, not including New Guinea, may have 150–175 million, the Indo-Chinese peninsula, including Malaya, may have 120–140 million, and the Philippines may have 30–35 million. If, then, there is still no sign of a decline in the birth rate, the world will have to face a new and serious problem of population pressure in this region.

In the meantime the populations of India and China can be expected to grow to the extent that their means of subsistence, their health services, and their internal civil order will permit. To believe that India and China may have 1,000–1,250 million people by the end of this century is not fantastic. It merely assumes the continuance of the modest checks on the death rate already achieved in India and the establishment of similar checks in China during the next two or three decades.

MIGRATION FROM CHINA, INDIA, AND JAPAN

Assuming a population of about 400 million in the Chinese Empire, the population of the three really crowded countries in this region—India, China, and Japan—was about 860 million in 1940–41. The rate of increase in Japan since 1920 has averaged about 1.4 per cent a year and in India about 1.2 per cent.

We do not know what has happened in China, but I at least, as already indicated, am among those who doubt that there has been much increase in China's population during the last forty or fifty years because I can find no evidence of any betterment in the conditions of life in China similar to that which has encouraged population growth in Japan and India. The argument here, however, rests not on the acceptance of any given figure for China's population but only on (a) the fact which no one questions that her population already is huge and (b) the assumption, entirely reasonable in the light of world experience since 1800, that if civil order is maintained and economic and sanitary conditions are even slightly improved, China's population will grow at about the same rate as in India and Japan. The only *proved* expansion of the Chinese in the last thirty to forty years has been in Manchuria, whither many millions have gone, of whom a considerable number have remained. Manchuria may now have 40 million, possibly more (see chap. v), and can provide a large annual contingent for its own "pioneer fringes" during the next few decades even without aid from China Proper.

Currently, there is also much interest among the Chinese in the possibilities of settlement in southwestern and northwestern China, but there is great uncertainty regarding the amount of land in these regions suitable for agricultural use. In much of the northwest the rainfall is both light and uncertain. Besides, hay farming and cattle-raising (grazing) must supplement grain farming in order to make the best use of the land, and in such types of farming the Chinese are quite inexperienced. The size of the population the northwest will support is highly debatable, but at most it cannot be more than a few million. Great care must be taken not to load this semiarid land to the point where it will provide merely a subsistence in good years and in bad years will be subject to devastating famines. It is a "dust-bowl" region.

But let us assume for the sake of argument that this northwest region of China is almost another Manchuria and can support 40–60 million people. How long will it afford real relief to China? With a population of 400 million, it would be possible for China to settle over 40 million people there in a single decade with a rate of increase of only 10 per 1,000 per year without reducing her population in other parts of the Empire. It would draw off only the increase of population on the farms; it would not reduce the farm population except in a few communities. At the rate of 15 per 1,000 per year (India's rate in 1931–41), China would have an increase of over 64 million in ten years and could almost fill the vacant spaces of all northern and northwestern China without reducing the population of the present settled areas.

Knowing as little as we do about northwestern China and even less about southwestern China, one cannot say categorically that China could not find a place for 40 million emigrants in a decade or possibly for even a larger number; but it does seem highly doubtful that such an amount of new agricultural land is available in the Chinese Empire, since the movement into these regions during the last forty years has been practically negligible except into Manchuria. It has been shown further that it is highly doubtful whether Chinese industry can be developed fast enough to absorb any considerable proportion of such an increase. Therefore, if emigration is to effect any substantial relief of population pressure in China, it must absorb a large part, perhaps all, of the actual population increase that will arise as living conditions improve because it must lead to a reduction in the present density of population on farms. Industrialization will help, but it will proceed too slowly to absorb more than a small proportion of the natural increase China will have when her death rate is reduced to the level of that of India, to say nothing of that of Japan.

The problem of relieving China's population pressure by migration, as long as the birth rate remains as high as we have reason to believe it now is, is simply insoluble. Every improvement in civil order, in economic conditions, and in sanitation will reduce the death rate and thus raise the rate of natural increase. New homes might be found for several millions of Chinese but not for the tens of millions who will need them during the next few decades. The size of the problem is hard to grasp because the numbers involved are so great.

Now if we add the populations of India and Japan to that of China, the total is so vast (about 860 million) that the impossibility of caring for such an increase for even a few decades by emigration is at once apparent even if the open spaces of tropical Africa are added to those of China and the colonies of Southeast Asia. India and Japan alone had fewer than 400 million in 1930 but by 1940 had about 460 million. These three countries combined might easily have an increase of 100 million in the ten years, which would grow to 175 million in each ten years by the end of the century. All that would be necessary to bring this about would be to find subsistence for them while maintaining India's modest health service and duplicating it in China. While with further industrialization Japan's population growth will probably decline and possibly become negligible before the end of the century, India's and China's populations will grow so greatly under any significant improvement in economic conditions that the failure of increase in Japan's will scarcely be noticed.

We have seen that there is no body of unused but usable land in Southeast Asia that can support such a vast migration for more than a few years; nor is it reasonable to expect industry, trade, and the services to absorb several million new workers each year. Even the huge and thinly settled parts of tropical Africa could afford only a few years' relief to a population increasing 10–15 million per year. It is not a question of the ability of the Indians and the southern Chinese to pioneer in the tropics; there is much evidence that all these people make good pioneers under conditions which are quite impossible to Europeans. They can settle on new land in the tropics and thrive in much the same way as the Europeans did in North America and elsewhere in the temperate climates when they left what seemed to them crowded Europe.

But while a vast migration from India, China, and Japan might conceivably be organized within a comparatively few years, it could hardly become great enough to relieve population pressure more than temporarily in a few localities. The very magnitude of the migration

needed to afford substantial relief to these crowded peoples precludes
it as a practicable solution of their population pressures. In the first
place, there is not the land; in the second place, there are not the
means of transport to effect such a mass movement; and, in the third
place, there is no organization powerful enough to direct and control
such a migration, nor is there likely to be. Thus even as a temporary
solution migration cannot be effective over this vast area, while as a
permanent solution it is out of the question to rely on migration to
solve the population problems of this area as long as the easing of pressure in India or China merely means that the home death rate declines a little so that soon there are just as many, or more, mouths to
feed than there were before.

Any rational view of the extent of relief to these poverty-stricken
peoples to be achieved through migration must be highly pessimistic,
because of the *local* and *temporary* nature of the consequent improvement. This is the real Malthusian dilemma facing India and China
and possibly Japan. So far as we can tell from human experience to
date, there is only one permanent and sure alternative to a high death
rate and that is a low birth rate.

MIGRATION AND EUROPE'S GROWTH

As already noted, Europe escaped the Malthusian dilemma after
1800 by three great developments: a relatively large migration to new
lands from which she then drew, indeed is still drawing, cheap food
and raw materials (colonial produce); a relatively rapid mechanization of both agriculture and industry which, because of abundance of
land and mineral resources, enabled her to increase per capita production very greatly; and, in recent decades, the control of the birth rate
when these other means began to show signs of lessening efficacy.

The first two of these means of caring for a growing population are
not open to South and East Asia to anything like the same extent in
1946, with a population of almost 1,000 million and no new continents
to settle, as they were to Europe in 1800, with a population one-fifth
to one-sixth as great and the New World and Australia almost un-
touched. A net migration from Europe between 1820 and World War I
of perhaps 40 million would have to be matched by a net migration
probably ten or fifteen times as great from this area during the next
fifty to sixty years, because already the measures to reduce deaths in
many of these Asiatic countries are as effective as those achieved in
most of Western Europe by the middle of the nineteenth century, and

the three countries we are especially concerned with here are now far more crowded in relation to their resources than any part of Europe ever was.

The rather easy optimism which assumes that emigration, industrialization, and improvement of agriculture can work the same wonders with the level of living in South and East Asia as they did in the West during the past century or century and a half is not justified. South and East Asia are not starting where we started when our ancestors finally broke through the cake of medieval custom. These Asiatics have handicaps which Europeans did not have, of which the greatest is a dense population with relatively small areas of new land available. Hence migration as an active factor in raising the level of living in South and East Asia can have far less effect than it did in the West during the nineteenth century. Because of this, more of the immediate burden of caring for an increasing population must be thrown on the development of industry and the improvement of agricultural practices on the land already in tillage, and for the same reason birth control becomes at once a far more urgent matter here than it was in the West at any time before World War I.

PSYCHOLOGICAL VALUE OF THE RIGHT TO EMIGRATE

The acceptance of this point of view does not mean, however, that emigration can be or should be left out of account in our consideration of the population problems of South and East Asia, nor that the present colonial policies toward immigration, if continued, will not affect the prospects for future peace. The doctrine that the unused lands of Oceania, Indonesia, the Indo-Chinese peninsula, and Africa are being held in trust for the natives cannot be used much longer to insure their continued colonial exploitation by Europeans while excluding these crowded Asiatic peoples from actual settlement in those areas which are thinly settled and little used. As things now are, these Asiatic peoples, or rather those few who think about such matters, regard this doctrine of trusteeship as sheer humbug, as a subterfuge intended to insure exclusive European exploitation of valuable natural resources (see chap. xix).

While there are unquestionably many able and sincere colonial administrators who are doing all they can to make the doctrine of trusteeship a reality, there is no gainsaying the accusations of the Indians that they are prevented from migrating to many parts of the British Empire where population is sparse while Europeans are allowed to hold vast areas of land which they do not cultivate and to exploit colonial mineral resources without hindrance. Is it surprising that the Indians regard the trusteeship doctrine merely as a convenient cloak for British exploitation? Though much less has been heard from China on this point, can there be any doubt that, once China herself has thrown off her semicolonial status, she will join India in denouncing a colonial policy which shuts her off from equal access with Europeans to the use of the lands and minerals of the thinly settled areas of Southeast Asia (and of Africa)?

Thus even though no great relief from population pressure is to be expected in this region by making migration to the unsettled lands of the Pacific and even to Africa relatively free, the very fact that it was permitted to Asiatics under conditions safeguarding the rights of the natives against both Europeans and Asiatics equally would go far to remove grievances already being felt and voiced by the Indians and Japanese, who will almost certainly soon be joined by the Chinese. The psychological effect of removing the discriminations against Asiatic migration to some of these relatively thinly settled areas would be very great. Dropping the bars to a moderate extent might not actually result in the emigration of any very considerable number of Chinese or Indians, but the acquisition of the right to do so under the same conditions as the Europeans would remove one very important grievance—the present discrimination in favor of Europeans.

This is not the place to discuss the measures needed to insure preservation of the rights of the natives in land, in mineral resources, and, above all, in the retention of their social organization. In the past no highly organized people with stronger military power has ever respected native rights to the possession of all their land and resources. It has commonly been assumed that the greater military strength gained by a more effective economic and social organization, of which modern industrialization is an example, conferred the right on its possessors to conquer and to exploit the lands of the weaker peoples. Recently the Japanese have demonstrated their acceptance of this doctrine. Can we assume that there will not be similar attempts from other sources when they have come to feel keenly the urge to expansion if there are still unsettled areas into which they might expand?

There is much reason to believe that for the near future the more crowded peoples of Asia, having no voice in the decision, will agree to such restrictions regarding the settlement and the exploitation of the mineral resources of the little-used lands of the western Pacific (and

Africa) as are needed to prevent hardship to the natives, that they will be content with equality of treatment and will not demand special privileges. It will behoove us to grant this equality while there is still time. It is certainly a little late in the day for the peoples of the West to insist on the rights of natives to the sole possession of their present lands and resources when these natives really do not need them and are not in position to make them available to the peoples who do need them. The equal right of migration (and exploitation) under suitable safeguards would do much to allay the bitterness felt by many Asiatics toward Europeans even if it did not afford much opportunity for actual migration. This is another important reason for abolishing the present colonial system and putting all these little-used or unused lands under an international commission for the "backward" peoples on which these crowded Asiatic peoples would have representation. Only some such scheme will convince both the natives and the more crowded Asiatics that the Westerner is no longer bent only on the most profitable exploitation of weaker peoples.

Of course, the uncontrolled entry of considerable numbers of Indians, Chinese, or Japanese into many of these thinly settled areas would create serious social and economic problems different in many respects from those arising under European control but equally difficult of solution. There are already the beginnings of race problems in several of these areas, as we have said. Until some satisfactory solution can be found for the problems created by the presence in the same territory of peoples generally thought of as different races, it would seem wise to avoid such situations where possible. But the Soviet Union seems to be making substantial headway in solving the problems of race contact, and perhaps such problems are not as difficult as we have generally assumed.

JAPANESE EMIGRATION

On several accounts the migration of Japanese to other parts of South and East Asia is a special case which must be considered separately from that of Indians and Chinese. For some time to come all Japanese immigrants will be suspected of political intentions. This has been true to some extent in the recent past but will be even more true in the future. There is little likelihood that even under international control Japanese immigrants would be allowed to enter the present colonial areas in the near future. As shown in chapter vi, however, the birth rate in Japan is declining faster than the death rate, and the chance is that her population will grow less and less rapidly during the next few decades. Since this decline in the birth rate is likely to be accelerated by any considerable migration which would lead to improvement in the level of living, Japan is the one country in all this region which might be helped by a large migration. This is quite different from the situation of India or China, in which a large migration would almost certainly lower the death rate but have little or no effect on the birth rate, thus increasing the margin between them and filling up any gap due to the loss by migration. Only after a country has reduced its death rate to reasonably low limits so that migration does not of itself lead to further reduction and after it has begun to control its birth rate can migration even on a large scale furnish any permanent relief to population pressure.

There is reason to believe that Japan has reached or soon will reach this condition, and consideration should be given to her need for emigration especially now that she is deprived of all colonies. Care needs to be taken not to create new race problems, and certainly no one wants any future growth of the Japanese to result in the strengthening of their military power; but it should be pointed out that it may be more dangerous to world peace to drive the Japanese into their home islands, and to force a very low standard of living on them by curtailing their industry, than to allow some of them to migrate into certain of the unsettled areas of Southeast Asia if such migration is properly supervised to prevent its becoming merely another arm of Japanese military power. This might be done by arranging a like migration of Chinese or Indians as a foil to the Japanese.

Of course, any large migration into these colonies will reduce the area into which the natives might expand at some future time. But, after all, we cannot hope to plan a world for a long future; we cannot look ahead at the needs and growth of population more than a few decades at most. We must use the means at our disposal now to avoid the difficulties which are almost certain to arise within the relatively short period we can foresee. We should therefore consider the needs of India and China and Japan for new areas of settlement in the light of what seems reasonable with conditions as they now are, using the best information at our disposal in arriving at our decisions. We should not allow some *principle* or *abstraction* to deter us from considering how the open spaces in tropical South and East Asia (and Africa) can be used in the near future to help in the establishment of a workable "peace in our time."

Chapter XXI

PEACE AND POPULATION GROWTH
IN THE PACIFIC

THIS survey of population and resources in the Pacific and South and East Asia is, of necessity, too brief to take up many points which should be considered, but, even so, it has covered a good deal of ground. It remains to gather together the many threads of fact and to present an over-all interpretation of them as they seem likely to affect the maintenance of peace in the next few decades.

One is tempted to say that the nub of the problem lies in the relatively densely settled countries of China, Japan, and India. But it might be as truly said that the real problem is the more efficient use of the more thinly settled areas in the Netherlands East Indies, Australia, New Zealand, the Indo-Chinese peninsula, and Africa. The little-used tropics of Africa must be included in the area, the better use of which should be planned if we are to provide a better living for the peoples of South and East Asia.

Whether the dangers to peace are considered to arise chiefly from the overcrowding of people or from the underuse of resources will depend on the approach. These two factors are merely two aspects of a single problem. Furthermore, if attention is focused entirely on the regions that have been surveyed here the problem is greatly oversimplified. The relation of population to peace in this whole area, which for convenience is called the Pacific Region, cannot be clearly understood unless we see it as part of the world problem in differential pressures of people on their resources.

A comprehensive picture of the situation cannot be drawn without some repetition; it is necessary if we wish to retain a clear view of the danger we face.

THE EAST AND THE WEST

To the best of our knowledge the world's population has considerably more than doubled in the last hundred and fifty years. In absolute numbers man's increase since about 1800 has been greater than in all the millenniums since his appearance on earth. But this great growth did not take place uniformly among the peoples of the world in

1800. The European peoples, and the Western Europeans in particular, staged a most remarkable growth in numbers for something over a century preceding World War I—a gain which almost no one living in 1800 would have believed possible and which resulted in more than tripling their numbers.

The information regarding population growth which has been accumulated during the last century and a half enables us to say with reasonable certainty how this great increase came about (see chap. ii). Briefly, this increase in population rests on the movement of Europeans into new and unused lands, on the increase in man's productive capacity associated with the agricultural and industrial revolutions, and on the development of modern sanitation and medicine. Once man learned how to produce more than mere subsistence, he could use this surplus in a variety of ways. The chief uses made of it with which we are concerned here were (a) for a general improvement of the level of living, in the agricultural population as well as in the nonagricultural population; (b) for sanitation and health; and (c) for capital. The first two of these uses contributed directly to the lowering of the death rate, and the third was probably no less important in this respect, although its effects were not so directly discernible. The consequences of these uses of the surplus production on population growth were truly amazing, but today we are not amazed because we have come to accept a rapid and continuous growth in numbers as normal and have adjusted our economy and our social life to it.

But since this increase in the productivity of human labor and the saving of human life it made possible did not affect all peoples at the same time, it resulted in a differential growth of population, the peoples of European stock growing rapidly for some decades before there was any comparable growth among non-Europeans. As soon as the factors underlying the growth of population came to be understood, it became clear that this was a *natural* response to certain economic and social conditions and would probably be duplicated in other populations as they, too, settled on new land, and/or gained in industrial and agricultural efficiency, and used their surplus products in ways which reduced the general death rate.

In our survey of population in the Pacific countries it is shown that the processes of population growth with which we have become familiar in the West as a result of the factors just mentioned, but particularly of the health measures reducing the death rate, are now becoming operative in many of the countries of South and East Asia, and that therefore they have several decades of rapid growth ahead of them. We have also seen that in recent decades the peoples of Western European origin have entered on a new stage of population growth and are now becoming stationary. As a consequence, the differential growth of peoples in the world today is favoring South and East Asia and seems likely to favor it still more in the near future.

This seems a conservative expectation because it took several decades for the Western peoples to develop a fairly adequate control over births after they had achieved such control over deaths. But there is some reason to believe that South and East Asia can achieve a like control over births in a shorter time than Western Europe. Japan seems to be doing so. But it cannot be assumed that the birth rate there will begin to fall faster than the death rate for several decades yet, probably not much before the end of the century, perhaps not even that soon, when the entire region is considered. Hence we may look for a still more rapid increase of population in most of these countries during the period immediately ahead if their production can be augmented to care for this increase. If production cannot be raised in this measure and if emigration remains small, the rate of increase will almost certainly be reduced by a higher death rate in the more densely settled areas. That there will be no significant reduction in the birth rate in any of these countries of South and East Asia, except Japan, within the next few decades is also a reasonable prediction.

AGRICULTURAL SUPPORT FOR A POPULATION INCREASE

In the light of the increase of population which seems probable in South and East Asia in the next few decades, the next important question is: Can this increase be cared for? An answer to this question was sought for the more important countries by examining their agricultural and mineral resources and their possibilities of industrial expansion in the near future.

It was found that the two great countries on the mainland of Asia— India and China—do not have large areas of new land which can be brought under cultivation. India in particular seems to have brought into use most of her good tillable land and to have extended her irrigation works to the point where it will be much more expensive to water new areas. China, with Manchoukuo and parts of Mongolia available for settlement, and with no extension of irrigation to her credit for several centuries, probably can extend her tilled area considerably once a strong central government comes into power and undertakes these jobs. But if China now has 400 million people, and if these people increase like the people of India as economic improvements take place, it will not be long before China will have used up her own tillable land and, like India, will have made but little headway in raising the per capita productivity of her agricultural population. The chief gain to the nation will consist in those public services which assist in lowering the death rate.

The chief hope of improvement in per capita agricultural production in both India and China in the immediate future lies in better farming —better tillage, better varieties of rice and other crops, better soil fertility practices, and better utilization of land not suited to annual tillage by raising cattle, trees, fruits, nuts, etc., on it. But with an increase in numbers of 10–15 per cent in a decade, as India has had since 1921 and which China may very well have as soon as the agricultural area is extended, as agricultural practices are slightly improved, as the internal order is improved, and as a modicum of public health service is established, the outlook for a larger sustained per capita agricultural production is not good. Population will grow about as fast as better and more extensive farming can be expected to increase production.

The agricultural situation in the Indo-Chinese peninsula, in the Netherlands East Indies, and in the Philippines is much more hopeful because there is a relative abundance of unused land within their own boundaries for these peoples to settle, certainly enough for several decades. If, however, Indians and Chinese numbering only a little under 800 million in 1940 (assuming China had 400 million) were allowed to move freely into these less densely peopled areas, the latter would soon be filled and India and China would be little better off thirty or forty years from now because of this migration (chap. xx).

There simply is not enough land in the Pacific Region (and tropical Africa combined) to accommodate the more than 2,000 million people that would result during the next five decades from a 15 per cent decennial increase among the more than 1,100 million now living there. I have used five decades in this calculation because this seems to be about the *minimum* period during which the continuance of the present high birth rates must be expected, to judge from Western and Japanese experiences, and because we cannot hope to look farther than this into the future with the knowledge now at our disposal.

In addition, even after the birth rate begins to come under voluntary control, population will go on growing almost as rapidly for at least two or three decades, since the death rate will continue to decline if the productivity of labor continues to increase only a little. Thus we are driven to the Malthusian conclusion that there is not a great deal of hope for any substantial improvement in the level of living in South and East Asia as long as it remains an agricultural region and depends on an extension of the tilled area and better farming for its existence. The crowding of people on the land, which now makes it impossible to enlarge the farms in much of the area and thus to use more animal or mechanical power, will continue unless some way is found to employ a large part of the future increase in numbers in some other type of production. This brings us to a consideration of the industrial possibilities of this region.

INDUSTRIAL SUPPORT FOR A POPULATION INCREASE

Taken as a whole, this region is not rich in mineral resources. India alone appears likely to develop any large basic industry—that is, large when compared with Europe and America. China, Japan, the Netherlands East Indies, and Australia can be expected to develop only relatively small amounts of heavy industry. None of them has large amounts of good iron ore, and Australia, in addition, has too small a population (a population unlikely to grow significantly in the future by natural increase) to support any considerable heavy industry even if she could export large quantities of manufactured goods. Thus iron and steel can never play the part in the industrialization and mechanization of work in this region that they have in the West. But it should not be supposed that they will not play a far larger part in the future than in the past. Japan has shown that this is possible, and all these countries are anxious to emulate her industrial expansion to the fullest extent of their resources.

If in the future iron and steel become less basic than they now are, the Pacific Region may become relatively more industrialized than now seems likely. The substitution of plastics for steel for many purposes would be advantageous to it, for it has coal in much greater relative abundance than iron; also, because much of it is tropical or semitropical, it should be able to produce an abundance of vegetable matter for plastics and for power alcohol when its rather scanty oil supplies fail.

Up to the present the machine industries of this region have been confined chiefly to the processing of agricultural products and the recovery and processing of mineral products for export. Only a beginning has been made in the manufacture of consumption goods. The one outstanding exception is, of course, Japan, although India may surpass her in the heavier industries within three or four decades. But when the industrial development of this region is considered in the light of the known mineral resources, we are forced to conclude that the Pacific Region can never become highly industrialized like Western Europe, North America, and now the Soviet Union. Its industries must occupy themselves far more with the working-up of their agricultural products into consumption goods than has been customary in the West.

Since South and East Asia will need much machinery even for its factories making consumption goods and much steel for its railways and ships, it must plan on the continuance of the export of its agricultural products and raw minerals for some time to come in order to get the capital goods to enable the manufacture of consumption goods to go ahead even at a moderate pace. If Japan is ever allowed to rebuild her heavy industries located in her home islands, she will have the facilities to supply a considerable part of the heavy good needed by China and the Netherlands East Indies and other countries, but she can do so only if she is also allowed to buy the raw materials of these countries by trading with them without much restriction. India should be able to proceed with a moderately rapid expansion of her steel industry and, in addition to supplying her own needs, to export some to neighboring lands. But even if the ambitious plans of some of the leading Indian industrialists are made effective, it is hard to see how India can hope to increase substantially the export of industrial products in the next two decades. China may also develop a modest steel industry in the near future with Japanese equipment, but at best her development of heavy industry will be slow.

The point of chief concern here is that we must not expect the expansion of the iron and steel industries and the closely related heavy industries to take place rapidly enough to absorb any considerable portion of the probable natural increase of population unless they are heavily subsidized, are protected by high tariffs, or are operated by the state. Even under these conditions they cannot be expected to attain large dimensions, according to our notions, because iron ore of good grade is lacking and because it is hard to see any such rapid expansion of the market as took place in the United States or even in Western Europe (for the reason that per capita agricultural production cannot expand at much more than a snail's pace).

This inability of South and East Asia to develop large basic industry in the near future should not be overemphasized, however, for, as our modern economy evolves, it employs relatively fewer workers in basic industry and relatively more in the elaboration of basic products into consumption goods and in the numerous services needed to maintain a high level of living. What we paid Japan for silk before the war amounted to far more than the cost of importing all the steel she was then using. In a peaceful world where trade is not too much fettered by tariffs, quotas, exchange restrictions, etc., the lack of basic mineral resources may not be as much of a handicap as it is often assumed to be. But in the world as it was in the inter-war period, such a lack was serious.

Although the lack of iron and coal may be serious in the long run, such quantities as are available may be exploited rapidly, and for the time being a relative abundance of production may thus be attained which can be used as the state sees fit; for war, as Japan did, or for the expansion of plants, or for consumption. But any rapid development of the steel industry can take place only if a highly centralized state control of the economy pumps a large part of the national income above mere subsistence into this and other industries, and perhaps into war supplies. The likelihood of such an effort by any state in this region (except perhaps Japan, if we allow her to) seems rather small at the present time, so it must be doubted that basic industry will progress rapidly enough in the near future in any of these countries to supply any considerable portion of their increasing millions with more productive jobs.

When we turn attention to the probable development of the consumption industries, the prospect looks somewhat brighter in spite of formidable obstacles to be overcome. Such industries are already being developed in most of these countries on a small scale. They can no doubt be expanded rather rapidly in the near future, but that they can absorb any considerable part of the increase in population which is to be expected is beyond rational hope.

TECHNOLOGICAL UNEMPLOYMENT

The outstanding characteristic of machine industry as contrasted with hand industry is its greater per capita productiveness. One worker in a spinning mill will produce many times as much yarn as a hand spinner, and it will be of superior quality. This is true of most machine industry and is the chief economic virtue of such industry. But we must not forget that if one worker in a mill produces ten times as much yarn as a hand spinner, nine of the latter will be thrown out of work unless a market can be found at once for a vastly increased product. Even if such a market is found, it may be at a price which will mean literal starvation to the hand spinners still at work. It is no solution of the practical difficulty faced by hand workers in being thrown out of jobs that in the long run people will be better off because of the increased productivity of the machine worker. Gandhi has urged the Indians to return to hand spinning and weaving because he believes that, by thus employing their time not needed on their small plots of ground, they can produce goods useful to themselves and thus improve their level of living. He does not urge it because it is more productive.

The fact is that even in the West the extension of machine industry was accompanied by much hardship and suffering among the hand workers, in spite of the fact that never in human history had it been so easy for man to move on to new land and thus find employment. Machine industry does displace hand workers, and, if land is scarce, as in India and China, these displaced workers find it far more difficult to make a living than was the case in Western Europe during its period of rapid displacement of such workers.

Furthermore, there is no real hope that the machine textile industry of India, for example, will be able to open up large foreign markets as that of England did when it began to expand rapidly. The same is true of most of the other consumption industries. There is very good reason to doubt, therefore, that the total volume of machine production can be expanded rapidly enough either by increase in domestic consumption or by export to absorb the hand workers that will be displaced. The displaced workers of India seem to be crowding on land already in use, thus nullifying the agricultural improvement which has taken place. The increase in population goes on, and there is at best only a small outlet in industry or on the land. It is not that these countries of South and East Asia will not expand their industries. They will. Of this there is no doubt. But some of them are already densely peopled and have no easy outlet to new land. Their farmers are living very close to subsistence level so that their purchasing power is small. They have very high birth rates, hence any temporary easing of pressure merely means another life saved and another mouth to share the product.

I am not arguing that this vicious circle of poverty arising from inefficient agriculture on tiny landholdings, and high birth rates leading to still more poverty on still tinier holdings, cannot be broken; nor am

I denying that industry is one of the most important means of breaking it. But I am saying that the birth rate being what it is and with sanitation being introduced to reduce the death rate, with land being scarce, and with certain basic natural resources also relatively scarce and costly to use, and with the level of living at near subsistence, we cannot reasonably expect industrialization, either in heavy industries or in consumption industries, to absorb more than a small part of the probable increase in population for several decades. The general level of living will rise slowly at best, and there is no assurance that the rise will be continuous. There is little hope of significant improvement as long as the birth rate remains at or near its present level.

If this conclusion is rejected because of the achievements of Japan, three points must be borne in mind. In the first place, Japan had a long head start in industry compared with these other lands of South and East Asia and was in a favorable position for some years (until about 1932–33) to exploit their markets for many types of cheap goods. With her cheap labor she could also exploit the large markets of Europe and America for certain luxury goods, silk being the chief. This enabled her to trade for the raw materials of this region on quite favorable terms, until special bars to Japanese trade were erected when the depression of the 1930's deepened. No other country in South and East Asia can hope to occupy this unique position for even two or three decades in the future.

In the second place, from the very beginning of her modern industrial development, Japan had a strong central government which worked in close co-operation with her capitalists and was willing to allow them fabulous profits if only they would give Japan an increasingly varied and a relatively efficient economy. Any of these countries could adopt the same policy, but none of them now has the strong central control by a native government that Japan had seventy-five years ago. It will be some time before they can develop such a government even if the colonial system is done away with in the near future. This now seems highly doubtful. Even war did not give China a strong central government, to say nothing of an efficient and unified one capable of giving substantial aid to those who might act as enterprisers; while, for all practical purposes, India is still a colony.

In the third place, it should be remembered that, with all Japan's industrial development, her people still lived at a very low level according to Western standards. A similar degree of industrialization for all of South and East Asia cannot be achieved for three to five decades at best, and, because they already have denser populations than Japan had sixty years ago, it is doubtful if they can achieve as much in the way of better living as Japan has.

POPULATION PRESSURE AND WAR

At this point I can well imagine the reader saying: "Suppose that the people of South and East Asia do increase so fast that there is only a very slow improvement in their level of living during the next several decades. How does that have any bearing on the problem of peace in the Pacific? Will it not merely mean that they will go on living about as they have been living for many decades, perhaps for centuries, and need it concern us as long as we can get the rubber and tin and oil we need from them?"

This would be so only if they did remain in exactly the same condition as in the past. But this is not the case and will be still less the case as time passes. Their fairly rapid growth in numbers is a relatively recent phenomenon and *is proof of one very important change now going on.* Their desire to industrialize, although largely confined to a small Western-educated group, *is proof of another important change:* a conscious dissatisfaction with their present status on the part of an influential segment of the population. Moreover, all these peoples have been given a very bitter lesson as to what it means to remain industrially and therefore militarily weak when other peoples are strong.

There are active groups in all these countries determined that they will not submit much longer to being ruled by European powers or to the unequal treaties which in effect make them semicolonial peoples. There is a growing understanding which did not exist in the past of how industry can strengthen a nation's political position; and, although none of these nations may become a first-class industrial power for a long time, if ever, there is no doubt that several of them can go far enough in industrial development to make themselves formidable powers in a comparatively few years.

Japan was a weak industrial power in 1921 when measured by Western standards. She had to withdraw from Shantung and forego the "Fifteen Demands." Indeed, she could scarcely have been called a great industrial nation even in 1941. Her capacity for producing steel at the time she attacked us was probably not over ten million tons, her merchant marine was possibly one-fifth as large as that of the United

Kingdom, her navy was much smaller than ours, and her capacity to turn out weapons and munitions of all kinds was only a fraction of our own. But when even such a relatively weak nation turned its energies to war production, she became a very formidable antagonist within a few years. If the other countries in South and East Asia become as strong industrially as Japan—and India and China could do so without absorbing more than a small part of their probable future population increase into industry—and if they had grievances as irritating as Japan felt hers to be, why should we think that they will be less willing to upset the status quo in order to secure an enlarged place in the sun?

DIFFERENTIAL POPULATION GROWTH AND WAR

No one would for a moment deny that Hitler, or Mussolini, or the army and navy clique in Japan, or the peculiar historical development of each of these countries was a factor in encouraging it to military aggression. On the other hand, I do not see how anyone can deny that the increase of population pressure—or, expressed differently, the lack, or the *felt* lack, of adequate resources—is frequently an aggravating factor in leading people to war. Nor do I see how we can fail to recognize that the increase in population pressure is often the consequence of differential population growth. Thus if Germany had not had a population much larger than that of France in 1914, and one which was then still growing rapidly while France's was almost stationary, and if she had not been industrializing rapidly, she would not have felt so keenly the need of larger resources, of more colonies in Africa and the Pacific, and of the wheat lands of the Ukraine; nor would she have been so sure that she possessed the power to take what she wanted.

Need, like most other human judgments, is a value judgment and is relative. The needs felt are quite different in an agrarian Germany of 1850 with a population of 35 million and in a rapidly industrializing Germany of 1914 with 60 million. Likewise the Japan of 1860 which wanted to avoid all possible contact with the outside world was, with only about 30 million people, quite content to live on her own resources in the traditional manner. She was a quite different Japan from the one which *felt* a very great need for more land and resources in 1930 after she had made considerable progress in establishing modern industry and had grown to 64 million, although she was not so poor absolutely as at the earlier period.

To fail to realize that such changes in numbers, in economy, and in social structure also change the values of peoples as regards their *needs* and what is worth fighting for is to be blind to what is happening in the world today.

We all recognize that World War II has altered the relative importance of many nations, but we do not seem to see that the enhanced power of the Soviet Union is due as much to her great increase in numbers as to her increase in industrial power, that increase in industrial power at any given stage of development has a very important relation to the increase of the population. Of course, if a country does not have the essential raw materials and cannot get them, manpower and industrial power do not march together; but, even though there may be a long-time shortage of certain basic minerals, as appears to be the case in China, and as certainly was the case in Italy and Japan and probably in Germany, there is always the possibility that, temporarily, enough can be found to make the attempt to conquer more appear likely to succeed. As long as this is the case and as long as we can be reasonably certain that pressure of population on resources is going to be *felt* more and more in China and India and Java and Japan, it seems only common sense to expect that they will increasingly resent any discriminations against them in the use of land and resources.

But the best evidence of the significance of differential population growth as a factor causing changes in the political importance of nations is found in the expansion of European influence since 1800. Certainly no one would maintain that, if Great Britain had remained a country of 12 million as in 1801, even a very high degree of industrialization would have enabled her to attain the dominance she achieved during the latter half of the nineteenth century and which she maintained until World War I. Nor could Germany have challenged the power of France in 1870, 1914, and 1939 if it had not been for the growth of her population from about 25 million in 1800 to 60 million in 1914, while France grew only from 27 million to 42 million. The differentials in population growth and size have been a powerful factor in determining the conduct of nations in the past, but they have been neutralized to some extent during the past century or century and a half by the differentials in industrial capacity. Industrialized populations like those of Great Britain or France were able to gain control over far larger populations of nonindustrialized lands with comparative ease.

If we assume, as I believe we are fully justified in doing, that India and China are going to industrialize as rapidly as possible, and that they have the raw materials for a considerable industrial development, although relatively far inferior to our own, we must expect that, with their probable growth of population, they are going to become relatively much more powerful within a few decades. Are these great countries going to be content to develop within their present boundaries while 600,000 or 700,000 square miles of Indonesia and Oceania are lying almost idle except for a few European plantations and a few mines worked by imported labor? Are the Indians going to submit for long to virtual exclusion from Natal, Kenya, and Tanganyika in Africa, while a few tens of thousands of white British subjects monopolize vast fertile areas and appeal to the doctrine of trusteeship to justify keeping the Indians out of many areas where the natives are making but little use of the land?

It is time that we recognized the very obvious fact that the present differentials in population growth in the world are working against Europe, west of Poland and the Balkans, and in favor of Eastern Europe and Asia. We must also recognize that the military strength conferred by industrialization is no longer the sole prerogative of Western Europe and North America, that it is now relatively easy to transfer industrial skills from one country to another, and that, if urgent, capital can be accumulated rather rapidly. Witness what both Japan and the Soviet Union have accomplished in these respects since World War I.

It would seem only the part of common sense for the Western Europeans, who are going to be on the losing end of power arguments in the near future, to try to find ways to satisfy the legitimate demands of the peoples who are growing relatively stronger and who, to judge by what has happened in the past, will use this strength to take what they *believe* they need. It is time for the Western Europeans, while still strong, to begin to make concessions to the future great powers of the East, but above all it would seem the part of wisdom for them to work diligently for some international authority which can deal with the problems of colonies and unused territories, with the problems of trade, with the problems of population growth, and with all the other manifold problems of living in a world where there are bound to be more and more conflicting national needs as population increases. If we leave these matters to the arbitrament of force, we will before many decades find ourselves the underdog. We are no longer a "swarming" people, and we no longer have a monopoly on machine production.[1]

If South and East Asia maintain their present birth rate indefinitely, there is probably no hope of avoiding a life-and-death struggle between these peoples and the low-birth-rate peoples. In the long run there can be but one issue to such a struggle. The high-birth-rate peoples will win. There is no good reason, however, to believe that these peoples are not as anxious to improve their level of living as our own European ancestors were, or to doubt that they will in time appreciate fully the relation between a high birth rate, a high death rate, and a low level of living. When they do, they will probably control their birth rates, much as has happened in the West. But we must not forget that they are already a numerous people, about five to six times as numerous as Europeans in 1800, and that considerable parts of the world suited to European settlement have been settled and developed in the meantime; nor should we forget that it takes some time, two or three decades at least, to effect any significant decline in the rate of natural increase even after urbanization and industrialization have resulted in a large decline in the birth rate. Hence, under the conditions likely to prevail in South and East Asia for the next several decades, the *felt* pressure of population is almost certain to grow in spite of all possible agricultural expansion and improvement and in spite of all that can be done to increase machine production.

It is because of this that it is the part of common sense to make some provision to open up a portion of the unused or little-used tropics to these "swarming" peoples who are largely tropical. Not only has the European shown no aptitude for tropical settlement, but he is not now

[1] As this goes to press, we are being shocked with tales of the incredible destructiveness of the atomic bomb and have great reason to be thankful that Germany or Japan did not beat us to its use. But we certainly cannot assume that, because we possess a monopoly on this bomb today, it will not become the common property of all nations within a few decades, possibly within a few years; nor can we assume that because it cost us two billion dollars to make a few of these weapons, the cost will remain prohibitive to these backward industrial lands. Indeed, the perfecting and cheapening of this weapon may, instead of cementing the hold of the West over the East, be the thing which will quickly make the peoples of South and East Asia our equals in war potential and may be decisive in arousing their determination not to put up with what they believe to be grave injustices in the use of the lands and resources of the Pacific Region. The lesson we should draw from the development of the atomic bomb is not that we no longer need to consider the possible growth of military power in the relatively weak nations of the East but rather that a few years hence even these weak peoples (that is, weak industrially) may be able to launch a sudden and decisive attack against much more powerful industrial nations, if they are goaded to desperation by injustice and by being treated as fit only to serve their present masters.

even settling the new lands in more temperate latitudes where Europeans are already settled. Again I ask: Can a strong India and China be expected to respect the "rights" of Europeans in regions where they do not settle and do not actually use their own labor in making a living? Will they continue to recognize the European master when they need these lands with their mineral resources, and when they have gained the strength to make successful conquest seem likely? Why should we think that these peoples are so different from ourselves that they will remain quiescent under what they cannot but regard as unjust discrimination? Let us recognize the facts of population growth and industrial development in South and East Asia and begin to make adjustments which will, as far as is in our power, render the forceful conquest of new lands unnecessary to these growing peoples. A genuinely disinterested and understanding helpfulness on the part of Western peoples at this time while they are yet relatively strong would create a greater willingness on the part of these Eastern peoples to undertake measures which might result in lower birth rates and in an adjustment of population to resources which would make a higher level of living possible without going out for conquest.

Already, however, the time is short and a beginning should not be delayed. The coming years of peace offer an opportunity to enter upon a new type of co-operation between West and East in the better use of the tropics. If we fail to use this opportunity, it may prove a blunder of the first magnitude—one which our children and our children's children will not forgive us.

Chapter XXII

THE STAKE OF THE UNITED STATES IN THE PACIFIC

WHAT DO WE WANT IN THE PACIFIC?

ONCE we had definitely decided upon the complete independence of the Philippines, our territorial stake in the Pacific consisted of Hawaii and a few small islands which might have been of strategic importance if we had developed them as strong naval stations. At the Washington Conference in 1922 we relinquished this privilege in return for a naval agreement which presumably gave us, in conjunction with the British, definite naval superiority over Japan. After this treaty lapsed and with the decision to allow the Philippines their independence, it seemed to Congress unnecessary to fortify Midway, Yap, Guam, and Samoa and the Philippines. It was assumed that Hawaii would never be attacked by Japan—that she would confine her aggression to Asia and the neighboring islands in which we felt but small interest.

Consequently, after 1934 it could be said that most people in the United States thought of our military job in the Pacific as being confined to the protection of Hawaii, which our naval authorities frequently told us was so easy as to require little effort or expenditure. We were led to believe that our navy was far more than a match for the Japanese navy, and quite obviously before 1940 our naval authorities did not consider naval aviation of any great importance, while Congress was even more indifferent. But all this is past. What we are interested in now is what our stake in the Pacific will be for the next few decades.

With the independence of the Philippines, our only territorial stake in the Pacific of any economic significance will be Hawaii. It is likely, however, that we will retain more and better strategic bases. Economically the Marshalls, the Carolines, the Marianas, and the Ryukyus are of little importance to us. Altogether the first three groups contain but a little over 1,000 square miles, and much of this is not suitable for agriculture. The known mineral deposits are likewise of little importance. There are some potash and bauxite deposits, but they do not appear to be large and will add little if anything to our economic strength. It can be assumed, however, that we will keep these islands, and perhaps Okinawa, because of their strategic value either entirely in our own power or that they will come under the control of an international organization which will allow us to use them as strategic bases. In either case, we will be responsible for the maintenance of whatever naval and army bases are deemed necessary. They certainly will not be allowed to revert to Japan in the foreseeable future, and it is scarcely likely that Australia and New Zealand will feel able to undertake their control and the policing duties that must go with it.

I believe that the average American will now see our stake in the Pacific as confined to the maintenance of whatever military establishments, including island bases, may be necessary to keep Japan harmless for as long as we remember vividly the danger from this quarter and to the building-up of a system of trade treaties which will insure us a fair share in Pacific trade, since we need rubber, tin, coconut oil, and many other products from this region.

For a time we shall probably be unwilling to intrust the preservation of peace and our trade interests wholly to the care of any international organization; later we may be willing to do so. In any event, we are not expecting to take on any new territorial obligations in the Pacific, except those necessary to accomplish our strategic purposes. Certainly we do not want any of the tropical islands on which large-scale settlement of tropical peoples might take place, nor, as a people, do we want any special trade privileges in this region, although certain groups and interested corporations may clamor loudly for them. This does not mean, of course, that we may not make a trade treaty with the Philippines granting special access to our markets in order to tide them over the difficult period of transition from almost complete dependence on trade with us to a time when their trade can take its natural place in world markets and their internal economy can be adjusted to the new conditions.

PEACE IN THE PACIFIC AND WORLD PEACE

If the interest of the American people in the Pacific is stated correctly, it will appear to most of us that, as far as our demands are concerned, it should not be difficult to achieve "peace in our day" if an adequate policing of Japan's (and Germany's) production is maintained long enough. This would be the case if the interests of all other Allied nations were as simple as our own and were as little likely to conflict with the interests of the peoples of South and East Asia during the next generation or two. Unfortunately, this is not the case. The allies will not long remain as closely united as they now are, and Japan certainly will not be slow to exploit any and all differences in policy which may and will develop from time to time, while the other countries of South and East Asia will likewise exploit these differences as soon as they develop the strength to do so if they continue to feel themselves the victims of unfair treatment by Westerners.

History shows that alliances are slender reeds on which to rest a peace, but history's teachings will probably be brushed aside with the brusque statement that *this time things are different*. We must not forget, however, that the nations which now constitute the United Nations stood aside when Japan took Manchoukuo in 1931, attacked China Proper in 1937, and later moved into French Indo-China. Japan timed her aggression against China to take advantage of the divergent interests of the powers that might take effective action against her and did not attack the interests of the European powers and the United States until she saw them very heavily involved elsewhere —so heavily involved that it seemed unlikely they would be able to challenge her in any strength until she had become well intrenched in their former colonies as well as in China. Peace in the Pacific proved not to be separate from peace in the world as a whole, and it will be even less so in the future. Surely at this time we do not need to argue that the aggression of one or two nations anywhere may plunge the world into war, or that this aggression need not be aimed directly at us when it is initiated, in order to compel us to defend ourselves and our interests by fighting in distant lands, although we claim no special rights and privileges there for ourselves.

It may seem useless, therefore, to talk of the stake of the United States in the Pacific while ignoring our stake in the world at large. But understanding the conditions which we have to face in the Pacific will help us to understand the larger problems of world peace. It does not mean that we are ignoring other danger spots if we devote our attention here to the Pacific. It is not assumed that the situation in the Pacific is more dangerous than in Europe, but, because there are certain very fundamental changes going on in this region which have been given far less consideration in the planning of peace than have the conditions in Europe, and because they are dangerous to the maintenance of peace, they need our attention.

The purpose of the remainder of this chapter is to show how the

United States must interest itself in the consequences of the population and economic changes now going on in the Pacific Region and help to find a way to render them less dangerous if we are not to be involved again in a war of whose active preparation we will be scarcely aware. This is not to deny that we bear a large share of responsibility for this war because of our indirect actions (e.g., tariffs) and passive attitudes (indifference) toward certain world problems which seemed remote but which really concerned us closely. In a word, the argument here is that the social and economic developments in the several parts of the Pacific Region, which have been described all too briefly above, do concern us vitally and that our ultimate stake in peace can be achieved only by helping to see that the explosive forces likely to accumulate are dissipated before they become dangerous.

THE SOVIET UNION IN THE PACIFIC

Nothing has been said up to this point about the Soviet Union as a Pacific power. This neglect was based on the assumption that for the next few decades the Soviet Union will be so busy with her own development and with securing her European frontier that she will not be interested in extending her power in the Pacific beyond what we will be glad to acquiesce in at the expense of Japan and possibly of China. The bases of this assumption are (*a*) the tremendous job of rebuilding all of western and southern European Russia which lies ahead of the Soviet Union; (*b*) the fact that the Union possesses within its present boundaries all the land and minerals needed for the continued rapid industrialization of the nation even though she may be expected to grow very rapidly in numbers for the next half-century;[1] and (*c*) the belief that there will be no Asiatic power which can seriously challenge the Union's position during this period of rebuilding and recovery which will certainly require two or three decades, possibly more.

How the growth of the Soviet Union will change the situation forty or fifty years hence need not give us much concern here because there is a good probability that the industrialization of the Union will in the meantime lead to a marked decline in the birth rate and that by the end of the century she, like the United States at present, can look ahead to a comparatively small future increase. Also, like the United

[1] One estimate is that, making no allowance for war losses, the Soviet Union will grow to about 250 million by 1970 (346, p. 56). By 1990, even assuming war losses of 10–15 million, the Soviet Union might be expected to have a population in the neighborhood of 300 million.

States, the Soviet Union need not worry greatly about the resources to care for her probable future population, provided she has opportunity to carry on a reasonably free trade with the rest of the world. The omission of further consideration of the position of the Soviet Union in the Pacific is not because she will not be a great military power, probably the greatest land power, during the ensuing half-century, but because, with the job she has to do at home and with relatively abundant resources within her own borders, she is not likely to engage in aggressive action during that time.[2]

MAINTENANCE OF THE COLONIAL SYSTEM AS IT AFFECTS OUR STAKE

The United States, as already indicated, belongs to the group of nations whose population is rapidly becoming stationary and after two or three decades may even begin to decline. Australia and New Zealand are in about the same situation, and Canada is only a little behind because her French population still has a high birth rate. By 1970 the combined populations of these countries of European stock with greatest direct interest in the Pacific Region will probably not exceed 180–190 million, while that of what we have called South and East Asia will almost certainly be well above the 1,000–1,100 million now living there. South and East Asia may easily have 1,300–1,400 million people by that time, with no sign of any decline in the birth rate, except in Japan.

Unless there is a definite movement now to modify and later to abolish the colonial system, about three million square miles of the territory of South and East Asia will remain under European control, including India and that under the control of Australia and New Zealand. In the past Great Britain has been able to exercise control over and to protect her colonies and dominions, but events have shown that she can no longer hope to do so alone. Her power will be weaker relative to that of South and East Asia in the future. Moreover, France and

---

[2] Just how the development of atomic power will affect the relations of the Soviet Union and the United States must remain a matter of opinion at present. Atomic power has not changed the basic fact that we can both proceed with our industrial development without getting in each other's way. Only if we stir up such distrust and fear of each other that we give up trying to come to an understanding is it likely that we shall clash over the treatment of Japan or China or the control of the islands off the coast of China. But, clearly, if two great countries like the Soviet Union and ourselves do reach the stage of distrust where we are unwilling to co-operate to control atomic warfare, there is a real danger that each will utterly destroy the other. On the other hand, if we deal with each other on the assumption that we both want peace and security in order to achieve a better life for ourselves and for the world, we should be able to find a basis of agreement for the control of this power. But, of course, we can never have security and peace unless we are willing to abate our claims of national sovereignty.

Holland have relied on the British navy more than on their own power to protect their colonies, and they will be even less able to perform this service to their colonies in the future. The inevitable result of this relative decline in the power of the European states in South and East Asia is that the colonial system in this region can be maintained in anything like its present form only during the next generation or two if the strength of the European colonial powers is buttressed directly by that of the United States and indirectly by that of the Soviet Union. The strengthening of China and India through industrialization about which we are hearing so much will certainly result in the relative weakening of European power. Quite obviously, Australia and New Zealand with eight to ten million people cannot supply either the manpower or the materials to fend off an attack by even a greatly weakened Japan, to say nothing of protecting the colonies of the Pacific Region from an industrializing India or China co-operating with each other or even with Japan.

Let us face the facts. Great Britain and France are now second-rate powers and will become relatively weaker as time goes on. It is absurd to talk of the 550 million people in the British Empire, or the 150 million of the French Empire, as though they would rise up in defense of a colonial system which keeps seven-eighths of those in the British Empire in leading strings and over two-thirds of those in the French Empire in much the same position. The Soviet Union certainly has a vital interest in keeping Japan weak for some time to come, perhaps three or four decades, while she is building up such economic strength in her Far Eastern territory that it would be folly for Japan to attack her. After that the situation may change.

The time may come when it will not be to the interest of the Soviet Union to keep Japan as weak as at present, and we, too, may be far less interested in keeping her weak by 1970–80 than we now are. It is by no means impossible that the Soviet Union, as well as ourselves, will in two or three decades have no special objection to a stronger Japan as a foil to growing strength in China and India. Japanese settlements in parts of Indonesia to forestall the expansion of China may then appear a shrewd political move. It must not be forgotten that in 1938 it was considered compatible with British interests to keep hands off Europe if Hitler saw fit to attack the Soviet Union. Why should the Soviet Union of 1970 or 1980 with an unassailable continental position go to any trouble to deny Japan settlements on New Guinea or Borneo? Indeed, why should we do so if it appears that Japan's expansion southward and eastward in the Pacific does not endanger us because China has become strong enough to handle the situation?

If there is to be a settlement in the Pacific which perpetuates the present colonial system and which guarantees Australia and New Zealand protection against any encroachments from Asiatic settlement on New Guinea for a generation, or possibly even for two generations, it will have to come from the United States. Great Britain cannot make good on any such undertaking by her own power, and the Soviet Union is more than likely to be uninterested in maintaining such a status for longer than she needs to consolidate her own position as an unassailable power in North Asia.

Are we ready to accept the responsibility for a settlement which will make it necessary for us to play the major role in policing Japan for more than a decade or two and also to enforce "no trespass" rules against China and India, as well as Japan, if they want to send people to settle on the unused lands of the Pacific, or to exploit their resources?

THE POSITION OF AUSTRALIA AND NEW ZEALAND IN THE PACIFIC

We must remember in this connection that Australia and New Zealand have shown no disposition in the recent past to adopt immigration and settlement policies likely to lead to the growth of their populations beyond possibly 8 million in the case of the former and 2.0–2.25 million in the case of the latter, a total population in the neighborhood of 10 million (see chap. iv). At the same time very low estimates of their ability to support people at a high level of living would not be less than 25 million, and many well-informed people would place the number at 40 million or more. This situation in which a small population with a high level of living occupies a land having resources far beyond its probable future needs is certain to raise many questions in the minds of less fortunate peoples.

But this is not the only or even the most disturbing aspect of the position of Australia and New Zealand in the Pacific. They expect to exercise colonial power over about 200,000 or more square miles of almost empty tropical land which they cannot possibly settle—land which they can only exploit feebly in the traditional colonial manner (see chap. iv). They also expect to have a decisive say in determining the settlement policies of the Dutch in their 150,000 square miles of New Guinea. They will do all this, of course, as a part of the British

Empire, or as a member of the organization set up in San Francisco. Furthermore, their purpose is less the economic advantage to be gained through colonial power than the prevention of large settlements of Asiatics too near their homelands.

But Australia and New Zealand know perfectly well, as do the Dutch, that their only hope of maintaining control over settlement in New Guinea and adjacent islands is to preserve the exclusive character of the present colonial system, and the leaders of the peoples of South and East Asia are also fully aware of this fact. These Asiatic peoples will acquiesce in any settlement of this war which tends to perpetuate their exclusion from equal access to the unused areas of the Pacific Region only because they cannot now do otherwise. When any of these peoples feels strong enough to challenge this colonial system, it will do so and it will pick the weakest point for attack. This weakest point seems very likely to be the "empire" which Australia and New Zealand, with the aid of Great Britain and Holland certainly, and that of the United States if it can possibly be secured, are establishing to keep the Asiatics at a distance. That this is given the name of a "regional" understanding does not make it less the customary colonial arrangement.

In the United States we should not ignore the fact that, although this "empire" can probably be erected without our consent, it certainly cannot be maintained for any length of time without our active assistance. It is a matter of very great importance to us, therefore, to inquire carefully into the commitments involved in the establishment of an Australasian Empire under the control of Australia and New Zealand and the Dutch, who control the western half of New Guinea and a number of the adjacent islands, and supported by Great Britain and France. It may easily become an additional *stake* in the Pacific for the United States which will require far more effort to maintain after a few years than the more direct stakes discussed above. Indeed, the support of such a "regional" arrangement may well prove the most dangerous commitment we shall be called upon to make.

It is not difficult to understand why the Australians do not want any of the Asiatic peoples to settle in Australia. We have a race problem of our own and should be very sympathetic to the desire of the Australians to avoid such a development. But this does not mean that we should make any commitments regarding the control by Australia and New Zealand of large colonial areas from which they intend to exclude all Asiatics unless they come in as temporary contract laborers working on European plantations and in European mines and factories; nor does it mean that we should make any commitments to a prolonged protection of these countries themselves against settlement by Asiatics if Australia and New Zealand continue to discourage the immigration of those European peoples who alone can settle the land and help them build up a population large enough to defend themselves from invasion in some not distant future.

Ten million people in Australia and New Zealand in 1980 probably cannot remain in control of their present homelands in the face of the increase in numbers in South and East Asia by that time without the support of the United States even if Japan is kept completely harmless by the big powers. The only hope of Australia and New Zealand for maintaining their independence in the long run is to encourage the growth of populations large enough to defend themselves.

This is a situation which we must recognize now. If we do not recognize it and limit our commitments to what it is feasible to carry through, either we shall find ourselves involved in squabbles in which we have little interest in the outcome or, more likely, we will become disgusted with the whole situation and withdraw all commitments. To do the latter would be to invite any strong Asiatic power to make encroachments on the Australasian "empire," just as our aloofness from European affairs gave encouragement to Hitler and Mussolini to hope that we "would not intervene this time" and therefore rendered their projects of conquest more likely of accomplishment.

THE "EMPIRE" OF AUSTRALIA AND NEW ZEALAND
AS IT AFFECTS OUR STAKE

What the United States wants in the Pacific is peace and the opportunity to carry on essential trade which only peace can assure. But if we are not extremely careful, we may find ourselves underwriting a settlement for Australasia which does not mean peace but war. It is the main thesis of this study that large differentials in population pressure which are *felt* will lead the more crowded peoples to attempt to equalize these pressures by force whenever and wherever the chance of success seems reasonably good if force remains the only method of securing larger resources.

It simply is not reasonable to suppose that China and India, when they have 200–300 million more people than at present and when they have become strong enough to equip and maintain strong armies and navies, will not look with covetous eyes upon the Australasian tropical empire which is practically certain to remain almost vacant under the present colonial system. Thus the United States may, if not extremely careful, create another stake in the Pacific by encouraging Australia and New Zealand to think that we will support them in their policy of excluding all Asiatics not only from their homelands but also from their "empire," while at the same time they make no serious effort to people even their homelands to reasonable density.

Any commitments we make to Australia and New Zealand beyond rendering Japan impotent for several decades, which is essential in our own interests, should be contingent upon their building up their own populations to the size where they can put up a strong defense of their homelands. This same position should be taken by the world organization which will attempt to maintain peace. Not even a strong world organization can insure peace if there are large and growing differentials in population growth leading to increasing differentials in population pressure which are felt to be unjust and unnecessary.

I have tried to explain above how great hardship may become customary and may be long endured without revolt but that the processes of modern economic development are changing this quiescent attitude and producing an awareness of differential pressures which will become increasingly dangerous as the "backward" peoples become stronger through industrialization. I am further contending here that if Australia and New Zealand, with 8–10 million people, make large claims to unsettled lands in New Guinea and other smaller islands in the neighborhood merely to protect themselves against Asiatic neighbors, they are inviting aggression in a world where military force is the only effective instrument of national policy, and even in a world with an incipient but only moderately effective international organization for the settlement of international grievances.

Undoubtedly the Big Four, or Five, nations are strong enough now to protect Australia and New Zealand and their "empire" from Japan and also from any other possible Asiatic aggressor until these Asiatic countries are much farther along the road to industrialization; yet it is time now to define our stake in the Pacific very precisely and to see that it is not enlarged without our knowledge and consent. If peace and opportunity to trade are what we want, and are all we want, for ourselves, then our policy should be directed solely to these ends. We should not allow our policy to be enlarged or to be shunted aside by issues of sentiment and chivalry which not only will not contribute to peace but will almost certainly lead to war. We should not actively support a settlement of the colonial system which is sure to arouse the antagonism of the growing peoples of Asia as soon as they become aware of its implications.

If the Australians and the New Zealanders wish to maintain their "white Australia" policy in the form it assumed before the war, it is up to them to take the consequences; it is not up to us to protect them indefinitely or to support a "regional" colonial system.

In the United States we have found that we can live in moderate comfort with large numbers of Italians and Germans and Poles and Serbs and a dozen other European groups and that their children make as good citizens as the descendants of the British. It is up to the Australians to learn how to live with some of these more backward European peasants and to modify their land policies to encourage closer settlement if they expect to be strong enough to carry any great weight in international affairs or even to guard themselves against conquest. The only other way to people their land is to raise large families of their own, and there is probably not time now to accomplish effective peopling of the country from that source alone. In the long run, if the Australians and New Zealanders do not think enough of their civilization, aside from the abundance of creature comforts it offers, either to raise the children to insure growth or to endure the inconveniences arising from allowing "other" Europeans to enter who will raise large families, they will necessarily go the way of the aborigines whom they replaced or will disappear in the multitude of their conquerors.

It is not the duty of the United States to guarantee them the possession even of their homelands any longer than is necessary to give them a chance to carry out a population policy calculated to render them able to defend themselves. Nor will a strong and effective world organization be able to give them such a guaranty for long. South and East Asia will not long abide by the decisions of any organization which attempts to fix the status quo when new differentials in population are arising which create the need for the better use of the lands of this region. It is clearly not to the interest of the United States to arouse the antagonism of the peoples of South and East Asia by supporting Australasian policies which are certain to perpetuate the evils of the present colonial system.

Lest I be misunderstood, I want to make it clear that Australasia has not asked us explicitly for such a guaranty of territorial integrity in the future, or for the support of her position as a colonial power controlling 200,000 or more square miles of tropical islands. But she does implicitly assume that the United States as a supporter of world organization will underwrite a colonial policy, now called a "regional understanding" but differing very little from the pre-war policy in this region. Such an assumption seems to me implicit in the joint declaration of policy by Australia and New Zealand signed at Canberra on January 21, 1944 (130, 1944, pp. 31–35), asking for the sanction of "regional agreements" increasing their colonial control in this region.

This belief is strengthened by the fact Australia and New Zealand and the Dutch are now proceeding with the governmental organization of the reconquered colonies in a way that clearly indicates their intention of controlling New Guinea and all the neighboring islands in the interest of their present "white Australia" policy. Nor is there any evidence in recent utterances regarding the "white Australia" policy that Australasians recognize the urgent need to promote European settlement or to increase their birth rate (115 and 130, 1944, p. 188) if they are to be assured of national existence in the future.

Since I feel that the enforcement of any Pacific settlement will rest primarily on the shoulders of the United States for the next three or four decades, I believe that we must study the implications of the colonial and population policies of Australia and New Zealand as well as those of Great Britain, France, and Holland very carefully. Our chief stake in the Pacific is peace and not the maintenance of the status quo. Of course, we want trade, but it can be assumed that we will get what trade we deserve if peace endures and if colonies are not made exclusive "spheres of influence."

It should be made clear at this point that I am not now questioning the right of any nation to determine its own immigration policy and its own efforts to increase or decrease its birth rate. I would admit at once that it is none of our business what Australasia does as regards the more adequate peopling of her territory, or the use she makes of the colonies she holds and will probably administer in the postwar world, if Australasia will admit that it is none of our business what happens to her when China and India, to say nothing of a rearming Japan in 1970 or 1980, begin to acquire industrial strength and are hard put to it to find the wherewithal to support their increasing populations.

It is very doubtful, however, whether the United States can remain indifferent to the fate of Australia and New Zealand forty or fifty years

hence or to the manner in which Asiatic countries may go about acquiring rights of settlement and exploitation in Australasian colonies
(or any other Pacific colonies). If this expansion is by force in the manner attempted by Japan, as it probably will be if we do not take measures to make force unnecessary, then we shall probably have to resist
it just as we have had to resist Japanese aggression. The only hope of
preventing future war for the possession of the present colonial areas
in the Pacific is to plan for their use by the peoples who can settle them
and exploit them with their own labor, while at the same time pointing
out to them that these lands, large as they are, cannot long afford them
any permanent relief and that ultimately they must learn how to adjust their numbers to their available resources if they would live well
and at peace with the world.

The interests of the United States in the Pacific will be best served
not only by the use of the land in this region by the peoples who need
it and can work it but also by aiding in the industrial development of
these peoples, since this is the quickest known way to induce a reduction of their birth rates. A low birth rate everywhere is the only way
in the long run to avoid the unbalancing of power relations arising
from differential rates of population growth. Nothing we can do will
reduce the population increases in South and East Asia for three or
four decades, but in the long run the situation need not be hopeless,
nor need we look for a solution of the problems posed by differential
population growth to the policies of Hitler and Mussolini—the raising
of the rate of growth in their countries as nearly as possible to that of
their probable opponents still having high birth rates. A race for numbers is a race for poverty and, with the growing awareness of differences in resources, is bound to involve us in new wars beside which
those of the past will appear humane and of little significance.

INDUSTRIALIZATION AND TRADE IN THE PACIFIC

A word should be said about the encouragement of industrialization
in South and East Asia as it will affect our trade interests in the Pacific,
since this is a matter of world concern. In the past it has quite commonly been assumed that it was to the interest of the more advanced
industrial countries to prevent the establishment of factories not only
in colonies but in independent countries to which the former wished
to export their manufactures (for example, China, Australia, New Zealand, Canada). The colonial policies of all the Western powers and of

Japan attest this attitude, and the control of the tariff policies of Japan until 1911 and China until 1929 by the Western powers manifest the same attitude. The question will be asked, therefore, whether, if we encourage industrial development in South and East Asia, we shall not be closing their doors to our trade.

Undoubtedly the industrialization of these lands will reduce certain kinds of trade—trade in cloth and clothing and in certain other kinds of light consumption goods—but it may very well increase total trade. Our trade with Japan has for some time been far more important than that with China and has grown with the increasing industrialization of Japan.

Likewise Great Britain and Germany have long been among our most important customers in spite of their high degree of industrialization. The sentiment for autarchy may become so strong that it will reduce trade in certain places and for a period, but the more complex the economy of any nation becomes, the more it trades with other nations if trade barriers are not made too formidable. Moreover, we do learn, albeit slowly, that we cannot sell our goods abroad or even loan money to foreign lands to buy our goods without taking their goods in payment of principal and as interest on our loans.

Modern trade experience would seem to show, then, that we need not fear that the industrialization of China and India and other Asiatic lands will reduce our trade with them. The character of the trade will change, and this will work hardship on certain manufacturers and merchants for a time, but the total volume of trade with these countries is likely to increase rather than to decrease once they really begin to industrialize. But we must be sensible about our tariffs, and we shall have to consider the national welfare rather than the interests of the particular groups of manufacturers and merchants which now have a large stake in keeping things as they are.

How, then, are we to serve our interests in the Pacific in the settlement of this war? If these interests are summed up in the words "peace" and "trade," we must keep in mind at all times the conditions essential to serving these ends and not allow ourselves to be swerved from the path they indicate. We must not allow our sentiments, our concern for the prosperity of particular economic groups, our desire to be a "good fellow," or even our hatred for the Japanese (see chap. xi) to move us from the course which has the best chance to establish peace.

THE CONDITIONS OF PEACE

Although I have argued that the problems arising from differential population growth, from holding large areas of land virtually unused by the "stationary" peoples, and from the growth of industrial power among the "backward" peoples are fundamental problems in the achievement of peace, I recognize that we must have the machinery to investigate these matters and to effect desirable changes. There can be no hope of effecting a redistribution of the earth's resources more in accordance with the needs of peoples or of regularizing trade relations between nations until we are willing to establish some international body with power to act in these and in many other matters of vital interest to all of us. The determination of each nation to go its own way regardless of the effect this may have on other nations can result only in more and greater wars in the future. The only way any nation can have its own way in the world of today is the way Germany and Japan have tried. The economic loss involved in trying to get one's way by force is beyond computation. The wholesale destruction of resources and goods involved in modern war is a thousand fold greater than any possible gain derived from going one's own sweet way in regard to tariffs, to international monetary funds, to colonies, to the establishment of airlines, etc., in times of peace.

This need for a world organization where the troubles of all peoples can be aired and can be adjudicated in the light of world interests would seem too obvious to require argument, but unhappily this is not the case. There are even now many people who believe so much in the *right* of their country's *might* that they prefer to trust to the traditional measures of diplomacy and to the ability of their country to make others bow to its power by measures short of war to joining with other nations in a common effort to maintain peace and further prosperity among all men.

The isolationist, who is also, as a rule, a strong nationalist, makes a great fetish of "sovereignty" and the "rights" of nations to control their own affairs and talks as though any right freely granted to a world organization by his nation were in some way a derogation of its basic rights. Man learned long ago that there is no safety for anyone in a community where anarchy prevails; where he does not give up certain privileges of arbitrary action in order to co-operate with his fellows in the maintenance of a stable social order in which all have a better chance not merely to survive but also to enjoy liberty and the pursuit of happiness. The irreconcilable anarchist generally gets short shrift from his fellow-men. It will be so in time as regards nations, but many people are not yet convinced that an international society which demands of each nation the yielding of a measure of the right to do as it pleases is just as essential to peaceful and profitable dealings between them as is the establishment of law and order in civil society.

Without some kind of closely knit international organization to which we and all other nations give allegiance and to which we give strength by our support, there is no hope of settling peaceably the problems of economy, of race, and of differentials in population increase which now confront us in the Pacific Region. It is not desirable or necessary to erect a superstate which can ride roughshod over all the rights of national groups, but it is necessary to give this world organization power with sanctions which will make any recalcitrant state think carefully before it wilfully goes counter to world opinion as developed in the give and take of a democratic world organization.

In the end, the power of this world organization must be and will be limited by world opinion just as in our own country the power of the government is limited by national opinion. But we must be willing to try new modes of international control of national actions and probably of certain types of personal actions and to learn how to accommodate national interests to world interests, or we shall continue to resort to force to secure our aims wherever and whenever we think we can get away with it.

This granting of power to an international organization is frequently opposed by asking the question: "Do you want some international body to tell your boy where he must fight and whom he must fight?" Of course, the answer is supposed to be, "No!" and the implication is that this international body has interests as foreign to our national interests as some other independent nation will have. There are two fundamental errors involved in such a question.

In the first place, we—the United States—would be a part of any international body exercising power, and we would have acquiesced in the establishment and use of this power because we decided it was in the common interest. It is not an alien body in the same way the governing body of Great Britain, or Germany, or France is alien to the people of the United States.

In the second place, and of greater importance, is the false assumption that if we do not have an international body to help us in deciding what to do in international relations, we can determine our own conduct to suit ourselves, that we can tell our boys when and where and whom they must fight or whether they must fight at all.

Can anyone seriously maintain that it was our own choice that our boys have fought all over the Pacific and Europe and Asia? This choice was made for us by Japan and Germany. We had nothing to say about where we would fight unless we were willing to stop with defense of our homeland. We had nothing to say about whom we would fight. We had nothing to say about when we would fight. We had to begin to fight both Japan and Germany on their own terms, at times and in places where they judged they had the advantage. Without an effective world organization, the nation which wishes to be peaceful is entirely at the mercy of the aggressive nation, which can call all the terms and determine all the rules of the game, at least in its early stages, which may well be decisive.[3]

Our choice is not between *complete* national sovereignty and self-determination and subservience to an international organization but between adhering to an international organization to which we freely grant certain powers to deal with international disputes and remaining at the mercy of any nation which is shrewd enough, strong enough, or ruthless enough to get the jump on the rest of us. Who will not prefer the *relatively* mild control of an international body, in whose decisions we actively participate, to the control of our life for several years every decade or two by a Germany or a Japan which decides when, where, and whom we shall fight and how much of our national wealth we will thus waste?

It must be admitted at once that we have no positive assurance that the international organization we are willing to establish now will be able to maintain peace, but we certainly will never get such an organization until we erect one and honestly try to make it work. Moreover, until this organization is given a considerable amount of power, each great nation will continue to rely on its own might and on the alliances it can make to insure its own interests, and this, as always, will provoke counteralliances and a race to build up still greater military strength, with the consequences we have observed these last thirty years.

In addition, we are going to have several new and powerful nations to take into account in the not distant future. India, China, and possi-

[3] This was written before the atomic bomb was used, but it is even more true now.

bly Indonesia and the people of the Indo-Chinese peninsula are growing in numbers and will grow in industrial strength and cannot much longer be treated as cavalierly as in the past. The day of Western European (and American) domination is past.

If this argument is sound, it would appear the height of folly to make commitments to any nation or group of nations which are inconsistent with our interests as a member of a world organization. If we do this, we may find before many decades have passed that we are on the side of the weaker alliance and have accumulated a fund of ill-will on the part of the growing nations which will endanger our future independence or even our existence. The balance of numbers and of power is now shifting, and while we are still strong and growing, albeit slowly, is the time to throw our influence on the side of a strong world organization which will deal justly with all peoples. If we try now to secure special privileges and rights of exploitation for ourselves and our friends by reason of our great present power, our children will live to rue this decision.

SELECTED BIBLIOGRAPHY

1. ABEND, HALLETT E. *Ramparts of the Pacific*. Garden City, N.Y.: Doubleday, Doran & Co., 1942.
2. ADAMS, ROMANZO. *The Peoples of Hawaii*. New York: Institute of Pacific Relations, 1933.
3. ADARKAR, B. D. *War Time Economic Trends and Post War Policy*. New York: International Secretariat, Institute of Pacific Relations, 1942.
4. AKAGI, ROY H. "Japan and the Open Door in Manchukuo," *Annals of the American Academy of Political and Social Science*, CLXVIII (July, 1933), 54–63.
5. ALLEN, G. C. *Japan: The Hungry Guest*. New York: E. P. Dutton & Co., 1938.
6. ———. *Japanese Industry: Its Recent Development and Present Condition*. New York: International Secretariat, Institute of Pacific Relations, 1940.
   ———. *See also* SCHUMPETER (403).
7. *Amerasia: A Review of America and Asia*. New York, March, 1937———. (A semimonthly, with articles on contemporary political and economic problems.)
8. AMERICAN ACADEMY OF POLITICAL AND SOCIAL SCIENCE. *Annals*. (This contains a number of volumes dealing with various social and economic aspects of life in the countries dealt with in this book.)
9. AMERICAN GEOGRAPHICAL SOCIETY OF NEW YORK. "Special Publications." New York, 1915———. (An important source of geographical information for all countries.)
10. AMERICAN IRON AND STEEL INSTITUTE. *American Iron and Steel Reports*. New York: American Iron and Steel Institute, 1930.
11. ANDERSON, KARL L. "Australian Trade in the Great Depression," *Far Eastern Survey*, IV, No. 18 (September 11, 1935), 140–44.
12. ANDREWS, JAMES MADISON. *Siam, Second Rural Economic Survey, 1934–1935*. Bangkok: W. H. Murdie (Bangkok Times Press), 1935.
13. ANDRUS, J. RUSSELL. "Burma," *Foreign Commercial World*, VII, No. 5 (May 9, 1942), 4–5, 29–32.
14. ANSTEY, VERA. *The Economic Development of India*. 3d ed. New York: Longmans, Green & Co., 1936.
15. ASAHI, ISOSHI. *The Economic Strength of Japan*. Tokyo: Hokuseido Press, 1939.
16. *Austral-Asiatic Bulletin* (Australian Institute of International Affairs). Victorian Division, Austral-Asiatic Section. Melbourne, April, 1937———.
17. AUSTRALIA BUREAU OF CENSUS AND STATISTICS. *Official Year Book of the Commonwealth of Australia*. Canberra, 1907———.
18. AUSTRALIA, NEW SOUTH WALES, BUREAU OF STATISTICS. *The Official Year Book of New South Wales*. Sydney, 1906———.
19. ———. *Statistical Register for 1939–1940*. Part VII: *Population and Vital Statistics, 1940*, pp. 401–559. Sydney: Acting Government Printer, 1942.
20. *Australia Official Handbook*. Issued with the authority of the Minister for Commerce by the Australian National Publicity Association. Melbourne, 1941.
21. AUSTRALIAN INSTITUTE OF INTERNATIONAL AFFAIRS. *Australia and the Pacific*. Issued under the auspices of the International Secretariat, Institute of Pacific Relations,

and the Australian Institute of International Affairs. Princeton, N.J.: Princeton University Press, 1944.

22. BAIN, H. FOSTER. *Ores and Industry in the Far East*. New York: Council on Foreign Relations, 1933.

23. BAKER, O. E. "Agriculture and the Future of China." Reprinted from *Foreign Affairs: An American Quarterly Review* (New York), April, 1928.

24. BANERJEA, PRAMATHANATH. *A Study of Indian Economics*. 5th ed. New York: Macmillan Co., 1939.

25. BARNETT, PATRICIA G. "The Chinese in Southeastern Asia and the Philippines," *Annals of the American Academy of Political and Social Science*, CCXXVI (March, 1943), 32–49.

26. ———. "Southeast Asia Increases Iron Exports to Japan," *Far Eastern Survey*, IX, No. 14 (July 3, 1940), 166–68.

27. BARNETT, ROBERT W. "Factors in Chinese Economic Reconstruction." New York: American Council, Institute of Pacific Relations, 1942. (Mimeographed.)

28. BEDEKAR, S. K. "Crop Reporting in India," *Indian Journal of Economics*, XIX, Part I (July, 1938), 87–97.

29. BELDEN, W., and SALTER, M. "The Iron Ore Resources of China," *Economic Geography*, XI (1935), 426–30.

30. BERGSMARK, DANIEL R. *Economic Geography of Asia*. New York: Prentice-Hall, Inc., 1942.

31. BISSON, T. A. *Japan in China*. New York: Macmillan Co., 1938. (A number of recent articles by Mr. T. A. Bisson on Far Eastern affairs will be found in *Foreign Policy Reports*.)

32. BLANCHARD, FESSENDEN S. *The Textile Industries of China and Japan*. New York: Textile Research Institute, 1944.

33. BOEKE, J. H. *The Structure of Netherlands Indian Economy*. New York: International Secretariat, Institute of Pacific Relations, 1942.

34. BORTON, HUGH. *Japan since 1931: Its Political and Social Developments*. New York: International Secretariat, Institute of Pacific Relations, 1940.

35. BOUSQUET, G. H. *A French View of the Netherlands Indies*. London and New York: Oxford University Press, 1940.

36. BOWMAN, ISAIAH. *Limits of Land Settlement*. New York: Council on Foreign Relations, 1937.

37. BOWMAN, ROBERT G. "Prospects of Land Settlement in Western Australia," *Geographical Review*, XXXII, No. 4 (October, 1942), 598–621.

38. BRADLEY, ANITA. *Trans-Pacific Relations of Latin America: An Introductory Essay and Selected Bibliography*. New York: International Secretariat, Institute of Pacific Relations, 1942.

39. BRAILSFORD, HENRY NOEL. *Subject India*. New York: John Day Co., 1944.

40. BRITISH MALAYA, STATISTICAL DEPARTMENT. *Malayan Year Book, 1937*. Singapore: Government Printing Office, 1937.

41. BRITISH MALAYA, SUPERINTENDENT OF CENSUS. *A Report on the 1931 Census and of Certain Problems of Vital Statistics*. London: Crown Agent for the Colonies, 1932.

42. BROEK, JAN O. M. *Economic Development of the Netherlands Indies*. New York: International Secretariat, Institute of Pacific Relations, 1942.

43. Brouwer, H. Albert. *The Geology of the Netherlands East Indies*. New York: Macmillan Co., 1925.

44. Brunner, Edmund deS. *Rural Australia and New Zealand*. New York: American Council, Institute of Pacific Relations, 1938.

45. Buck, John L. *Chinese Farm Economy*. Chicago: University of Chicago Press, 1930.

46. ———. *Land Utilization in China*. Chicago: University of Chicago Press, 1937.

47. Buer, M. C. *Health, Wealth, and Population in the Early Days of the Industrial Revolution*. London: George Routledge & Sons, 1926.

48. Burt, Bryce. "India's Agricultural Progress," *Asiatic Review*, XXXVIII (April, 1942), 134–51.

49. Butler, Harold. *Problems of Industry in the East*. London: P. S. King & Son, 1938.

50. Byas, Hugh. *The Japanese Enemy*. New York: Alfred A. Knopf, 1942.

51. Bywater, Hector C. *Sea-Power in the Pacific: A Study of the American-Japanese Naval Problem*. Boston: Houghton Mifflin Co., 1921.

52. California University Committee on International Relations. *The Renaissance of Asia: Lectures Delivered under the Auspices of the Committee on International Relations on the Los Angeles Campus of the University of California, 1939*. Berkeley and Los Angeles: University of California Press, 1941.

53. ———. *World Resources and Peace*. Berkeley and Los Angeles: University of California Press, 1941.

54. Callis, Helmut G. *Foreign Capital in Southeast Asia*. New York: International Secretariat, Institute of Pacific Relations, 1942.

55. Campbell, Edward T. "The Dutch East Indies," *Proceedings of the Royal Institute of Great Britain*, XXXII, Part I, No. 147 (1942), 122–30.

56. Carbonel, William de. "Mining Industry of the Philippines," *Far Eastern Review*, XXXVI, No. 1 (January, 1940), 32–34.

57. Carr-Saunders, A. M. *World Population*. Oxford: Clarendon Press, 1936.

58. Carus, Clayton D., and McNichols, Charles L. *Japan: Its Resources and Industries*. New York: Harper & Bros., 1944.

59. Chamberlin, William Henry. *Modern Japan*. St. Louis: Institute of Pacific Relations and Webster Publishing Co., 1942.

60. Chand, Gyan. *India's Teeming Millions*. New York: W. W. Norton & Co., 1939.

61. Chandrasekhar, S. "Food and Population in Asia," *Asia and the Americas*, XLIII, No. 6 (June, 1943), 338–42.

62. ———. "Growth and Characteristics of India's Population," *Scientific Monthly*, LVII, No. 3 (September, 1943), 260–72.

63. ———. "Population Pressure in India," *Pacific Affairs*, XVI, No. 2 (June, 1943), 166–84.

64. ———. "Why Are Indians Poor?" *Asia*, XLII, No. 1 (January, 1942), 37–41.

65. Chao, Ch'eng-Hsin. "Familism as a Factor in the Chinese Population Balance." Reprinted from the *Yenching Journal of Social Studies* (Peking), Vol. III, No. 1 (September, 1940).

66. ———. "Recent Population Changes in China." Reprinted from the *Yenching Journal of Social Studies*, Vol. I, No. 1 (June, 1938).

67. CHEN, C. C. "The Rural Public Health Experiment in Ting Hsien, China," *Milbank Memorial Fund Quarterly*, XIV, No. 1 (January, 1936), 66–80.

68. CH'ENG-K'UN, CHENG. "Regionalism in China's Postwar Reconstruction," *Social Forces*, XXII, No. 1 (October, 1943), 1–20.

69. CHETTY, SHAUMUKHAM. "India's Fighting Strength," *Foreign Affairs*, XX, No. 3 (April, 1942), 410–20.

70. CHIAO, CHI-MING. "A Study of the Chinese Population." Reprinted from the *Milbank Memorial Fund Quarterly*, Vol. XI, No. 4 (October, 1933), and Vol. XII, Nos. 1–3 (January, April, and July, 1934).

———. *See also* THOMPSON, WARREN S., and CHIAO, C. M. (445).

71. *The China Economic Annual 1941*. Tokyo: Asia Statistics Co., 1941.

72. *China Handbook, 1937–1943*. Compiled by the Chinese Ministry of Information. New York: Macmillan Co., 1943.

73. *China Year Book*. Peking: Tientsen Press, 1912———.

74. CHINA. *Poverty and Progress in China*. Planning Broadsheet No. 209. London: Political and Economic Planning, July 20, 1943.

75. CHINGYNAN, Y. LI. "Strategy of Mineral Resources in the Sino-Japanese Conflict," *Amerasia*, III, No. 9 (November, 1939), 413–18.

76. CHOW, S. R. *Winning the Peace in the Pacific*. New York: International Secretariat, Institute of Pacific Relations, 1943.

77. CHRISTIAN, JOHN L. "Burma," *Annals of the American Academy of Political and Social Science*, CCXXVI (March, 1943), 120–28.

78. ———. *Modern Burma*. Berkeley and Los Angeles: University of California Press, 1942.

79. CHU HSIAO. "Manchuria: A Statistical Survey," in *Problems of the Pacific, 1929*, pp. 380–422. Chicago: University of Chicago Press, 1930.

80. CLARK, COLIN. *The Economics of 1960*. London: Macmillan & Co., 1942.

81. CLARK, GROVER. *Economic Rivalries in China*. New Haven: Yale University Press, 1933.

82. ———. *A Place in the Sun*. New York: Macmillan Co., 1936.

83. CONDLIFFE, JOHN B. *China Today: Economic*. Boston: World Peace Foundation, 1932.

84. ———. *The Economic Pattern of World Population*. "Planning Pamphlets," No. 15. Washington, D.C.: National Planning Association, 1943.

85. *Contemporary Japan: A Review of Japanese Affairs*. Tokyo: Foreign Affairs Association of Japan, 1932———. (A quarterly written from the Japanese point of view.)

86. COULTER, JOHN W. *Fiji, Little India of the Pacific*. Chicago: University of Chicago Press, 1942.

87. ———. *Land Utilization in the Hawaiian Islands*. Honolulu: Univerity of Hawaii, 1933.

88. COUNCIL ON FOREIGN RELATIONS. *Political Handbook of the World*. New York: Council on Foreign Relations, 1941.

89. COUPLAND, R. *The Indian Problem*. London: Oxford University Press, 1944. (Report on the constitutional problem in India.)

90. CRAWFORD, R. M. *Ourselves and the Pacific*. London: Melbourne University Press in association with Oxford University Press, 1941.

91. CRESSEY, GEORGE B. *Asia's Lands and Peoples.* New York: McGraw-Hill Book Co., 1944.
92. ———. *China's Geographic Foundations: A Survey of the Land and Its People.* New York: McGraw-Hill Book Co., 1934. (Excellent detailed bibliography.)
93. CROCKER, W. R. *The Japanese Population Problem.* London: George Allen & Unwin, 1931.
94. CRUZ, CORNELIO C. *Philippine Demography from the Geographic Point of View.* Manila: Institute of Pacific Relations (University of Philippines Press), 1933.
95. ———. "Population and Land Utilization in the Philippines," in *Problems of the Pacific, 1933,* p. 384. Chicago: University of Chicago Press, 1934.
96. CUTSHALL, ALDEN. "The Philippine Islands and Their People," *Journal of Geography,* XLI, No. 6 (September, 1942), 201–11.
97. DANIEL, HAWTHORNE. *Islands of the Pacific.* New York: G. P. Putnam's Sons, 1943.
98. DAVIDSON, ALFRED C. *The Economics of Peace.* Sydney: Angus & Robertson, 1941.
99. DAVIS, KINGSLEY. "Demographic Fact and Policy in India," *Milbank Memorial Fund Quarterly,* XXII, No. 3 (July, 1944), 256–78.
100. DEAN, VERA MICHELES. "Industry and Agriculture in the U.S.S.R.," *Foreign Policy Reports,* Vol. XIV, No. 6 (June 1, 1938).
101. ———. *Russia at War.* "Headline Books." New York: Foreign Policy Association, 1942.
102. ———. "The U.S.S.R. and Japan," *Foreign Policy Reports,* Vol. XVIII, No. 9 (July 15, 1942).
103. DEHAAS, J. ANTON. *Our Allies: The Nethe. lands East Indies.* New York: Oxford University Press, 1942.
104. DE WILDE, A. NEYTZELL, and MOLL, J. THOMAS. *The Netherlands Indies during the Depression.* Amsterdam: J. M. Menlenhoff, 1936.
105. DEIGNAN, HERBERT G. *Burma, Gateway to China.* "War Background Studies," No. 17. Washington, D.C.: Smithsonian Institution, 1943.
106. ———. *Siam—Land of Free Men.* "War Background Studies," No. 8. Washington, D.C.: Smithsonian Institution, 1943.
107. DENNERY, ÉTIENNE. *Asia's Teeming Millions and Its Problems for the West.* London: Jonathan Cape, 1931.
108. DENNETT, TYLER. *Security in the Pacific and the Far East.* New York: American Council, Institute of Pacific Relations, 1942.
109. DIETRICH, ETHEL B. "Closing Doors against Japan," *Far Eastern Survey,* VII, No. 16 (August 10, 1938), 181–86.
110. ———. *Far Eastern Trade of the United States.* New York: International Secretariat, Institute of Pacific Relations, 1940.
111. DUBEY, R. N. *Economic Geography of India.* Allahabad: Kitab-Mahal, 1939.
112. DUFFETT, W. E. *India Today.* "Contemporary Affairs," No. 10. Toronto: Ryerson Press, 1942.
113. DULLES, FOSTER RHEA. *Behind the Open Door.* New York: American Council, Institute of Pacific Relations, and Webster Publishing Co., 1944.
114. DUNBAR, SIR GEORGE. *India at War.* London: H.M. Stationery Office, 1940.

115. DUNCAN, W. G. K. "White Australia and the Atlantic Charter," *Austral-Asiatic Bulletin*, February, 1943, pp. 43–49.

116. DUTT, R. PALME. *The Problem of India*. New York: International Publishers, 1943.

117. EARLE, FRANCES M. "Geography of the Southeast Tropics," *Annals of the American Academy of Political and Social Science*, CCXXVI (March, 1942), 1–8.

118. EGGLESTON, F. W., *et al*. *The Peopling of Australia*. New York: American Council, Institute of Pacific Relations, 1933.

119. ELLINGER, BARNARD and HUGH. *Japanese Competition in the Cotton Trade*. London: Royal Statistical Society, 1930.

120. ELLINGER, WERNER B., and ROSINSKI, HERBERT. *Sea Power in the Pacific, 1936–1941: A Bibliography*. Princeton, N.J.: Princeton University Press, 1942.

121. EMBREE, JOHN F. *The Japanese*. "War Background Studies," No. 7. Washington, D.C.: Smithsonian Institution, 1943.

122. ———. *The Japanese Nation*. New York: American Council, Institute of Pacific Relations, 1945.

123. EMENY, BROOKS. *The Strategy of Raw Materials*. New York: Macmillan Co., 1936.

124. EMERSON, RUPERT. *The Netherlands Indies and the United States*. Boston: World Peace Foundation, 1942.

125. ———. "The Outlook in Southeast Asia," *Foreign Policy Reports*, Vol. XV, No. 17 (November 15, 1939).

126. EMERSON, RUPERT; MILLS, LENNOX A.; and THOMPSON, VIRGINIA. *Government and Nationalism in Southeast Asia*. New York: International Secretariat, Institute of Pacific Relations, 1942.

127. FAHS, C. B. *Government in Japan: Recent Trends in Its Scope and Operation*. New York: International Secretariat, Institute of Pacific Relations, 1940.

128. *Far Eastern Quarterly: A Review of Eastern Asia and the Adjacent Pacific Islands*. Menasha, Wis.: Far Eastern Association, 1941———.

129. *Far Eastern Review*. New York, 1939———. (Reviews of articles on the Far East appearing in current periodicals.)

130. *Far Eastern Survey: A Fortnightly Research Service*. New York: American Council, Institute of Pacific Relations, 1932———. (Excellent short studies on contemporary developments, primarily economic.)

131. FARLEY, MIRIAM S. *The Problem of Japanese Trade Expansion in the Post-war Situation*. New York: International Secretariat, Institute of Pacific Relations, 1940.

132. ———. *Speaking of India*. New York: American Council, Institute of Pacific Relations, 1943.

133. FIELD, FREDERICK V. (ed.). *Economic Handbook of the Pacific Area*. New York: Doubleday, Doran & Co., 1934.

134. ———. *An Economic Survey of the Pacific Area*. Part I: "Population and Land Utilization," by KARL J. PELZER; Part II: "Transportation," by KATRINE R. C. GREENE, and "Foreign Trade," by JOSEPH D. PHILLIPS. New York: International Secretariat, Institute of Pacific Relations, 1941.

135. FONG, H. D. *The Post-war Industrialization of China*. Chungking, China: Nankai Institute of Economics, Nankai University, 1942.

136. FONG, H. D. "The Prospect of China's Industrialization," *Pacific Affairs*, XV, No. 1 (March, 1942), 44–60.

137. *Foreign Affairs: An American Quarterly Review*. New York: Council on Foreign Relations, 1922——.

138. FOREIGN AFFAIRS ASSOCIATION OF JAPAN. *How the North China Affair Arose*. Tokyo: Kenkyusha, 1932——.

139. *Foreign Commerce Weekly*. Washington, D.C.: United States Department of Commerce. (Contains information on foreign trade.)

140. *Foreign Policy Reports*. New York: Foreign Policy Association. (A semimonthly containing many good articles on Far Eastern affairs.)

141. FORSYTH, WILLIAM D. *The Myth of Open Spaces*. Melbourne and London: Melbourne University Press in association with Oxford University Press, 1942.

142. ——. "Population Growth: Some Comparisons," *Economic Record*, XVII, No. 33 (December, 1941), 248–52.

143. ——. "Stability in the Pacific," *Pacific Affairs*, XVI, No. 1 (March, 1943), 7–18.

144. FRANCE, BUREAU DE LA STATISTIQUE GÉNÉRALE: *Annuaire statistique 1938*. Paris: Imprimerie Nationale, 1939. (A good statistical annual with an international section.)

145. ——. *Statistique international du mouvement de la population d'après les Registres d' Etat Civil ... .* 2 vols. Paris: Imprimerie Nationale, 1907–13.

146. FRANCE, GOUVERNEMENT GÉNÉRAL DE L'INDOCHINE. *L'Indochine française*. Paris: Exposition Coloniale Internationale, 1931.

147. FRANCIS, E. V. *Britain's Economic Strategy*. London: Jonathan Cape, 1939.

148. FRECHTLING, LOUIS E. "Oil and the War," *Foreign Policy Reports*, Vol. XVII, No. 6 (June 1, 1941).

149. ——. "Replacement of Strategic Materials Lost in Asia," *ibid.*, Vol. XVIII, No. 7 (June 15, 1942).

150. FREE THAI COMMITTEE. *Recent Developments in Thailand*. Washington, D.C., 1942.

151. FREYN, HUBERT. *Free China's New Deal*. New York: Macmillan Co., 1943.

152. FRIEDMAN, IRVING S. *British Relations with China: 1931–39*. New York: American Council, Institute of Pacific Relations, 1940.

153. FURNIVALL, J. S. *Educational Progress in Southeast Asia*. "Inquiry Series." New York: Institute of Pacific Relations, 1943.

154. ——. *Progress and Welfare in Southeast Asia*. New York: International Secretariat, Institute of Pacific Relations, 1941.

155. GEDDES, ARTHUR. "Half a Century of Population Trends in India," *Geographical Journal*, XCVIII, Nos. 5–6 (November–December, 1941), 228–52.

156. ——. "The Population of India," *Geographical Review*, XXXII, No. 4 (October, 1942), 562–73.

157. GERMANY, STATISTISCHES REICHSAMT. *Statistisches Jahrbuch für das Deutsche Reich*." Berlin: Reimar Hobbing, 1880——.

158. GHATE, B. G. "A Study of Population Movement in India," *Indian Journal of Economics*, Vol. XX (January, 1939).

159. GHURYE, G. S. (ed.). *Indian Population Problems*. Bombay: Karnatak, 1940.

160. GLOVER, PATRICIA. "Malayan Tin Products Clash with Agricultural Interests," *Far Eastern Survey*, VIII, No. 14 (July 5, 1939), 169–70.

161. GOODRICH, L. CARRINGTON. *A Short History of the Chinese People.* New York: Harper & Bros., 1943.

162. GOSHAL, KUMAR. *The People of India.* New York: Sheridan House, 1944.

163. GRAJDANZEV, ANDREW J. *Formosa Today.* New York: International Secretariat, Institute of Pacific Relations, 1942.

164. ———. "Formosa (Taiwan) under Japanese Rule," *Pacific Affairs*, XV, No. 3 (September, 1942), 311–24.

165. ———. "India's Wartime Economic Difficulties," *ibid.*, XVI (June, 1943), 189–205.

166. ———. "Japan's Ideological Front," *ibid.*, XII, No. 9 (May 3, 1943), 89–92.

167. ———. "Memorandum on Korea's Agriculture and Resources." New York: International Secretariat, Institute of Pacific Relations, November, 1942. (Mimeographed.) (Incorporated in a book entitled *Modern Korea.* See Item 168.)

168. ———. *Modern Korea.* New York: International Secretariat, Institute of Pacific Relations, 1943.

169. ———. "Statistics of Japanese Agriculture." New York: International Secretariat, Institute of Pacific Relations, November, 1941. (Mimeographed.)

170. GRATTAN, C. HARTLEY. *Introducing Australia.* New York: John Day Co., 1942.

171. ———. *Lands Down Under.* St. Louis: Institute of Pacific Relations and Webster Publishing Co., 1943.

172. GREAT BRITAIN, BOARD OF TRADE. *Statistical Abstract for the British Empire, 1928 to 1937.* 67th No. London: H.M. Stationery Office, 1938.

173. ———. *Statistical Abstract for the Several British Oversea Dominions and Protectorates.* London: H.M. Stationery Office, 1865–19——.

174. ———. *Statistical Abstract for the United Kingdom, 1912–1926.* 71st No. London: H.M. Stationery Office, 1928.

175. GREEN, JAMES FREDERICK. "Australia in the World Conflict," *Foreign Policy Reports*, Vol. XVI, No. 24 (March 1, 1941).

176. ———. *The British Empire.* "Headline Books." New York: Foreign Policy Association, 1940.

177. GREENE, MARC T. "Lifeblood of the Netherlands," *Asia*, XXXIX, No. 12 (December, 1939), 705–8.

178. GULL, E. M. "The Future of British Economic Interests in the Far East." London: Royal Institute of International Affairs, 1942. (Mimeographed.)

179. HAILEY, LORD. "A Colonial Charter," *Fortnightly*, No. 907 (new ser., July, 1942), pp. 1–7.

180. ———. "India in the Modern World," *Foreign Affairs*, XXI (April, 1943), 401–11.

181. ———. "Problems of the Post-war Settlement in the Far East: Great Britain and Her Dependencies: Note on General Policy." London: Royal Institute of International Affairs, 1942. (Mimeographed.)

182. HARRIS, H. L. "The Economic Resources of Australia." Sydney: Angus & Robertson, 1934.

183. HART, G. H. C. "Recent Development in the Netherlands Indies," *Geography Journal*, XCIX, No. 2 (February, 1942), 81–102.

184. ———. *Towards Economic Democracy in the Netherlands Indies*. New York: Netherlands and Netherlands Indies Council, Institute of Pacific Relations, 1942.

185. HAWAII. UNITED STATES DEPARTMENT OF COMMERCE, BUREAU OF THE CENSUS. *Hawaii—Agriculture, 1940*. Washington, D.C.: Government Printing Office, 1942.

186. HAYDEN, JOSEPH R. *The Philippines: A Study in National Development*. New York: Macmillan Co., 1942.

187. HECKER, J. F. C. *Epidemics of the Middle Ages*. 3d ed. London: Trübner & Co., 1859.

188. HERRE, ALBERT W. C. T. "Japanese Fisheries and Fish Supplies," *Far Eastern Survey*, XII, No. 10 (May 17, 1943), 99–101.

189. HIGGINBOTTOM, SAM. *India's Agricultural Problems*. New York: International Secretariat, Institute of Pacific Relations, 1942.

190. HINDER, ELEANOR M. *Life and Labour in Shanghai*. New York: International Secretariat, Institute of Pacific Relations, 1944.

191. HOAR, H. M. *The Coal Industry of the World*. "United States Department of Commerce Trade Promotion Series," No. 105. Washington, D.C.: Government Printing Office, 1930.

192. HOFFMANN, WALTER GAILEY: *Pacific Relations: The Races and Nations of the Pacific Area and Their Problems*. New York: McGraw-Hill Book Co., 1936.

193. HOLCOMBE, ARTHUR N. *Dependent Areas in the Post-war World*. Boston: World Peace Foundation, 1941.

194. HOLTOM, DANIEL C. *Modern Japan and Shinto Nationalism*. Chicago: University of Chicago Press, 1943.

195. HONJO, E. *The Social and Economic History of Japan*. Kyoto: Institute for Research in Economic History of Japan, 1935.

196. HOWARD, HARRY PAXTON. *America's Role in Asia*. New York: Howell & Soskin, 1943.

197. HSU, Y. Y. "Chinese Views of Wartime Economic Difficulties." New York: International Secretariat, Institute of Pacific Relations, 1942. (Mimeographed.)

198. HU, T. Y. *Japan's Economy under War Strain*. Washington, D.C.: Chinese Council for Economic Research, 1941.

199. HUBBARD, G. E. *British Far Eastern Policy*. New York: Institute of Pacific Relations, 1943.

200. HUBBARD, G. E., and BARING, DENZIL. *Eastern Industrialization and Its Effect on the West*. London: Oxford University Press, 1935.

201. HUDSON, G. F., and RAJCHMAN, MARTHE. *An Atlas of Far Eastern Politics*. New York: John Day Co., 1942.

202. HUTTON, J. H. *Census of India, 1931*. Delhi: Manager of Publications, 1933.

203. ICHIHASHI, YAMATO. *Japanese in the United States*. Stanford, Calif.: Stanford University Press, 1932.

204. INDIA. *India in the Years 1917–18———: A Statement Prepared for Presentation to Parliament*. Delhi: Manager of Publications, 1919———.

205. ———. "India To Produce Aluminum," *Indian Information*, VII, No. 60 (September 15, 1940), 214.

206. ———. "Industrial Employment in India," *International Labour Review*, XLIX, No. 2 (February, 1944), 234–35.

207. ———. CENSUS COMMISSIONER. *India (Census of India, 1921)*. 2 vols. Calcutta: Superintendent of Government Printing, 1924.

208. ———. *Census of 1931*. 2 vols. Delhi: Manager of Publications, 1933.

209. ———. *Report of the Royal Commission on Agriculture in India*. London: H.M. Stationery Office, 1928.

210. ———. *Statistical Abstract for British India, 1929–30 to 1938–39*. 71st No. London: H.M. Stationery Office, 1942.

211. *Indian Information*. New Delhi, 1937———. (An Indian information journal published twice a month.)

212. *The Indian Year Book: A Statistical and Historical Annual of the Indian Empire with an Explanation of the Principal Topics of the Day*. Bombay and Calcutta: Bennett, Coleman & Co., 1914———.

213. INDO-CHINA. *Economic Resources of French Indo-China*, XXXVI, No. 11 (November, 1940), 400–401.

214. ———. "Indo-China Treaty with Japan Likely," *China Weekly Review*, LIX, No. 11 (February 13, 1932), 342.

215. INOUYE, MASAJI. *Population of Japan*. Tokyo: Bureau of Social Affairs, 1937.

216. L'INSTITUTE INTERNATIONAL DE STATISTIQUE. *Annuaire international de statistique*. La Haye: W. P. Van Stockum & Fils, 1916.

217. ———. *Aperçu de la démographie des divers pays du monde, 1929–1936*. La Haye: Office Permanent de l'Institute International de Statistique, 1939.

218. INSTITUTE OF PACIFIC RELATIONS. (Publishes a large amount of material on Pacific lands. Citations here are only to a few specific points.) "Australia and Japan Seek Trade Treaty," *Far Eastern Survey*, IV, No. 11 (June 5, 1935), 86–87.

219. ———. *Eighth Conference of the Institute of Pacific Relations, Mount Tremblant, Quebec, Canada, December, 1942*.

220. ———. "Indian Labour at War," *Far Eastern Survey*, XIII, No. 2 (January 25, 1943), 19–24.

221. ———. *Industrial Japan*. New York: International Secretariat, Institute of Pacific Relations, 1941.

222. ———. *Korea for the Koreans*. New York: American Council, Institute of Pacific Relations, 1943.

223. ———. *The Peopling of Australia*. Melbourne: Melbourne University Press in association with Oxford University Press, 1933.

224. ———. *Problems of the Pacific, 1927*———. Chicago: University of Chicago Press, 1927———.

225. INSTITUTE OF PACIFIC RELATIONS, NEW SOUTH WALES BRANCH. *Studies in Australian Affairs*. Melbourne: Macmillan & Co. in association with the Melbourne University Press, 1928.

226. INTERNATIONAL CONGRESS FOR STUDIES ON POPULATION. *Proceedings of the International Congress for Studies on Population, Rome, 7th–10th September 1931*. 10 vols. Edited by Dr. CORRADO GINI. Rome: Istituto Poligrafico dello Stato Libreria, 1933–34.

227. INTERNATIONAL LABOUR OFFICE. "India and the Pacific Region." Montreal, Can.: International Labour Office, n.d. (Mimeographed.)

228. INTERNATIONAL LABOUR OFFICE. "News in Brief," *International Labour Review*, XLIV, No. 3 (September, 1941), 350.

229. ———. "Social and Economic Reconstruction in the Pacific Colonies." Montreal, Can.: International Labour Office, 1942. (Mimeographed.)

230. *International Labour Review*. Geneva: International Labour Office, 1921———. (Monthly magazine containing many interesting articles on Pacific countries.)

231. *International Year Book of Agricultural Statistics*. Rome, 1912———.

232. ISHII, RYOICHI. *Population Pressure and Economic Life in Japan*. London: P. S. King & Son, 1937.

233. JAPAN, BANK OF. *Economic Statistics of Japan*. Tokyo: Bank of Japan, 1923———.

234. JAPAN, BUREAU DE LA STATISTIQUE. *Résumé statistique de l'Empire du Japon*. Tokyo, 1880———.

235. ———. *Résumé statistique du mouvement de la population de l'Empire du Japon*. Tokyo, 19———?

236. JAPAN, DEPARTMENT OF FINANCE. *Financial and Economic Annual of Japan*. Tokyo: Government Printing Office, 1901———.

237. JAPAN, IMPERIAL GEOLOGICAL SURVEY OF JAPAN. *The Geology and Mineral Resources of the Japanese Empire*. Tokyo, 1926.

238. JAPAN. *Japan in the Beginning of the Twentieth Century*. Tokyo: Imperial Japanese Commission to the Louisiana Purchase Exposition, 1904.

239. "Japan in Manchuria," *Foreign Commercial World*, XIV, No. 7 (February 12, 1944), 7.

240. *Japan-Manchoukuo Year Book*. Tokyo: Japan-Manchoukuo Year Book Co., 1933———.

241. *The Japan Times Year Book*. Tokyo, 1933.

242. *The Japan Year Book*. Tokyo, 1906———.

243. JOHNSON, STANLEY C. *A History of Emigration*. London: George Routledge & Sons, 1913.

244. JOHNSTONE, WILLIAM C. *America Faces Japan*. New York and Toronto: Oxford University Press, 1941.

245. ———. "Australia and New Zealand Agree." *Far Eastern Survey*, XIII, No. 4 (February 23, 1944), 31–35.

246. JONES, CLARENCE F. *Economic Geography*, New York: Macmillan Co., 1941.

247. JONES, WILLIAM R. *Tinfields of the World*. London: Mining Publications, Ltd., 1925.

248. JONG, ELLEN VAN ZYLL DE. *The Netherlands East Indies and Japan*. New York: Netherlands Information Bureau, 1942.

249. KAWAI, TATSUO. *The Goal of Japanese Expansion*. Tokyo: Hokuseido Press, 1938.

250. KEESING, FELIX M. *The Philippines: A Nation in the Making*. Shanghai: Kelly & Walsh, 1937.

251. ———. *The South Seas in the Modern World*. New York: John Day Co., 1941.

252. KEETON, GEORGE W. *Some Factors in a Far Eastern Peace Settlement*. New York: International Secretariat, Institute of Pacific Relations, 1942.

253. KENNEDY, RAYMOND. *The Ageless Indies*. New York: John Day Co., 1942.

254. ———. *Islands and Peoples of the Indies*. "War Background Studies," No. 14. Washington, D.C.: Smithsonian Institution, 1943.

255. KILLOUGH, HUGH B. and LUCK W. *Raw Materials of Industrialism.* New York: Thomas Y. Crowell Co., 1929.

256. KIMBLE, G. H. *The World's Open Spaces.* London and New York: Thomas Nelson & Sons, 1939.

257. KING, FRANKLIN H. *Farmers of Forty Centuries.* London: Jonathan Cape, 1927.

258. KIRK, WILLIAM. "Social Changes in Formosa. II," *Sociology and Social Research,* XXVI, No. 1 (September–October, 1941), 10–26.

259. KISER, CLYDE V. *Group Differences in Urban Fertility.* Baltimore: Williams & Wilkins Co., 1942.

260. KIZER, BENJAMIN H. "Industrialization *versus* Feudalism," *Far Eastern Survey,* XII, No. 3 (February 8, 1943), 31–32.

261. KOBAYASHI, USHISABURO. *The Basic Industries and Social History of Japan 1914–1918.* New Haven: Yale University Press, 1930.

262. KRANOLD, HERMAN. *The International Distribution of Raw Materials.* London: George Routledge & Sons, 1939.

263. KRIEGER, HERBERT W. *Peoples of the Philippines.* "War Background Studies," No. 4. Washington, D.C.: Smithsonian Institution, 1942.

264. KUNO, YOSHI S. *Japanese Expansion on the Asiatic Continent.* Vols. I–II. Berkeley, Calif.: University of California Press, 1937–40.

265. KUYKENDALL, RALPH S. *A History of Hawaii.* New York: Macmillan Co., 1926.

266. *Kyoto University Economic Review: Memoirs of the Department of Economics in the Imperial University of Kyoto.* Kyoto: Kyoto Imperial University, 1926——. (The best journal in English on Japanese economic history.)

267. LADEJINSKY, W. I. "Australia's Agricultural Resources," *Foreign Agriculture,* VII, No. 1 (January, 1943), 3–21.

268. LA FOY, MARGARET. "India's Role in the World Conflict," *Foreign Policy Reports,* Vol. XVIII, No. 4 (May 1, 1942).

269. LAMOTT, WILLIS. *Nippon: The Crime and Punishment of Japan.* New York: John Day Co., 1944.

270. LANDHEER, BARTHOLOMEUS (ed.). *The Netherlands.* Berkeley, Calif.: University of California Press, 1943. Chap. 22: "The Dutch in the Far East," by AMRY J. VANDENBOSCH.

271. LANDON, KENNETH PERRY. *The Chinese in Thailand.* London and New York: Oxford University Press, 1941.

272. ——. "The Problem of the Chinese in Thailand," *Pacific Affairs,* XIII, No. 2 (June, 1940), 149–61.

273. ——. *Siam in Transition.* Chicago: University of Chicago Press, 1939.

274. LASKER, BRUNO. "Asia on the Move." New York: Institute of Pacific Relations, 1943. (Mimeographed.)

275. ——. *Peoples of Southeast Asia.* New York: Alfred A. Knopf, 1944.

276. ——. *Populations Adrift.* "Education and National Defense Series," No. 11. Washington, D.C.: Government Printing Office, 1941.

277. ——. "Post-war Migration Problems: The Far East," *Social Forces,* XXII, No. 2 (December, 1943), 130–36.

278. ——. "Welfare and Freedom in Postwar Southeast Asia." New York: American Council, Institute of Pacific Relations, 1942. (Mimeographed.)

279. LASKER, BRUNO, and HOLLAND, W. L. *Problems of the Pacific, 1933*. Chicago: University of Chicago Press, 1934.

280. LATOURETTE, K. S. *The Development of Japan*. New York: Macmillan Co., 1918.

281. LATTIMORE, OWEN. "Asia in a World Order," *Foreign Policy Reports*, Vol. XVIII, No. 12 (September 1, 1942).

282. ———. *Inner Asian Frontiers of China*. London and New York: Oxford University Press, 1940.

283. ———. *Manchuria: Cradle of Conflict*. New York: Macmillan Co., 1932.

284. LATTIMORE, OWEN and ELEANOR. *The Making of Modern China*. New York: W. W. Norton & Co., 1944.

285. LAWRENCE, CHESTER H. (ed.). *New World Horizons*. New York: Duell, Sloan & Pearce, 1942.

286. LEAGUE OF NATIONS. *International Statistical Year-Book*. Geneva, 1927——.

287. ———. *Monthly Bulletin of Statistics*. Geneva, 1920——.

288. ———. *The Transition from War to Peace Economy*. Geneva, 1943.

289. LEE, HOON K. *Land Utilization and Rural Economy in Korea*. Shanghai: Kelly & Walsh, 1936.

290. LEITH, C. K., *et al. World Minerals and World Peace*. Washington, D.C.: Brookings Institution, 1943.

291. LEVY, ROGER; LACAM, GUY; and ROTH, ANDREW. *French Interests and Policies in the Far East*. New York: International Secretariat, Institute of Pacific Relations, 1941.

292. LIBRARY OF CONGRESS, DIVISION OF BIBLIOGRAPHY. *The Japanese Empire: Industries and Transportation*. Washington, D.C., 1943.

293. LILIENTHAL, PHILIP E., and OAKIE, JOHN H. *Asia's Captive Colonies*. New York: American Council, Institute of Pacific Relations, 1944.

294. LIND, ANDREW WILLIAM. *An Island Community: Ecological Succession in Hawaii*. Chicago: University of Chicago Press, 1938.

295. LIPPINCOTT, ISAAC. *The Development of Modern World Trade*. New York: Appleton-Century Co., 1936.

296. ———. *Economic Resources and Industries of the World*. New York: D. Appleton & Co., 1929.

297. LOCKE, ALAIN L. *World View on Race and Democracy*. Chicago: American Library Association, 1943.

298. LORWIN, LEWIS L. *Postwar Plans of the United Nations*. New York: Twentieth Century Fund, 1943. Chap. 9, "Australia"; chap. 10, "New Zealand."

299. LOVERING, T. S. *Minerals in World Affairs*. New York: Prentice-Hall, Inc., 1943.

300. LOWDERMILK, W. C. "Forestry in Denuded China," *Annals of the American Academy of Political and Social Science*, Vol. CLII (November, 1930).

301. LOWER, A. R. M. *Canada and the Far East*. New York: International Secretariat, Institute of Pacific Relations, 1940.

302. MCCLEARY, G. F. "Australia's Population Problem," *Milbank Memorial Fund Quarterly*, XX, No. 1 (January, 1942), 23–34.

303. MCCUNE, SHANNON. "Recent Growth of Japanese Cities," *Geographical Review*, XXXII, No. 1 (January, 1942), 164–65.

304. MACFADDEN, CLIFFORD H. *A Selected Bibliography of Pacific Area Maps*. New York: Institute of Pacific Relations, 1940.

305. McGuire, Paul. *Australia: Her Heritage, Her Future.* New York: Frederick A. Stokes Co., 1939.

306. ———. *Westward the Course!* New York: William Morrow & Co., 1943.

307. McWilliams, Carey. *Brothers under the Skin.* Boston: Little, Brown & Co., 1943.

308. Maisel, Albert Q. *Africa, Facts and Forecasts.* New York: Duell, Sloan & Pearce, 1943.

309. Mallory, Walter H. *China: Land of Famine.* New York: American Geographical Society, 1926.

310. Mandel, William. "The Soviet Far East." New York: International Secretariat, Institute of Pacific Relations, 1942. (Mimeographed.)

311. Marres, Paul. "The Problem of Overpopulation in French Indo-China and the Far East according to Pierre Gouron and Charles Robequain," *Annales de géographie,* LI, No. 285 (January–March, 1942), 52–57.

312. Masani, Minocheher R. *Our India.* New York: Oxford University Press, 1942.

313. Meikel, G. H. *Report on the Age Distribution and Rates of Mortality Deduced from the Indian Census Returns of 1921 and Previous Enumerations.* Calcutta: Government of India Central Publishing Branch, 1926.

314. Merrill, Fred T. "The Outlook for Philippine Independence," *Foreign Policy Reports,* Vol. XV, No. 13 (September 15, 1939).

315. Mikami, Harry M. "World Iron-Ore Map," *Economic Geology,* XXXIX, No. 1 (January–February, 1944), 1–24.

316. Mills, Lennox A. *British Rule in Eastern Asia.* Minneapolis, Minn.: University of Minnesota Press, 1942.

317. ———. "The Future of Western Dependencies in Southeastern Asia and the Pacific," *American Political Science Review,* XXXVII, No. 5 (October, 1943), 909–19.

318. Mills, Lennox A. (ed.). "Southeastern Asia and the Philippines," *Annals of the American Academy of Political and Social Science,* Vol. CCXXVI (March, 1943).

319. Milner, Ian F. G. *New Zealand's Interests and Policies in the Far East.* New York: Institute of Pacific Relations, 1939.

320. Misshima, Yasuo, and Goto, Tomio. *A Japanese View of Outer Mongolia.* Translated by Andrew J. Grajdanzev. New York: International Secretariat, Institute of Pacific Relations, 1942.

321. Mitchell, Kate L. *India without Fable.* New York: Alfred A. Knopf, 1942.

322. ———. "India's Economic Potential," *Pacific Affairs,* XV, No. 1 (March, 1942), 5–24.

323. ———. *Industrialization of the Western Pacific.* New York: International Secretariat, Institute of Pacific Relations, 1942.

324. ———. *Japan's Industrial Strength.* New York: Alfred A. Knopf, 1942.

325. ———. "United States Technical Mission to India," *Far Eastern Survey,* XI, No. 6 (March 23, 1942), pp. 71–72.

326. Mitchell, Kate L., and Holland, W. L. (eds.). *Problems of the Pacific, 1939.* New York: Institute of Pacific Relations, 1940.

327. Moore, Harriet L. *A Record of Soviet Far Eastern Relations, 1931–42.* New York: International Secretariat, Institute of Pacific Relations, 1943.

328. Moulton, Harold G. *Japan: An Economic and Financial Appraisal.* Washington, D.C.: Brookings Institution, 1931.

329. MOWRER, EDGAR ANSEL, and RAJCHMAN, MARTHE. *Global War.* New York: William Morrow & Co., 1942. (Seventy maps and charts.)

330. MUKHERJEE, B. "Conservation of Coal Resources in India: Its Economic Aspects," *Indian Journal of Economics*, XIX (October, 1938), 307–20.

331. MUKERJEE, RADHAKAMAL (ed.). *Economic Problems of Modern India.* 2 vols. London: Macmillan & Co., 1939.

332. ———. *Food Planning for Four Hundred Millions.* London: Macmillan & Co., 1938.

333. NARAIN, BRIJ. *Indian Economic Life, Past and Present.* Lahore: Uttar Chand Kapur & Sons, 1929.

334. ———. *The Population of India.* Anarkali, Lahore: Rama Krishna & Sons, 1925.

335. NASU, SHIROSHI. "Aspects of Japanese Agriculture." New York: International Secretariat, Institute of Pacific Relations, 1941. (Mimeographed.)

336. ———. *Land Utilization in Japan.* Tokyo: Research Department of Japanese Council, Institute of Pacific Relations, 1929.

337. NATIONAL RESOURCES PLANNING BOARD. *Estimates of Future Population of the United States, 1940–2000.* Washington, Government Printing Office, 1943.

338. NETHERLANDS, DIVISION OF COMMERCE. *1930 Handbook of the Netherlands East-Indies.* Batavia, Java: G. Kolff & Co., 1930.

339. NETHERLANDS EAST INDIES. *Indisch Verslag.* Batavia: Landsdrukkerij, 1916———.

340. ———. "Japan's Trade with the Netherlands Indies," *Foreign Affairs*, XV (January, 1937), 381–83.

341. NEW ZEALAND, CENSUS AND STATISTICS OFFICE. *New Zealand Official Yearbook.* Wellington: Government Printer, 1892———.

342. NOMA, KAIZO. "Japanese Capacity for Colonizing the Tropics," *Contemporary Japan*, X, No. 3 (March, 1941), 400–405.

343. NORMAN, E. HERBERT. *Japan's Emergence as a Modern State.* New York: International Secretariat, Institute of Pacific Relations, 1940.

344. NORMANDO, J. F. *Asia between Two World Wars.* New York: Iranian Institution and School of Asiatic Studies, 1944.

345. NORMANDO, J. F., and GERBI, ANTONELLO. *The Japanese in South America.* New York: International Secretariat, Institute of Pacific Relations, 1943.

346. NOTESTEIN, FRANK, *et al. The Future Population of Europe and the Soviet Union.* Geneva: League of Nations, 1944.

347. NUGENT, DONALD R., and BELL, REGINALD (eds.). *The Pacific Area and Its Problems.* New York: American Council, Institute of Pacific Relations, 1936.

348. OAKIE, JOHN H. *America's Economic Interest in the Far East.* New York: American Council, Institute of Pacific Relations, 1944.

349. O'MALLEY, L. S. (ed.). *Modern India and the West.* London: Oxford University Press, 1941.

350. ORCHARD, JOHN E. and D. J. *Japan's Economic Position.* New York: McGraw-Hill Book Co., 1930.

351. *Oriental Economist: A Monthly Journal of Practical Finance and Economics for Japan and Eastern Asia.* Tokyo: Oriental Economist, Ltd., 1934———. (An independent journal containing many valuable tables and articles.)

352. OSBORN, FREDERICK. *Preface to Eugenics.* New York: Harper & Bros., 1940.

353. *Pacific Affairs: Journal of the International Secretariat.* New York: Institute of Pacific Relations, 1929———. (A quarterly containing valuable book reviews and many comprehensive and objective articles on modern politics and economics.)

354. *Pacific Islands Yearbook.* Sydney, Australia: Pacific Publications Pty., 1932———.

355. PANIKAR, K. M. *The Future of South-east Asia.* New York: Macmillan Co., 1943.

356. PEFFER, NATHANIEL. *Basis for Peace in the Far East.* New York: Harper & Bros., 1942.

357. ———. *Prerequisites to Peace in the Far East.* New York: International Secretariat, Institute of Pacific Relations, 1940.

358. PENDLETON, ROBERT L. "Land Utilization and Agriculture of Mindanao, Philippine Islands," *Geographical Review*, XXXII, No. 2 (April, 1942), 180–210.

359. PENROSE, E. F. *Food Supply and Raw Materials in Japan.* Chicago: University of Chicago Press, 1929.

360. ———. "Japan's Basic Economic Situation," *Annals of the American Academy of Political and Social Science*, CCXV (May, 1941), 1–6.

361. ———. *Population Theories and Their Application.* Stanford, Calif.: Food Research Institute, 1934.

———. *See also* SCHUMPETER (403).

362. PHILIPPINE ISLANDS, BUREAU OF COMMERCE AND INDUSTRY. *Statistical Bulletin.* Manila: Bureau of Printing, 1918———.

363. ———. *Census of the Philippine Islands, 1918.* Manila: Bureau of Printing, 1920–21.

364. ———. *Census of the Philippines, 1939.* 5 vols. Manila: Bureau of Printing, 1940–43.

365. PHILIPPINE ISLANDS, DEPARTMENT OF AGRICULTURE AND COMMERCE. *Statistical Handbook of the Philippine Islands.* Manila: Bureau of Printing, 1933———.

366. PHILIPPS, J. D. *An Economic Survey of the Pacific Area.* New York: International Secretariat, Institute of Pacific Relations, 1941.

367. PHILLIPS, P. D., and WOOD, G. L. (eds.). *The Peopling of Australia.* Melbourne: Macmillan & Co. in association with Melbourne University Press, 1928.

368. POPPER, DAVID H. "Progress of the Sino-Japanese Conflict," *Foreign Policy Reports*, Vol. XIV, No. 5 (May 15, 1938).

369. *Population Index.* Princeton: Princeton University, School of Public and International Affairs, and the Population Association of America. 1935———. (A quarterly containing much current population information and many articles dealing with the population of different areas.)

370. PORTER, CATHERINE L. *Crisis in the Philippines.* New York: Alfred A. Knopf, 1942.

371. ———. *Filipinos and Their Country.* New York: American Council, Institute of Pacific Relations, 1944.

372. ———. *Philippine Emergency.* "Far Eastern Pamphlets," No. 3. New York: American Council, Institute of Pacific Relations, 1941.

373. PRENTICE, EZRA PARMALEE. *Hunger and History.* New York: Harper & Bros., 1939.

374. PRICE, A. GRENFELL. *White Settlers in the Tropics.* New York: American Geographical Society, 1939.

375. QUIGLEY, HAROLD S. *Far Eastern War, 1937–1941*. Boston: World Peace Foundation, 1942.

376. RAGER, FRITZ A. "Japanese Emigration and Japan's Population Pressure," *Pacific Affairs*, XIV, No. 3 (September, 1941), 300–321.

377. RAMAN, T. A. *Report on India*. New York: Oxford University Press, 1943.

378. RANADIVE, B. T. *Population Problem of India*. London: Longmans, Green & Co., 1930.

379. READ, THOMAS T. "Economic-Geographic Aspects of China's Iron Industry," *Geographical Review*, XXXIII, No. 1 (January, 1943), 42–55.

380. REID, CHARLES F. *Overseas America*. "Headline Books." New York: Foreign Policy Association, 1942.

381. ROBEQUAIN, CHARLES. *The Recent Economic Evolution of French Indo-China*. New York: International Secretariat, Institute of Pacific Relations, 1943.

382. ROBERTS, STEPHEN H. *History of Australian Land Settlement (1788–1920)*. Melbourne: Macmillan & Co. in association with Melbourne University Press, 1924.

383. ——. *Population Problems of the Pacific*. London: George Routledge & Sons, 1927.

384. ROCKHILL, WILLIAM WOODVILLE. *Diary of a Journey through Mongolia and Tibet in 1891 and 1892*. Washington, D.C.: Smithsonian Institution, 1894.

385. ROSINGER, LAWRENCE K. "China's War Economy," *Foreign Policy Reports*, Vol. XVIII, No. 17 (November 15, 1942).

386. ——. *China's Wartime Politics, 1937–44*. New York: International Secretariat, Institute of Pacific Relations, 1944.

387. ——. "Japan as an Economic Power," *Foreign Policy Reports*, Vol. XVIII, No. 2 (April 1, 1942).

388. ——. "Strategy of the War in Asia," *ibid.*, Vol. XIX, No. 3 (April 15, 1943).

389. ——. "What Future for Japan?" *ibid.*, No. 12 (September 1, 1943).

390. ROUSH, G. A. *Strategic Mineral Supplies*. New York: McGraw-Hill Book Co., 1939.

391. ROY, M. N. "Indian Labour and Post-war Reconstruction." New York: International Secretariat, Institute of Pacific Relations, 1942. (Mimeographed.)

392. ROYAL INSTITUTE OF INTERNATIONAL AFFAIRS. (In addition to the *Bulletins* and *Reports* listed here, this institute issues a great deal of other material relating to the western Pacific.) "British Reactions to the War in the Far East, 1941–42." London: Royal Institute of International Affairs, 1942. (Mimeographed.)

393. ——. "Japan's Co-prosperity Sphere," *Bulletin of International News*, XVIII, No. 9 (May 3, 1941), 548–52.

394. ——. "Malaya and Its Communications," *ibid.*, December 27, 1941, pp. 2003–7.

395. ——. *Netherlands Overseas Territories*. "Information Department Papers," No. 28. New York: Oxford University Press, 1941.

396. ——. "Problems of the Post-war Settlement in the Far East: Burma." London: Royal Institute of International Affairs, 1942. (Mimeographed.)

397. ——. "Problems of the Post-war Settlement in the Far East: North Borneo, Sarawak and Brunei." London: Royal Institute of International Affairs, 1942. (Mimeographed.)

398. ———. "Problems of the Post-war Settlement in the Far East: The Pacific Island Dependencies." London: Royal Institute of International Affairs, 1942. (Mimeographed.)

399. ———. *Raw Materials.* "Information Department Papers," No. 18A. London: Royal Institute of International Affairs, 1939.

400. ———. *World Agriculture, an International Survey.* London: Oxford University Press, 1932.

401. SANSOM, GEORGE B. *Japan, a Short Cultural History.* New York: D. Appleton–Century Co., 1943.

402. SARKAR, BENOY K. *Postwar World Economy.* Calcutta: Chuckervertty Chatterjee, 1941.

403. SCHUMPETER, ELIZABETH B. (ed.). *The Industrialization of Japan and Manchoukuo, 1930–1940.* New York: Macmillan Co., 1940. (Contributors: G. C. Allen, E. F. Penrose, M. S. Gordon, and E. B. Schumpeter.)

404. SHEPHERD, JACK. *Australia's Interests and Policies in the Far East.* New York: International Secretariat, Institute of Pacific Relations, 1940.

405. ———. *Industry in Southeast Asia.* New York: International Secretariat, Institute of Pacific Relations, 1941.

406. SHIH, HU. "Two Papers on Post-war Asia." China Council, Institute of Pacific Relations, 1942. (Mimeographed.)

407. SHIMOJO, YASWARO. "An Inquiry concerning the Numerical Evolution of Population," in GINI (ed.), *Proceedings of the International Congress for Studies of Population,* I, 293–321. 10 vols. Rome: Istituto Poligrafico dello Stato Libreria, 1933–34.

408. SIAM. *Statistical Year Book of the Kingdom of Siam.* Bangkok: Ministry of Finance, 1916——.

409. SIMONDS, FRANK H., and EMENY, BROOKS. *The Great Powers in World Politics.* Rev. ed. New York: American Book Co., 1937.

410. SITSEN, PETER H. W. *Industrial Development of the Netherlands Indies.* New York: Netherlands and Netherlands Indies Council, Institute of Pacific Relations, 1944.

411. SMITH, GUY-HAROLD, and GOOD, DOROTHY. *Japan: A Geographical View.* New York: American Geographical Society, 1943. (Gives map showing growth of population 1920–35 by smallest available civil divisions.)

412. SOUTH SEA ASSOCIATION. "Mineral Resources of the South Sea Countries," *Far Eastern Review,* XXXVI, No. 1 (January, 1940), 38–41.

413. SPATE, O. H. "Beginnings of Industrialization in Burma," *Economic Geography,* XVII, No. 1 (January, 1941), 75–92.

414. SPATE, O. H., and TRUEBLOOD, L. W. "Rangoon: A Study in Urban Geography," *Geographical Review,* XXXII, No. 1 (January, 1942), 56–73.

415. SPURR, WILLIAM ALFRED. *Seasonal Variations in the Economic Activities of Japan.* Lincoln, Neb.: University of Nebraska, 1940.

416. SPYKMAN, NICHOLAS JOHN. *America's Strategy in World Politics.* New Haven: Institute of International Studies, Yale University; New York: Harcourt, Brace & Co., 1942.

417. STALEY, EUGENE. *Raw Materials in Peace and War.* New York: Council on Foreign Relations, 1937.

418. STAMP, L. D. *Asia: An Economic and Regional Geography*. New York: E. P. Dutton & Co., 1938.

419. ———. "Burma: An Undeveloped Monsoon Country," *Geographical Review*, XX, No. 1 (January, 1930), 86–109.

420. ———. "Siam before the War," *Geographical Journal*, Vol. XCIX, Nos. 5–6 (May–June, 1942).

421. STANDING, PERCY C. "Progress in Siam," *Contemporary Review*, CXXV (June 24, 1924), 762–68.

422. *The Statesman's Year-Book: Statistical and Historical Annual of the States of the World*. London, 1864———.

423. STEWART, MAXWELL S. (ed.). *Our Neighbors across the Pacific*. St. Louis: American Council, Institute of Pacific Relations, and Webster Publishing Co., 1943.

424. ———. *War-time China*. New York: American Council, Institute of Pacific Relations, 1944.

425. SWEDEN, STATISTISKA CENTRALBYRÅN. *Statistisk Årsbok för Sverige*. Stockholm, 1914———.

426. SWETTENHAM, SIR FRANK. *British Malaya*. New York: John Land Co., 1920.

427. TAEUBER, IRENE, and BEAL, EDWIN G. "The Dynamics of Population in Japan," *Milbank Memorial Fund Quarterly*, XXII, No. 3 (July, 1944), 222–55.

428. TANG, CHI YU. *An Economic Study of Chinese Agriculture*. London: Arthur Probsthain, 1924.

429. TATEYANIA, Y. "A Japanese View of Thailand's Economic Independence," *Pacific Affairs*, XIV, No. 4 (December, 1941), 469–73.

430. TAWNEY, R. H. *Land and Labour in China*. New York: Harcourt, Brace & Co., 1932.

431. TAYLOR, GEORGE E. *The Struggle for North China*. New York: International Secretariat, Institute of Pacific Relations, 1940.

432. TAYLOR, GRIFFITH. *Australia*. New York: E. P. Dutton & Co., 1943.

433. ———. *Australia: A Study of Warm Environments and Their Effect on British Settlement*. New York: E. P. Dutton & Co., 1940.

434. ———. *Australia in Its Physiographic and Economic Aspects*. Oxford: Clarendon Press, 1928.

435. TAYLOR, HENRY C., and TAYLOR, ANNE DEWEES. *World Trade in Agricultural Products*. New York: Macmillan Co., 1943.

436. THOMAS, DOROTHY SWAINE. *Social and Economic Aspects of Swedish Population Movements, 1750–1933*. New York: Macmillan Co., 1941.

437. THOMPSON, VIRGINIA. *French Indo-China*. New York: Macmillan Co., 1937.

438. ———. *Postmortem on Malaya*. New York: Macmillan Co., 1943.

439. ———. "Siam Manoeuvering towards Self-sufficiency," *Far Eastern Survey*, VII, No. 25 (December 21, 1938), 289–94.

440. ———. "Thailand Irredenta—Internal and External," *ibid.*, IX, No. 21 (October 23, 1940), 243–49.

441. ———. *Thailand the New Siam*. New York: Macmillan Co., 1941.

442. THOMPSON, WARREN S. *Danger Spots in World Population*. New York: Alfred A. Knopf, 1929.

443. ———. *Plenty of People*. Lancaster, Pa.: Jaques Cattell Press, 1944.

444. ———. *Population Problems*. New York: McGraw-Hill Book Co., 1942.

445. THOMPSON, WARREN S., and CHIAO, C. M. *An Experiment in the Registration of Vital Statistics in China.* Oxford, Ohio: Scripps Foundation for Research in Population Problems, 1938.

446. TIMPERLEY, H. J. *Australia and the Australians.* New York: Oxford University Press, 1942.

447. ———. *Japan: A World Problem.* New York: John Day Co., 1942.

448. UNITED STATES DEPARTMENT OF COMMERCE. *Channels of Distribution of American Merchandise in India.* Trade Information Bull. No. 817. Washington, D.C.: Government Printing Office, 1933.

449. ———. *Economic Review of Foreign Countries 1939 and Early 1940.* Washington, D.C.: Government Printing Office, 1941.

450. ———. *Iron and Steel Industry and Trade of India.* Trade Information Bull. No. 816. Washington, D.C.: Government Printing Office, 1933.

451. ———. *The Marketing of Manganese Ore.* Trade Information Bull. No. 599. Washington, D.C.: Government Printing Office, 1929.

452. ———. *Mineral Raw Materials.* "Trade Promotion Series," No. 76. Washington, D.C.: Government Printing Office, 1929.

453. ———. *Statistical Abstract of the United States, 1942.* Washington, D.C.: Government Printing Office, 1943.

454. ———. *The United States in India's Trade.* "Trade Promotion Series," No. 200. Washington, D.C.: Government Printing Office, 1939.

455. UNITED STATES DEPARTMENT OF COMMERCE, BUREAU OF THE CENSUS. *Monthly Summary of Foreign Commerce of the United States.* Washington, D.C.: Government Printing Office, 1914———.

456. ———. *Sixteenth Census of the United States, 1940.* Washington, D.C.: Government Printing Office, 1943.

457. UNITED STATES DEPARTMENT OF COMMERCE, BUREAU OF FOREIGN AND DOMESTIC COMMERCE. *Coal Industry of the World.* Washington, D.C.: Government Printing Office, 1930.

458. ———. *Commerce Yearbook.* Washington, D.C.: Government Printing Office, 1922———. (Contains many special articles on trade in particular commodities.)

459. ———. *Economic Review of Foreign Countries, 1937———.* Washington, D.C.: Government Printing Office, 1938———.

460. UNITED STATES DEPARTMENT OF THE INTERIOR. *Hawaii and Its Race Problem.* Washington, D.C.: Government Printing Office, 1932.

461. UNITED STATES DEPARTMENT OF THE INTERIOR, BUREAU OF MINES. *Minerals Yearbook Review.* Washington, D.C.: Government Printing Office, 1933———.

462. UNITED STATES TARIFF COMMISSION. *Colonial Tariff Policies.* Washington, D.C.: Government Printing Office, 1922.

463. ———. *The Foreign Trade of Japan.* Washington, D.C.: Government Printing Office, 1922.

464. ———. *Iron and Steel.* Report No. 128. 2d ser. Washington, D.C.: Government Printing Office, 1938.

465. ———. *Recent Developments in the Foreign Trade of Japan.* Washington, D.C.: Government Printing Office, 1936.

466. ———. *Trade during the War.* Washington, D.C.: Government Printing Office, 1919.

467. UYEDA, TEIJIRO. *Future of the Japanese Population*. Tokyo: Nippon Press, 1933.

468. ———. *The Small Industries of Japan*. New York: International Secretariat, Institute of Pacific Relations, 1938.

469. VAKIL, C. N., *et al. Growth of Trade and Industry in Modern India*. New York: Longmans, Green & Co., 1931.

470. VAKIL, C. N., and MUNSHI, M. C. *Industrial Policy of India*. New York: Longmans, Green & Co., 1934.

471. VANDENBOSCH, AMRY. *The Dutch East Indies*. Berkeley, Calif.: University of California Press, 1942.

472. VLIELAND, C. A. "The Population of the Malay Peninsula," *Geographical Review*, XXIV, No. 1 (January, 1934), 61–78.

473. VOSKUIL, WALTER H. *Minerals in Modern Industry*. New York: John Wiley & Sons, 1930.

474. WALLACE, B. B., and EDMINSTER, L. R. *International Control of Raw Materials*. Washington: Brookings Institution, 1930.

475. WALLACE, HENRY A. *Our Job in the Pacific*. New York: American Council, Institute of Pacific Relations, 1944.

476. WANG, CHUNG YU. "China's Position in the World of Minerals," *Far Eastern Review*, XXXI, No. 6 (June, 1935), 212–15.

477. *War and Peace in the Pacific*. Prepared by the International Secretariat, Institute of Pacific Relations. New York: International Secretariat, Institute of Pacific Relations, 1943.

478. WATTAL, P. K. *The Population Problems in India*. Bombay: Bennett, Coleman & Co., 1934.

479. WEIL, ELSIE. "Facts on the Indian Famine," *Asia and the Americas*, XLIV, No. 1 (February, 1944), 74–75.

480. WELD, WILLIAM ERNEST. *India's Demand for Transportation*. "Studies in History, Economics, and Public Law," Vol. XC, No. 206. New York: Columbia University, 1920.

481. WENTWORTH, EDNA CLARK. *Filipino Plantation Workers in Hawaii*. New York: American Council, Institute of Pacific Relations, 1941.

482. WHITE, DAVID. "The Petroleum Resources of the World," *Annals of the American Academy of Political and Social Science*, LXXXIX (May, 1920), 111–34.

483. WHYTE, SIR FREDERICK. *India: A Bird's Eye View*. New York: Oxford University Press, 1943.

484. WICKIZER, V. D., and BENNETT, M. K. *The Rice Economy of Monsoon Asia*. Stanford University, Calif.: Food Research Institute, 1941.

485. WILKINSON, H. L. *The World's Population Problems and a White Australia*. London: P. S. King & Son, 1930.

486. WILLCOX, WALTER F. *Studies in American Demography*. Ithaca, N.Y.: Cornell University Press, 1940.

487. WINSTEDT, RICHARD O. "Malaya," *Annals of the American Academy of Political and Social Science*, CCXXVI (March, 1943), 97–111.

488. WOLFE, HENRY C. *Human Dynamite*. "Headline Books." New York: Foreign Policy Association, 1939. (The story of Europe's minorities.)

489. WONG, H. D. *The Post-war Industrialization of China*. "Planning Pamphlets," Nos. 12–13. Washington: National Planning Association, 1942.

490. WONG, W. H. *The Distribution of Population and Land Utilization in China.* New York: China Council, Institute of Pacific Relations, 1933.

491. WORCESTER, D. C., and HAYDEN, R. *The Philippines Past and Present.* New York: Macmillan Co., 1930.

492. WORTH, W. J. "Notes on Mineral Research in North Borneo," *Far Eastern Review,* XXXVI, No. 9 (September, 1940), 335–39.

493. WRIGHT, PHILIP G. *The American Tariff and Oriental Trade.* Chicago: University of Chicago Press, 1931.

494. ———. *Trade and Trade Barriers in the Pacific.* London: P. S. King & Son, 1935.

495. WU, LEONARD T. K. "The Crisis in the Chinese Cotton Industry," *Far Eastern Survey,* IV, No. 1 (January 16, 1935), 1–4.

496. YAMASAKI, KAKUJIRO, and OGAWA, GOTARO. *The Effect of the World War upon the Commerce and Industry of Japan.* New Haven: Yale University Press, 1929.

497. YEATTS, M. W. M. "The Indian Census of 1941," *Journal of the Royal Society of Arts,* XCI (March, 1943), 182–87.

498. YOUNG, ARTHUR N. "China's Financial Progress," *Foreign Policy Reports,* Vol. XIV, No. 3 (April 15, 1938).

499. ZIMMERMAN, CARLE C. *Siam Rural Economic Survey 1930–31.* Bangkok: Bangkok Times Press, 1931.

500. ———. "Some Phases of Land Utilization in Siam," *Geographical Review,* XXVII, No. 3 (July, 1937), 378–93.

501. ZIMMERMANN, E. W. *World Resources and Industries.* New York: Harper & Bros., 1933.

502. ZON, RAPHAEL, and SPARHAWK, WILLIAM N. *Forest Resources of the World.* New York: McGraw-Hill Book Co., 1923.

INDEX

[Page references to tables or to illustrations are indicated by italic figures; numbers in parentheses refer to the Bibliography.]

Acland, T. G., on deficiencies in India's vital statistics, 223

Africa, population growth in, *23*

Agriculture
  in Australia, *52–53*, 56–63
  in China, 184–91, 209–10
  in the Fiji Islands, 44, 49
  in Formosa, 117–18
  in Hawaii, 43–44, 48–49
  in India, 226–35
  in Japan, 95, 109–13
  in the Japanese Mandate, 46
  in Java, 261–63
  in Korea, 102 n., 113–15
  in Manchoukuo, 81–82
  in New Guinea, Territory of, 45–46
  in New Zealand, 72–74
  in Oceania, 42–45
  in the Pacific Region
    population engaged in, 14
    and population support, 331–33
  in the Philippine Islands, 276–78

Alienated landholdings
  in Australia, *57, 61*
  in New Zealand, 73–74

Allen, G. C. (6), on Japanese labor, 141

Alloy minerals, in Japan and Korea, 130–31

Aluminum
  Japanese source of supply of, *123*, 129
  in Manchoukuo, *83–84*, 91, 129

Alunite, in Korea, 129. *See also* Bauxite

Amboina and Ternate, area, density, and population of, *260*

Antimony, in China, 195

Asahi, Isoshi (15), on Japanese labor market, 153–54

Asia, Southeast
  birth control in, 276
  colonial system in, 297–318
  colonies of, 251–96. *See also* Burma; Indo-China; Malaya; Netherlands East Indies; Philippine Islands
  industry in
    capital for, 15–16, 139
    markets for, 153–55
  land settlement possibilities in, 108
  population of, 13, *23*
    future growth in, 329–31
    and land scarcity, 13–16
  See also Pacific Region

Atlantic Charter, on trade freedom, 168

Atomic bomb, and military strength, 342 n.

Australia, 52–71
  agriculture in, 56–63
    and alienated landholdings, *57, 61*
    contrasted with United States, 52
    crop area of, 67–68
    expansion of, 56–58, 68
    and temperate zone, 56–59
    and tropical zone, 59–60
  climate and rainfall in, *52–53*
  gold rush in, 62–63
  habitability of, *52–53*
  immigration to, *54–55*, 68–71
  industry, growth of, 65–66
  land utilization in, 61–63, 66–68, 77
    a temptation to crowded countries, 351–56
  livestock in, 58
  and military policing in Japan, 172
  mineral resources of, 63–65
  population of, *54–56*
    carrying capacity of, 60, 350
    future growth of, 55, *100*
    policy of, 66–71, 354
    racial composition of, 68–69
    urban, 55–56
  trade of, 65–66
  vital statistics of, *54–55*

Bain, H. Foster (22)
  on China's minerals, 192–95, 202
  on India's manganese, 237
  on the Netherlands East Indies, minerals in, 263–64

Balance of power
  and population growth, 348–50
  shift in, 17, 341–43

Bali and Lombok, area, density, and population of, *260*

Bananas
  in Australia, 59
  in the Fiji Islands, 44

Banditry, in Manchoukuo, 86

Bangka and Billiton, area, density, and population of, *260*

Baring, Denzil (200)
  on China's industry, 198, 201, 205
  on demand for Japanese products, 156 n.–157 n.

Barley yields, by countries, *229*

385

Bauxite
  in China, 196
  in India, 237
  in Malaya, 292
  in Sumatra, 265
  See also Aluminum
Beal, Edwin G. (427), cited, 97 n.
Bengal Iron and Steel Company, production of, 241
Bennett, M. K., on rice yields, 261, 296
Bergsmark, Daniel R. (30), on Thailand's rice culture, 295
Bilateral treaties to curb Japanese trade, 158–59
Billiton. See Bangka
Birth control
  in China, 217
  in India, 226, 235, 250
  in Japan, 97
  in the Philippine Islands, 276
  probability of, in Southeast Asia, 276, 314, 328
  and the standard of living, 342
Birth rate
  Australia's upheld by favorable age composition, 55
  decline of, in the West, 26, 30–31
  and differential growth, 27
  in Japan, 95–97
  in stationary countries, 29
  in Sweden, 26
  urban and rural, 30–31
  See also Ratio of children to women; Vital statistics
Bismarck, on Poles in Prussia, 107
Blanchard, Fessenden S. (32), Chinese- and Japanese-operated mills compared, 201
Borneo
  area, density, and population of, 252, 260
  land utilization in, 13
  mineral resources of, 263–64
  See also Netherlands East Indies
Bowman, Isaiah (36), on Australia's future settlement, 53
British Empire, Churchill on liquidation of, 298
British India. See India
British Malaya. See Malaya
Broek, Jan O. M. (42), on Netherlands East Indies, 258–59, 261–62, 267, 269, 271
Brouwer, H. Albert (43), on iron ore in Netherlands East Indies, 264
Buck, John L. (46), on China, 176, 179, 184
Burgdörfer, Friedrich, on future population of Germany, 100
Burma, 285–89
  agriculture in, crop yields of, 229
    rice, 261, 286
    sesame, 286
  area of, 286
  forests of, 286
  immigrants in, 285–86
  Japanese exclusion from exploitation of minerals, 163
  mineral resources of, 287–88
  population statistics of, 285
  trade of, 287–88
Burt, Sir Bryce (48), on culturable waste land in India, 230

Cairo Declaration
  as a basis for peace, 170–71
  and the future of Japan, 165
Capital reserves, in Japan since World War I, 139
Cartel-like organization of Japanese trade, 160
Carus, Clayton (58), on Korean fisheries, 119
Caste system, as impediment to progress, 15
Cattle, in India, 231–32
Celebes
  area, density, and population of, 253, 260
  iron ore in, 264
  land settlement possibilities of, 13
  See also Netherlands East Indies
Central America, population growth in, 23
Ceylon, rice yields in, 261
Chand, Gyan (60), on India's vital statistics, 223–24
Charles, Enid, on future population of England and Wales, 100
Chemicals, Japan's production of, 124
Chen, C. C. (67), on vital statistics in China, 180
Chetty, Shaumukham (69), on India's iron, 237, 241–42
Chiao, C. M. (445), on vital statistics in China, 180
China
  agriculture in, 184–91
    and crop yields, 187–88, 229, 261
    and erosion, 186
    expansion possibilities of, 176–77, 184–87
    and irrigation, 185
  area and location of, 176
  Central government in, 198–99
  climate of, 176
  colonial status of, 199
  economic future of, 207–17
    in relation to Japan, 212–13
    wealth of, exaggerated, 192
  forests, lack of, 190–91
  hydroelectric power in, 193–94
  industry in, 198–206
    and capital, 213–14
    and coal reserves, 192–93
    and factories, 205

future development of, 206, 213
and hand labor, 198
and iron and steel, 202-3
jobs for displaced farmers in, 208-10
limitations of, 195, 197-200, 204-6
and standard of living, 215-17
and textiles, 200-202
and transportation, 213
Malthusian dilemma in, 210
migration in, 321-24
to Manchoukuo, 79-80, 82
and population growth, 189-90
military policing of, in Japan, 172
mineral resources of, 192-98
antimony, 195
bauxite, 196
coal, 192-93
copper, 196
inadequacy of, 197-98
iron ore, 194-95
magnesium, 196
petroleum, 193
tungsten, 195-96
population in, 176-83
future of, 182-83, 216
resources of, future attitude toward, 20-21
standard of living in, 181-82
topography of, 176-77
trade of, 128, 193, 215
transportation in, 203-4
vital statistics of, 178-81
in Kiangyin, *181*

Chinese Eastern Railway, in Manchoukuo, 84-85

Chinese labor
in Hawaii, 38-39
in Malayan tin industry, 291
in the Netherlands East Indies, 265
in Thailand, 294-95

Chinese social attitudes, and industrialization, 15

Chosen. *See* Korea

Christian, John L. (77 and 78), on Burma, 163, 286-87

Chrome, in the Philippine Islands, 279

Churchill, Winston, on British Empire, 298

Clark, Grover (82), on colonial system, 302-3

Coal
in Australia, 63-64
in China, 192-93
in India, 236
in Indo-China, 283
Japanese supply of, 122-26
in Manchoukuo, *83*-84, 89-90
in the Philippine Islands, 278
world production of, by countries, *125*

Coal liquefaction
in Australia, 64
in Japan, 124, 126-27, 140-41
in Manchoukuo, 90

Coconut industry. *See* Copra

Colonial areas, for development by settlers, 13-14, 356

Colonial system
advantages of, to colony, 298-302
from native viewpoint, 306-8
advantages of, to holding power, 297-98, 302-5, 308-9
in Burma, 285-86, 288-89
as detriment to peace, 18, 310-11, 354-55
effect of, on noncolonial powers, 304-6
and exploitation, 297-98, 306-7
European and Japanese contrasted, 167, 297, 302
future of, 308-10, 348-50
in Hawaii, dilemma of, 42
and the Malthusian dilemma, 313-15
in the Netherlands East Indies, 252-53, 268
in Oceania, 50-51
and population trend, 18, 255, 313-15
in South and East Asia, 297-318
versus free trade, 303-4
and world citizenship, 317-18

Colonies
internationalization of, 305
need of, as reason for aggression, 316
of Southeast Asia, 251-96
as spheres of influence, 312
trade advantages of, 162
trusteeship of, from native viewpoint, 305

Communication and transportation, mental attitudes toward, 14-15

Consumption industries, colonial areas' need for, 293, 333-34

Contraception. *See* Birth control

Copper
in Australia, 64-65
in China, 196
in Japan, *123*, 127-28
in the Philippine Islands, 279

Copra
in the Fiji Islands, 44
in the Japanese Mandate, 46
in Oceania, 42-43, 48
in the Philippine Islands, 280

Cressey, George B. (91), on Thailand, 294-95

Crop yields, countries compared, 229

Crops, commercial, European domination of, 42-43

Dairy products of Australia, 58

Davis, Kingsley (99), on India's vital statistics, 225 n.

Death rate
and emigration, 13
and India's population growth, 222
Japanese decline in, 97-98
and population growth, 34-35

Death rate—*continued*
in pre–Industrial Revolution days, 23, 26
in Sweden, *26*
See also Vital statistics

Depression, and Japan's trade, 155

Dietrich, Ethel B. (109), on curbing Japanese trade, 158

Economic dominance, in commercial agriculture, 41–42, 45

Economic future
of China, 207–17
of Japan, 165–75

Economic nationalism, and Japan's trade, 158

Economic needs, as war incentive, 16–17, 19–21, 174, 316–17

Economic oligarchy, in Japan, 146

Economy of backward peoples, 243–45

Electric power, in Manchoukuo, 91. *See also* Hydroelectric power

Emigration. *See* Migration

England and Wales
crop yields in, *229*
decline in birth rate in, 30
future population of, *100*

Europe, population growth of, *23*
contrasted with Asiatic, 12–13

Expanding population, 27–33

Exploitation, under colonial system, 37–38, 45–47, 50–51, 115–16, 119, 297–98, 301

Exports. *See* Trade

Factories. *See under* name of country

Family ideals, in China as obstacle to industrialization, 15

Family size, in countries with stationary population, 29

Famine
in India, 220–22
and population growth, 22–23

Farley, Miriam S. (132), on India's iron ore, 237

Federal Capital, agricultural area of, *57*. *See also* Australia

Fertilizer, Japan's supply of, 131

Field, Frederick V. (134)
on Chinese immigration to Manchoukuo, 79
on Koreans in Japan, 101 n.
on trade restrictions, 159

Finland, population of, 22, 25

Fire clay, in Manchoukuo, *83*

Fishing, in Japan and Korea, 119–20

Five-year plan, in Manchoukuo, 89–90

Fong, H. D. (135)
on China's copper production, 196
on Manchoukuo's coal, 192–93

Food supply
in China, 187–88
in Formosa, 118–19
in India, 232–34
in Japan, 109–21
without colonies, 166, 168–69
in Korea, 115–16
in Manchoukuo, 81–82
in Oceania, 49

Foreign trade. *See* Trade

Forests
in Burma, 286
China's lack of, 190–91

Formosa
agriculture in, 117–18
rice yields, *261*
food supply of, 118–19
Japanese colonists in, 105
and Japanese economy, 103–4, 166, 212–13
population in, 102–4
standard of living in, 105
vital statistics of, 103–4, 179, 299

France
decline in birth rate in, 30
future population of, *100*

Frechling, Louis E. (148), on shale oil in Manchoukuo, 90

Free trade, as compensating for lack of mineral resources, 334–35. *See also* Trade

French Establishments, in Oceania, area of, 36

French Indo-China. *See* Indo-China

Freyn, Hubert (151)
on China's forests, 190
on China's pig-iron production, 203

Fuel. *See* Coal; Petroleum

Future population
of Australia, *100*
of China, 182–83, 188–90, 216
of England and Wales, *100*
of Formosa, 103–4
of France, *100*
of Germany, *100*
of India, *100*, 225–26, 234–35
of Japan, 98–*100*
of Korea, 102
of Manchoukuo, 80, 121
of the Netherlands East Indies, 272–73
of the Pacific Region, 320–21, 348–50
of pre-industrial countries, 34
of the Soviet Union, 32, *100*, 347 n.
of the United States, *100*

Germany
decline in birth rate in, 30
future population of, *100*
war preparation of, 172

Gold
in Australia, 64–65
in Japan, 130
in Manchoukuo, *83*
in Oceania, 47–48
in the Philippine Islands, 279

Government participation in industry
in Japan, 134–38
in the Netherlands East Indies, 269–72
in the Philippine Islands, 280–81

Grajdanzev, Andrew J. (163, 165, 167, and 169)
on Formosa, 103, 105, 117–18
on India's aluminum production, 237
on Japan's irrigated land, 110 n.–111 n.
on Korea, 101 n., 104, 114–15, 128

Graphite, in Korea, 130

Hailey, Lord (179), on the colonial system, 302

Handworkers, jobs for, in India, 247–48, 335–37

Hart, G. H. C. (184), on industry in the Netherlands East Indies, 268–69

Hawaii
agriculture in, 38–40, 42–45, 48–49
area of, 36
economic position of races changing in, 41–42
labor supply of, 38–40, 43
population in, growth differential of, 38, *40–42*
ratio of children to women in, 41
strategic importance of, to the United States, 42, 344
trade of, 48–50
See also Oceania

Health, under the colonial system, 299

Heroy, W. B., on lack of oil in China, 193

Herre, Albert W. C. T., on Japanese fishing industry, 120

Hubbard, G. E. (200)
on China's industry, 198, 200–201, 205
on Japanese products, 156 n.–157 n.

Hydroelectric power
in China, 193–94
in India, 236–37
in Japan, 126, 140 n.
See also Electric power

Ichihashi, Yamato (203), on native population in Hawaii, 38

Immigration. *See* Migration

Imports. *See* Trade

Independence
disadvantages of
to Formosa, 119
to Korea, 116–17
of the Philippine Islands, 281–82

India
agriculture in, 226–35
cattle, 231–32
crop acreage, 228
crop yields, 228–*29*, 231, 234, *261*
culturable waste, 230
improvement in, and population growth, 232–35
milk production, 231
persons employed in, 227
tillable land, 230
area, climate, and location of, 218
birth control in, 235
economic outlook for, 236–50
famine in, 220–22
as future aggressor, 249–50
hydroelectric power in, 236–37
industry in, 236–50
and capital, 247
and expansion and health, 245–46
expansion possibilities for, 248–49
factory employees in, 239–41
handwork in, 238–39
and iron and steel production, 241–42
and jute, 241
and population growth, 234–35
power reserves in, 236–37
and production, 238–43
reconstruction of, a plan for, *246*
and sugar production, 241
and textiles, 240–41
trained personnel in, need of, 246
influenza in, in 1918, 221–22
marriage taboos in, 225
mineral resources of, 236–50
bauxite, 237
coal reserves, 236
iron ore, 237
manganese, 237–38
petroleum, 236
population of, 218–26
accuracy of censuses of, 219
future of, *100*, 225–26, 234–35, 248–50
growth of, 11, 250
social betterment in, retarding factors, 247–48
standard of living in, 232–33, 248–50
trade, history of, 239
vital statistics of, 222–25

Indo-China, 282–85
agriculture in, crop yields, *229, 261*
rice production, 284
area of, 282
consumption industries in, 284–85
mineral resources in, 283–84
population in, 282–83

Industrial Revolution, and population growth, 23

Industry
aptitudes among peoples for, 243–45
in Australia, 65–66
in Burma, 288
capital for, 15–16

Industry—*continued*
in China, 198–206, 213
and consumption goods, 333–34
and decline in birth rate, 30–31
in the Fiji Islands, 49
fishing, diminishing returns of, 120
in Hawaii, 48–50
in India, 15, 238–43, *246*
in Japan, 123–26, 132–47, 167–68
jobs for displaced handworkers in, 335–37
in Korea, 102
limiting factors of, 15–17
machine production in, in backward
lands, 244–45
in Malaya, 293–94
in Manchoukuo, 86–91
need of co-operation with Japan, 210–
11
in the Netherlands East Indies, 265–73
in New Guinea, Territory of, 50
in Oceania, 48–50
in the Philippine Islands, 280–82
plastics for steel, use of, 333
and population, 26–27, 333–35
and standard of living, 14–16
in Thailand, 295–96
and trade in the Pacific Region, 356–57
in the United States, production and exports of, 150

Influenza, in India, contrasted with United
States, 221–22

International organization. *See* United Nations Organization

Investment abroad, and trade, 161–63

Iron ore
in Australia, 64
in China, 194–95
in Indo-China, 283–84
in Japan, source of supply, 123–24, 128
in Malaya, 292
in Manchoukuo, *83*–84
in the Netherlands East Indies, 264–65
in the Philippine Islands, 278–79
world production of, by countries, *125*

Irrigation
in China, 185
in Formosa, 117–18
in Japan, 111–12
in Korea, 113–14
in New Zealand, 72–73

Japan
aggression of, as a consequence of economic organization, 316
agriculture in, 109–13
yields of, 112, *229*, *261*
and the Asiatic market, 153–55
birth control in, 97
birth rate in, differential of, 95–97
capital reserves in, 139
capitalist interests in, 146
in China's future economy, 212–13

and colonies, 99–108, 114–17, 121–30,
159–60, 165–70, 212–13
denuded of industry, 147
economic future of, 165–75
economy
and industrialization in, 132–33
and peace, 170–71
and fertilizer, 131
food supply of, 109–21
from colonies, 112–13, 115, 118, 121
from fish, 119–20
meat consumption of, 113
fuel supply of, 122–27
in future Asiatic economy, 334, 337–38
hydroelectric production in, 126, 140
industry in
and capital, 153
development of, 134–47, 155–56
factories, growth of, 138–40
and fuel, 122–27
Fujiwara, on future possibilities of, 132
government participation in, 134–38
heavy industry, handicaps to, 144–45
Komura, on population problem, 132
labor in, 141–42, 153–54
in Manchoukuo, 80–83, 86, *88*–89, 91–
92, 167–68
markets for, 153–57
military influence on, 145–46
monopolistic tendencies of, 152–53
normal growth of, 145–47
production and exports of, 150
production indices of, *142*
research in, 140–41
and textiles, 141
value of, *143*
and a just peace, 173–74
and migration, 327–28
mineral resources of, 122–33
coal supply, 122–26
copper, 127–28
future outlook for, 131–33, 138
iron ore, 128
petroleum production, 124–26
source of supply, *123*
tin, 130
political control versus free trade in, 164
population
of the Empire, 93–108
future of, 98–*100*
urban, 95
poverty and war in, 173
production and exports of, 149–50
Russo-Japanese War and subsequent industrialization, 136
standard of living and trade in, 164
trade of, 148–64
by commodities, 148–*51*
by countries, *156*
dependence on, 149–52
history of, 148–55
and iron ore from the Philippine
Islands, 278
restrictions on, 157–60, 163–64

vital statistics of, 94–98
world depression as a benefit, 155
See also Japanese Empire; Manchoukuo

Japan Cotton Spinners Association, report of, on increasing efficiency, 141

Japanese Empire
dissolution of, 165
and industrial expansion, 167–69

Japanese labor, in Hawaii, 39

Japanese Mandate, 36, 46–47. *See also* Oceania

Java and Madura
agriculture in, 261–63
area, density, and population of, *260*
migration possibilities in, 258–60
population of, 253–57
production per capita of, 257–58
size of, 253
standard of living, in, 261–62
vital statistics of, 255–56
See also Netherlands East Indies

Justice, in a lasting peace, 173

Jute, India's production of, 241

Kessing, Felix M. (251), on Oceania, 37–38, 43, 47

Kimble, G. H. (256), on land in China, 187

King, Franklin H. (257), on China's agriculture, 177–78

Korea
agriculture in, 113–15
crop yields, *229, 261*
persons employed by, 102 n.
fishing industry in, 120
food supply of, 115–16
independence of, 116–17
since Japanese occupation, 101–2, 104, *105*, 114, 116, 166
and migration, number living abroad, 101 n.
mineral resources in, 128–31
population of, 99–102
standard of living in, 105, 116
trade in rice, 115
vital statistics of, 101–2, 299

Kwantung Army, as military authority in Manchoukuo, 87

Kwantung Leased Territory, area of, 86

Labor supply
in Australian tropics, 59–60
in China, 200
in the Fiji Islands, 44
in Hawaii, 38–40, 43
in Japan, 141–42, 153–54
in New Guinea, Territory of, 45–46

Ladejinsky, W. I. (267), on Australia's agriculture, 56

Lamott, Willis (269), on Japanese co-operation toward peace, 174

Land, opened to settlement, 312–13, 342–43
scarcity of, 13, 16
a temptation to crowded countries, 351–56

Land settlement
in Australia, 61–63
in China, 176–77, 187
in the Netherlands East Indies, 319–20
in South and East Asia, 108

Land utilization
in Asia, 328, 332
attitude of backward peoples toward, 315–16
in Australia and New Zealand, 77
in the Netherlands East Indies, 272–73

Landheer, Bartholomeus (270), on economy in the Netherlands East Indies, 268, 271

Landon, Kenneth Perry (271), on Thailand, 294

Leith, C. H. (290)
on India's iron ore, 237
on Japanese in Mindanao, 163

Level of living. *See* Standard of living

Lind, Andrew William (294), on Filipino labor in Hawaii, 39

Livestock
in Australia, 58
in India, 231–32
in Korea, 113, 115
in New Zealand, 73

Living conditions. *See* Standard of living

Lombok. *See* Bali

Lowdermilk, W. C. (300), on forests in China, 190

Machine economy, 243–45

McNichols, Charles L. (58), on Korean fisheries, 119

Madura. *See* Java

Magnesite, in Manchoukuo, *83–84*

Magnesium
in China, 196
Japanese supply of, 129–30
in Manchoukuo, 91, 130
from sea water, 130

Malaria in Southeast Asia, 252
retards industrialization, 245–46

Malaya, 289–94
agriculture in, rice yields, *261*
industry in, 293–94
mineral resources of, 292–93
population of, 289, 294
race conflict in, 291–92
rubber holdings of, 290
and trade, iron ore, 128
quotas on Japanese goods, 158

Malthusian dilemma
  Asiatic escape from, 325
  in China, 210
  European escape from, 324–25
  in India, 234–35
  in Java, 257
  in Southeast Asia, 14
Manchoukuo, 78–92
  agriculture in, 81–82
  area and climate of, 78
  banditry in, 86
  Chinese migrants in, 322
  industry in, 84, 86–91, 202
    five-year plan of, 89–90
    investments in, 88–89
  in Japan's economy, 83, 91–92, 123–26,
    166–68, 212–13
  land settlement of, 186–87
  mineral resources of, 83–84, 86, 89–91
    coal reserves, 124, 193
    iron ore, 128, 194–95
    shale oil, 90, 126, 193
    in Tungpientao region, 84, 90
  population of, 78–82, 105–6, 121
  transportation in, 84–86
  vital statistics of, 79–80
  after World War II, 80–81, 210–11
  See also China; Japan
Manchuria. See Manchoukuo
Manchuria Industrial Development Company, 88–89
Manganese
  in India, 237–38
  in Malaya, 292–93
  in Manchoukuo, 83
  in the Philippine Islands, 279
Markets
  India's lack of, 247
  for Japan's products, 153–57
Meat consumption, in Japan, 113
Meat production, in Australia, 58
Melanesia, population trends in, 37. See also
  Oceania
Micronesia, population trends in, 37. See
  also Oceania
Migration, 319–28
  in Australia, 54–55, 68–71
  basic principle of, 107
  in Burma, 285–86
  in China, 79–80, 82, 189–90
  and the death rate, 13–14
  in Hawaii, 38–39
  in Japan, 104–8, 327–28
  in Java, 258–60
  in Korea, 101 n.
  in Malaya, 289
  in New Zealand, 72
  in the Philippine Islands, 275–76
  and population pressure, 321–24
  psychological effect of, 13–14, 326
Militarism and capitalism, in Japan, 146

Military policing, of Japan, 171–73
Milk production, in India, 231
Mills, Lennox A. (316), on Malaya, 158,
  289–90
Mineral production of the world, 125
Mineral resources
  of Australia, 63–65
  of Burma, 287–88
  of China, 192–98
  of India, 236–50
  of Indo-China, 283–84
  of Japan, 122–33
  limiting factor in industrialization, 15–
    17
  in Malaya, 292–93
  of Manchoukuo, 83–84
  of the Netherlands East Indies, 263–65
  of New Caledonia, 47–48
  of New Guinea, 47–48
  of New Zealand, 74–76
  of Oceania, 47–48
  of the Philippine Islands, 278–79
  See also Alloy minerals; and under name of
    country
Mitchell, Kate L. (323)
  on bauxite near Sumatra, 265
  on Malay population, 289
  on minerals in the Philippine Islands,
    278–79
  on the Netherlands East Indies' need for
    industrial strength, 271
Molybdenum, in Korea, 130–31
Monopoly, and Japan's foreign trade, 137
Mortality rates. See Death rate; Vital statistics
Mukerjee, Radhakamal (331), on India,
  230–31, 236–37, 240
Munitions industry, Japan's early history
  of, 136

Nasu, Shiroshi (335)
  on Formosa's tillable land, 117
  on irrigated land in Japan, 110 n.
  on per cent of Japanese in agriculture,
    109
National Resources Planning Board, on future population of United States, 100
National unity, and felt needs, 16–17
Natural increase
  in Australia, 54–55
  in Finland, 25
  general trend in, 25
  in New Zealand, 72
  in Sweden, 25–26
Natural resources, scarcity of, and war, 20–
  21. See also Mineral resources
Nauru, 47. See also Oceania
Nepotism, in China, 204
Netherlands, wheat yields of, 229

Netherlands East Indies
demarcated, 252–53
exploitation of, 160
industry in, 265–72
Dutch capital in, 270
factory workers in, 266–67
government control of, 269–72
native, 268–69
and textiles, 269
Japanese concessions in, 163
land settlement in, 108, 272–73, 319–20
mineral resources of, 263–65
population of, *254*, *260*, 272–73
and trade, 267–69
See also under name of islands

New Britain. *See* New Guinea

New Caledonia, 36, 47–48. *See also* Oceania

New Guinea, Territory of (Australia), 36, 45–46, 48
land-settlement possibilities in, 13
trade of, 50
See also Netherlands East Indies; Oceania

New Hebrides, area of, 36. *See also* Oceania

New Ireland, area of, 36. *See also* New Guinea

New South Wales, agricultural area of, *57*. *See also* Australia

New Zealand, 71–77
agriculture in, 72–76
area and climate of, 71
immigration in, *72*, 76
industry in, limiting factors of, 75–76
mineral resources of, 74–76
population of, 71–*72*, 76–77

North America, population growth in, *23*

Northern Territory, agricultural area of, *57*. *See also* Australia

Notestein, Frank, on future growth of Europe, 32, *100*

Occupations, of Japanese colonists in Korea, *105*

Oceania (Tropical), 36–51
agriculture in, 42–45, 50–51
demarcated, 36
exploitation of, 37–38, 45–47
future economy of, 50–51
mineral resources of, 47–48
population of, *23*, 36–38
trade of, 48–50
See also under name of country

Office of Population Research, on future growth of Europe, 32

Oil. *See* Petroleum

Outer Provinces, area, density, and population of, *260*

Pacific colonies, and the peace structure, 310–11

Pacific Region
danger spot to peace, 11–21
demarcated, 11
future population of, 12–13, 348–50
industrial expansion in and standard of living of, 14–16
See also Asia, Southeast

Palau Laut, iron ore in, 264

Peace
and a balanced economy, 312
and the Cairo Declaration, 170–71
and the colonial system, 18, 310–11
conditions of, 358–61
danger to, 11–21
and equality of peoples, 311–12
through justice, 147, 165, 171, 173–75
and land utilization, 21, 312–13, 328
and the new order in Asia, 17–18
and the Pacific Region, 345–47
and population control, 313–15
and population growth, 11–12, 19, 329–43
poverty as threat to, 19, 21
and United States attitude toward an underpopulated Australia, 351–56
universal, 11

Pelzer, Karl J. (134)
on irrigated land in Japan, 110 n.–111 n.
on Javanese migration, 259 n.

Petroleum
in Australia, 64
in Burma, 287
in China, 193
in India, 236
in Japan, 124–27
source of supply, *123*
in the Netherlands East Indies, 264
world production of, by countries, *125*
See also Coal liquefaction; Shale oil

Philippine Islands, 274–82
agriculture in, 276–78
rice yields, *261*
co-operation of, in World War II, 308
demarcated, 274
independence of, 281–82
industry in, 280–82
ownership of mining corporations, 163
internal migration in, 275–76
Japanese colonists in, 107
mineral resources of, 278–79
population in, 274–75, 277–78
trade, in iron ore, 128
with United States, 277
vital statistics of, 274–75

Phosphates
in Malaya, 293
in Nauru, 47

Pineapples, in Oceania, 42–43, 48

Plantation system, in Oceania, 50–51

Plastics, use of, for steel, in Asia, 333

Polynesia, population trends in, 37. *See also* Oceania

Population
and agricultural improvement, 331–33
of Australia, *54–56*
of Burma, 285
of China, 177–*79*
in colonial areas, 13–14
of Finland, 22
of Formosa, 102–4
of Hawaii, 38–42
of India, 218–26
real increase in, *219*
of Indo-China, 282–83
and industry, 34–35, 333–35
of Japan, 93–95, 98–99, 109
of Java, 253–57
of Korea, 99–102
of Malaya, 289
of Manchoukuo, 78–81
and means of subsistence, relation between, 176
of the Netherlands East Indies, *260*
of New Zealand, *72*
of Oceania, 36–38
of the Philippine Islands, 274–76
significance of growth of
Asiatic, 11–12
and balance of power shifting, 17
decline of, in stationary countries, 26, 29–30
differential, 22–35
emigration, 13–14
European, 12
expanding countries, 32–33
in Japan, 132–33
modern cycle of, 22–23
position of nations with regard to, 26–29
in pre-industrial countries, 33–34
social and economic factors, 12
and war, 11–12, 339–43
stationary, children necessary to maintain, in United States, 41
of Thailand, 294–95
world, by continents, *23*
countries classified by position in growth cycle, 26–29, 32–33
present and future distribution of, 34–*35*
See also Future population; Vital statistics

Population-carrying capacity
of Asia, 14
of Australia, 60
of Malaya, 294
of New Zealand, 74

Population control, and industrialization, 314–15

Population policy
in Australia, 66–71, 350–56
in New Zealand, 76–77, 350–56

Population pressure, 319–28
and emigration, 13–14
felt needs of, 18–21, 339–40
in India, 250
and war, 18, 338–43

Porter, Catherine L. (370), on food production in the Philippine Islands, 277

Portuguese, as laborers in Hawaii, 39

Potatoes, in Korea, 113

Poverty and population pressure, a vicious circle, 336–37

Power. *See* Balance of power

Pre-industrial population, 27, 33–35

Psychological effect of opening unused land, 13–14, 18–19

Puerto Ricans, as laborers in Hawaii, 40

Queensland, agriculture in, *57*, 67. *See also* Australia

Quezon, Manuel L., on Philippine government in industry, 280–81

Quota system, trade effects of, 269
on Japan, 158–59

Race conflict, in Malaya, 291–92

Racial composition
in Australia, 54, 68–69
in Hawaii, 38, *40*
in Nauru, 47
in New Guinea, Territory of, 45
in Oceania, 36–38

Railroads, in Manchoukuo, 84–85

Ratio of children to women, in Hawaii, by race, 41. *See also* Birth rate

Raw materials, colonies as source of, 303

Rayon, Japanese production of, 141

Reciprocity agreements, as curb to Japanese trade, 158

Regional agreements, and peace, 355

Rice
in Burma, 286
in China, 184–85
by countries, *229, 261*
in Formosa, 118
in India, 228
Indo-China's exports of, 284–85
in Japan, 112
in Java, 261
in Korea, 113–14
as staple diet in colonies of Southeast Asia, 251–52
in Thailand, 295–96

Riouw, area, density, and population of, *260*

Roads, in Manchoukuo, 85–86

Roberts, Stephen H. (383), on exploitation in Oceania, 37

Roush, G. A. (390), on antimony supplies, 195

Rubber, in Malaya, 290
Russia. *See* Soviet Union
Russo-Japanese War, 104, 136

Samoa, area of, 36
Sauvy, Alfred, on future population of France, *100*
Schumpeter, Elizabeth (ed.). (403)
  on alloy minerals, 130–31
  on electric power in Manchoukuo, 91
  on industrialization of Manchoukuo, *88*
  on iron ore in Manchoukuo, *83*
  on irrigated land in Japan, 110 n.–111 n.
  on Japanese concessions in the Netherlands East Indies, 163
  on the Japanese fish industry, 120
  on Japanese industrialization, 141
  on Japanese occupations, 109
  on Korea's iron-ore exports, 128
Sesame, Burma's exports of, 286
Shale oil
  in Australia, 64
  in Manchoukuo, *83*, 90, 126, 193
  See also Petroleum
Shensi, shale oil in, 193
Shepherd, Jack (405)
  on Netherlands East Indies
    Chinese labor in, 264
    industry in, 266, 268–69, 271
    mineral resources in, 265
  on tin in Indo-China, 284
Shimojo, Yaswaro (407), on Japan's population, 93
Siam. *See* Thailand
Sino-Japanese War
  and Japan's economic development, 136
  and Korea, 104
Solomon Islands, area of, 36. *See also* New Guinea
South America, population growth in, *23*
South Australia, agricultural area of, *57*. *See also* Australia
South Manchuria Railway, as economic power in Manchoukuo, 85–*88*
Soviet Union
  future population growth of, 32, *100*, 347 n.
  in the Pacific Region, 347–48
  and relations with United States, 348 n.
Soybeans, in Manchoukuo, 81
Spate, O. H. (413), on Burma, 288
Stamp, L. D. (418), on Burma's forests, 286
Standard of living
  in Australia, 60
  and birth control, 314–15
  in China, 181–82, 188–89, 207–8, 215–17
  and competition between classes, 104–5, 107

in India, 227–28, 232–33, 235, 247–50
  and industrial expansion, 14
  in Japan, as determined by trade, 164
  in Java, 261–62
  in Korea, 116–17
  and population control, 16
  and population increase, 215–17, 320–21
  in Southeast Asia, 251–52
  and subsistence farms, 319–20
Staple fiber. *See* Rayon
State enterprises. *See* Government participation
Stationary population, 27, 29–31
Steel production
  in China, 202–3
  in India, 241–42
  in Japan, 124
  in Manchoukuo, 90–91
Straits Laut, iron ore in, 264
Strategic bases, United States' need of, 344–45
Sugar
  in Australia, 59, 70
  in the Fiji Islands, 44
  in Formosa, 118
  in India, 241
  in the Japanese Mandate, 46
  in Oceania, 42–43, 48
  in the Philippine Islands, 280
Sulphur, in Japan, 129
Sumatra
  area, density, and population of, 253, *260*
  land-settlement possibilities of, 13
  mineral resources of, 264–65
Sweden, vital statistics of, 25–*26*

Taboos, in India, 225
Taeuber, Irene (427), cited, 97 n.
Taiwan. *See* Formosa
Tariff autonomy, in Japan after 1911, 136
Tariff-free trade, of the Philippine Islands with United States, 277
Tariffs, as curb to Japanese imports, 159
Tasmania, agricultural area of, *57*. *See also* Australia
Tata Iron and Steel Company production, 241
Taylor, Griffith (434), on Australia's agricultural area, 52, 56
Teakwood
  Burma's export of, 286
  in East Java, government control of, 269
Tegengren, F. R., on China's iron ore, 194
Ternate. *See* Amboina
Textiles
  in China, 200–202
  in India, 240–41

Textiles—*continued*
in Japan, 141
in the Netherlands East Indies, 269

Thailand, 294–96

Thompson, Virginia (438 and 441)
on Malaya, 289
on Thailand, 294–96

Thompson, Warren S. (445), on vital statistics in China, 180

Timor, area, density, and population of, *260*

Tin
in Australia, 64–65
in Indo-China, 284
Japan's supply of, *123*, 130
in Malaya, 291–92
in the Netherlands East Indies, 265

Trade
advantage of colonies for, 162, 169–70
of Australia, 65–66
of Burma, 287–88
of China, 128, 193, 215
factors determining, 304
of the Fiji Islands, 49
of Formosa, 118
of Hawaii, 48–50
of India, 239
of Indo-China, 284
and industry in the Pacific Region, 356
of Japan, 148–64
foodstuffs, 115, 120–21
monopoly, 136–37
of Korea, 115, 128
of Malaya, 128
need for balance of, 159–64
of the Netherlands East Indies, 267–69
of New Guinea, Territory of, 50
of New Zealand, 75–76
of Oceania, 48–50
of the Philippine Islands, 128, 277
South and East Asia's need of, 334–35
of Thailand, 295–96

Trade restrictions, 152–53, 157–60, 162, 169–70, 303–4

Transportation
in China, 203–4
under colonial system, 300–301
in India, and famine relief, 220, 222
in Manchoukuo, 84–86

Trusteeship and European exploitation, 325–26

Tungpientao region, mineral resources of, 84. *See also* Manchoukuo

Tungsten
in Australia, 64–65
in Burma, 287
in China, 195–96

United Nations Organization
and early Japanese aggression, 346

and loans to backward peoples, 213
need of, 341–42
and status quo as regards colonies, 310–11
to study grievances of nations, 358–61
for supervision of colonial areas, 317–18
and trade interests, 345

United States
agriculture of, contrasted with Australia, 52
crop yields, *229*
attitude toward colonies, 355–56
commitments to an Australasian Empire, 351–54
decline in birth rate of, 30
future population of, *100*
and military policing of Japan, 171
production and exports of, 150
relations of, with Soviet Union, 348 n.
stake of, in the Pacific Region, 344–61

Uyeda, Teijiro (215), on future population of Japan, 99–*100*

Vandenbosch, Amry (471)
on Java's population, 253–54, 258–59
on the Netherlands East Indies, exploitation in, 160

Victoria, agricultural area of, *57*. *See also* Australia

Vital statistics
Australia, *54*–55
China, 178–81
Formosa, 103–4
India, 222–25
Japan, 94–98
Java, 255–56
Korea, 101–2
Manchoukuo, 79–80
New Zealand, 71–*72*
Philippine Islands, 274–75
Sweden, *26*
See also Birth rate; Death rate

War
Australia and New Zealand a temptation to aggression, 77
causes of, 11–12, 18–21
economic motive for, 174
future possibility of, under colonial system, 310–11
Pacific Region as future cause of, 11–12
and population pressure, 338–43
time involved in preparation for, 172–73

Washington Conference, and stake of the United States in the Pacific, 344

West Australia, agricultural area of, *57*. *See also* Australia

Western civilization
declining power of, 317, 341–43
and democratic development in Asia, 17–18

Western industry in the Netherlands East Indies, 269

Wheat
in Australia, 56–57
in India, 228
yields by countries, *229*

White Australia, 68–71, 354

Whyte, Sir Frederick (483), on cloth production in India, 240–41

Wickizer, V. D. (484), on rice yields, *261*, 296

Wilkinson, H. L. (485), on agricultural area in Australia, 56

Willcox, Walter F. (486)
on population of China, 177–78
on population growth by continents, *23*

Wolstenholme, S. H., on future population of Australia, *100*

Wool, Australian production of, 58

World organization. *See* United Nations Organization

World peace. *See* Peace

World War I, and Japanese industry, 137–40

World War II
attitude of colonial peoples in Southeast Asia toward, 306
in the Philippine Islands, 308
for trade or freedom, 171

Youth volunteers, in Manchoukuo, 106

⟦ PRINTED IN U·S·A· ⟧

U. S. S. R.
ASIA
MANCHOUKUO
KOREA
JAPAN
CHINA
FORMOSA
INDIA
BURMA
THAILAND
FRENCH INDO-CHINA
PHILIPPINES
MARIANAS
GUAM
CAROLINE ISL
JAPANESE
BRITISH MALAYA
SUMATRA
BORNEO
CELEBES
NETHERLANDS INDIES
JAVA
NEW GUINEA
INDIAN OCEAN
AUSTRALIA